MW00440514

Reinhold Niebuhr and His Circle of Influence

Reinhold Niebuhr, the prominent American theologian, was one of the few religious figures who had a significant impact on the broader society outside the theological community in the United States during the twentieth century. Niebuhr's influence was most pronounced among those associated with historical studies and politics. This book presents Niebuhr in dialogue with seven individuals who each had a major influence on American life: the theologian Paul Tillich, philosopher/educator John Dewey, socialist activist Norman Thomas, historian Arthur Schlesinger Jr., international political theorist Hans Morganthau, diplomat George Kennan, and Supreme Court Justice Felix Frankfurter. Through a detailed examination of Niebuhr's interactions with these figures, Daniel F. Rice's study offers a survey of mid-twentieth-century theology, political thought, and culture.

Daniel F. Rice is Professor Emeritus of Philosophy and Religious Studies at the University of Wisconsin, Eau Claire. He is the author of *Reinhold Niebuhr and John Dewey: An American Odyssey* (1993) and editor of *Reinhold Niebuhr Revisited: Engagements with an American Original* (2009).

Reinhold Niebuhr and His Circle of Influence

DANIEL F. RICE
University of Wisconsin, Eau Claire

Frankmas 2012

Dear Frank —

Happy reading! I think there are less than six degrees of separation between Niebuhr and Lippman...

Luigi

CAMBRIDGE
UNIVERSITY PRESS

CAMBRIDGE UNIVERSITY PRESS
Cambridge, New York, Melbourne, Madrid, Cape Town,
Singapore, São Paulo, Delhi, Mexico City

Cambridge University Press
32 Avenue of the Americas, New York, NY 10013-2473, USA

www.cambridge.org
Information on this title: www.cambridge.org/9781107653092

© Daniel F. Rice 2013

This publication is in copyright. Subject to statutory exception
and to the provisions of relevant collective licensing agreements,
no reproduction of any part may take place without the written
permission of Cambridge University Press.

First published 2013

Printed in the United States of America

A catalog record for this publication is available from the British Library.

Library of Congress Cataloging in Publication Data
Rice, Daniel F., 1935–
Reinhold Niebuhr and his circle of influence / Daniel F. Rice.
    p.   cm.
ISBN 978-1-107-65309-2 (pbk.)
1. Niebuhr, Reinhold, 1892–1971 – Influence.   I. Title.
BX4827.N5R525   2012
230.092–dc23   2012012499

ISBN 978-1-107-02642-1 Hardback
ISBN 978-1-107-65309-2 Paperback

Cambridge University Press has no responsibility for the persistence or accuracy of URLS for external
or third-party Internet Web sites referred to in this publication and does not guarantee that any
content on such Web sites is, or will remain, accurate or appropriate.

To Judy
for everything
and
to Dick Behling,
valued friend and colleague

Contents

Acknowledgments   *page* ix

   Introduction   1

1   Paul Tillich (1886–1965)   13

2   John Dewey (1859–1952)   46

3   Norman Thomas (1884–1968)   80

4   Arthur Schlesinger Jr. (1917–2007)   113

5   Hans Morgenthau (1904–1980)   145

6   George Kennan (1904–2005)   174

7   Felix Frankfurter (1882–1965)   205

   Afterword   247

Index   251

Acknowledgments

I wish to thank my wife Judith and my former colleague Dick Behling for their dedication and labor in readying this manuscript prior to submitting it to Cambridge University Press for publication. My wife's experience as an editor and teacher of English and Professor Behling's skill in all things linguistic served me well in the task of writing this book.

The willingness of Cambridge University Press to consider and finally decide to publish the book is, of course, paramount to its seeing the light of day. I am most grateful for the diligence and patience of Eric Crahan who as Editor of History and Politics steered this project to completion. Thanks also go to Abby Zorbaugh, Cherline Daniel, and Adam Schwartz.

Because the relationship between Reinhold Niebuhr and each of the seven individuals dealt with in this book involved a substantial degree of correspondence material, I extend my gratitude to the numerous named and unnamed individuals whose assistance proved invaluable. Thomas Lannon of the Manuscripts and Archives Division at the New York Public Library located and sent me correspondence between Niebuhr and Arthur Schlesinger Jr. from the newly opened Schlesinger Papers. Archivists Stephen Plotkin and Meridith Roy at the John F. Kennedy Library in Boston also made their Niebuhr–Schlesinger correspondence available to me. Maurice Klapwald was able to provide me with correspondence between Niebuhr and Norman Thomas from the New York Public Library's archive containing the Norman Thomas Papers. Resource people at the Seeley G. Mudd Manuscript Library at Princeton sent me the correspondence between Niebuhr and George Kennan from the Kennan Papers. The help provided to me by the staff at the Manuscript Division of the Library of Congress was crucial in giving me access to the Reinhold Niebuhr Collection and the Felix Frankfurter Collection. Finally, several individuals at the Morris Library of Southern Illinois University at Carbondale offered valuable assistance in accessing their collection of the John Dewey Papers.

Several institutions were kind enough to provide me with photographs of the seven individuals comprising this volume's representation of Niebuhr's "circle of influence." Wayne Geist at the Graduate Center of the City University of New

York supplied me with the photograph of Arthur Schlesinger Jr. The University of Chicago is to be credited for the photographs of Paul Tillich and Hans Morgenthau. Photographs of Norman Thomas, George Kennan, and Felix Frankfurter were provided by the Library of Congress. The photograph of John Dewey came from the Morris Library of Southern Illinois University at Carbondale.

Introduction

The theologian Reinhold Niebuhr was among the few members of what Paul Tillich called the "theological circle" to make a significant impact on the secular world. Within this world, Niebuhr's influence was most pronounced among those associated with historical studies and politics. This book presents Niebuhr's dialogues and interactions with seven influential individuals from fields as diverse as theology, philosophy, political theory, diplomacy, and jurisprudence – men whose careers took them to the pinnacles of their professions.

Paul Tillich was the dominant philosophical theologian in mid-twentieth-century America. John Dewey, a staunch defender of democracy and icon of social liberalism, was America's leading educator and successor to William James as the preeminent exponent of American pragmatism. Norman Thomas established a reputation as the most influential voice of socialism in the United States. Arthur Schlesinger Jr. was a brilliant and prolific historian, as well as a political activist and presidential adviser. Hans Morgenthau, after his arrival in America, quickly became the leading authority in international political theory and a forceful advocate of political realism. George Kennan, an expert on Soviet affairs and author of the United States' post–World War II "containment theory," was one of America's most able diplomats. Felix Frankfurter was a giant on the Supreme Court and was considered by many to possess a brilliance matched by very few in the history of that august body.

Three factors were involved in choosing these individuals for detailed examination: the degree of interaction each had with Niebuhr; the availability of source material, including abundant correspondence, connecting each to Niebuhr; and the impact each made on American life and thought.

The sequence of the chapters is based on both chronological and developmental factors. The chronological factor relates to the time during which Niebuhr's interaction with each person came into focus. The developmental factor relates to the changes in Niebuhr's thought over the course of his career. The relationship between Niebuhr and Tillich began in 1933, arising out of the situation in Nazi Germany when Niebuhr played an instrumental role in helping Tillich establish himself at Union Theological Seminary in New York City. Paul

Tillich, Norman Thomas, and John Dewey were ardent socialists at the time Niebuhr first gained public notice with the publication of *Moral Man and Immoral Society* in 1932. Niebuhr and Dewey worked together in the arena of progressive politics from the time Niebuhr arrived at Union, although their relationship became increasingly adversarial after Niebuhr held him up to criticism in *Moral Man and Immoral Society*. Niebuhr and Norman Thomas shared a socialist history that spanned the period between Thomas's first run for the presidency in 1928 and Niebuhr's resignation from the Socialist Party in 1940. The beginning of Niebuhr's relationship with Schlesinger occurred at a transitional period when Niebuhr was moving away from his socialist-radical period. Schlesinger, a generation younger, became aware of Niebuhr at the beginning of the 1940s, and their relationship reached its zenith during their support of Adlai Stevenson during his presidential campaigns of 1952 and 1956. Niebuhr met Hans Morgenthau at the University of Chicago in 1944, and together they helped shape the emerging political realism that spanned the 1940s and 1950s. Although George Kennan and Niebuhr had little face-to-face contact, Kennan, referring to the political realists, once called Niebuhr "the father of us all" and conscripted Niebuhr to serve as one of the outsiders on the State Department's policy planning committee in 1949. The book concludes with Felix Frankfurter, whose relationship with Niebuhr spanned the quarter-century prior to Frankfurter's death in 1965 and was the most intimate of all Niebuhr's associations among these seven individuals.

The underlying thread that connects Niebuhr's relationships with all of these luminaries is the political and social history that gave shape and substance to life in the United States in the period between the 1930s and the time of Niebuhr's death in 1971. The world in which they interacted and were so very influential covered the decades between the Great Depression of 1929 and the peak of the Cold War in the 1960s. Niebuhr came to Union Seminary in 1928 as the era of the old GOP – with the pro-business conservatism of Warren Harding, Calvin Coolidge, and Herbert Hoover – was about to implode. This was the America into which Niebuhr, John Dewey, and Norman Thomas launched their attacks on laissez-faire capitalism, advocating socialism as a sensible option for America's future. During the late 1920s and early 1930s, the three worked together on numerous causes, served together on various committees, and published articles in socialist-leaning journals such as *The World Tomorrow*. Norman Thomas, running on the Socialist Party ticket, was the presidential candidate of choice in 1928 for both Niebuhr and Dewey.

Niebuhr, Dewey, and Thomas were strong advocates and defenders of democracy. By the mid-1930s, they became more convinced than ever that democracy itself could survive only if some form of socialism replaced a capitalist order that they saw drifting inexorably toward fascism. Niebuhr was in his most radical phase at this time, propelled in large measure by the rapid success of fascist movements in Europe. During these years, while aligning himself with the socialist causes and the presidential ambitions of Norman Thomas, Niebuhr's controversy with Dewey continued to grow and occupy space in journals such as

The World Tomorrow, *The New Republic*, and, in Niebuhr's case, scattered throughout his publications.

Amid the rising tide of fascism in Hitler's Germany, Paul Tillich's long-standing advocacy of democratic socialism there, his intellectual openness, and his defense of his students from Nazi harassment led to his dismissal from the teaching position he held in Frankfurt. Tillich came to America in 1933 under the auspices of Union Theological Seminary and Columbia University. Niebuhr aided in arranging the move by introducing Tillich to various intellectual circles, and, with his wife, assisting the Tillichs in their adjustment to life in America. The friendship between Niebuhr and Tillich easily survived what became a highly public theological dispute in the 1940s and 1950s.

Niebuhr's relationships with Schlesinger, Morgenthau, Kennan, and Frankfurter date from the early to mid-1940s. The historian Arthur Schlesinger Jr. was drawn to Niebuhr at the time Niebuhr broke with the Socialist Party in 1940, on the eve of America's entry into World War II. Niebuhr voted for Roosevelt that year after gaining increasing appreciation for Rooseveltian pragmatism and its New Deal reforms. Niebuhr was also so convinced that the country must enter the war against Hitler that, in 1941, he launched his own journal, *Christianity and Crisis*. While chiding Niebuhr for his failure to appreciate Roosevelt's pragmatic approach earlier, Schlesinger came to highly value Niebuhr's realistic assessment of human nature and his running commentary on world events. Both Schlesinger and Niebuhr were active in the ADA (Americans for Democratic Action) and worked diligently in support of Adlai Stevenson's failed efforts to capture the presidency in 1952 and 1956.

Hans Morgenthau, entering the American scene in the mid-1940s, met Niebuhr at the University of Chicago in 1944. They quickly became friends and allies based on their mutual commitment to realism in politics. Morgenthau emerged as the major authority on international political theory with the publication of his *Politics Among Nations* in 1948. He, together with Niebuhr and George Kennan, fought the radical swing in America between isolationism, on the one hand, and zealous interventionism, on the other. All three sought to redirect international political thinking in America away from the overly idealistic pathways that, they were convinced, would lead only to disaster in global politics. The urgency of their writings reflected the realities of the time – the Cold War and the nuclear age when the post–World War II rivalry between the United States and the Soviet Union threatened again and again to bring the world to the brink of atomic war.

Niebuhr's relationship with Supreme Court Justice Felix Frankfurter was at its core a personal friendship, as the trove of correspondence left by Frankfurter reveals. Frankfurter first encountered Niebuhr when the latter was preaching in Heath, Massachusetts, where both resided during the summers. Frankfurter's tenure on the Supreme Court began in 1939. In 1941, he was called upon to intervene on Niebuhr's behalf in a case wherein Niebuhr's loyalty was being questioned by the FBI. They became friends and over the decades repeatedly found themselves in each other's intellectual debt. Frankfurter read Niebuhr's books and articles, often sharing views and even consulting him on theological matters. Niebuhr, in turn, both consulted and engaged Frankfurter on a variety of judicial matters. The many issues over which they exchanged views covered the entire range of events that shaped the period between World War II and the mid-1960s.

It was clearly a credit to Niebuhr that there were those individuals among this august group who not only held him in high regard but also turned to him for advice and friendship. Although having varying reactions to Niebuhr's religious convictions, they all recognized and responded to the religious basis on which his insights and analyses were grounded. In the late 1920s and throughout the 1930s, Niebuhr shared the religious views of Social Gospel liberals, although he soon became a major critic of the Social Gospel and what he came to view as the simplistic idealism and moralism of American liberalism in both its religious and secular forms. This is the Niebuhr who engages and is engaged by both John Dewey and Norman Thomas. Later on, in the 1940s and 1950s, Niebuhr had discovered and appropriated the insights of the Protestant Reformers Luther and Calvin, and, most especially, those of St. Augustine. This gradually led to what has been called "Christian realism," and it is this Niebuhr who is predominant in his relationships with Schlesinger, Morgenthau, Kennan, and Frankfurter.

Niebuhr had a rather distinctive standing among theologians. In the wake of his memorable statement "I cannot and do not claim to be a theologian,"[1] Niebuhr carefully honed his disclaimer by admitting that he was interested neither in the "fine points of pure theology" nor in being a "theologian" in the sense that his European critics might have expected from him. Niebuhr found himself quite comfortable with Alexis de Tocqueville's observation that, "in comparison with European Christianity," American Christianity bore a "strong pragmatic interest." He declared that his own competence in "Christian social ethics" and "in the ancillary field of 'apologetics'" had "prompted an interest in the defense and justification of the Christian faith in a secular age, particularly among what Schleiermacher called Christianity's 'intellectual despisers.'"[2]

Niebuhr's overriding interest was to distill insights about human nature from both biblical faith and subsequent theological resources and apply them to the full range of social and political life. He struggled constantly with the problem of how to relate Christian love (*agape*) and political justice, and how that relationship could be applied to social communities. From the beginning Niebuhr was

---

[1] R. Niebuhr, "Intellectual Autobiography" in C. W. Kegley, *Reinhold Niebuhr: His Religious, Social and Political Thought* (New York: Pilgrim Press, 1984), p. 3. The first edition, edited by C. W. Kegley and R. W. Bretall, was published by Macmillan in 1956.

[2] Ibid. By his own admission, Niebuhr was not doing what theologians characteristically do; namely, either write dogmatic theology, as Karl Barth did for the church, or construct a systematic theology aimed at covering the full range of Christian belief, as was the case with Paul Tillich. Indeed, one of Tillich's mistakes (made in his 1941 review of the first volume of Niebuhr's *The Nature and Destiny of Man*) was expressing the expectation that "we shall have a theological system" when the second volume appeared. See P. Tillich, review of *The Nature and Destiny of Man* in *Christianity and Society* (Spring, 1941), 34.

involved in a variety of political activities that, in turn, fed into his teaching of social ethics. Roger Shinn pointed out that, as Niebuhr became actively involved in the world of politics and public affairs on both national and international levels, he developed "what might be called a bilingual ethics. That is, he was resolutely Christian" with an "immersion in Scripture, the Augustinian heritage, the theology of the Reformation, and in the social gospel. At the same time he was showing the relevance of those insights to audiences that thought themselves indifferent or hostile to them."[3] Although he denied being a "theologian" in any systematic manner, George Lindbeck is correct in pointing out that Niebuhr was "perhaps the last American theologian who in practice (and in some extent in theory) made extended and effective attempts to redescribe aspects of the contemporary scene in distinctively Christian terms."[4]

Niebuhr's appeal to individuals in the secular world also was owed to the fact that his theological apologetics was rooted in, and reflected, the pragmatic tradition of James and Dewey. His connection to and appropriation of American pragmatism is evident from the earliest days and continued throughout his changing views, albeit in somewhat different ways. Niebuhr was consistently pragmatic in the obvious sense that his thought was consistently related to what Dewey called the "problems of men." On a deeper level, however, his very conception of both theology and the theological enterprise came to bear the mark of pragmatism. Roger Shinn is certainly correct in pointing out that Niebuhr's highly touted pragmatism was definitely "a pragmatism in a theological context."[5] It is also the case that Niebuhr was doing theology in a pragmatic context. In sharing Dewey's distrust of the metaphysical and epistemological certainties associated with Western intellectual tradition, Niebuhr engaged in what Richard Rorty labeled an "edifying" activity. He ably performed the role which Rorty so valued in our society; namely, "that of the informed dilettante, the polypragmatic, Socratic intermediary between various discourses" in whose "salon, so to speak, hermetic thinkers are charmed out of their self-enclosed practices" and where "disengagements between disciplines and discourses are compromised or transcended in the course of conversation."[6] Niebuhr knew he was drawing upon a theological tradition that had been ignored, rejected, or

---

[3] R. L. Shinn, "Reinhold Niebuhr as teacher, colleague, and friend" in D. F. Rice (ed.), *Reinhold Niebuhr Revisited: Engagements with an American Original* (Grand Rapids, MI: Eerdmans, 2009), p. 8. In choosing to function from within the theological tradition in the role of a theological apologist, Niebuhr's manner was often polemical. Because his criticisms were aimed primarily at the overly optimistic rationalism that was predominant in America's secular and religious circles, he was frequently vilified by members of both communities. From many within his own religious tradition, his polemics often received rejection and expressions of wounded pride. From secular quarters, he was often accused of misrepresenting the persons or positions he criticized, or was simply dismissed as being a supernatural "irrationalist."

[4] G. A. Lindbeck, *The Nature of Doctrine: Religion and Theology in a Post-Liberal Age* (Philadelphia: Westminster Press, 1984), p. 124.

[5] R. L. Shinn, "Realism, radicalism, and eschatology," *Journal of Religion* (October, 1974), 415.

[6] R. Rorty, *Philosophy and the Mirror of Nature* (Princeton, NJ: Princeton University Press, 1979), p. 317.

simply marginalized by many who nonetheless found compelling what he had to say. To use Rorty's term, Niebuhr functioned as a "peripheral" theologian whose theological discourse was used to engage the secular culture in an attempt to keep conversational spaces open against unwarranted closures. That he did so with some measure of success is witnessed to by the caliber of influential individuals touched by both his life and his thought. A brief sketch of the seven men dealt with in this volume follows.

PAUL TILLICH (1886–1965)

The one theologian with whom Niebuhr had a significant and lasting relationship was his friend and colleague Paul Tillich. Born the son of a Lutheran minister in Germany in 1886, Tillich came to America in 1933 at age forty-seven after losing his teaching position during the Nazi regime. With Niebuhr's assistance, he began teaching at both Union Theological Seminary and Columbia University in New York City. After developing his existentialist-based philosophical theology, Tillich became one of the twentieth century's most influential Protestant theologians. His monumental three-volume *Systematic Theology* was published between 1951 and 1963. Among his more popular works are *The Shaking of the Foundations* (1948), *The Courage to Be* (1952), and *Dynamics of Faith* (1957). Tillich remained Niebuhr's colleague at Union until 1955, when he went to Harvard University. In 1962, Tillich took a position at the University of Chicago, where he remained until his death three years later.

Together, Niebuhr and Tillich occupied center stage among Protestant theologians in America in the decades surrounding the mid-twentieth century. The tradition of nineteenth-century Protestant liberalism – the tradition of Adolf von Harnack, Albrecht Ritschl, and Friedrich Schleiermacher – had come under devastating attack in Europe in the 1920s by the Swiss Reformed theologians Karl Barth and Emil Brunner. A decade later Niebuhr launched his own scathing attack on the vapidity of the liberal tradition – both religious and secular – in his 1934 book *Moral Man and Immoral Society*. Niebuhr's attack, combined with Tillich's role in bringing European developments in theology to the United States, resulted in their being identified as the leading exponents of what was labeled "Neo-orthodoxy" in America. To a large extent the label was misapplied. Whereas Niebuhr and Tillich drew upon similar theological resources in criticizing Protestant liberalism, they were sharply critical of Barth for his narrow view of the relation between theology and culture with its lack of appreciation for broader theological and philosophical traditions.

Soon after coming to Union Theological Seminary, Niebuhr voiced appreciation for the liberating role Tillich's interpretation of religious symbols had for the churches in America. Tillich had been active in social and political struggles in Germany, and he joined with Niebuhr in the Fellowship of Socialist Christians during their early years together in America. Gradually, however, Tillich's and Niebuhr's intellectual worlds diverged. Niebuhr's focus was on politics, history, and social ethics, while Tillich's interests were in philosophy, psychology, and the arts. Tillich and Niebuhr eventually engaged in a decade-long dispute over the role of ontological analysis in theological discourse.

From the time between Tillich's arrival in America and the post–World War II decade of the mid-1940s, Niebuhr and Tillich made occasional trips to Europe and wrote extensively on the Nazi situation that engulfed Germany. The first part of Chapter 1 deals with their mutual involvement with events in Germany and elsewhere in Europe before, during, and after the rise of Nazism. The second part focuses on theological issues and the controversy in which they became involved after they had gained prominence in the American theological scene.

JOHN DEWEY (1859–1952)

Chapter 2 focuses on John Dewey, who was born in Vermont in 1859. Dewey became the dominant intellectual figure in America during the first half of the twentieth century. His reputation as an innovator in educational theory was established early in his career both at the University of Chicago and at Columbia University. Dewey's impact on democratic thought in the United States was unexcelled, and he became the most articulate defender of democratic requirements in the context of industrial America. A few of his major books relating to politics include *Democracy and Education* (1916), *The Public and Its Problems* (1927), and *Liberalism and Social Action* (1935). As America's ranking philosopher, Dewey viewed philosophy as relating first and foremost to "the problems of men." He was the major successor to Charles Sanders Peirce and William James in furthering the tradition of American pragmatism, although he chose to label his version "instrumentalism." In the years since his death, his name has again come to the fore in the resurgent reevaluation of pragmatism and its role in contemporary philosophical trends.

Niebuhr's and Dewey's lives overlapped only briefly between Niebuhr's arrival at Union Theological Seminary in New York City in 1928 at age thirty-five and Dewey's official retirement from Columbia University in 1930 at age seventy-one. The only occasions in which Niebuhr and Dewey had personal contact were when they served together in various social and political organizations. Niebuhr, who was a generation younger than Dewey, launched an attack on Dewey beginning in 1932 when, in his book *Moral Man and Immoral Society*, he singled out Dewey as the quintessential embodiment of the naïve, utopian, and excessively rationalistic views of American liberalism. Beyond their disputes over the merits and weaknesses of American liberalism, Niebuhr and Dewey also differed in their approaches to religion, naturalistic philosophy, human nature, and democracy.

NORMAN THOMAS (1884–1968)

Chapter 3 traces the interesting and somewhat tumultuous relationship between Niebuhr and Norman Thomas, who succeeded Eugene Debs as the head of the

Socialist Party of America. This chapter focuses primarily on the twenty-year span between Thomas's first and sixth runs for president of the United States. During the 1930s, after Niebuhr had moved to New York City, he was drawn into the orbit of Norman Thomas and became an ardent supporter of socialist causes. Ohio-born and Princeton-educated, Norman Thomas started out as a Presbyterian minister. A product of the emphasis on the Social Gospel gained at Union Theological Seminary, he developed an acute social consciousness that drew him to a ministry in East Harlem. Thomas was a member of the pacifist Fellowship of Reconciliation (FOR), and his opposition to America's participation in World War I led to his resignation from his pastorate and later to a departure from the Presbyterian Church. His status as a conscientious objector was the deciding factor in his joining the Socialist Party of America in 1918. That same year Thomas became editor of the Fellowship's journal *The World Tomorrow*, and four years later he became codirector of the League for Industrial Democracy.

Running unsuccessfully on the Socialist ticket for a variety of political offices during the 1920s, Thomas became the Socialist Party candidate for president of the United States in 1928. His brand of socialism grew out of a Christian framework and was democratic to the core. Although socialism never gained traction in the United States, Thomas gained a measure of respect and admiration among his fellow Americans. Amid ever-increasing factional disputes within socialist ranks, he would run as the Socialist Party's presidential candidate five more times, finally ending his bid after the 1948 election.

After arriving at Union Theological Seminary in 1928, Niebuhr, eight years younger than Thomas, was drawn to the socialist movement that the older man led. Thomas gave forceful expression to socialist thought during the late 1920s and 1930s, when economic conditions in America were deteriorating. In their reactions to the Great Depression, both Thomas and Niebuhr saw capitalism as being bankrupt and intractably decadent. Thomas and Niebuhr came to believe that American capitalism was doomed and that the nation was rapidly moving toward the kind of fascism that had overtaken much of Europe. Niebuhr became a staunch supporter of Thomas, backing his presidential campaigns in 1928, 1932, and 1936. However, in 1940 an insurmountable break occurred when, after repudiating the pacifism of the Socialist Party and gaining increasing appreciation for the accomplishments of the New Deal, Niebuhr supported Franklin Roosevelt for the presidency. His support for American involvement in World War II was a primary factor in his resignation from the Socialist Party and resulted in his founding of the publication *Christianity and Crisis* in 1941. Thomas unsuccessfully implored Niebuhr to return to the ranks of the Socialist Party. However, he took some solace in the fact that by the 1948 election many of his recommendations and reforms had been taken up by America's mainstream political parties. Although Niebuhr and Thomas would go their separate ways politically, they remained on friendly terms.

ARTHUR M. SCHLESINGER JR. (1917–2007)

One of the most prolific historians in America, Arthur Schlesinger Jr. combined a scholarly yet exciting historical writing with a committed political activism. He not only wrote history but also wrote forceful analyses and interpretations of issues affecting the contemporary body politic. Born in Ohio, Schlesinger was heir to the historical talents of his father. He first came into prominence in 1945 as a historian with the publication of his Pulitzer Prize–winning book *The Age of Jackson*, and he later secured his reputation as one of America's ranking historians with the publication of his three-volume work *The Age of Roosevelt* (1957–60). In addition to writing biographies of both John and Robert Kennedy, many of Schlesinger's later writings combined historical writing with social and political activism, including books such as *The Vital Center* (1949), *The Imperial Presidency* (1973), *The Cycles of American History* (1986), and *The Disuniting of America* (1991).

A generation younger than Niebuhr, Schlesinger's active life ranged from serving in the Office of Strategic Services (OSS) during World War II, through involvement in Cold War-era politics, to witnessing the dawn of the twenty-first century. Schlesinger's political activities were legend – ranging from his involvement in Americans for Democratic Action (ADA) and participation in the two Democratic presidential campaigns of Illinois Governor Adlai Stevenson to his service to the Kennedy administration when, on leave from Harvard, he accepted the position of special assistant to the president. After the tragedies affecting the Kennedys, he returned to teaching at the Graduate Center of the City University of New York until retiring in 2004. Schlesinger recorded this journey in two books: *A Life in the Twentieth Century: Innocent Beginnings, 1917–1950* (2000) and *Journals 1952–2000*.

From the time Schlesinger's wife prodded him to listen to Niebuhr preach at Harvard in the early 1940s until Niebuhr's death in 1971, each man exerted significant influence on the other. In terms of political action, they worked together in Democratic politics, particularly in support of the twice-defeated Stevenson. In terms of intellectual influence, Schlesinger was profoundly impacted by Niebuhr's realism, especially in its devastating analysis of the limits of human reason and its indictment of the naïve idealism then so prevalent in American society. While benefiting from Niebuhr's understanding of human nature, Schlesinger remained at a comfortable distance from the theological convictions that Niebuhr found so important. Niebuhr, meanwhile, deferred to Schlesinger on historical matters, and he admitted to Schlesinger that he had come rather late in appreciating Roosevelt and his pragmatic New Deal measures. After Niebuhr's first stroke in 1952, Schlesinger involved himself personally in Niebuhr's life, much to the benefit and appreciation of Niebuhr and his family. In the last decade of his life, with his health in rapid decline, Niebuhr deeply valued his continuing friendship with Schlesinger.

HANS J. MORGENTHAU (1904–1980)

Chapter 5 deals with Niebuhr's remarkable relationship with Hans Morgenthau, who, within six years of his 1943 arrival in America, gained the well-deserved reputation as America's preeminent international political theorist. Morgenthau was not only one of the architects of modern international politics but also instrumental in the move to obtaining a home for the study of foreign affairs and diplomacy in the political science departments of most universities. Born in Coburg, Germany, to a Jewish family, Morgenthau was educated in Germany and Switzerland. After a variety of teaching positions ending in Frankfurt, he immigrated to the United States in 1937 during the Nazi era. Morgenthau secured a position at the University of Chicago, where he taught for twenty-five years until, in 1968, he took up a teaching post at the New School for Social Research and at City University of New York.

The twenty-five-year relationship between Niebuhr and Morgenthau began in 1944 when Niebuhr was invited to Chicago to give a lecture. Niebuhr was then at the apex of his career, having recently published *The Nature and Destiny of Man*. For both men, American political thought was betrayed by the false notion that the methods appropriate to the natural sciences were applicable to understanding the much more complicated realities of human nature. In 1946, Morgenthau published his first important book since arriving in America, *Scientific Man Versus Power Politics*, which, in its attack on what both men labeled "scientism," was in complete accord with Niebuhr's own thinking. In addition, both Niebuhr and Morgenthau agreed that American political thought was wedded to a naïve idealism that consistently misjudged the realities of power and self-interest in both domestic and international politics. In 1948, seeking to redirect political thought toward a more realistic basis, Morgenthau published his monumental *Politics Among Nations*, a work that would undergo numerous editions and become the definitive book on international politics for decades.

Niebuhr and Morgenthau expressed their mutual indebtedness, each insisting that the other had influenced him more. Niebuhr had become one of the major voices in America in defense of what has been called "political realism," and, although his form of realism was rooted explicitly in the Christian theological tradition whereas Morgenthau's realism was not, they usually found themselves on the same side of an issue. Having moved to New York City at the time Niebuhr was nearing the end of his life, Morgenthau was among those whose effort to maintain close personal contact meant so much to Niebuhr.

GEORGE F. KENNAN (1904–2005)

George Kennan was a superb diplomat who emerged as the most astute observer and interpreter of Russia during the critical years of the post–World War II conflict between the United States and the Soviet Union. He was born in Milwaukee, Wisconsin, graduated from Princeton University, and entered the newly formed Foreign Service in 1926. Along with immersing himself in the Russian language, he studied the politics, history, and culture of Russia. Kennan continued his study of Russia while serving in Latvia and in 1933 became one of the best-trained Russian experts at the U.S. embassy in Moscow. After holding several other diplomatic posts throughout the war, in 1944 Kennan was appointed deputy chief of the U.S. mission in Moscow. His knowledge of Russia and its culture had made him quite cynical about U.S.-Soviet relations, and he came to advocate a sphere-of-influence approach in post–World War II Europe rather than an increased cooperation with Russia. His 1946 "long telegram" to the State Department set forth an assessment of how to deal with Russia's mixture of historic insecurity, conspiratorial speculations, and Marxist ideology. A year later he authored, under the imprimatur "X," an article in the journal *Foreign Affairs* on "The Sources of Soviet Conduct," an essay that outlined the famous "containment theory." After retiring from the Foreign Service in 1953, Kennan became a permanent professor at the Institute for Advanced Study at Princeton until his retirement in 1974.

Kennan not only served with distinction as one of America's premier diplomats but also authored numerous articles and official papers relating to his professional positions. Kennan's published books include *American Diplomacy: 1900–1950* (1951), *Realities of American Foreign Policy* (1954), *Russia, the Atom and the West* (1957), and *The Cloud of Danger: Current Realities of American Foreign Policy* (1977). His personal publications include *Memoirs, 1925–1950* (1967) and *Around the Cragged Hill: A Personal and Political Philosophy* (1993).

Niebuhr never had a close relationship with this prestigious statesman and diplomat. However, Kennan acknowledged Niebuhr's influence on him, and he summoned Niebuhr to participate as one of several outsiders in State Department staff meetings. Kennan identified with political realists such as Niebuhr and Morgenthau and, according to a conversation with Kenneth Thompson, Kennan went so far as to claim that "Niebuhr is the father of us all."[7] Niebuhr, in turn, admired Kennan's diplomatic skills and appreciated the fact that Kennan understood "containment" of Soviet influence primarily in political and economic terms, rather than in the predominantly military terms in which it was soon couched. Kennan was chosen by Kenneth Thompson to deliver the memorial tribute to Niebuhr before the American Academy of Arts and Letters in 1971.

FELIX FRANKFURTER (1882–1965)

Chapter 7 of the book deals with Niebuhr's close and personal relationship with Supreme Court Justice Felix Frankfurter. Born in Vienna, the twelve-year-old

---

[7] See K. W. Thompson, "Niebuhr and the foreign policy realists" in D. F. Rice (ed.), *Reinhold Niebuhr Revisited: Engagements with an American Original* (Grand Rapids, MI: Eerdmans, 2009), p. 139.

Frankfurter moved with his family to the Lower East Side of New York City in 1894. After receiving a degree from the City College of New York, he attended Harvard Law School, graduating with highest honors. After a diverse career in law and political activism, including helping found the American Civil Liberties Union, Frankfurter was appointed to a chair at Harvard Law School. His illustrious career reached its zenith in 1939, when President Roosevelt appointed him to the United States Supreme Court, replacing the recently deceased Benjamin N. Cardozo. Considered to be one of the most brilliant minds in the Court's history, Frankfurter's advocacy of judicial restraint after having held liberal-progressive social views disappointed Roosevelt and bewildered Frankfurter's political friends. While Niebuhr's commitment to progressive justice generally found him sympathetic to the decisions of the Warren Court, he genuinely appreciated the rationale behind Frankfurter's defense of judicial restraint.

The extent of our knowledge of Niebuhr's relationship with Frankfurter is the result of Frankfurter's commitment to writing and saving letters. With Niebuhr based in New York City and Frankfurter in Washington, DC, they had only occasional personal contact. However, they spent many summers together in Heath, Massachusetts, enabling them to establish a close personal friendship, which created a hiatus in their otherwise frequent correspondence.

This chapter covers the relationship between Niebuhr and Frankfurter between the early 1940s and Frankfurter's death in 1965 – a relationship revealing not only the vast range of intellectual interests Niebuhr and Frankfurter shared, but also various aspects of the personal life that existed between their two families.

Daniel F. Rice
Chicago, Illinois

CHAPTER I

Paul Tillich (1886–1965)

NIEBUHR, TILLICH, AND "THE GERMAN SITUATION"

Paul Tillich and Reinhold Niebuhr became the two most influential and widely read theologians in American Protestantism during the middle third of the twentieth century. The historian Van Harvey claimed that "it can safely be said that Reinhold Niebuhr and Paul Tillich were the last two public theologians in this country, that is, theologians whose names were recognized because they contributed to those types of discourse that seriously engage American intellectuals."[1] The relationship between Niebuhr and Tillich began not in the realm of theology, as one might suppose, but rather in the cauldron of pre–World War II German politics.[2] Tillich, at age forty-seven, arrived in New York from Germany with his family on November 4, 1933, by way of an arrangement made between Union Theological Seminary and Columbia University.[3] In the midst of this arrangement, Union president Henry Sloane Coffin had Reinhold Niebuhr obtain "more personal information concerning [Tillich] – the nature of Hitler's hostility to him, the size of his family, his academic record, and the probable date of his arrival should we cable him to come."[4] Each faculty member contributed five percent of his wages in support of Tillich's first year salary, and the Board of Directors voted him the use of a small apartment. Niebuhr sent a cable to Tillich informing him of the decision and urged Columbia University professor of philosophy Horace S. Friess to meet with Tillich while Friess was in Germany that summer. Tillich was told that he need not teach a course during the fall, while being given time

---

[1] V. A. Harvey, "On the intellectual marginality of American theology" in Michael J. Lacey (ed.), *Religion and Twentieth-Century American Life* (Cambridge: Cambridge University Press, 1989), p. 172.

[2] An earlier version of this section on Niebuhr, Tillich, and the situation in Germany can be found in *Union Seminary Quarterly Review*, 62 (2010), 152–86.

[3] A committee at Columbia University was formed that year with Union Theological Seminary president Henry Sloane Coffin as Union's representative. On the condition that Columbia would utilize Tillich in its philosophy program, Coffin agreed to find a position for Tillich at Union.

[4] H. S. Coffin, *A Half-Century of Union Theological Seminary 1896–1945: An Informal History*, p. 135.

FIG. 1 Tillich
Courtesy of the University of Chicago

to study English, but he would teach one course during the spring semester. Upon his arrival in New York in November, 1933, Tillich was met by Friess and, soon after, was welcomed to his new apartment at Union Theological Seminary by Niebuhr's wife Ursula.

In his 1952 autobiographical sketch, Tillich wrote that when "shortly after my dismissal by Hitler I was asked by Reinhold Niebuhr (who happened to be in Germany that summer) to come to Union Seminary," Tillich was prevented "from becoming a refugee in the technical sense." Moreover, he credited Niebuhr for extending an invitation that provided him "a shelter at the moment when my work and my existence in Germany had come to an end."[5] Unlike so many émigrés from Germany who were prevented from taking up their careers regardless of their previous professional status, Tillich entered the United States by way of an unfilled quota – a status that, along with the invitation from Union/ Columbia, enabled Tillich to continue in his profession while assisting others less fortunate.[6] Niebuhr had also "been his informal sponsor in this country" and,

[5] P. Tillich, "Autobiographical reflections" in C. W. Kegley and R. W. Bretall, *The Theology of Paul Tillich* (New York: Macmillan, 1952), p. 16.

[6] Hannah Tillich recounted how "friends sent their emigrating friends to Paulus as the head of Selfhelp for German Emigres. At first he brought everybody to our house for a meal, but after a while it became too much, in amount of people as well as of money. Of course they were all poor – doctors who had to take a special examination here, philosophers, economists, psychologists, the intellectual elite of Germany, businessmen, bankers." She concluded that while "many of the old

soon after Tillich's arrival, "arranged for the publication of *The Interpretation of History* (1936)."[7] Paul Tillich made the United States his home from the time he arrived in New York in 1933 until his death in Chicago in 1965.

The vast intellectual accomplishments Tillich achieved after his arrival in the United States established Tillich's reputation for most Americans. The contributions he made to the social and political struggles in Germany, both before and after his arrival in the United States, began to receive significant attention only long after Tillich's death.[8] Tillich was the first non-Jew to be dismissed from a teaching post by Hitler. Tillich's suspension from his chair in philosophy at Frankfurt am Main on April 13, 1933, was occasioned by his warnings that the Nazis jeopardized academic freedom, Nazi opposition to his 1932 book *The Socialist Decision* (proposing a socialist alternative to the German crisis), his active defense of his university from an attack by Nazi thugs, and his refusal to take an oath of submission to Hitler.[9] The relationship between Niebuhr and Tillich began during the period 1930–3 and centered almost entirely on the political situation in Germany during the rise of Nazism in the wake of the collapse of the Weimar Republic. This mutual involvement with the German situation extended well into the post–World War II era. Their interaction operated on both personal and literary levels – moving along parallel, intersecting, and overlapping paths.

Pre-Nazi Germany

In the mid-1920s, while Tillich was making the transition from a teaching post in Berlin to a position in Marburg and giving shape to what became known as

---

friends were responsible for the founding" of Selfhelp for German Emigres, "Paulus was obliged to carry the burden as president in the first years." See *From Time to Time*, p. 181.

[7] R. Shinn, "Reinhold Niebuhr as teacher, colleague, and friend" in D. F. Rice (ed.), *Reinhold Niebuhr Revisited: Engagements with an American Original* (Grand Rapids, MI: Eerdmans, 2009), p. 11. In 1932, prior to Tillich's coming to America, Reinhold Niebuhr's brother, H. Richard Niebuhr, had introduced Tillich to an American audience through his translation of Tillich's book *The Religious Situation* (New York: Holt, 1932). Reinhold reviewed this book a few months prior to his trip to Germany in 1933. His review was given the title "Eternity and Our Time" and appeared in *The World Tomorrow* (December 21, 1932).

[8] Notable among these are W. and M. Pauck, *Paul Tillich: His Life and Thought* (New York: Harper & Row, 1976); J. R. Stumme, *Socialism in Theological Perspective: A Study of Paul Tillich 1918-1933*, (Missoula, MT: Scholars Press, 1978); R. H. Stone, *Paul Tillich's Radical Social Thought* (Atlanta, GA: John Knox Press, 1980); and R. H. Stone and M. L. Weaver (eds.), *Against the Third Reich: Paul Tillich's Wartime Radio Broadcasts into Germany* (Louisville, KY: Westminster/John Knox Press, 1998).

[9] A detailed account of the period leading up to Tillich's dismissal is to be found in W. and M. Pauck's *Paul Tillich: His Life and Thought*, pp. 129–38. Of the Nazi attack at the university, Tillich's wife, Hannah, wrote "It was a last triumph of reason when the attack on the university by Nazi hoodlums and a few students was unsuccessful. The university senate, fighting back, managed to insist on the punishment of the intruders. Paulus, who had been lecturing during the attack, had helped to carry battered students into a room behind his office." Hannah Tillich, *From Time to Time* (New York: Stein and Day, 1973), p. 149. The section on "Frankfurt" in Hannah Tillich's book also provides a highly personal view of the period prior to their departure for America.

"religious socialism," Niebuhr, serving Bethel Church in Detroit, traveled twice to Germany with a study group called the "American Seminar" under the leadership of Sherwood Eddy. Niebuhr's exposure to the situation in Weimar Germany afforded him the opportunity of witnessing firsthand the massive suffering that the Treaty of Versailles had imposed on Germany after World War I. In the course of his two trips Niebuhr contributed a total of eight articles to *The Evangelical Herald*.[10] In an August 9, 1923, article he described immense German suffering in the Ruhr caused by the vindictive aims of a French policy that sought the destruction of the German nation itself through the occupation of Germany's key industrial area and the confiscation of its crucial resources.[11] Writing in September on "Germany in Despair," Niebuhr reiterated how "the Ruhr invasion has opened up the jugular vein of the patient and seems to make his recovery impossible." At the same time the combination of ignorance and a persistent isolationist policy prevented America, "the only hope of Germany," from assuming a responsible role in preventing European disaster.[12]

Niebuhr's hopes for Germany wavered between his learning that while the Weimar constitution was being celebrated, there were "millions of Germans who will have nothing of the republic," on the one hand, and believing it was "probable that the republic has weathered the worst storms" on the other. He was still holding out hope that the enemies of the republic were "not united" and had "no clear program" and that "the defenders of the republic are resolute and determined and are probably in the majority."[13]

Tillich, of course, had lived through the events leading up to those that Niebuhr was interpreting for his American audience. Having witnessed the abdication of Kaiser Wilhelm and the hesitant assumption of power by the Social Democratic Party, Tillich began voicing socialist ideas that went beyond merely reforming post–World War I society.[14] Between 1919 and 1933, Tillich developed his socialist thinking through lectures, writings, and, most importantly, in a variety of communal settings. These included meetings in

---

[10] Articles published in 1923 include: "A trip though the Ruhr," *The Evangelical Herald* (August 9, 1923); "Germany in despair," *The Evangelical Herald* (September 13, 1923); "The despair of Europe," *The Evangelical Herald* (September 20, 1923); "America and Europe," *The Evangelical Herald* (November 1, 1923); and "The youth movement in Germany," *The Christian Century* (November 1, 1923). The 1924 articles are: "The dawn in Europe," *The Evangelical Herald* (August 7, 1924); "Berlin notes," *The Evangelical Herald* (September 18, 1924); and "Is Europe on the way to peace?" *The Evangelical Herald* (September 25, 1924). All of these articles appear in W. G. Crystal's *Young Reinhold Niebuhr: His Early Writings, 1911–1931* (New York: Pilgrim Press, 1977).

[11] R. Niebuhr, "A trip through the Ruhr" in W. G. Chrystal (ed.), *Young Reinhold Niebuhr: His Early Writings, 1911–1931* (New York: Pilgrim Press, 1977), pp. 124–7.

[12] R. Niebuhr, "Germany in despair," Ibid., 128–9.

[13] Niebuhr, "Berlin notes," Ibid., 154.

[14] R. H. Stone chronicles a brief history of Tillich's socialist activities and involvements from 1919, when Tillich was in Berlin through his moves to Marburg, Dresden, Leipzig, and finally Frankfurt. See R. H. Stone, *Paul Tillich's Radical Social Thought* (Atlanta, GA: John Knox Press, 1980), chapters 4, 5, and 6.

1919 with a group of intellectuals which dealt with the relationship of the church to socialism, membership in the "Berlin group" or "*kairos* circle" starting in 1920, and while active involvement in the Institute of Social Research (*Institut fur Sozialforschung*) in Frankfurt after 1929. During this period there would appear such key works as Tillich's 1922 essay "Kairos," his 1923 essay "Basic Principles of Religious Socialism, *The Religious Situation* (1926), and *The Socialist Decision* (1932–3).

Niebuhr next visited Germany in 1930 as an established figure at Union Theological Seminary, having the task of reporting back to America on the rapidly developing religious and political situation in Germany. He found that the situation had worsened. A socialist himself at that time, Niebuhr wrote on the "German Election Prospects," expressing concern for the socialist movement there. He pointed out how, "having worked for international conciliation within the terms of the Versailles treaty" with its "impossible reparations," German Socialism was placed at a severe disadvantage to the Communists "who could make the plausible argument that the Socialist has helped to make the German worker the slave of international capital."[15] Meanwhile, democratic prospects were dashed by the splintering of the fragile coalition of liberal and centrist parties as it fell victim to attacks from all sides for its complicity in the national humiliation caused by the harsh economic reparations and truncated borders meted out by the Allies in the Versailles Treaty. While underestimating the appeal of National Socialism, Niebuhr was convinced that "the policy of conciliation with other former enemy nations which the parliamentary Republican parties have been following" was "bound to color political thought for decades."[16] His hope for a large Social Democratic vote in the September election along with the survival of German parliamentary government proved illusory. In writing for *The Nation* on "The German Crisis" in October, Niebuhr reported how unhealthy the political situation was in Germany, lamenting how the National Socialists – "a party of demagogues" – had successfully exploited "the discontent of the worker and the outraged pride of the Nationalists" and had drawn strength from exciting "in the breast of German citizens" a racially based hatred of the Jews.[17]

The year 1930 also saw the appearance of Tillich's "Sozialismus: II. Religioser Sozialismus," later published in English as "Religious Socialism" in the 1971 book *Religious Expectation*. In this essay, Tillich formulated an approach that he hoped would "resolve the static opposition of the concepts of religion and socialism by demonstrating their dialectical relationship."[18] He wanted an understanding of religion wherein religion was freed from "bondage

---

[15] R. Niebuhr, "German election prospects," *The New Leader* (August 1, 1930), 5.

[16] R. Niebuhr, "Political currents in Germany," *The New Leader* (July 26, 1930), 5.

[17] R. Niebuhr, "The German crisis," *The Nation* (October 1, 1930), 359–60.

[18] P. Tillich, "Religious socialism," *Political Expectation* (New York: Harper & Row, 1971), 41. Tillich's original essay, "Socialismus: II. religioser sozialismus" appeared in *Die Religion in Geschichte und Gegenwart*, 2nd ed. (Tubingen, 1930), vol. V, pp. 637–48.

to the religious sphere as a sphere apart," creating in the process "an openness for the religious understanding of the profane." His immediate aim was to achieve room for "a religious analysis of secular forms of socialism." Conversely, Tillich sought to overcome socialism's hostility to religion by formulating a "religious socialism" that "does not abandon the theoretical and practical forms of socialist life to their apparent secularity, but penetrates to the religious character of their basis."[19] Niebuhr's own awareness of Tillich's involvement in the socialist cause found expression that same year in his August, 1930, article in the *Christian Century* where he made reference to "an organization of religious leaders calling themselves 'religious socialists,' in which, among others, the young philosopher of religion, Paul Tillich is active."[20]

Hitler's Rise to Power

Tillich's hope for democratic socialism continued to find powerful expression in a book he was working on in 1932. Published in 1933 as *Die sozialistische Entscheidun* and translated as *The Socialist Decision*, its appearance coincided with Hitler's assuming power. It was banned and ended up playing a major role in Tillich's dismissal from his teaching position at Frankfurt.[21] Tillich had turned against the quietistic and nationalistic teaching of his Lutheran heritage after having been aroused from his indifference to politics by the sufferings and class prejudices he witnessed as a chaplain during World War I. While later acknowledging that his involvement with socialism in Germany was more theoretical than practical,[22] his 1933 book again sought to overcome both the reticence of Christians to actively engage in needed social reform and the reluctance of secular-minded Marxian socialists to make common cause with the spiritual virtues of Christian ethics.

Speaking out of the Kairos Circle to which he belonged, Tillich had expected a *kairos* moment in Germany that would bring the "in-breaking" of the eternal

---

[19] P. Tillich, "Religious socialism" in *Political Expectation*, 54. Tillich appealed to the "prophetic-Protestant principle" as a way of highlighting the affinity the prophetic, world-changing orientation of socialism had with the biblical prophetic tradition. He also wanted to set the anti-absolutistic principle of Protestantism against the utopian elements in socialist visions of a heaven on earth. The "prophetic-Protestant principle," as Tillich understood it, not only operated as a "guardian against the attempts of the finite and conditioned to usurp the place of the unconditioned in thinking and acting," but it also functioned as a "prophetic judgment against religious pride, ecclesiastical arrogance, and secular self-sufficiency and their destructive consequences." P. Tillich, *The Protestant Era* (Chicago, IL: University of Chicago Press, 1957 abridged edition), p. 163. Tillich applied the same criticisms against later trends he saw in Marxism. See "Marx and the prophetic tradition," *Radical Religion* (Autumn, 1935), 21–9, and his "Marxism and Christian socialism," *Christianity and Society* (Spring, 1942), 13–18.

[20] R. Niebuhr, "Church currents in Germany," *The Christian Century* (August 6, 1930), 959.

[21] See J.R. Stumme's "Introduction" in P. Tillich, *The Socialist Decision* (Washington, DC: University Press of America reprinted by arrangement with Harper & Row, 1977), pp. ix–xxvi.

[22] P. Tillich, "On the boundary: An autobiographical sketch" in *The Interpretation of History* (New York: Charles Scribner's Sons, 1936), p. 17.

into the temporal. Distinguishing between *kronos* (quantitative, formal time) and *kairos* (qualitative time, the time of fullness and significance), Tillich saw the moment in which he lived as a time "when temporal forms are in need of transformation and an eternal meaning is imminent, waiting to break through in temporal fulfillment."[23] Tillich believed that a decisive and world-altering engagement with the eternal was about to occur in Europe in the wake of the debris of sacred symbols and the catastrophic instability of modern civilization.[24] Upon Niebuhr's return to Germany in the summer of 1933 in the wake of the collapse of the Weimar Republic and the Nazi victory of March 5 – at the very time Tillich was extended an invitation to come to Columbia/Union – it was clear that the prospect of a *kairos* moment had definitely disappeared.

Three decades later at a colloquium in honor of Niebuhr held in New York in 1961, Tillich spoke of the role Niebuhr played leading up to the time they first met. Commenting on "our common start in and after the First World War," Tillich stated that Niebuhr, "with his ability of empathetic participation in far removed historical events, was with us at that time, although we did not know him and we did not know that he was with us."[25] Niebuhr had revealed that empathy many times, most recently in a 1932 article "America and Europe," in which he accused America of "selfishness and pharisaism" for having withdrawn from Europe. He pleaded that those "who know the facts in regard to European conditions ought to do everything in their power to sting the American conscience and arouse it out of its present apathy. ... It is time that we think straighter on this whole European issue and cease to strengthen the hands of those who are making the doom of European civilization inevitable."[26]

By 1933, however, the inevitable had happened. Niebuhr's return to Europe that year enabled him once again to bring home to Americans insight into the conditions in Germany. Writing from Germany in April, 1933, Niebuhr lamented the demise of the Social Democrats. While acknowledging that the causes for the "crash" of German socialism were complex, he saw all of them reflecting the lengths to which an imperiled capitalism would go to avoid dissolution. Hitler proved supremely capable of deflecting the resentments of a defeated people away from the financial crisis affecting the middle classes, and welding "the lower and impoverished middle classes politically to the interests of

---

[23] P. Tillich, "Religious socialism," p. 55. Tillich opposed the aspect of his Lutheran heritage that believed only in "Kairos in its *unique* and universal sense [in] the appearing of Jesus as the Christ" – a belief relating *kairos* solely to the eschatological age when Christ would return. See P. Tillich, "Kairos" in *The Protestant Era* (Chicago, IL: University of Chicago Press, 1957 abridged edition), p. 46.

[24] Tillich did not see this as a utopian vision involving an achievable, perfect future, as it tended to be with secular socialists and Marxists. While fervently hoping for the possibility of transformative actions in history, he insisted that our finite human situation was always susceptible to demonic disruption. Therefore, no social order could be expected to lead to the kind of fulfillment meant by the Kingdom of God.

[25] P. Tillich's essay in H. R. Landon (ed.), *Reinhold Niebuhr: A Prophetic Voice in Our Time* (Greenwich, CN: Seabury Press, 1962), p. 31.

[26] R. Niebuhr, "America and Europe" in W. G. Chrystal (ed.), *Young Reinhold Niebuhr*, p. 144.

the industrialists," ending up securing both "votes from the poor and money from the rich."[27] In addition, Hitler "was so effective because he could secure the money of the big industrialists on the promise that he would protect Germany from communism and at the same time he could secure the votes of the poor on the promise that he would proceed against big capital. To weld the poor and the rich into a common political instrument," Niebuhr pointed out, "requires demagogic abilities of a high order."[28]

Niebuhr saw the primary reasons for the failure of German socialism as being twofold: first, that the "parliamentary Socialist party ... was sleepily constitutional in a day when its enemies, both Right and Left, were unconstitutional," and, second, because the party had supported the "the policy of trusting the Allies to be reasonable if Germany fulfilled the conditions of the Treaty of Versailles."[29] Meanwhile, Fascism succeeded in Germany in part because strategic means were successfully employed in order to use and then abuse democratic forms for the purpose of gaining power before eliminating democratic, parliamentary systems altogether.

Both Niebuhr and Tillich abhorred the rise of anti-Semitism then prevalent in Germany, although what was occurring in 1933 was only a prelude to the extermination policies and death camps to come. Tillich, of course, had experienced Nazi inhumanities against the Jews while in his academic position in Frankfurt. Niebuhr's judgment at this time saw "Hitlerism" as "a devil's brew" comprised of the combination of "resentments of a defeated nation against the exactions of its foes, anti-Semitism and economic reaction." While noting that anti-Semitism was "most publicized at the present moment," he thought that it was "secondary to the economic aspect of the movement." Niebuhr's opinion was that the "really important element in fascism" resided in "its toryism and reaction," and that anti-Semitism was used as "merely the tool of its reactionary policies."[30] At the same time, Niebuhr had begun to see German anti-Semitism as the racial bigotry it was. In an August, 1933, article entitled "Germany Must Be Told" published in *The Christian Century*, he claimed that evidence was mounting that Nazi Germany's "effort to extirpate the Jews in Germany is proceeding with unexampled and primitive ferocity."[31] Niebuhr lamented the fact that the German people – left largely in the dark and often mouthing the view that the alleged atrocities were nothing but Jewish propaganda – were in a state of denial as to what was actually happening in their own country. After citing some of the more inhumane details of Jewish persecution, he remarked

---

[27] R. Niebuhr, "Hitlerism – A devil's brew," *The World Tomorrow* (April 19, 1933), 369.

[28] R. Niebuhr, "Why German socialism crashed," *The Christian Century* (April 5, 1933), 452.

[29] R. Niebuhr, "The opposition in Germany," *The New Republic* (June 28, 1933), 170.

[30] R. Niebuhr, "Hitlerism – A devil's brew," 369. Paul Merkley argued that Niebuhr's early Marxism led him to underestimate anti-Semitism as "a marginal aspect of the [Nazi] movement, a transparent devise which Hitler exploited to neutralize class division in the hope of strengthening national unity behind him." See Merkley, *Reinhold Niebuhr: A Political Account* (Montreal: McGill-Queen's University Press, 1975), p. 130.

[31] R. Niebuhr, "Germany must be told," *The Christian Century* (August 9, 1933), 1014.

that "the total situation is such a dismal one that one wonders whether anything can be done to prevent one of the darkest pages in modern history from becoming even more tragic."[32] After Tillich's move to New York both men became increasingly involved in laboring on behalf of Jewish victims of the Nazi regime.

By the time Niebuhr traveled to Germany in 1930 and again in 1933 his own increasingly radical convictions found him in agreement with many of Tillich's views. Both Tillich and Niebuhr believed that bourgeois civilization was doomed to destruction. Niebuhr published an article in *The American Scholar* in 1933 insisting that German fascism was but an extreme example of what was occurring in all of modern civilization, even going so far as to suggest that "the Rooseveltian program in our own county reveal [sic] elements roughly analogous to Hitler's movement."[33] In his most radical book *Reflections on the End of an Era*, published in 1936, he was fully persuaded that fascism was coming to America as "a declining capitalist economic system," and that after making futile efforts to make concessions to socialism, would revert to "sheer force against its foes" as a "dying social order hastens its death in the frantic effort to avoid or postpone it."[34] Meanwhile, Tillich identified as one element of "the political faith of Religious Socialism" its "conviction that the bourgeois period of history is coming to a catastrophic end and that a new fundamentally different period is at hand."[35]

Tillich and Niebuhr repeatedly addressed the church situation in Germany at the time of the Nazi rise to power. With few exceptions they were disillusioned with the response of German Protestantism to this crisis. In early August, 1930, Niebuhr sent an editorial to *Christian Century* from the Netherlands in which he cited the "quietism and pessimism" associated with the strong influence Barthian theology was having in Germany. While praising its recovery of "spiritual treasures" in the Reformation and its repudiation of what was bad in the Enlightenment, Niebuhr expressed an "uneasy feeling" that Barthians were not only turning their backs "on all that was good" coming out of the Enlightenment, but also becoming "quite irrelevant to every ethical effort" by becoming "destructive of every moral energy."[36]

The "confessional" dogmatism both Tillich and Niebuhr saw in Barthianism was one disturbing thing. Patriotic nationalism on the part of the German church was another. Tillich saw Barth's "purely transcendent" view of the Kingdom of God resulting in "indifference toward what is social." He also saw the "Modern Lutheran consecration of Nationalism" as a contributing factor to the churches'

---

[32] Ibid., 1015.

[33] R. Niebuhr, "The Germans: Unhappy philosophers in politics," *The American Scholar* (October, 1933), 409.

[34] R. Niebuhr, *Reflections on the End of an Era* (New York: Charles Scribner's Sons, 1936), pp. 18–19.

[35] P. Tillich, "Man and society in religious socialism," *Christianity and Society* (Fall, 1943), 10.

[36] R. Niebuhr, "Europe's religious pessimism," *The Christian Century* (August 27, 1930), 1032. In his report to *The Christian Century* a month earlier Niebuhr had written of "the tendency toward theological conservatism in this mother-nation of theological liberalism," citing "a new emphasis ... in the case of the Barthians, upon a new dogmatism." R. Niebuhr, "Church currents in Germany," 960.

having capitulated to the Nazi regime.[37] Niebuhr, too, recognized that in some sections of the German church there was "an unlovely penchant for making a most thoughtless identification of 'Christentum und Deutchtum,' of religion and nationalism" that produces a violent anti-Semitism that "feeds on the idea that the Jew is responsible for the pacifistic and international 'sentimentality' which [is believed to have] destroyed the robust German patriotism of other days."[38]

The early 1930s saw the establishment of the Fellowship of Socialist Christians – an organization that Niebuhr helped found and of which Tillich became a member and ardent supporter once safely in the United States.[39] The change of name to Frontier Fellowship in 1948[40] reflected the fact, as Charles Brown put it, that many of the members of the Fellowship of Socialist Christians "had, like Niebuhr, come to accept the New Deal as much better than either socialism or laissez-faire capitalism."[41] Tillich, along with Niebuhr, knew that conditions in the United States did not fit the European mold. In a rejoinder to Clark Kucheman's essay published in 1966, Tillich commented that while "the main problem" in the early years "was the conflict created by the dehumanization of the proletariat in the capitalistic society," the situation – especially in America – was different. Thus, "When after World War II the movement of 'Christian Socialists' under the leadership of Reinhold Niebuhr discussed the future of our group we realized that a self-restriction to the ideas developed in the first half of this century (and before) would be impossible in a totally changed situation. So I agreed that we must change our focus into an attitude of readiness for speaking and acting whenever and wherever a situation of dehumanization and structure injustice is given."[42]

---

[37] P. Tillich, *The Interpretation of History*, 55.

[38] R. Niebuhr, "Church currents in Germany," 960.

[39] Niebuhr's treatment of the relationship between Christianity and socialism at this time is found in his article "The Fellowship of Socialist Christians," *The World Tomorrow* (June 14, 1944), 297–8.

[40] This organization, which changed its name over the years – first to Frontier Fellowship in 1948 and then to Christian Action in 1951 – endured until 1956. Niebuhr claimed that this was an organization whose "primary loyalty" was "to Christianity." In its early incarnation its members looked forward to the demise of capitalism and accepted some version of the class struggle, while opposing strict Marxist ideology. Both Tillich and Niebuhr published in the Fellowship of Socialist Christians' journal *Radical Religion* (renamed *Christianity and Society* in 1940), which, under Niebuhr's founding and editorship in 1935, moved away from a pacifist position and focused more on defending democracy in opposition to fascism.

[41] C. C. Brown, *Niebuhr and His Age: Reinhold Niebuhr's Prophetic Role and Legacy* (Harrisburg, PA: Trinity Press International, 2002), pp. 189–90.

[42] P. Tillich, "Rejoinder" (in response to C. A. Kucheman's article "Professor Tillich: Justice and the economic order"), *The Journal of Religion*, 46:1 (1966), 191. In 1949 Tillich and Niebuhr both reflected on the change of the name Fellowship of Socialist Christians to The Frontier Fellowship. Tillich suggested that because "socialism" lacked the meaning and symbolic power in the United States that it had among Europe's "Religious Socialists (the European predecessor and analogue of our group)," the word socialism "can be dropped as a matter of expediency." Even though the European form alone "represented a comprehensive vision of a creative and meaningful society in which the destructive implications of modern industrial technology would be minimized or overcome," we need a "second focus" – a "social existentialism" that can address the problems

Returning to Europe in 1936

However optimistic Tillich had been in the past about the prospects of religious socialism, by 1936 he was forced by events to abandon his conviction that this was the time of *kairos*. Diagnosing the situation in an article on impressions derived from his 1936 European trip, Tillich was convinced that "Europe has missed her providential moment, her *kairos* ... and tried in vain to escape the destructive consequences of this failure." He saw this providential moment occurring with the disarmament and the democratization of Middle Europe after World War I. However, "the tragic power of fate and destiny were too strong; the old fatal curses, lying like a dark cloud over the whole European history, proved to be inescapable and turned down every new beginning."[43] Tillich saw Europe, having missed her *kairos*, as rushing headlong toward self-destruction. He saw only a mood of "fear, uncertainty and meaninglessness" in all the countries through which he traveled: Great Britain, the Netherlands, Belgium, Luxemburg, France, Switzerland, and Italy.[44]

In 1936, both Niebuhr and Tillich were back in Europe, at the chronological midpoint between the Nazi triumph of 1933 and the beginning of World War II in 1939. This was Tillich's first appearance in Europe since his move to America and came the year prior to the Oxford Conference on Church, Community, and State which was to be held in July, 1937. During this trip Tillich kept a diary. The May 21st entry found him in the Netherlands overlooking the Rhine "where," he noted, "we can see all the way to Germany" – poignantly adding, "I see it without any feeling of homesickness. Dead, destroyed: barbed wire and Gestapo."[45] On July 28 while in Strasbourg, Tillich recorded in some detail his meeting with Niebuhr:

After lunch Niebuhr appears. He has been asked to come from Stuttgart by air because the other Americans have canceled. He is deeply preoccupied with thoughts of Germany and England. He feels that, for the moment, the danger of war has been averted. He thinks it inescapable that Germany will get everything she wants – peacefully, since none dare resist. He describes Eden as an inept functionary for Baldwin and Chamberlain. The

of dehumanization and the destruction of community provided" in the American context. See "The second focus of the Fellowship," *Christianity and Society* (Winter, 1949–50), 19. Niebuhr admitted that the negative requirement to drop the name related to the fact that the name "socialism is too intimately identified with Marxism." Yet he saw that admission of the errors and illusions of Marxism risked sacrificing "some of the truth which Marxism has taught our culture and our Christian faith," namely, its "emphasis upon the social character of human existence and the consequent social dimension of man's redemption." Niebuhr insisted that we must both "take the political and economic structure seriously" and "recognize that, although the 'class struggle' is infinitely more complex than Marxism assumes, there is such a struggle. We must, in other words, reject the illusion that any human society is or can be a simple harmony of all interests." Ibid., 21.

[43] P. Tillich, "An historical diagnosis," *Radical Religion* (Winter, 1936), 11–12.
[44] Ibid., 12.
[45] P. Tillich, *My Travel Diary: 1936* (New York: Harper & Row, 1970), p. 72.

treaty with Austria is nicknamed "The Trojan Horse." He feels that Germany is now more settled. Much rejoicing over the Olympics, little depression. . . .

Niebuhr had brought along the manuscript of a memorandum by the Confessing Church's synod, protesting against concentration camps, lies, rigged elections, the evil of putting children under oath, the persecution of the Jews, etc. The memorandum was read to Hitler by [Third Reich Finance Minister Hjalmar] Schacht. In the middle of the reading, Hitler got up and walked out. Never came back. His secretary told Schacht that Hitler was taking a walk.[46]

Tillich and Niebuhr had both delivered lectures. With a definite sense of humor, Tillich wrote, "I have to translate [Niebuhr] into German in minute detail, which gives me a chance to overstress his anti-Nazi points a bit. His personality makes a great impression." The next day, July 29, they had breakfast and lunch together. During the afternoon Tillich sat "by the lake with Niebuhr, each of us on a different bench, preparing our lectures [with] Niebuhr's second lecture, again being translated by me." That evening Tillich reported "there is a discussion of Niebuhr's lecture," adding that the "theological battle lines are drawn." On July 30, Tillich recorded that "Niebuhr gives his final lecture" which was "the best and most impressive one" he had given. Prior to Niebuhr's urgent departure for London, Tillich mentioned that they had discussed both "a possible offer from Ann Arbor, and the definite order from Manchester which Loewe has sent me in the meantime." Niebuhr's advice was that "I should use both, and stay at Union, where my position is secure and 'we will found a school of theology there.' I have a feeling of warmth with him, such as I had never experienced before."[47]

In 1970, five years after Tillich's death, Niebuhr wrote a review of the English translation of Tillich's 1936 diary. It was his judgment that, while Tillich's "influence on our religious life [in America] was maximal, upon our political thinking and upon our political life, it was minimal."[48] Niebuhr saw Tillich's symbolic account of Biblical faith as having played a major role in emancipating the "intellectually questioning in the [American] churches." He even thought that the catastrophic note Tillich sounded during the Nazi threat registered with Americans, who, after World War II, amid the fears of the nuclear age, were experiencing the failure of their optimistic creed. Niebuhr credited the minimal impact Tillich's thought had on American political life to the contrast between the political situation in Europe and America. He insisted that the same catastrophism, which proved so religiously effective, "was also the reason that [Tillich] neither fully understood nor contributed to political thinking or political life in this country."[49] Tillich's catastrophic socialism, with its appeal to a historic conflict between proletariat and bourgeoisie, was largely irrelevant to the situation in America. In the United States the combination of its form of labor

[46] Ibid., 143.

[47] Ibid., 144–5.

[48] R. Niebuhr, "A window into the heart of a giant," *The New York Times Book Review* (May 10, 1970), 6.

[49] Ibid.

and the fluid mobility between the working class and the middle class due to the growing wealth of the nation reflected cultural differences for which Tillich's political ideas had minimal connection.

In 1936, amid the growing strength of the Nazi regime, Tillich, recognizing the desperation Europe faced about its future, expressed the conviction that Europe's focus must be on developing "hope and strength for the day after tomorrow" rather than the possibilities of the day. Indeed, "preparing for the day after tomorrow" was one of the "therapeutic attitudes" he found during his travels.[50] Several years later, after America's entry into World War II when the outcome of the war was still unsure, Tillich and Niebuhr began reflecting on the problems facing postwar reconstruction. Many of their writings on postwar issues were published between 1942 and 1944.

Reflections on Postwar Germany

Early in 1941 Niebuhr was addressing issues of the postwar world in his article "The World After the War." Niebuhr claimed that any effort to "speak responsibly on problems of postwar reconstruction" involved supplying "specific answers to five great problems: 1. The reconstruction of Europe and the place of Germany in this new order. 2. Economic reorganization in both domestic and international terms. 3. Disarmament. 4. The future of small, weak, or less-developed nations, [and] 5. A world political order and the abridgment of national sovereignty."[51]

Niebuhr was ready in late 1942 to explore the issues involved in postwar reconstruction and did so that year in his examination of various "Plans for World Reorganization." He identified "two general types of approach to the problems of international politics" – one "the historical and realistic school of politics," and the other school, "rationalistic in method and idealistic in temper." He discounted the latter approach largely on the basis that it underestimated the role of power in political life. Rationalists and idealists simply ignored the fact that "some dominant power is the basis of every social organization" – a precondition for "whatever justice is achieved in human relations." Always expecting their rational analysis of moral values and ideals to be clearly recognized and easily implemented, the idealists devise endless programs for a "federation of the world" that are abstract and unrealistic.[52] Within the realist camp Niebuhr favored what he called "imperial realists" over "balance of power realists" for the basic reason that he did not think a postwar balance-of-power approach occurring within a postwar environment of international anarchy could work. He found the "imperialistic realists" advancing a "more hopeful program" because they recognized the need for a small group of dominant nations to supply a viable organization for the postwar world.

[50] P. Tillich, "An historical diagnosis," 17.
[51] R. Niebuhr, "The world after the war," *Christianity and Crisis* (February 10, 1941), 3.
[52] R. Niebuhr, "Plans for world organization," *Christianity and Crisis* (October 19, 1942), 3.

Given the existing power relations at that time, Niebuhr assumed that any realistic step taken after the war would require Anglo-American solidarity. At the same time, he cautioned that Anglo-Saxon hegemony posed the threat of a new menace and more resentment in spite of the fact that the fabric of its political forms is generally more compatible with required international justice than any other previous historical powers.[53] Niebuhr feared that even if the vision of imperialism offered by the imperial realists was expanded to include Russia and perhaps China, the resulting world organization would prove insufferably heavy-handed. In the process, urgent problems of justice would not be adequately addressed.[54]

Niebuhr, of course, did not believe that a perfect democracy would come out of a postwar settlement. He insisted that "if a stable peace depended altogether upon the achievement of an ideal democracy in the constituent nations, we would have to resign ourselves to decades of further purgatory." Niebuhr knew that any realistic chance of solving any of these complex problems must be linked to the type of internal structure that participating nations possess. His realistic bent of mind led him to conclude that it was "almost axiomatic that anything like a perfect world organization is bound to elude us." The organizing center required for a political implementation of a tolerable equilibrium seemed out of reach. Such organization "must include many regional arrangements; and yet these regional arrangements must not run counter to the basic fact that the economic and political life of the nations is integrated in world, rather than regional terms." Niebuhr regarded "the hazards to success" to be "so great that we must be prepared to accept anything which keeps the future open; but we must also be prepared to contend for everything which represents a basic requirement of justice."[55]

Tillich certainly shared Niebuhr's judgment that the "final health of Germany depends upon the creation of a healthy continent; just as a healthy continent also requires an ultimately healthy and sane Germany; and as a tolerably healthy world community requires a decently reorganized European continent."[56] The situation was inherently reciprocal. Tillich had a different way of putting it. Having emphasized that, whether the future situation involved "a European federation or a world federation or an alliance of different federations," he emphasized that "it will then be about the politics of the human race." Indeed,

---

[53] R. Niebuhr, "Anglo-Saxon destiny and responsibility," *Christianity and Crisis* (October 4, 1943), 2.

[54] For Niebuhr, the pressing question regarded the degree to which smaller nations could be drawn into the post-war reconstruction constitutionally so that their voices and power would be fitted into the whole scheme so that it would prevent the power of the dominant elements in the organization from becoming vexatious. Sadly, he saw "little indication that any of the larger powers" were seriously thinking about "how their combined power is to be used for the achievement of Justice." R. Niebuhr, "The possibility of a durable peace," *Christianity and Crisis* (October 4, 1943), 9–10.

[55] R. Niebuhr, "Plans for world prganization," 5–6.

[56] R. Niebuhr, "The German problem," *Christianity and Crisis* (January 10, 1944), 3.

"for all nations – but particularly for Germany, the country of Middle Europe – everything will depend on the fact that the national remains subordinated to the human race as a whole. Otherwise nation and humanity will be lost."[57]

Niebuhr identified another dimension to the problem – namely, that the prospect of postwar reconstruction of Europe was imperiled by the "mood of outraged national sentiment in all the enslaved nations." Although "the various subjugated nations know intellectually that their final security must be found in a system of mutual security [their] sense of outraged national pride is a more powerful force in their life than their rational international convictions."[58] Also, "the general preoccupation in the western world with the problem of what kind of punishment should be meted out to Germany" posed another serious and volatile issue. Niebuhr was definitely convinced that as perplexing as the German problem was, a "wholesome German political life [cannot] be achieved by punishment alone."[59]

Niebuhr struck an extremely pessimistic note on this issue in a 1944 article on "The Plight of Germany." Responding to the Yalta agreement, he voiced concern that the combination of fear and retribution coming out of the Yalta deliberations portended that any future threat to world peace posed by Germany "is to be overcome by the essential destruction of Germany."[60] Niebuhr saw evidence of so little wisdom and grace vis-a-vis the horrendous evils Nazi Germany delivered upon the world that the Allied response was "bound to unleash untold forms of retaliatory evil into history."[61] In the same issue, while reviewing his book *Re-Educating Germany*, Niebuhr applauded the former Minister of Culture of Prussia during the Weimar Republic for laying out "what the internal and external conditions for a possible reclamation of a criminal nation are." Niebuhr, however, believed that the "spiritual, as well as political and economic breakdown in Germany will be so great that the nation is more likely to be driven to despair rather than repentance." Moreover, he expressed fear that the self-righteous and vindictive pride of the victorious nations "will quite likely aggravate the despair which a general breakdown will produce."[62]

While Niebuhr confined himself to complex political problems, Tillich, who had witnessed deep spiritual disintegration while in Germany, believed that what was needed most was a postwar spiritual reconstruction. He saw World War II as "a part of world revolution" rooted in "the loss of an ultimate meaning of life by the people of Western civilization." With a loss of both personality and community associated with this loss of meaning came an oscillation "between a

---

[57] R. H. Stone and M. L. Weaver (eds.), *Against the Third Reich*, p. 134; in Tillich's March 23, 1943 address "Germany's rebirth into the human race."

[58] R. Niebuhr, "Nationalism and the possibilities of internationalism," *Christianity and Society* (Fall, 1943), 5.

[59] R. Niebuhr, "The possibility of a durable peace," *Christianity and Society* (Summer, 1943), 10–11.

[60] R. Niebuhr, "The plight of Germany," *Christianity and Society* (Winter, 1944), 6–7.

[61] Ibid., 7.

[62] R. Niebuhr, review of Werner Richter's book *Re-Educating Germany* in *Christianity and Society* (Winter, 1944), 37.

cynical and fanatical surrender to powers, the nature of which nobody can fully grasp, or control, and the end of which nobody can foresee."[63] Tillich was convinced that spiritual reconstruction would require a restatement of symbols expressing the meaning of life. Only on this basis could a reestablishment of personality and community be achieved. As Tillich viewed it the task at the moment was to "make as many people as possible realize where they are, what they are missing, what has happened to them, what they have lost, why they are lonely, insecure, anxious, without ultimate purpose, without an ultimate concern, without a real self and without a real world."[64]

Niebuhr and Tillich had both focused serious attention on trying to discover those aspects in German thought and tradition that gave rise to Nazi fanaticism. In his 1933 article on "The Germans: Unhappy Philosophers in Politics" published for *The American Scholar*, Niebuhr maintained that fascism in Germany was "derived ... in part from unique characteristics in the German nature." He decided this included the fact that German intellectuals "permit the development of one theory of government and politics to a degree of consistency which renders it absurd." Because of this "philosophic temper" Niebuhr found the improvization and compromise, so characteristic of the politically more successful English, sorely lacking in Germany. He also insisted that the preeminence given to "the organic relations of life, race, family and nation," combined with the subservience of the individual to the collective – rooted, in part, in German romanticism – had been "given a consistent elaboration unknown in other countries and therefore [made] for a fanatic state absolutism."[65]

Tillich, in a 1942 radio address broadcast into Germany, stressed the tragic habit of German thought to separate "internal" from "external" freedom. While forever emphasizing the essential freedom of the human spirit, the great German poets and thinkers never had in mind the freedom to determine the future of one's own people. "German poets created their realm of freedom in the land of fantasy, but not in the land of real life," Tillich insisted, while "German philosophers fell back on internal freedom without making serious efforts toward external freedom. Freedom in spirit, bondage in life: this contradiction rests as a curse over German history."[66]

---

[63] P. Tillich, "Spiritual problems of post-war reconstruction," *Christianity and Crisis* (August 10, 1942), 3.

[64] Ibid., 4–5.

[65] R. Niebuhr, "The Germans: Unhappy philosophers in politics," *The American Scholar* (October, 1933), 409–10.

[66] P. Tillich's April 20, 1942 address "Internal and External Freedom" in R. H. Stone and M. L. Weaver (eds.), *Against the Third Reich*, p. 21. In a 1944 broadcast, Tillich went so far as to state that "the German poets and philosophers were concerned with the freedom of thought one can have even in chains. And so, the entire German nation could be chained up, first by the nobles, then by the princes, then by the magistrates, then by the property owners, and then by the Nazi authorities. They took consolation in the fact that the spirit was still free even if life remained enslaved. That is what first went wrong in Germany. That is the ultimate foundation of everything else that went wrong." Ibid., 248 in Tillich's April 18, 1944, address "The cost of surrendering freedom."

Tillich and Niebuhr shared the view that a major reason for the problem related to the Prussian military tradition. Niebuhr, concurring with writers whose books he was reviewing at that time, stated that "the height and depth of evil achieved in Nazism was partly the consequence of compounding the more obvious evil of Nazi nihilism with the older evil of a predatory militarism, deeply rooted in Prussian history and borne by the aristocratic class."[67] He also noted "that one of the most potent causes of the German worship of the state, of German cynicism and moral nihilism, which finally culminated in Nazism was the failure of the German middle classes to break the power of the feudal military classes."[68] Tillich, in his 1942 address on "Germany's Past, Present, and Future Fate," spelled out the broader links German subservience had to an earlier history. "The Prussian state," Tillich reported,

developed in the colonial northeast, which, under the leadership of the *Junker* class, created German unification and naturally imposed its character on the united nation. But even before, the feeling for personal freedom had been taken from the German people through countless minor princes and potentates. In distinction from the western countries, there has been no effective, revolutionary middle class in Germany. The German middle class wanted to be just like the German aristocrat, and the German laborer imitated the German middle class; and the German peasant has never recovered from the crushing consequences of the Peasant's Revolution. That was fate and that has formed their character. And character has then called in fate anew: the unresisting subjugation beneath the Nazi dictatorship. Here as well [alongside the aggressive, warlike tendencies] is a tragic cycle between fate and character. This cycle must also be broken in two if the German nation is to live. It will be almost more difficult to break than that between warlike character and warlike fate.[69]

Despite visiting Europe in 1936 and returning to London in 1937, Niebuhr did not return to Germany between 1933 and the end of the war. During that time he had broken with Norman Thomas's Socialist Party over the pacifist issue and was active in the attempt to arouse Americans to the Nazi threat. The latter effort involved him in vehement opposition to anti-Semitism and relentless efforts to find ways of helping German émigrés. Niebuhr helped found, and was chairman of, the group called American Friends of German Freedom. He characterized its aim as that of helping "prepare the way for a peace which will give German democracy a new opportunity."[70] Tillich was also a member of this group, which sought to assist Germans inside Germany to resist the Nazi regime.

Niebuhr knew that the democracies shared guilt for the catastrophic events in Germany because they had backed away when democratic voices in Germany hoped they would resist Hitler. In the aftermath of the war, he feared that war passions would block any serious evaluation of the relationship between

---

[67] R. Niebuhr, "The German question," *The Nation* (November 4, 1944), 563–6.
[68] R. Niebuhr, "The Germans and the Nazis," *The Nation* (April 14, 1942), 398–9.
[69] R. H. Stone and M. L. Weaver (eds.), *Against the Third Reich*, 84, in Tillich's November 3, 1942 address "Germany's past, present, and future fate."
[70] R. Niebuhr, "Group here urges integrity of Reich," *The New York Times* (November 15, 1941), 6.

Germans and Nazis. And late in 1943, Niebuhr cautioned against viewing a victory in World War II as validation of America's own virtue. What was required was that Germany be brought "into the world community on terms which will bring health both to them and to the total community." What we must not do is "give ourselves to the illusion that this war was a simple contest between right and wrong; and that the victory was a simple triumph of right over right and wrong." The democracies should never "fail to understand to what degree Nazi tyranny grew on the soil of our general international anarchy," and that "if we lack the spiritual humility to see those facts of history, we shall be bound to corrupt the peace by vindictiveness."[71]

Niebuhr was not, however, exempting Germans from their involvement in the catastrophe. In a 1940 editorial note, he had stated that "if the Germans had had as much political wisdom as they have specialized intelligence, they would not have let the Nazis come to power. In that sense the Germans are responsible for the Nazis. But one must not forget that millions of Germans are as much the victims of this fury as the other nations of Europe and that many of them understood the meaning of Hitler long before those who now resist him understood it."[72] Again in 1944, he commented that, while "we are fools if we think that all Germans are Nazis," we are "only a little less foolish if we imagine the German tragedy can be explained merely as a Nazi conspiracy against a good Germany." In the end "the 'good' Germany was inept in politics and contributed to the rise of Hitlerism by this ineptness."[73] Tillich agreed that the Germans were not blameless for the tragedy that had befallen them. He insisted that "the double tragedy for Germany is that it surrendered itself to [the work of tragic destruction] – half willingly, half unwillingly – and became its instrument and, as a result, was itself the instrument of a destroying and self-destroying destiny."[74]

Both Tillich and Niebuhr were adamant, however, in insisting that the key to postwar German health depended on the German people themselves. Niebuhr, in a 1942 review struck a hopeful note in heartily agreeing with one author that "there are men of good will in Germany just as there are such men everywhere in the world."[75] And a year later he praised the author of the *The Silent War* – a book on the underground movement in Germany – for refuting "the rising

---

[71] R. Niebuhr, "Anglo-Saxon destiny and responsibility," 4.

[72] R. Niebuhr, "Editorial notes," *Christianity and Society* (Winter, 1940), 8–9.

[73] R. Niebuhr, "The German problem," 2.

[74] R. H. Stone and M. L. Weaver (eds.), *Against the Third Reich*, 49–50; Tillich's August 1942 address "The German tragedy." In pondering why a land so highly developed culturally as Germany had allowed itself to become complicit in this self-destruction, Tillich pointed to a variety of factors including, first, the "retreat of the German, particularly the German Protestant, religion from this life into the life to come"; second, "the escape of [Germany's] spiritual leaders into the inwardness of the heart from the external realm of political action"; and finally, Germany's "separation of nation and authority" in which the "political" is separated from the "human," the result being that German "humanity was not fully developed and its politics fell into the hands of inhuman powers."

[75] R. Niebuhr, "The German tragedy," *The New Republic* (December 7, 1942), 764.

prejudice of those who profess to believe that all Germans are Nazis."[76] Tillich, meanwhile, had been recruited to broadcast a series of radio addresses beamed inside Germany to the German people – addresses commencing in March, 1942 and ending in mid-May, 1944.[77] His overriding purpose was to bolster opposition and resistance to the Nazi regime. Like Niebuhr, he was convinced that equating all Germans with Nazis was both wrong and unjust. In a 1942 address he expressed the view that if "a politically responsible, and with it, an intellectually serious, Germany" is to "spring forth from the ruins of present-day Europe" it will ultimately depend "on the struggle of the German Opposition, and on it alone."[78] Similarly, in his 1943 introduction to the book *The Silent War*, Niebuhr credited the author with convincing "all but the politically stupid that the reconstruction of Germany life cannot be achieved without a political program which will allow the forces of residual health in Germany freedom to achieve the rebirth of Germany from within."[79]

In his radio broadcasts Tillich kept appealing to the "German Opposition," proclaiming that it bore the burden of showing that the "German character . . . has the power for self-renewal; that the inclinations that one rightfully hates in the Germans do not determine the complete picture." However, the task it had of breaking "the cycle between subservient character and the fate of becoming subjugated" was a cycle Tillich admitted was "so greatly bound with the German being that it will be like a rebirth if it is conquered."[80] He continually urged non-Nazi Germans to oppose the Nazi regime and marshal the will to forge ahead in helping shape a post–World War II world. Tillich implored Germans to "take from [the German haters] the basis for hating the Germans, and unite with them in hatred toward the Nazis."[81]

THE AFTERMATH OF WAR

After the war Niebuhr and Tillich both returned to Germany. They published articles in *Christianity and Crisis* on their indelible impressions. Niebuhr returned in 1946 as part of the United States Government Commission to

---

[76] R. Niebuhr, "Introduction" to *The Silent War, The Underground Movement in Germany* (New York: J. B. Lippincott, 1943), 9.

[77] According to R. H. Stone and M. L. Weaver, to whom we are indebted for Tillich's wartime broadcasts, "Paul Tillich prepared 112 five-page addresses in German for broadcast into occupied Europe" and "even his closest friends in the United States did not know of his secret work for the Allied cause." See Stone and Weaver (eds.), *Against the Third Reich: Paul Tillich's Wartime Radio Broadcasts into Nazi Germany* (Louisville, KY: Westminster John Knox Press, 1998), p. 1.

[78] Tillich's August 28, 1942 address "Bringing Germany to political maturity" in R. H. Stone and M. L. Weaver (eds.), *Against the Third Reich: Paul Tillich's Wartime Radio Broadcasts into Nazi Germany*, p. 53.

[79] R. Niebuhr, "Introduction" in J. B. Jansen and S. Weyl (eds.), *The Silent War: The Underground Movement in Germany* (Philadelphia: J. B. Lippencott, 1943), p. 9.

[80] Ibid., 84 in Tillich's November 2, 1942, address "Germany past, present, and future fate."

[81] Ibid., 176 in Tillich's July 19, 1943, address "The defeated cheer the victors," and on page 186 of his August 16, 1943, address "Guilt – atonement – expiation."

Investigate the Occupied Territories. In his October 14th "Report on Germany" Niebuhr recorded that, given the threatening presence of Russia, the Germans were reluctant to have us leave in spite of their ambivalence regarding American occupation. Yet the inevitable arrogance of American power amid German weakness – sometimes manifesting as condescension, at other times as brutality – were difficult realities for a suffering population. This reaction was compounded by the raw feelings engendered by so much American luxury amid Germany poverty. Finally, while the German citizenry mostly understood and approved of the punishment of the Nazis, they quite rightly resented the vindictive passions and oft-times arbitrary retributive actions on the part of the victors.[82]

One week later on October 21, Niebuhr wrote an article published in *Life* titled "The Fight for Germany." He reiterated his view – here directed against the naïve illusions about Russia perpetrated by what he labeled the "Henry Wallace school of thought" – that "the Russians are not, and will not be, satisfied with any system of eastern European defenses but are seeking to extend their power over the whole of Europe." Yet while advocating strategic firmness, he stressed the need for "an economic strategy ... most obvious in the case of Germany, a nation which our policy thus far ... had permitted to become an economic shambles and morass of wholly unnecessary human misery."[83] Niebuhr urged the United States to refrain from obsessive concern with diverse groups within Germany that held economic views different from those held in this country. Rather, we should understand and embrace the common anti-Communist stance of these diverse groups. Neither should we succumb to liberal opposition to establishing policy and taking action independent of the United Nations. Niebuhr reminds critics that "significant decisions of policy are obviously not being made through the United Nations" and while "nothing must be done ... to destroy this organ" we should understand its limited but important role "as a minimal bridge over a wide chasm." Niebuhr agrees with Secretary Byrnes that we should proceed toward a reexamination of our entire position, including our policy on reparations. For Niebuhr, "it is now high time to [establish] a clear policy of economic reconstruction" for Western Europe, including "a first step" of reopening "the ordinary channels of trade between Germany and the West."[84]

When Tillich reported on his 1948 trip to Germany, his first in fifteen years,[85] he informed his readers that the catastrophic situation in Germany had "created

---

[82] R. Niebuhr, "A report on Germany," *Christianity and Crisis* (October 14, 1946), 6–7.

[83] R. Niebuhr, "The fight for Germany," *Life Magazine* (October 21, 1946), 66.

[84] Ibid., 70.

[85] Apparently Tillich's trip to Germany in 1948 was quite successful. In a letter Niebuhr wrote to his wife from Woudschoten, the Netherlands, on August 20th of that year he reports: "Last night we went to a nearby pub and Barth, Bishop Neil, t'Hooft, Pierre Maury, and Bill Pauck and I had some beer. Bill reports that [Paul] Tillich has had indeed a triumph in Germany and is enjoying himself hugely." In U. M. Niebuhr (ed.), *Remembering Reinhold Niebuhr: Letters of Reinhold and Ursula M. Niebuhr* (San Francisco: Harper, 1991), p. 259.

a latent hostility of everyone against everyone and of all of them against the world outside of Germany." He provided vivid impressions of "a superhuman burden in the faces of almost everybody" arising out of severe food shortages and miserable housing conditions. The most "transforming experiences" were those Tillich received from his numerous personal contacts. He reported seeing the depth of suffering the German people had experienced, first under the terror of the Nazis, and subsequently in connection with the Russian invasion and Allied bombing. Tillich wrote with power and feeling of their "disappointment about those whom they expected to come as liberators and who came, naturally, first of all as conquerors; then under the continuation and even sharpening of the hunger and other miseries after the downfall of Hitler; and finally in the hopelessness of their political situation, caused most by their own political inability, but partly caused by the occupation and the world situation."[86]

The failure "of the occupation and the world situation" to which Tillich referred relates to the sad failure of the last of his own active political involvements. Tillich had participated in the founding of the Council for a Democratic Germany at a May 3, 1944, meeting in New York, heading the organization until late 1945, when it ended because of deep divisions over policy. As the war was winding down the aim of the council was to enlist the aid of German refugees, including many intellectuals, in establishing a peaceful, democratic postwar Germany. According to Tillich's biographer, "a letter of invitation had been sent out to a large group of refugees on April 27, sent by Reinhold Niebuhr," among others, "asking them to support the newly-formed council." The council's declared program, formulated by Tillich, stressed the need for practical measures for postwar political reconstruction of a democratic Germany, measures for purging Nazi racist teachings from educational institutions, libraries, theaters, and so on, and a program of political unity to which all anti-Nazi forces in Germany could eventually adhere.[87] Virtually none of the proposals received unanimous support. Some refugees opposed German self-government while others demanded harsh, retributive punishment. The work of the Council for a Democratic Germany – whose proposals Niebuhr judged to be "one of the ablest and soundest proposals for postwar Germany yet formulated" – also suffered virulent attack from the outside.[88] Sadly, because of America's deep suspicions of the involvement of German emigrants in postwar German reconstruction as

---

[86] P. Tillich, "Visit to Germany," *Christianity and Crisis* (November 1, 1948), 147.

[87] W. and M. Pauck, *Paul Tillich: His Life and Thought*, p. 202.

[88] Niebuhr informed us that one organization, the Society for Prevention of World War III, went so far as to issue a denunciation of Tillich's program in advance of its publication "warning the American public against the Council for a Democratic Germany. Its proposals included a wholesale indictment of the German nation, virtual emasculation of German economy, and reeducation of the German people by foreign supervision." Niebuhr, citing the "folly of their proposals and the menace of their propaganda," concluded that "were their views to prevail, history might rechristen their organization 'Society to Assure World War III.'" R. Niebuhr, "Editorial notes," *Christianity and Crisis* (June 26, 1944), 2.

well as suspicions that communist sympathizers were involved, Tillich, for a time, was "blacklisted by the U.S. Army and excluded from democratization projects for postwar Germany."[89]

Fear of Germany was widespread both in Europe and in the United States. This deep fear, along with both a lack of courage and unwillingness to face the post–World War II German situation creatively, made it impossible to effectively move postwar policy toward supporting measures for achieving a democratic Germany. For Tillich, however, the issues were much broader. The combination of a failure to find a solution to postwar Germany, changing conditions brought about by the Cold War, and the receding prospects for socialism resulted in Tillich's withdrawing from active politics. In announcing "a decrease of ... participation in political activities" in his 1949 article "Beyond Religious Socialism," Tillich felt that a vacuum to be merely "accepted and endured" had replaced the hope of "a creative kairos." No "premature solutions" should be expected, only the "sacred void" of waiting."[90] According the Roger Shinn, such an attitude reflected not only Tillich's detachment from the world of politics but also his inability or unwillingness to see creative approaches to the problems of justice in American society. In 1953, Shinn posed the question: "May it not be that as he probably overestimated the potentialities of [the period following World War I], he may be underestimating the present?"[91]

Niebuhr, meanwhile, voiced fear that there was "a fateful significance in the fact that America's coming of age coincides with the period of world history when the paramount problem is the creation of some kind of world community."[92] Recognizing the urgent need for a workable system of mutual security in the postwar world in order to avert a return to international anarchy, he worried that the two contradictory impulses in American political history, which he labeled "isolationist imperialism," might come together to produce an arrogant and irresponsible policy. Niebuhr was already observing signs that "the isolationists of yesterday are the imperialists of today" and were threatening to use America's emerging power as an instrument for avoiding mutuality and compromise. With all the other difficulties facing the achievement of a workable arrangement for postwar Europe, America's contradictory impulses and its inexperience in matters of foreign policy simply compounded an already complex situation. With all the other difficulties facing the achievement of a workable arrangement for postwar Europe, America's contradictory impulses

---

[89] R. H. Stone and M. L. Weaver (eds.), *Against the Third Reich*, p. 223. Stone reveals some aspects of the FBI's interest in Tillich in his article "Tillich and Niebuhr as Allied public theologians," *Political Theology* (October, 2008), 508–9. Stone also writes about the FBI's dealings with Niebuhr in his book *Professor Reinhold Niebuhr: A Mentor to the Twentieth Century*, 181–5.

[90] P. Tillich, "Beyond religious socialism," *The Christian Century* (June 15, 1949), 733.

[91] R. L. Shinn, *Christianity and the Problem of History* (New York: Charles Scribner's Sons, 1953), p. 218, n. 7.

[92] R. Niebuhr, "American power and world responsibility," *Christianity and Crisis* (April 5, 1943), 2.

and its inexperience in matters of foreign policy simply compounded an already complex situation.[93]

PERSONAL RELATIONS AND THEOLOGICAL ISSUES

Personal Relations

Tillich received help in his desire to become known to a wider community in America from two primary sources – Reinhold Niebuhr and philosophers at Columbia University. Niebuhr's wide-ranging social and political connections, as well as his contacts in church organizations, helped Tillich receive acceptance as well as speaking engagements. Soon after Tillich's arrival in New York, Niebuhr saw to it that he joined the Fellowship of Socialist Christians. This organization, in which Niebuhr exerted a considerable influence, enabled Tillich to meet new friends, sustain contact with other recent German exiles, and pursue his political interests. Tillich's eventual membership in the Theological Discussion Group – which originated in 1931 as the Discussion Group of the Younger Theological Thinkers – introduced him to many among the most active of America's theologians. Meanwhile, Tillich's friendly association with Columbia University philosophers, such as John Herman Randall Jr., with whom he taught a course, resulted in his being invited to join the prestigious Philosophy Club in the early 1940s. This group, which met monthly throughout the academic year, allowed him both entre into the world of American philosophers and acquaintance with the diverse range of philosophical currents in America.

The personal relations between Niebuhr and Tillich during their years at Union were, by all accounts, friendly. Roger Shinn, who claims that Niebuhr and Tillich each "had a genuine admiration for the other," points out that "when Tillich arrived in this country, knowing no English, Reinie was one person with whom he could converse. As late as my time, I heard them occasionally exchange comments, in German, as they passed each other in the halls."[94] Ever thankful for Niebuhr's role in Tillich's new life in the United States, Wilhelm and Marion Pauck claimed that he liked to call Niebuhr "his colleague and 'savior.'" The Paulks went on to say that "Niebuhr unfailingly

---

93 In 1951 Niebuhr contributed a chapter to a book Hans J. Morgenthau was editing. He reiterated many of his pervious themes including his warning that Germany ought not be held responsible for all the ills of Western civilization, that German political ineptness was a factor in its tragic failure to make democracy viable, and that our pride of victory stands as an impediment to making a useful contribution to the reeducation of German society. Niebuhr also cautioned against our vindictiveness and its resultant punitive excess, the ill-conceived policy of denazification, and the failure to recognize the limits of our own way of life in relation to other nations. See Niebuhr, "Germany and Western civilization" in H.J. Morgenthau (ed.), *Germany and the Future of Europe* (Chicago, IL: University of Chicago Press, 1951), p. 11.

94 Quoted in M.A. Stenger and R.H. Stone, *Dialogues of Paul Tillich* (Macon, GA: Mercer University Press, 2002), p. 48.

encouraged Tillich in the early years when he was often depressed by his professional situation," adding that "especially in the 1930s the two men shared a warm camaraderie" and often took walks together on Riverside Drive.[95] Writing in 1977, Niebuhr's wife Ursula expressed the view that "Paul Tillich and my husband were congenial colleagues and became good, rather than close or intimate, friends. Reinhold accorded Paul affectionate admiration, and regarded him as a great scholar whose philosophical and theological knowledge he greatly respected."[96] Even in the midst of their sharp disagreement regarding the place of ontology in theological understanding, Niebuhr agreed that

Paul Tillich's influence on American theology has been a very profound and creative one, ever since Hitler unwittingly enriched our whole culture, and our theology in particular, by forcing him to emigrate to our shores. He has labored for two decades in the American theological vineyard and his influence has been a constantly growing one. His unique contribution was partly derived from his very great gifts of both mind and heart and partly from his complete mastery of both the philosophical and theological disciplines.[97]

Several people have provided interesting and humorous anecdotes involving the relationship between Niebuhr and Tillich. Roger Shinn, referring to one of the monthly discussion groups he attended, writes, "usually, following the presentation of one professor, Niebuhr was quick to leap into the discussion and usually spoke as much as anybody present, although making some effort not to dominate the conversation. Paul Tillich was an utter contrast. He usually sat in silence through most of the discussion, then when he sensed that the evening was about to end, made an extended comment, suggesting that this was the last word on the subject."[98]

Ronald Stone delivered an address to the North American Paul Tillich Society, published in 2005 under the title "Tillich and Niebuhr as Allied Public Theologians," where he provided examples from responses to a questionnaire he sent out to 400 Union graduates in 1990. Robert McAfee Brown responded with one version of a well-known and widely circulated story of Niebuhr and Tillich:

You know the story about a student referring to Tillich in Niebuhr's class in relationship to nature, creation or something like that. Reinhold Niebuhr responded in an offhanded way, "See Tillich is nothing but a damned nature mystic." The word rapidly made its way to Tillich, and the next morning, after chapel, as Reinhold is bustling along Claremont Ave., there was Tillich admiring the spring crocuses. "Ah yes, Reinie," he said, "Ze damn nature mystic is worshipping ze flowers."[99]

---

[95] W. and M. Pauck, *Paul Tillich: His Life and Thought*, p. 178.
[96] U. M. Niebuhr, review of W. and M. Pauck, *Paul Tillich: His Life and Thought*, Volume I, *Life* in *Religious Studies Review* (October, 1977), p. 200.
[97] R. Niebuhr, review of Tillich's *Biblical Religion and the Search for Ultimate Reality* in *Union Seminary Quarterly Review* (January, 1956), 59.
[98] R. L. Shinn, "Reinhold Niebuhr as teacher, colleague, and friend," 10–11.
[99] R. H. Stone, "Tillich and Niebuhr as Allied public theologians," *Political Theology* (October, 2008), 504.

Evidently, Niebuhr and Tillich's friendship was such that that they could often engage in such banter. Another example from Stone's questionnaire came from John Dillenberger, who claimed that Niebuhr and Tillich "played out games with each other wondering if they really knew what the other was thinking. Once in the hall, Reinie said to Tillich, 'Paulus, that's nothing but Schleiermacher,' to which Tillich, beaming, said, 'Of course.' So the chiding ... was received by the other as if that was not all that was being done. Deception, no. I think deep respect, not letting or assuming that the other was saying anything negative."[100]

Theological Issues

Looking back from the vantage point of 1970, when Niebuhr claimed that Tillich had little influence on American political thought, he was profoundly aware that Tillich had made a major impact on religious life in America. There was, especially early on, wide-ranging agreement between Niebuhr and Tillich in their understanding of religion. Indeed, in large part because of their central roles in first introducing European "Neo-orthodox" (or better, Neo-Reformation) thought to America, Niebuhr and Tillich were closely identified with each other. Certainly, at Union Theological Seminary, according to Roger Shinn, "so closely associated were they that in theological conversation the phrase 'Niebuhr 'n' Tillich' became almost one word."[101] Niebuhr, whose own view of religious symbols was influenced by Tillich, credited Tillich's symbolic account of Biblical faith as having played a major role in emancipating the "intellectually questioning in the [American] churches."[102] Both men opposed Karl Barth and the Barthians on the relation of theology and culture. Unlike Barth, they were committed to an apologetical theology that sought open and creative engagement with the entire range of cultural life. In this latter commitment both Niebuhr and Tillich sought to correlate theology to culture, albeit in somewhat different ways. According to Langdon Gilkey, whereas Tillich thought the theological tradition had validity as "an interpretation of [its] traditional symbols in the terms of a modern ontology," for Niebuhr correlation "meant exhibiting the relevance of a Biblical symbol to contemporary experience ... helping both to understand and to validate that symbol."[103]

Over time, however, two important developments occurred that would result in a parting of the ways and reveal a theological fissure between them. The parting of the ways was simply a reflection of the divergent intellectual worlds in

---

[100] Ibid., 505.

[101] R. L. Shinn, "Reinhold Niebuhr as teacher, colleague, and friend," 11.

[102] Gary Dorrien correctly observes that Niebuhr's thinking about religious myth was "crucially influenced by Paul Tillich" whose "emphasis on myth and his view of religion as the dimension of depth in life were amply reproduced in Niebuhr's writings of the mid-1930s." G. Dorrien, *Soul in Society: The Making and Renewal of Social Christianity* (Minneapolis: Fortress Press, 1995), pp. 94–5.

[103] L. Gilkey, *On Niebuhr: A Theological Study* (Chicago, IL: University of Chicago Press, 2001), p. 226.

which Niebuhr and Tillich moved. While Niebuhr had focused on the area of social ethics and politics, Tillich moved increasingly into the domain of psychology and the arts. This did not result in conflict, but only in the fact that their engagements in the public sphere diverged. Niebuhr's public voice was directed toward historians, social ethicists, and politicians. Tillich, meanwhile, gained the attention of philosophers of religion and metaphysics, psychoanalytic psychologists, and artists. The theological fissure came in the early 1950s when Tillich and Niebuhr openly engaged in what would prove to be a decade-long dispute over major theological and philosophical issues.

When Niebuhr published his account of "The Contribution of Paul Tillich" in 1937 he saw Tillich as "not only one of the most brilliant theologians in the Western world, but one whose thought is strikingly relevant to every major problem of culture and civilization."[104] Five years later when Tillich was reviewing the first volume of Niebuhr's *Nature and Destiny of Man*, we find him looking forward to the publication of the second volume when, he believed, "we shall have a theological system."[105] Both that expectation on Tillich's part, as well as specific criticisms he made in his review, initiated, however tentatively, the theological differences between Niebuhr and Tillich. Although Tillich described Niebuhr's book "a masterpiece" full of "penetrating thought" that "will reintroduce large sections of the present theological generation into the profounder problems of Christian theology,"[106] his anticipation of a "theological system" was clearly alien to Niebuhr's objective. And while largely in agreement with the later chapters of Niebuhr's book, Tillich found himself at odds with the first chapter, "Man as a Problem to Himself." Here we see Tillich giving voice to an issue that would emerge full-blown a decade later as the core conflict between them. Tillich held that Niebuhr wrongly contrasted the classical, Christian, and modern doctrines of human nature in his comparison of Biblical religion with Greek philosophy. Tillich believed such a comparison is impossible because philosophy "is directed towards the forms and structures of being in a theoretical attitude of distance, while religion, although receiving philosophical elements, is an expression of our ultimate concern about the meaning of being for us, demanding an existential attitude of decision."[107]

Roger Shinn, who was at Union in the late 1940s, pointed out that there were significant differences between Niebuhr and Tillich that Niebuhr became aware of only rather late. Relating a story about Niebuhr in the mid to late 1940s when he was Niebuhr's colleague at Union Theological Seminary, Shinn wrote:

---

[104] R. Niebuhr, "The contribution of Paul Tillich," *Religion in Life* (Autumn, 1937), p. 581. At the same time Niebuhr believed that "Tillich's thought may have to be mediated for some time because, even when he speaks English, his rarified abstractions of German philosophy and theology are not always understood. Sometimes his terms, understood in Germany, where they have a particular-history, completely mystify his English and American readers." Ibid.

[105] P. Tillich, review of "The nature and destiny of man" in *Christianity and Society* (Spring, 1941), 34.

[106] Ibid., 37.

[107] Ibid., 35.

One night (somewhere in my 1945–9 period at Union) I found myself helping Reinie and Ursula clean up their kitchen after a party. We combined intellectual conversation with dishwashing in a very Niebuhrian way. Something led Reinie to comment, "You know, I've just begun to realize how really different Paul and I are." I replied brashly – it was easy to be brash around Reinie – "Your students have known it for a long time." He laughed in his friendly way. We students knew it because we were getting Tillich's "system" in his lectures. Niebuhr, reading Tillich's early publications and entering conversation with him, was slower in getting the impact of "the system."[108]

Shinn was quite aware that students at Union enrolled in the Tillich courses that would provide the basis for his three-volume *Systematic Theology* were way ahead of Niebuhr in the knowledge of the direction Tillich's thought had taken.

Tillich's 1941 review of Volume One of Niebuhr's *Nature and Destiny of Man* gives us a glimpse into an area of contention that first gained prominence in the 1952 Kegley-Bretall volume on *The Theology of Paul Tillich* and continued on for a decade through Tillich's essay in the 1962 book *Reinhold Niebuhr: A Prophetic Voice in Our Time.* Tillich's classes at Union, of which Niebuhr had little awareness, resulted in the publication of the first volume of his *Systematic Theology* in 1951. Niebuhr gave voice to the major problem he had with Tillich a year later. The crux of Niebuhr's criticism came in his chapter in the Tillich volume entitled "Biblical Thought and Ontological Speculation in Tillich's Theology." Niebuhr poignantly took on two of the most influential theological voices of the time – Tillich and Barth – by stating that "if Karl Barth is the Tertullian of our day, abjuring ontological speculations for fear that they may obscure or blunt the *kerygma* of the Gospel, Tillich is the Origen of our period, seeking to relate the Gospel message to the disciplines of our culture and to the whole history of culture."[109]

Niebuhr always valued Tillich for the creative power with which he related theology to human experience and the disciplines of human culture, and he claimed that "there is no one in our generation who so completely masters the stuff, philosophical and theological with which he is dealing, as Tillich."[110] Yet, while acknowledging Tillich's greatness in exploring the boundary between theology and metaphysics, Niebuhr proposed that "the difficult task of 'walking

---

[108] Roger Shinn's report of this incident was made in his response to the 1990 question Ronald Stone had sent out to former Union Students and is found in R. H. Stone, "Tillich and Niebuhr as allied public theologians," 508. Langdon Gilkey, a student of both Niebuhr and Tillich during the late 1940s claimed that "it was commonly understood that Tillich's frequent arguments against a 'mainly' biblical symbolism and for ontology in theology were also directed at Niebuhr. And we all were familiar with the latter's usually gentle chiding of 'those who depended too much on the abstractions of philosophy' in doing theology, and we knew he meant Tillich." Gilkey added, however, that "it was also understood how long they had been friends, how active Niebuhr had been in securing Tillich a place on the faculty at Union, and ... how much theologically and politically they had in common." L. Gilkey, *Gilkey on Tillich* (New York: Crossroad Press, 1990), p. 202.

[109] R. Niebuhr, "Biblical thought and ontological speculation in Tillich's theology" in C. W. Kegley and R. W. Bretall (eds.), *The Theology of Paul Tillich* (New York: Macmillan, 1952), p. 217.

[110] Ibid.

the tightrope' is not negotiated without the peril of losing one's balance and falling over on one side or the other. If Barth refuses to approach the vicinity of the fence because he doesn't trust his balance, Tillich performs upon it with the greatest virtuosity, but not without an occasional fall."[111] Niebuhr was convinced that in a fashion similar to Origen, Tillich's ontological speculations "falsified the picture of man as the Bible portrays it, and as we actually experience it."[112] Niebuhr contended that while there are ontological presuppositions for the biblical drama involving man and God, biblical thought sees that drama as pointing to a mystery "of will and personality which is not simply contained in the structures [of being]." Ontological speculation into the structures of being falsifies this divine/human drama by reducing it to the limits of rational intelligibility. Both God's freedom and man's self-transcending freedom are lost by being subject to ontological necessity.

Niebuhr recognized that there is a paradox between fate and freedom in the Bible that is embedded in the mystery of the myth of original sin in the fall of Adam (fate) and human responsibility (freedom). He approvingly noted that biblical thought insists on leaving the paradox a mystery while emphasizing freedom and responsibility. However, according to Niebuhr, "in Tillich's thought the emphasis upon the ontological basis of this 'paradox' seems subtly to shift the meaning of the fate, contained in the idea of 'original sin,' from a historical to an ontological one. With this shift the emphasis falls upon the fatefulness of sin rather than upon our responsibility." In other words, Niebuhr insisted that "Tillich's description of the Fall is close to that of Origen," picturing it "as one aspect of creation" and not as an event in history.[113] Tillich's reply to Niebuhr at the end of the volume faulted him for thinking that one can safeguard the personal-historical realm by using dramatic-poetic forms of expression and avoiding ontological analysis. Tillich believed Niebuhr was dividing life and thought, and insisted that "ontological analysis is just as open for the element of freedom as it is for that of destiny, for the characteristics of personality and history as well as for those of life and nature, for the meaning of symbols and images as well as for that of concepts and ideas."[114]

Tillich denied that he, like Origen, had identified finitude with evil. He admitted that he had asserted "that the fulfillment of creation and the beginning of the fall are, though logically different, ontologically the same." The fall, as an act of finite freedom, happened universally, thus unavoidably, as Niebuhr himself would contend. Tillich chided Niebuhr for appealing to dramatic-paradoxical language as a way of refusing to accept an ontological explanation of the symbols of a transcendent fall. He cited both philosophical sources and biblical indications (e.g., "cosmic powers," "the serpent," "the beast of the chaos," "Satan," "demonic-angelic figures," "the irrational forces of nature")

[111] Ibid., 226–7.
[112] Ibid., 218.
[113] Ibid., 219.
[114] P. Tillich, "Reply to interpretation and criticism" in *The Theology of Paul Tillich*, p. 338.

that contributed to the myth of the transcendent fall. Tillich's conclusion was that "if words like 'universal sinfulness' have any meaning, they point to something in finite freedom which makes the fall unavoidable, though something for which we are responsible at the same time." This requires of us "a theological interpretation which itself is not dramatic but ontological."[115]

Tillich's main point against Niebuhr's criticism was that, if it has any justification at all, he should not have pointed "to the danger of ontology as such, but to special mistakes of a special ontology."[116] Four years later, in a review of Tillich's book *Biblical Religion and the Search for Ultimate Reality*, Niebuhr provided his answer by suggesting that "if we define as 'ontological' everything which concerns 'being' there need not be any conflict between Biblical-poetic and philosophical ways of apprehending the divine." However, Niebuhr maintained that "if 'ontology' means the 'science of being' it may be questioned whether the mystery and meaning of the divine can be comprehended 'scientifically' or rationally and philosophically." He saw Tillich admitting this "when he declares that the theologians were right in speaking of creation '*ex nihilo*' thereby defining creation as a mystery beyond the bounds of rational thought." However, Niebuhr viewed Tillich as bringing "it within the bounds of reason" whereby "God is always transmuted into either the 'structure' of being or into the 'ground' of being from which particular beings emanate."[117]

The dispute between Niebuhr and Tillich resumed in 1956, when Tillich was asked to write for the Kegley-Bretall volume on *Reinhold Niebuhr: His Religious, Social and Political Thought*. Tillich, writing on "Reinhold Niebuhr's Doctrine of Knowledge," took a swipe at Niebuhr at the very beginning by stating that "the difficulty of writing about Niebuhr's epistemology lies in the fact that there is no such epistemology. Niebuhr does not ask, 'How can I know?'; he starts knowing."[118] Tillich was convinced that, in omitting

---

[115] Ibid., 343.

[116] Ibid., 339.

[117] R. Niebuhr, review of Tillich's *Biblical Religion and The Search for Ultimate Reality*, in *Union Seminary Quarterly Review* (January, 1956), 59–60. Niebuhr chided Tillich when he went on to say, "The real problem with Tillich's very imposing system of thought is, for one admiring colleague at least, that he interprets the religious problem correctly as the problem of the 'meaning of our existence' but somewhat dubiously equates the question of meaning with the question of being and non-being. He would overcome despair by proving to men that their contingent being is grounded in ultimate being. This may be an answer for the metaphysically inclined and gifted. But it is more probable that the real question about meaning is not whether the world rationally coheres in some structure of being but whether the coherence can give meaning to the strange drama of human existence, considered either individually or collectively. This drama has tangents of meaning and suggestions of meaninglessness. The threats of meaninglessness are not overcome by a faith which asserts the ultimate coherence of things, but by a faith which takes the incoherences into its system of meaning. That is why the love and trust of our fellows as indices of the character of ultimate reality may more frequently save us from despair than metaphysical speculations about being and non-being." Ibid., 60.

[118] P. Tillich, "Reinhold Niebuhr's doctrine of knowledge" in C. W. Kegley and R. W. Bretall (eds.), *Reinhold Niebuhr: His Religious, Social and Political Thought* (New York: Macmillan, 1956), p. 36 (p. 90 of the 1984 Pilgrim Press edition edited by C. W. Kegley).

epistemological support for his position, Niebuhr ends up with an unjustifiable "rejection of the ontological question within theology" that leads him to "retaining only [Jewish thought] as theologically sound."[119] With respect to the analysis of "reason," Tillich insisted that Niebuhr emphasized only technical reason, thus disregarding the kind of reason that participates in being and which enables the mind to both grasp and to transform reality. On Tillich's account, technical reason is the capacity for reasoning – Aristotle's "deliberate reason" – which calculates means to ends. Tillich was convinced that Niebuhr never appreciated the higher, or *logos*-type of reason, which is present in the structure of the mind and corresponds to an element in the divine life. What was once understood as critical reason – a derivative of reason as *logos* – was gradually "reduced to the cognitive function" and "became technical reason: scientific, calculating, arguing." Tillich claimed that "Niebuhr is right when he denies the ability of reason, in this sense, to attain knowledge of God," but "Niebuhr is wrong when he asserts that this is all one can say about the relation of reason to man's knowledge of God. For reason is more than arguing reason."[120]

Niebuhr replied to Tillich's charge by denying Tillich's claim that he had failed to distinguish between the *logos*-type reason and calculating reason, stating that such a claim "is a serious misunderstanding on Tillich's part. In point of fact it is with the classical rationalism that I am chiefly concerned." Niebuhr agreed that while the *logos* type of reasoning that Tillich (via Aristotle) talked about is something we also possess, he persisted in making the claims that "the self has a freedom which cannot be equated with this reason; and God has freedom beyond the rational structure," and that "the idea of creation points to a mystery beyond any system of rational intelligibility." In this respect Niebuhr sided with the nominalists who rejected the Thomistic notion that God is bound by natural law. Niebuhr knew that to speak of being one speaks ontologically. However,

since ontology is the "science of being, it has its limitations in describing any being or being per se which contains mysteries and meanings which are not within the limits of reason. Among these are both the human self in its mystery of freedom within and beyond the rational structure of mind, and the divine mystery which certainly implies the "power of being"; but the mystery of God's creative power is certainly beyond the limits of a rational ontology.[121]

Along with the issue of human freedom, therefore, the freedom and personality of God emerged as a central issue for Niebuhr in his dispute with Tillich. Niebuhr had claimed that "the Christian faith" holds two propositions that "are absurd from a strictly ontological standpoint," namely, that God "is a person and that He has taken historical action to overcome the variance between

---

[119] Ibid.
[120] Ibid., p. 37 (p. 91).
[121] R. Niebuhr's "Reply to interpretation and criticism" in C. W. Kegley and R. W. Bretall (eds.), *Reinhold Niebuhr: His Religious, Social and Political Thought* (New York: Macmillan, 1956), p. 432–3 (pp. 508–9 of the 1984 Pilgrim Press edition by C. W. Kegley).

men and God."[122] Roger Shinn commented that, as surprising as Niebuhr's emphasis on the Personhood of God was to many, Niebuhr "used the word *person* as a conscious protest against those who denied the freedom and personal love of God. ... Niebuhr of course, often said that all language about God is symbolic. But, with an eye to Tillich, he decided that the symbols of personality are less dangerous than the more 'ontological' symbols."[123]

Niebuhr certainly valued Hellenistic thought, without which there would not have been science or philosophy. However, he insisted that the assumptions and applications of science, so successful in understanding nature, had severe limitations in understanding human nature. To put it more accurately, they resulted in a misunderstanding of human nature. In its attempt to define what is uniquely human, Niebuhr believed that Hellenistic thought did so in too exclusively rational terms, often going so far as to equate what is divine in us with our reason. For Niebuhr, all classical definitions fail to describe the unique capacity for freedom, thus "when we deal with aspects of reality which exhibit a freedom above and beyond [rational] structures, we must resort to the Hebraic dramatic and historical way of apprehending reality. Both the divine and the human self belong to this category." So, he acknowledged, Tillich was quite correct in pointing to "my preoccupation with the nature of the self. That is indeed the cause of the difference between our respective viewpoints."[124]

---

[122] R. Niebuhr, "Intellectual biography" in C. W. Kegley and R. W. Bretall (ed.), *Reinhold Niebuhr: His Religious, Social and Political Thought* (New York: Macmillan, 1956), p. 19.

[123] R. L. Shinn, "The ironies of Reinhold Niebuhr" in D. F. Rice (ed.), *Reinhold Niebuhr Revisited: Engagements with an American Original*, p. 79. Shinn wrote that the "declaration that God is a person took some interpreters of Niebuhr by surprise. That was the talk that one expected, at that time, from the Boston personalists. Niebuhr thought they claimed to know too much abut God. Dealing with those who easily called God a person, Niebuhr often emphasized *Deus absconditus*, accenting the infinity and eternity of God, the vastness of the divine mystery, the ways in which God is *not* like the persons we meet from day to day." Ibid.

[124] R. Niebuhr, "Reply to interpretation and criticism" in *Reinhold Niebuhr: His Religious, Social and Political Thought*, p. 433 (p. 509). Niebuhr's view of the personhood of God and his "preoccupation" with the nature of the self reflected the influence that the Jewish thinker Martin Buber had made upon him. In his 1955 book, *The Self and the Dramas of History*, Niebuhr acknowledged his "indebtedness to the great Jewish philosopher, Martin Buber, whose book *I and Thou* first instructed me and many others on the uniqueness of human selfhood and on the religious dimension of the problem." [*The Self and the Dramas of History* (New York: Charles Scribner's Sons, 1955), p. ix.]. Niebuhr took what Buber saw as the three dialogues the self has with itself, with his neighbors, and with God as better serving the objective of "self-understanding" than the rationalistic accounts offered by philosophy. He would no doubt have concurred with Buber who, regardless of seeing the place and value of traditional philosophical analysis, concluded that "there are many methods of evading the vision and practice of the life of dialogue through theoretical discussions of the dialogical principle." [M. Buber in S. and B. Rome (eds.), *Philosophical Interrogations* (New York: Holt, Rinehart and Winston, 1964), p. 18.] Niebuhr saw biblical faith as embodying several crucial presuppositions such as "the personality of God: the definition of the relationship between the self and God as a dialogue; and the determination of the form of that dialogue in terms of a previous historic 'revelation' which is an event in past history, discerned by faith to give a key to the character and purpose of God and of His relationship to man" [*The Self and the Dramas of History*, p. 68].

The decade-long controversy between Tillich and Niebuhr was given renewed voice in Tillich's contribution to a colloquium in honor of Niebuhr held in 1961. Tillich, with a note of sarcasm, pointed out that Niebuhr, whose "writings continuously refer to the Biblical foundations of the Christian faith ... has a rather low evaluation of the non-Biblical literature, especially if this literature has the bad luck to have been written by a philosopher from Plato on."[125] He found Niebuhr's tactic of setting an alleged "Biblical truth" over against what he saw as a particular "philosophical error to be both unfair and fallacious," and charged Niebuhr with being an "anti-philosophical" theologian. Whereas Tillich claimed Niebuhr was an ontologist against his will, Tillich said he preferred "to be an ontologist with my will, because then you can avoid things."[126] John Hutchinson responded to Tillich by saying that he felt Niebuhr has "rejected the word [ontology] as you have used it sometimes, when he has felt that it has been a particular kind of ontology – namely, Neo-Platonic. The word *ontology* covers a lot of different kinds of metaphysics and ontologies, and perhaps in his attacks upon you he has been concentrating on what he has thought to be your preoccupation with a particular ontology."[127]

As correct as Hutchinson's comment was, Niebuhr's notable comment that Tillich "knows too much" also reflected his pragmatic distrust of metaphysical extravagance – distrust he shared with both James and Dewey. He certainly identified Tillich with Neo-Platonism when labeling him the "Origen of our day" and, as John Herman Randall recognized, Tillich's use of the term the "structure of being" – reflecting "the goal of Platonic and Neo-Platonic aspiration" as it does – "exposed [Tillich] to all the philosophical attacks directed against such a block universe from Peirce and James on."[128] As a theological pragmatist, Niebuhr was convinced that the kind of ontological reasoning Tillich engaged in was itself subject to the relativities of history. Niebuhr, as John E. Smith noted, resisted all "philosophies of coherence and rational systems" because of his awareness of the "incongruities both in man and in human history." For Niebuhr, "Christian truths can be seen as valid when they are made

---

[125] P. Tillich in H. R. Landon (ed.), *Reinhold Niebuhr: A Prophetic Voice in Our Time*, p. 33.
[126] Ibid., p. 36.
[127] Ibid., p. 42.
[128] J. H. Randall Jr., "The ontology of Paul Tillich" in C. W. Kegley and R. W. Bretall (eds.), *The Theology of Paul Tillich* (New York: Macmillan, 1952), pp. 139–40. A question Wilhelm Pauck raised at the end of the colloquium seems apropos. Pauck asked: "Isn't the opposition to ontology, on the part of a man like Niebuhr, more an opposition to the system, to the tendency on the part of the metaphysician to want to say something about everything, so that the whole universe, the whole cosmos is somehow penetrated by this reason, or whatever it is that the ontologist or the metaphysician uses to explain the mysteries of life? And the opposition of Niebuhr is against the pretension, the presumptuousness, the *hubris*, the pride of the system in the ontologist and the metaphysician, and not so much to their language." W. Pauck in H. R. Landon (ed.), *Reinhold Niebuhr: A Prophetic Voice in Our Time*, p. 43.

to appear as solutions not to the problems of ontology or cosmology, but to the perplexities of historical life."[129]

In spite of all their disputes over ontology, Niebuhr and Tillich remained on cordial terms. As Tillich put it after his rather sharp criticisms of Niebuhr in 1956, "The preceding discussion is a continuation and a summary of many theological disputes I have had with my great friend, to whom I owe more for life and thought than I can express in this place."[130] Niebuhr, in his reply to Tillich, chose to respond in the same vein stating: "Before engaging in a debate with my friend Paul Tillich, I want to express my gratitude to him for the education I received at his hands in two decades of teaching on the same faculty." Then Niebuhr added: "Tillich is a great metaphysician, but he will not think too much of my gratitude because he feels that I have not learned the philosophical lessons too well."[131] Even as the controversy persisted between these two men, so too did their friendship. Tillich recounted their "walks along Riverside Drive" during the time Niebuhr was working on *The Nature and Destiny of Man* and pointed out that, although "we worked together ... talked together ... and lived together ... we also developed independently of each other." In reflecting on how their "different characteristics became clearer and sharper" over time, Tillich said:

His background was a social-ethical passion from the very beginning of his ministerial work in a parish. My development, on the basis of the German background and German classical philosophy, went in another direction, more in the individual, psychological, and metaphysical, or ontological direction. This different basic interest, this fundamental difference in the structure of our being, came out also in those controversies which we had in public: my criticism of his book and his criticism of my book *Systematic Theology*. Our conversation developed, as a good conversation should, in a mixture of agreement and disagreement.[132]

Paul Tillich died in Chicago on October 22, 1965. The month after his death, Niebuhr, writing in the *Union Seminary Quarterly Review*, called for the celebration of "the life and massive achievements of Paul Tillich." He noted how Tillich had "purged religious thought of literalist and obscurantist tendencies and related Christian theology to every discipline of modern culture" and expressed "indebtedness to [Tillich] for his creative thrust in the context of the traditional habits of thought in the liberalism of the pre-war culture of the twentieth century." Niebuhr regarded himself as "an old friend and admirer" of Tillich, and he took "some pride in his small part in transferring this genius from Germany to our nation."[133]

---

[129] J. E. Smith, "Philosophies of religion" in P. Ramsey (ed.), *Religion* (Englewood Cliffs, NJ: Prentice Hall, 1965), pp. 425–6.
[130] P. Tillich, "Reinhold Niebuhr's doctrine of knowledge," p. 43 (p. 97).
[131] R. Niebuhr, "Reply to interpretation and criticism," p. 432 (p. 508).
[132] P. Tillich in H. R. Landon (ed.), *Reinhold Niebuhr: A Prophetic Voice in Our Time*, pp. 30–1,
[133] R. Niebuhr, "Paul Tillich in memoriam," *Union Seminary Quarterly Review* (November, 1965), 11.

CHAPTER 2

John Dewey (1859–1952)

John Dewey was the most well-known and respected liberal voice in America throughout the early twentieth century. Born in 1859, the year Charles Darwin published *The Origin of Species*, Dewey was Niebuhr's senior by a full generation. The American historian Henry Steele Commager accurately characterized Dewey as a "pioneer in educational reform, organizer of political parties, counselor to statesmen, champion of labor, of women's rights, of peace, of civil liberties [and] interpreter of America abroad [having] illustrated in his own career how effective philosophy could be in that reconstruction of society which was his preoccupation and its responsibility."[1] However critical Niebuhr became of Dewey, he always admired and shared Dewey's role as a public intellectual. Niebuhr saw Dewey as *the* preeminent American philosopher, and in his review of the book *Living Philosophers: A Series of Intimate Credos*, Niebuhr pointed out that among those mentioned only "John Dewey and Lewis Mumford both give themselves constructively to the social problem."[2] In his estimation of Dewey, what Niebuhr chose to emphasize was Dewey's membership among that rare breed of philosophers willing to "descend from their ant-hill of scholastic hairsplitting to help the world of men regulate its common life and discipline its ambitions and ideals."[3]

Although the relationship between Niebuhr and Dewey was one of the most interesting in twentieth-century American intellectual history,[4] the two men had

---

John Dewey's works are cross-referenced whenever possible. Jo Ann Boydston edited the multi-volume edition of Dewey's works published by Southern Illinois University Press. When my citation is not solely from this source, I have listed Dewey's major text followed by a cross-reference to the proper volume in the *Early, Middle,* or *Late Works of John Dewey* (abbreviated: *EW, MW,* or *LW,* as required), Southern Illinois University Press, 1967–91.

[1] H.S. Commager, *The American Mind: An Interpretation of American Thought and Character Since the 1880s* (New Haven, CT: Yale University Press, 1950), p. 100.

[2] R. Niebuhr, *The World Tomorrow* (September, 1931), 298.

[3] R. Niebuhr, "John Dewey," *The World Tomorrow* (November, 1929), 472.

[4] A more extensive treatment of the relationship between Niebuhr and Dewey can be found in my book *Reinhold Niebuhr and John Dewey: An American Odyssey* (Albany, NY: State University of New York Press, 1993).

FIG. 2 Dewey
Courtesy of the Morris Library, Southern Illinois University

little personal contact outside of their common involvement with various political activities during the late 1920s and 1930s.[5] They did share political causes
and occasional forums with the socialist Norman Thomas and were actively
involved in support of Thomas's presidential bid in 1932 – the same year
Niebuhr himself was conducting a failed run for Congress from his own home
district in New York. Both men were members of the League for Independent
Political Action in company with University of Chicago economist and future
United States Senator from Illinois Paul Douglas – an organization in which

[5] On occasion Dewey and Niebuhr either joined in or wrote about celebratory events held in each
other's honor. Dewey, for example, spoke at a banquet in Niebuhr's honor on October 2, 1932,
while Niebuhr, in a 1929 review, took the opportunity of noting that Dewey's recent seventieth
birthday celebration "gave his friends an opportunity to rejoice in the triumphs of his spirit and
purpose in philosophy, in education and in social reform"(R. Niebuhr, "John Dewey," *The World
Tomorrow*, 473). Niebuhr was also a signatory of the New York Philosophy Club's letter to
Dewey celebrating his eighty-fifth birthday in 1944. Both men no doubt saw each other's articles,
having written for Norman Thomas's journal *The World Tomorrow* as well as for broad-based
publications such as *The New Republic* and *The Nation*. They also contributed to the 1945–6
Commentary series on "The crisis of the individual." Dewey and Niebuhr belonged to the famed
New York Philosophy Club, although by the time Niebuhr came on the scene Dewey was not very
active and rarely came to meetings during the 1940s when Niebuhr and his colleague at Union,
Paul Tillich, were invited into membership.

Dewey served as chairman for five years. And, along with other members of LIPA, Niebuhr and Dewey seriously considered third-party alternatives, although Niebuhr soon came to the conclusion that a new political party would not be successful. Both Dewey and Niebuhr belonged to and served as presidents of the League for Industrial Democracy, and both men were members of New York's Liberal Party (Dewey was honorary chairman). As late as the early 1950s, Sidney Hook managed to get Dewey and Niebuhr to serve as successive honorary chairmen in his Congress for Cultural Freedom – a group that gained the reputation of being composed of "cold war liberals" by many of its detractors.[6]

Aside from the practice and promotion of progressive politics, Niebuhr and Dewey also had a kinship in the pragmatic tradition stemming from William James – a tradition to which Dewey gave new shape and direction and to which Niebuhr gave unique theological expression. Dewey, of course, was a major architect of American pragmatism. Niebuhr can be understood, in part, as a second-generation pragmatist who, having learned well from both James and Dewey, was actively forging his own unique species of theological pragmatism. Yet the conflicts that arose between them often obscured the degree to which Niebuhr shared common ground with Dewey. This was the case for two reasons: first, because many within Niebuhr's theological world were hostile to Dewey's secular humanism, and, second, because of Dewey loyalists who scrambled to disassociate themselves from Niebuhr both for his religious orientation and for what they viewed as his unjust attacks on their friend and mentor Dewey.

The differences between Niebuhr and Dewey were sharp and sometimes reached acrimonious levels. Part of the acrimony was no doubt the result of the relatively youthful Niebuhr's polemical tone in targeting America's intellectual elder statesmen. Late in life, Niebuhr made a general confession in an interview that his polemical approach was overdone, if not unnecessary, claiming that his "polemics were of an impatient young man who had certain things to say, and wanted to get them said clearly and forcefully."[7] At about this same time he made the specific admission that he had been too severe in his criticism of Dewey, suggesting that they had actually had far more common ground than Niebuhr had been aware early on. Professor James A. Martin Jr. gave his account of this event:

It is my recollection that, on an evening some time in the early sixties, a few of us gathered in the apartment of Roger Shinn for some informal conversation with Reinhold Niebuhr. It is also my recollection that, in the course of the conversation, some of us remarked on what we perceived to be similarities between some positions that Niebuhr had taken on public issues, and the process through which he arrived at those positions, and positions taken by John Dewey on those and similar issues. In response Niebuhr remarked, as I recall, that perhaps his criticisms of Dewey at an earlier time were too harsh – that perhaps

[6] Sidney Hook's account of this organization can be found in chapter 27 of his book, *Out of Step: An Unquiet Life in the 20th Century* (New York: Harper & Row, 1987), pp. 432–60.

[7] P. Granfield, "An interview with Reinhold Niebuhr," *Commonweal* (December 16, 1966), 316.

they had more in common on many matters than he had realized at the time. [Martin added]: This would certainly have coincided with the view that some of us who had worked at both Union and Columbia in the early forties had come to hold.[8]

And how did Dewey feel about Niebuhr? I once posed that question to the philosopher Sidney Hook. Hook, a Dewey loyalist who described himself as "Dewey's bulldog" (i.e. Dewey's defender in the manner of Huxley's pugnacious defense of Darwin), was also a friendly albeit disagreeable admirer of Niebuhr.[9] Hook's impression was that "Dewey did not feel that N[iebuhr] was like B[ertrand] Russell who during most of his life was hostile. After all, Dewey knew that [John Herman] Randall, [Horace] Friess, [Herbert] Schneider, and possibly at long remove [James] Gutmann, his colleagues for whom D[ewey]'s views were gospel, admired N[iebuhr] and were always building bridges to Dewey." Hook did suggest, however, that "possibly although D[ewey] was a very modest man he may unconsciously have been annoyed that a relative newcomer to the philosophical community in N.Y. should command such admiration and sympathy among a group which regarded Dewey and [Frederick J.] Woodbridge as the twin peaks of modern American philosophy."[10]

In spite of their common ground within America's pragmatic tradition, the controversies between Niebuhr and Dewey are what stand out in stark relief and involved a range of issues, including naturalism, scientific method, the "human studies," religion, the liberal tradition, and democracy itself. The boundaries of their controversy were essentially anchored at one end by the publication of Niebuhr's groundbreaking book *Moral Man and Immoral Society* in 1932 and at the other end by the events surrounding Sidney Hook's inclusion of Niebuhr in Hook's allegation of a "new failure of nerve" in the early 1940s.

NATURALISM, SCIENTIFIC METHOD, AND THE "HUMANISTIC STUDIES"

One of the major disagreements Niebuhr had with Dewey regarded Dewey's naturalism and the ease with which he believed scientific method could be applied to human studies. Niebuhr's choice of terms to describe Dewey's position was *naturalistic rationalism*.[11] Dewey was indeed a thoroughgoing, consistent naturalist, but his understanding of naturalism was a broad one, sharply at odds with both the empiricist tradition that saw experience made up of discrete disconnected sensations devoid of relatedness, and all those who

---

[8] J. A. Martin to D. F. Rice, March 5, 1992. I am indebted to Steven C. Rockefeller for bringing the informal gathering to which Professor Martin refers to my attention. In his book *John Dewey: Religious Faith and Democratic Humanism* (New York: Columbia University Press, 1991), Professor Rockefeller cites this important incident which was based on his own interview with Professor Martin on November 21, 1988. See Rockefeller's book pp. 464 and 620, note 44.

[9] See my article "Reinhold Niebuhr and the philosophers II: Sidney Hook," *Union Seminary Quarterly Review* 62:1–2 (2009), 17–45.

[10] S. Hook to D. F. Rice, August 27, 1986.

[11] R. Niebuhr, *Interpretation of Christian Ethics* (New York: Harper & Brothers, 1935), p. 218.

advocated a strictly materialistic naturalism. In his article "Anti-Naturalism in Extremis," he charged that opponents of naturalism "identify naturalism with 'materialism'" and then "charge naturalists with reduction of all distinctive human values, moral, esthetic, logical, to blind mechanistic conjunctions of material entities." According to Dewey, such identification "permits anti-naturalists to substitute name-calling for a discussion of specific issues in their proper terms in connection with concrete evidence."[12] Paul Conkin correctly notes that Dewey's aim was to achieve "a tremendously broad and humane form of naturalism"[13] – a naturalism that would be true to a view of experience that reflected what was recognizably human. Dewey's contention was that "if experience actually presents esthetic and moral traits, then these traits may also be supposed to reach down into nature, and to testify to something that belongs to nature as truly as does the mechanical structure attributed to it in physical science."[14] He certainly sought a broader, deeper, and more highly textured view of human nature than reductionist versions of naturalism would allow.

Regardless of what Dewey's intentions might have been, Niebuhr was convinced that Dewey's naturalism remained both restrictive and metaphysically dogmatic. Niebuhr's criticism of naturalism was not based upon an opposition to science or the attempt of the natural sciences to expand our understanding of human life.[15] However, he believed that scientific naturalism, as Dewey represented it, could not adequately account for the full range of human experience, and that it made extravagant claims for a methodology that spawned its own dogmatic rigidity. Niebuhr felt that certain metaphysical presuppositions were operating behind the very naturalism out of which the sciences operated. He saw in Dewey's adulation of naturalism and the incessant appeal to scientific method an exaggerated claim to be able to see experience plain and direct, unencumbered by prejudicial bias. Such a claim becomes insidious precisely at the point of its pretention to possess an unfiltered and undistorted view of experience. As late as 1954, during an interview for Columbia University's Oral History Collection, Niebuhr – specifically citing Dewey – stated that "presuppositions are the

---

[12] J. Dewey, "Anti-naturalism in extremis," *Partisan Review* (January–February, 1943), 25–6.

[13] P. K. Conkin, *Puritans and Pragmatists: Eight Eminent American Thinkers* (New York: Dodd, Mead and Co., 1968), p. 345.

[14] J. Dewey, *Experience and Nature, LW*, vol. 1. 13.

[15] Niebuhr abhorred the obscurantism with which some Christians resisted modern science when that science conflicted with some cherished belief. What he had to say specifically on the issue of Darwinian evolution applied across the board to all of the contributions of the natural sciences. Writing in 1955, he was adamant in his repudiation of "the pathetic efforts to refute undoubted discoveries about biological evolution by illicit appeals to the Biblical doctrine of creation, as if it were an alternative to scientific analysis of causes rather than a reference to the mystery which lies beyond all causal sequences and prompts reverence for the emergence of any novelty in the temporal flux, particularly the emergence of such a novelty as the human being. ... There can be no question about the futility of the effort to guard the idea of the uniqueness of the human person by resisting and defying the evidence of the biological scientists in regard to the evolution of natural forms." R. Niebuhr, *Self and the Dramas of History* (New York: Charles Scribner's Sons, 1955), p. 110.

dogmas of our life. They are the spectacles by which we see things. Professor Dewey and all these other people talk about experience, nothing but experience should determine truth, but this is fantastic because we don't see except through our spectacles [which] color things very much."[16]

Dewey was committed to a program of extending a scientific approach that had, over a long history, been under prolonged siege from religious quarters. Niebuhr, however, knowing how victorious the scientific view had become in the modern age, found himself doing battle against what he insisted was a scientific dogmatism. Dewey saw pragmatic naturalism, via the language and methodology of the sciences, to be the only way of establishing a truly rational explication of the world. As Hilary Putnam put it, "the key idea, which Dewey makes very explicit, is that if we assume that there is such a thing as truth in ethics or truth in politics, then it must be subject to the same constraints as scientific truth. That is to say, we must test it and retest it and allow others to test it. And we must constantly discuss the methods of verification."[17] Niebuhr, however, saw recent naturalism as having taken leave of its empirical moorings, absolutizing a method, and indulging in ontological assumptions which it denied having. Niebuhr insisted that "a justified empiricism in regard to the natural order may become so dominated by ontological presuppositions that it becomes impossible to be genuinely empirical about facts of a different order which do not fit into the ontological presuppositions."[18]

Dewey firmly believed that a scientifically informed philosophy would operate as a "critique of prejudices"[19] and that the empirical naturalism he was espousing was the only firm foundation for the philosophical enterprise. Niebuhr remained unconvinced. In his view, so common and deep-seated was the commonsensical view of scientific method among the intellectuals of the time that Dewey was simply unable to see the need for the self-application of his own principle. Dewey's recognition of the possibility of an idolatrous science turned on both the tendencies to claim "a privileged relation to the real" and to see science as an "exclusive and esoteric" activity. But for Niebuhr what Dewey removed as an obstruction on the metaphysical level in the first tendency, he handed back as a methodological obstruction in the second tendency. He was suspicious that Dewey's naturalism trafficked off the presupposition that something called *the* scientific method existed and that this method operated as model of rationality adequate for whatever is intended by the term "knowledge." Niebuhr was resisting what he saw as the tyranny of scientific methodology and calling for a broadly based cultural criticism of the inordinate claims made

[16] R. Niebuhr, "The reminiscences of Reinhold Niebuhr," *Columbia University Oral History Collection*, Part 1, p. 93.
[17] Hilary Putnam's remark came in an interview recorded in G. Borradori, *The American Philosopher: Conversations with Quine, Davidson, Putnam, Nozick, Danto, Rorty, Cavell, MacIntyre, and Kuhn* (Chicago, IL: University of Chicago Press, 1994), p. 63.
[18] R. Niebuhr, *Self and the Dramas of History*, pp. 110–1.
[19] J. Dewey, *Experience and Nature*, *LW*, vol. 1, 40.

on behalf of scientific philosophy. For Niebuhr the scientific culture itself was what stood in need of "the criticism of wider philosophical disciplines."[20]

Dewey found it "incredible that men who have brought the technique of physical discovery, invention, and use to such a pitch of perfection will abdicate in the face of the infinitely more important human problem."[21] For Niebuhr the "human problem" was, as Dewey claimed, "infinitely more important" and also infinitely more complex largely because of factors that defied the rational expect-ations of an idealized "scientific intelligence." The nature and extent of the fundamental human problem was precisely what was at stake and, as we noted earlier, for Niebuhr the method employed in the natural sciences was inadequate for an understanding of the range and depth of human life and experience.

The dispute over naturalism and scientific method thus came to focus on what Willhelm Dilthey saw as the crucial distinction between "nature studies" (*Naturwissenschaften*) and "human studies" (*Geisteswissenschaften*). As Niebuhr saw it, Dewey's naturalism failed to recognize the distinction, subsum-ing human studies under the model of the natural sciences. As *the* preeminent representative of a *social science* naturalism, his advocacy and defense of naturalism – aimed as they were on *the human* in nature the *human* in social contexts – became the prime target for Niebuhr. Thus Dewey's role as the undisputed champion of the cause to extend the methods of the natural sciences to the personal and social life drew the most intense fire from Niebuhr's pen. Dewey, in the latter stages of his life, summed up his long-standing position in his introduction to a collection of essays published in 1946 as *Problems of Men*. He saw that today "social subjects, as far as concerns effective treatment in inquiry, are in as much the same state as physical subjects three hundred years ago." What he wanted was to see was for social subjects to receive "the kind of systematic and comprehensive methods and habits and the same projection of generous hypotheses as, only a few hundred years ago, set going the revolution in physical knowledge."[22] Dewey vehemently believed that the social sciences could achieve a truly *scientific* character and that they should be given the inside track in guiding human affairs. The hit-and-miss successes science had achieved in the domain of the social world could be transformed and expedited only when the "directed intelligence" of science was systematically and comprehensively applied in such as way as to foster a genuine *social science*. In a 1948 article, Niebuhr summarized Dewey's notion of the "cultural lag" position:

Professor John Dewey believes that the only reason why we have not used these methods of mind in the realm of human affairs or why we have not achieved the attitude of disinterestedness which characterises pure science is because the struggle for the emanci-pation of the sciences resulted in a compromise rather than in a clear cut victory for

[20] R. Niebuhr, *Faith and History* (New York: Charles Scribner's Sons, 1949), p. 53.

[21] J. Dewey, "Science and society" (1931) in *Philosophy and Civilization* (New York: Capricorn Books, 1963), p. 330; *LW*, vol. 6, 63.

[22] J. Dewey, *Problems of Men* (New York: Greenwood Press, 1961), p. 17 ; *LW*, 166 and 167.

science. In that compromise the natural sciences were given their freedom while the humanities remained under the restraints of traditional authorities, particularly Church and State. All we need is one more movement of emancipation. All we need according to other wise men is a little more time to give the social sciences a chance to mature.[23]

Niebuhr was concerned with what got distorted, overlooked, or ruled out by means of the terms naturalism set forth as boundaries that enclose inquiry. When he remarked that "science which is only science cannot be scientifically accurate"[24] he was suggesting that the wisdom that comes from the method-ologies/operations characteristic of the natural sciences is not always wise if it claims to exhaust our understanding of the particular life we live as human beings. While concurring with the judgment that the attitude generated by the scientific revolt was of great importance to a better understanding of experience, human and nonhuman, he found irony at the point where "the 'spirit of science' as 'humility before the fact' is transmuted into a denial of obvious 'facts' so that the inconvenient facts will not seem to invalidate the 'methods of science.'"[25] For Niebuhr the "facts" obscured by advocates of social science naturalists such as Dewey were anthropological ones – including, according to Niebuhr, "the self's freedom, the self-corruption of the self in self-concern" and, finally, "the self's historical character."[26] In effect the "self" as an object *in* nature – in the manner Dewey tended to place it – missed the self as one whose "nature" defies such simple placement. The issue finally came down to the nature of experience, or more aptly put, the issue turned on just what presuppositions about experience lie behind the supposedly neutral word *experience* – a word, as Alfred North Whitehead noted, that "is one of the most deceitful in philosophy."[27] Niebuhr was clearly convinced that there were aspects of experience that were either ignored or distorted through the lens of the type of naturalistic empiricism that Dewey's thought represented.

As Niebuhr saw it, the Hellenistic culture that had given us our philosophy and science had led to a tragic and widespread misunderstanding of both human nature and human history. In doing so, it maligned and discredited the Hebraic culture whose insights into those realities were so profound by reducing them to outmoded superstitions. He saw "The Hebraic tradition" as being "more *'empirical'* than the Greek tradition. Its superior accuracy consists in its under-standing of the wholeness of the human self" and "in the appreciation of

---

[23] R. Niebuhr, "Our spiritual pilgrimage from a century of hope to a century of perplexity," *Current Religious Thought* 8:9 (November, 1948), 23.

[24] J. Dewey, *Problems of Men*, p. 78.

[25] R. Niebuhr, "The tyranny of science," *Theology Today* 10:4 (January, 1955), 469.

[26] R. Niebuhr, *Self and the Dramas of History*, p. 128.

[27] A. N. Whitehead, *Symbolism, Its Meaning and Effect* (New York: Macmillan, 1927), p. 16. Nancy Frankenberry wrote, "The selection of what is to count as empirical criteria is, of course, never philosophically neutral. Empiricism has always stood for the justificatory need to ground all knowledge in experience. But as such it is a thesis in search of an adequate *theory* of experience." Nancy Frankenberry, *Religion and Radical Empiricism* (Albany, NY: State University of New York Press, 1987), p. ix.

the dramatic variety of the self's encounter with other selves in history."[28] Niebuhr appealed to the "dramatic-historical approach" and "imaginative-poetic language" of the Hebraic tradition because he believed they more adequately captured the uniqueness of the self and its ambiguous relationship to nature than did the dominant naturalistic languages. He knew the self was a part of nature, but he also saw the self, in its radical freedom, as possessing the capacity for self-transcendence – a capacity in which the self made itself its own object in the sense of discerning itself as an actor in a drama of which it is a part. This capacity enables the self to transcend "not only the processes of nature but the operations of its own reason, and to stand, as it were, above the structures and coherences of the world." This pointed to the mystery of the self that made it, in part, impervious to "all purely rationalistic interpretations, not to speak of purely naturalistic ones."[29]

For Niebuhr, naturalism tended "to ascribe to the realm of the biological and the organic what is clearly a compound of nature and spirit, of biological impulse and rational and spiritual freedom"[30] – "spiritual" here referring to the self in its awareness of its freedom over its functions. Dewey definitely found objectionable all self-descriptive language that either resulted in the belief that the self was discontinuous with nature, or assumed things "beyond" nature or saw within nature irreconcilably discordant elements. Dewey quite obviously knew something of the "uniqueness" of the human being and the qualitative differences between human life and the pre- or subhuman biological life forms. But he maintained that experience, understood within a naturalistic framework, provides suitable means for adequate self-descriptions. He understood those aspects of human life that differ from lower life forms, but remained steadfastly "opposed to idealistic spiritualism [and] to super-naturalism [as well as] to that mitigated version of the latter that appeals to transcendent *a priori* principles placed in a realm above Nature and beyond experience."[31] Dewey did see that a cultural as well as a biological template was operative in understanding and interpreting human beings. However, he cautioned that the extraordinary differences the cultural matrix shows between the achievements of human beings and other biological forms is precisely what has "led to the [erroneous] idea that man is completely separated from other animals by properties that come from a non-natural source."[32]

Niebuhr placed the emphasis elsewhere. In a book review he wrote that "most scientists . . . are inclined to define the difference between man and animals as one of degree rather than kind." If this be the case, "it ought to be possible to point to

[28] R. Niebuhr, *Self and the Dramas of History*, 84.
[29] R. Niebuhr, "Intellectual autobiography" in C. W. Kegley (ed.), *Reinhold Niebuhr: His Religious, Social and Political Thought* (New York: Pilgrim Press, 1984), p. 17. An earlier version was co-edited with Robert W. Bretall and published in 1956.
[30] R. Niebuhr, *Nature and Destiny of Man-I*, p. 42.
[31] J. Dewey, "Experience, knowledge and values," *LW*, vol. 14, 63–4.
[32] Ibid., *LW*, vol. 14, 49.

some history of animal institutions. Animals have no such history. Their mode of life is bound by nature and is therefore involved in endless repetition. Only man has a history because he only has the freedom to rise above nature and fashion and refashion the modes of his life and the forms of his society."[33]

This dispute over the human nature and the extent to which it fits into the nature that science understood so well spilled over into those unique domains of the human life, politics and history. Niebuhr had rigorously indicted the social engineering approach to political life with its tendency to reduce the self's historical character to the dimensions of the scientific model that proved so effective in the natural sciences. Both Niebuhr and political theorist Hans Morgenthau strongly agreed that this model and the view of human nature it implied radically misunderstood the very human nature it purported to explain. Niebuhr used the term "scientism," not to denigrate science, but to refer to the unwarranted belief in scientific method as the exhaustive approach for under-standing human nature and as a curative solution for what Dewey had called "the problems of men" (the title of an anthology of articles ranging from 1935 to 1944 that he published in 1946). Morgenthau echoed Niebuhr in defining scientism as "the belief that the problems of social life are in essence similar to the problems of physical nature and that, in the same way in which one can understand the laws of nature ... one can understand the facts of society."[34] Dewey seemed to be an exemplar of this approach.

Niebuhr chided Dewey for his view of the translatability of method from the natural to the social sciences and for refusing to seriously entertain any wisdom in human affairs at odds with the scientific model to which he made incessant appeals. He lamented that

Professor John Dewey, the most typical of modern naturalistic philosophers, never tired of insisting that the "experimental method" must be rigorous enough to re-examine its own hypothesis. But it never occurred to him that his insistence that the "methods of science" could be transferred from the field of nature to that of history, and that only the intrusion of irrelevant religious and political authority prevented this consummation, rested upon an erroneous and unexamined presupposition. That was the universally held belief of modern culture that the realm of history was essentially identical with the realm of nature.[35]

The degree of objectivity achievable or desirable in the natural sciences was simply untranslatable to the realm of human events. In such a realm, the self is both situated within and is an interested participant in the events that define his being as historical. The self, qua self, has an existential, not a spectator-observer,

[33] R. Niebuhr, "Review of [Edwin Conklin's] *Man: Real and Ideal*" *Religion in Life* (Spring, 1944), 297.
[34] H. J. Morgenthau, "The escape from power" in *Politics in the Twentieth Century* (Chicago, IL: University of Chicago Press, 1962), vol. I, p. 312. First published in L. Bryson et al. (eds.), *Conflicts of Power in Modern Culture*. Seventh Symposium of the Conference on Science, Philosophy and Religion (New York: Harper & Brothers, 1947), pp. 1–10.
[35] R. Niebuhr, *Self and the Dramas of History*, p. 115.

relationship to the realities that "human studies" themselves address. Historical and cultural life constitutes the fabric and setting of life that is distinctively unique to human existence. Nature may well have a history, but the "self" is its history, for history is in the self and the self is in history in ways that have no comparison in subhuman nature. "Historical time," on Niebuhr's view, "is to be distinguished from natural time by the unique freedom which enables man to transcend the flux of time, holding past moments in present memory and envisaging future ends of actions which are not dictated by natural necessity."[36] It is "the freedom of the human spirit over the natural processes" that "makes history possible."[37]

Niebuhr claimed that Dewey had fallen victim to the most persistent and misguided error of interpreting social conflict in accordance with the folly of the "cultural lag" theory – a theory that was framed largely in terms of the last stage in the Comptean reading of historical progression. Dewey used the theory as both an indictment of the past and as an explanation for the delay for his much desired future. Religious dogma and authoritarian politics had been responsible for the initial resistance to the social sciences and thus explain the delay in finding solutions to social problem by bringing the social sciences into line with the sophisticated developments of the natural sciences. The divisive elements in our culture were considered vestigial remnants of outdated religious prejudices – prejudices that would eventually yield to progressive education.

Niebuhr saw Dewey's use of the cultural lag theory as blinding him to the character and extent of evil because of its over-exaggeration of the possibility of rational control, a sometimes utopian overestimation of the prospects of hope, and an unfounded belief in the likely success of scientific objectivity in matters of personal and historical life. He saw that "complete rational objectivity in the social situation is impossible," insisting "since reason is always, to some degree, the servant of interest in a social situation, social justice cannot be resolved by moral and rational suasion alone, as the educator and social scientist usually believes. Conflict is inevitable, and in this conflict power must be challenged by power."[38]

Niebuhr, we recall, labeled Dewey a "naturalistic rationalist." As to "rational knowledge," Niebuhr was convinced that Dewey, being a stepchild of the Enlightenment, sought refuge in a "'free cooperative inquiry' which is involved in the natural-historical process and yet has a vantage point of pure disinterestedness above it."[39] When Niebuhr called such a claim made on behalf of social-scientific intelligence an illusion, Dewey responded by suggesting that when the alternative to the method of intelligence is considered, namely "dogmatism, reinforced by the weight of unquestioned custom and tradition," then the

---

[36] R. Niebuhr, *Faith and History*, p. 55.
[37] R. Niebuhr, *Children of Light and Children of Darkness: A Vindication of Democracy and Critique of Its Traditional Defense* (New York: Charles Scribner's Sons, 1944), p. 49.
[38] R. Niebuhr, *Moral Man and Immoral Society: A Study in Ethics and Politics* (New York: Charles Scribner's Sons, 1932), pp. xiv–v.
[39] R. Niebuhr, *The Nature and Destiny of Man-I*, p. 121.

method of intelligence should be tried even more strenuously. After all, "illusion for illusion, this particular one may be better than all those upon which humanity has usually depended."[40] Dewey's suggestion that the choice is only between the influence of intelligence and a capitulation to habit, custom, and tradition, missed Niebuhr's point entirely. The issue for Niebuhr was not between intelligence and the absence thereof. Rather, it was between a view of scientific rationality that Niebuhr took to be extremely naïve, and a more circumspect intelligence that gauges the facts of sociopolitical life more realistically and more in line with the complexity and type of experience being considered. Human reason, Niebuhr charged, was never free from self-interest or local perspective. Dewey's mistake was to think that the model of reason perhaps reasonably attainable in the natural sciences was equally applicable to the domain of human affairs. The political realism in men such as Niebuhr and Hans Morgenthau found Dewey's overconfidence in reason and moral suasion simply naïve as regards the need for balancing power amid conflicting interests.

According to Niebuhr, not only are the moral conscience and the rational faculty severely limited in resolving social conflict, but the crux of the situation is that class domination and the imperial impulse can be prevented from exploiting weakness only if countervailing power is set against them. The kind of liberal moral idealism that Dewey and his fellow liberals espoused is always embarrassed by the existence of power in social relationships, and its inability to take this factor into the center of its thinking rendered its social policy recommendations dangerous and misleading. At best, conscience and reason can only ameliorate but never abolish the conflicting struggle between social groups, and even then they can do so only in a highly stable and homogeneous cultural context.

For Niebuhr, the social wisdom stemming from the liberal era was plagued by an inordinate, if not almost exclusive, emphasis upon either "higher intelligence" or "sincere morality." Reason and love were continually offered up as panaceas for resolving social conflict; whereas political justice, Niebuhr kept insisting, demands setting power against power precisely because the entrenched self-interest of privileged and powerful groups would not yield to either moral or rational persuasion. Those possessing power, wealth, or prestige seldom relinquish their advantage through an appeal to reason or conscience. The problem was that American culture was far too "enmeshed in the illusions and sentimentalities of the Age of Reason."[41] And Dewey's faith in the applicability of scientific rationality to the historical and political life of man was an extreme case of such illusions carried over into the twentieth century.

RELIGION

The religious character of Dewey's humanistic naturalism found its most explicit formulation in lectures delivered at Yale University in 1933 and published the

---

[40] J. Dewey, "Intelligence and power," *The New Republic* (April 25, 1934), 306; *LW*, vol. 9, 108.
[41] R. Niebuhr, *Moral Man and Immoral Society*, p. xxv.

following year as *A Common Faith*. He saw religion in its traditional and institutional forms inhibiting the achievement of religious values within the confines of natural experience. It was thus Dewey's aim to disassociate and thereby rescue the "religious" from "religion" in order to naturalize and humanize the religious life – the life of "natural piety." His defense of the "religious" from "religion" had the polemical force of attacking "the association of religion with the *supernatural*" which "tends by its own nature to breed the dogmatic and the divisive spirit."[42]

When Dewey spoke of the "religious," he was not pointing to an experience which is itself religious. His position was that the religious is a quality of experience which may conceivably belong to any or all experiences as such. This meant that although the actual experiences underlying religion are not to be questioned, we must forever question the various interpretations of the religious which have been "imported by borrowing without criticism from the ideas that [are] current in the surrounding culture." In essence, the "religious" is a generic and enduring change in attitude involving the means whereby the more inclusive and deep-seated changes of our being in its entirety toward the world are effected. Dewey was willing to say that a religious outlook is discovered whenever and wherever such a change in attitude occurs. The "religious" thus arises out of the plethora of experience and is neither tied to a religion nor occasioned by any object regarded as intrinsically religious.

Dewey saw himself as a "humanistic naturalist" and not one who espoused a religious humanism. Although he signed "A Humanist Manifesto" the year prior to the publication of *A Common Faith*, he had problems with the term "humanism" as applied to religious convictions. Uncomfortable with the subjective turn given to the term by Schiller, Dewey insisted that his philosophical position, properly understood, was that of a naturalist. Goaded by Corliss Lamont to label his position "humanism" – or at least "naturalistic humanism" – Dewey firmly declined. He preferred "cultural" or "humanistic naturalism" as a more adequate designation of his point of view. Dewey allowed the term *humanism* as an adjective prefixed to *naturalism* essentially as a *religious* counterpoint to supernaturalism. He was adamant about this limited use of the term *humanism* for another reason. Aside from humanism's subjectivist connotations – that is, its tendency to conceive religious experience as "inner" experience – Dewey was also convinced that "some humanists are inclined to minimize the natural basis of human life in comparison with what is contributed by the distinctively human factor." Expressing this concern to Bernard Meland in 1935, Dewey showed his major concern to be with the "danger of 'anthro-inflation'

---

[42] J. Dewey, "Experience, knowledge and value: A rejoinder" in P. A. Schilpp (ed.), *The Philosophy of John Dewey* (Evanston, IL: Northwestern University Press, 1939), p. 595. Dewey elsewhere wrote, "The opposition between religious values as I conceive them and religions is not to be bridged. Just because the release of these values is so important, their identification with the creeds and cults of religions must be dissolved." Dewey, *A Common Faith* (New Haven, CT: Yale University Press, 1934), p. 28.

[borrowing Meland's term] in any theory that isolates man from his natural matrix."[43] Even though Dewey had no compunction about affixing his name to "The Humanist Manifesto" of 1933, he consistently backed away from the term *humanism* because, as he put it in *A Common Faith*, "A humanistic religion, if it excludes our relation to nature, is pale and thin, as it is presumptuous, when it takes humanity as an object of worship."[44]

It is quite obvious that Dewey would have difficulties with Niebuhr's religious commitments. In point of fact, Dewey and others of his friends who worked with Niebuhr on political matters were shocked to find Niebuhr's voice giving aid and comfort to those they judged as experiencing a "failure of nerve." In the wake of a resurgence of what humanists saw as religious arrogance in the early 1940s, Sidney Hook arranged for a series of articles on what he called "the new failure of nerve" to be published in successive issues of the *Partisan Review*. Dewey was assigned to take on Catholic conservatives in their supernaturalism and strident anti-naturalism, while Hook focused on Niebuhr as a representative of and rallying point for what they saw as a revival of irrationalism within Protestant circles.[45]

Dewey and Hook respected Niebuhr's intelligence and political astuteness. Their awareness of his reputation and influence within broad intellectual circles led them to attack him for lending credibility to the resurgence of irrationalism and obscurantism that they saw in America. In his 1942 article "Theological Tom-Tom and Metaphysical Bagpipe," Hook indicted his fellow secular intellectuals for being "swept away on a tidal wave of irresponsibility, bad logic and obscurantism," and urged "both humanists and genuine democrats to establish "bulwarks against this surging flood of irrationalism."[46] Perhaps the pinnacle of such sentiment came in 1954 when the philosopher and Dewey loyalist Morton White, appalled at Niebuhr's following among respectable secular thinkers, coined the derogatory phrase for this group as "Atheists for Niebuhr."[47]

---

[43] J. Dewey, Remarks on "Mystical naturalism and religious humanism," *The New Humanist* 8 (April–May, 1935), 74. Dewey was resisting Bernard Meland's position that *mystical* naturalism was a necessary factor in religious humanism relative to safeguarding against "anthro-inflation."

[44] J. Dewey, *A Common Faith* (New Haven, CT: Yale University Press, 1934), p. 54.

[45] Part I of the series appeared in *Partisan Review* 10:1 (January–February, 1943) and included the following articles: S. Hook, "The new failure of nerve"; J. Dewey, "Anti-naturalism in extremis"; and E. Nagel, "Malicious philosophies of science." Part II of the series appeared in the subsequent issue of *Partisan Review* 10:2 (March–April, 1943). It contained the following essays: R. Benedict, "Human nature is not a trap"; R. V. Chase, "The Huxley-Head paradise"; and N. Guterman, "Kierkegaard and his faith." In addition Hook added a follow-up essay in "The failure of the left," in which he shifted attention to political issues.

[46] S. Hook, "Theological tom-tom and metaphysical bagpipes," *The Humanist* (Autumn, 1942), p. 96.

[47] White suggested that those who thought religion could bring "insight into man's nature" could best be described as members of "a group that might be called 'Atheists for Niebuhr.'" With a tone of derision, he saw these "atheists for Niebuhr, like Niebuhr himself [thinking] of their insight as transcending scientific psychology." M. White, "Religion, politics, and the higher learning," *Confluence*, 3:4 (1954), 404–5.

The novelist James T. Farrell once wrote to Dewey telling him that he had read the first volume of *Nature and Destiny of Man*. Farrell called Niebuhr "a disgusting spectacle." He then reminded Dewey: "You know, he is a man of keen intelligence, and broad background" being "the most intelligent man in the Socialist Party. His fiddling around with Christianity is abhorrent and repellent. ... But the man is no fool. You can't dismiss him the way you can Brooks and these people."[48] Dewey's opinion of Niebuhr was put somewhat differently six years later when, in a letter to Robert V. Daniels, he wrote: "I have the impression that both he [Niebuhr] and Kierkegaard have both completely lost faith in traditional statements of Christianity, haven't got any modern substitute and so are making up, off the bat, something which supplies to them the gist of Christianity – what they find significant in it and what they approve of in modern thought – as when two newspapers are joined. The new organ says 'retaining the best features of both.'"[49]

Dewey, of course, was correct in stating that Niebuhr "had lost faith in traditional statements of Christianity." Niebuhr's view was that religious symbols could only be taken "seriously" to the extent that they were not taken "literally." His aim was to get at the "permanent" as opposed to the merely "primitive" in mythic language. Only in this way could the substantive "truth" in myths be distinguished from the unacceptable story forms in which such "truth" was couched. Niebuhr viewed myths as both pre- and supra-scientific, and far more than useful fictions. They are ways into the truth about the human condition with respect to both self-understanding and life's ultimate meaning. Dewey found the kind of claims Niebuhr was making on behalf of the myths and symbols reflected in the dramatic-poetic language of the Hebraic tradition troublesome, if not absurd. In *A Common Faith*, he claimed that however much religious language might free itself from literalism, "the conception that faith is the best available substitute for knowledge in our present estate still attaches to the notion of the symbolic character of the materials of faith; unless ascribing to them a symbolic nature we mean that these materials stand for something that is verifiable in general and public experience.[50]

The radical opposition between Niebuhr and Dewey on religion and myth is evident in their respective objectives: Whereas Niebuhr sought to *rehabilitate* religious language, Dewey's aim was to *reconstruct* religious language. Niebuhr sought to reformulate and reassert the specific ways in which biblical symbols represented the "eternal in time." Dewey sought to translate the religious tradition into terms appropriate to the limits of his "humanistic naturalism." The myths and symbols Niebuhr strove to salvage were for Dewey simply pre-scientific, devoid of "truth." One of Dewey's trenchant indictments of religion

---

[48] J. T. Farrell to J. Dewey, March 31, 1941, *John Dewey Papers*, Special Collections, Morris Library, Southern Illinois University at Carbondale.

[49] J. Dewey, "Letters of John Dewey to Robert V. Daniels, 1946–1950" (November 17, 1947), *Journal of the History of Ideas* (October–December, 1959), 571.

[50] J. Dewey, *A Common Faith*, p. 41.

focused on religion as a false set of intellectual claims. We live in a world, he claimed, where "nothing less than a revolution in the 'seat of intellectual authority' has taken place," a world in which "new methods of inquiry and reflection have become for the educated man today the final arbiter of all questions of fact, existence, and intellectual assent."[51] There was only "one sure road of access to truth – the road of patient, cooperative inquiry operating by means of observation, experiment, record and controlled reflection."[52] The kind of thing Niebuhr was after struck Dewey as being nothing other than another form of dualism appearing in contemporary culture that employs variations of the two-realm language such as the terms *dimensions* or *aspects* of reality" – simply restatements "of the old dualism between the natural and the supernatural, in terms better adapted to the cultural conditions of the present time."[53]

The publication of *A Common Faith* occasioned a controversy over Dewey's willingness to employ the word "God" – a term that for Dewey only referred to the "*active* relation between ideal and actual."[54] Although Sidney Hook advised him not to use the term, Dewey used it nonetheless. Niebuhr's 1934 review did not join the pseudo-issue as to whether Dewey was or was not a theist. Indeed, Niebuhr fully acknowledged that "Dr. Dewey's criticism of supernaturalism is most central to his own philosophical position."[55] Three years later, when writing his essay on "The Contribution of Paul Tillich," Niebuhr noted that the "extreme left of American liberalism, which describes its theism by insisting that John Dewey is a theist, against the gentleman's embarrassed disclaimers."[56]

In general, Dewey saw the combination of belief in the advance of scientific intelligence and democracy as the substantive ideals commanding a religious response. This was the case because intelligence and democracy afford the best opportunity for the "deeper and enduring adjustments in life" that effect fundamental "changes in ourselves in relation to the world in which we live that are more inclusive and deep seated."[57] Lacking the finality aspired to by traditional religions, Dewey did wonder whether a religion based on natural piety and devoted to the task of working toward earthly ends could generate the devotion and fervor required. Knowledge based upon intelligence had a tentative and hypothetical character, and it was always accompanied by the doubts with which intelligence is moved. However, Dewey saw such doubts as "signs of faith, not of a pale and impotent skepticism. We doubt," Dewey exclaimed, "in order that we may find out, not because some inaccessible supernatural lurks

---

[51] Ibid., 31.

[52] Ibid., 32.

[53] Ibid., 38.

[54] Ibid., 51. For a detailed account of the controversy over Dewey's use of the term "God," see D. F. Rice, *Reinhold Niebuhr and John Dewey: An American Odyssey* (Albany, NY: State University of New York Press, 1993), pp. 148–51.

[55] R. Niebuhr, "A footnote on religion," *The Nation* (September 26, 1934), 358.

[56] R. Niebuhr, "The contribution of Paul Tillich," *Religion in Life* 6:4 (Autumn, 1937), 575.

[57] J. Dewey, *A Common Faith*, 16.

beyond whatever *we* can know."[58] Dewey's aim in *A Common Faith* was to give voice to his natural piety and not to offer a philosophy of religion. Aware of the limited scope of Dewey's book, Niebuhr in his review published in *The Nation* saw "this little volume [as] something of a footnote on religion added by America's leading philosopher to his life work in philosophy." He found Dewey's effort "disappointing only in the sense that it is too brief to do full justice to the problem or allow the author scope in elaborating his thesis on religion."[59]

In terms of its practical and moral import, "religious" faith, for Dewey, acknowledged the "intimate connection of imagination with ideal elements in experience."[60] Mistakes occurred when such faith was given epistemological status and viewed as "a kind of anticipatory vision of things that are now invisible because of the limitations of our finite and erring nature."[61] Faith, for Dewey, was not some kind of "knowledge" having definite contents guaranteed by an appeal to their alleged "supernatural" author. He saw faith in terms of "the unification of the self through allegiance to inclusive ideal ends, which imagination presents to us and to which the human will responds as worthy of controlling our desires and choices."[62] It is a practical affair in that it has wholly to do with the "conviction that some end should be supreme over conduct."[63]

What lifted Dewey's account of religion onto a different plane was his insistence that the "religious" dimension requires that there be ends so inclusive that they unify the self. Dewey thus related the "religious" to a unified sense of self in a meaningful and purposeful universe, and it is crucial to realize that for him only by an imaginative extension is human life experienced as teleological – as having aims and purposes. The capacity enabling us to project ideas or "wholes," be they the whole of self or a universe, clearly belongs to the province of imagination rather than to the domain of knowledge. Dewey insisted that "neither observation, thought, nor practical activity can attain that complete unification of the self which is called a whole. The *whole* self is an ideal, an imaginative projection. Furthermore, the idea of a thoroughgoing and deep-seated harmonizing of the self with the Universe (as a name for the totality of conditions with which the self is connected) operates only through imagination."[64]

Niebuhr valued Dewey's view of the religious as "whatever introduces genuine perspective ... into the piecemeal and shifting episodes of existence" and the religious quality of "any activity pursued in behalf of an ideal and against obstacles and in spite of threats of personal loss because of conviction of its general and enduring value." For Niebuhr this reflected a "kind of faith" that "is

---

[58] Ibid., 86.
[59] R. Niebuhr, "A footnote on religion," 358.
[60] J. Dewey, *A Common Faith*, 86.
[61] Ibid., 20.
[62] Ibid., 33.
[63] Ibid., 20.
[64] Ibid., 19.

not arrived at by a scientific observation of the detailed facts of existence. It is an a priori involved in all knowledge and action, since both knowledge and purposeful action presuppose a meaningful world." To use Dr. Dewey's own phrase, Niebuhr concluded, "The imagination feels that [the world] is a 'universe.'"[65] As Niebuhr saw it, Dewey's awareness of the fact of the "feeling of exquisite intelligibility and clarity" associated with the "larger, all-inclusive whole which is the universe in which we live" was accompanied by a blissful unawareness of Dewey's part that he was operating in the province of mythic imagination.

Dewey, as Niebuhr saw it, clearly accepted as legitimate aspects of religion both the trans-rational "poetic perspective which brings order and meaning into the total experience and the moral vitality expressed in devotion to ideals." He even went so far as to claim that Dewey's emphasis brought him "closer to qualified theists than to humanistic dualists" because of his insistence upon the inclusion of "nature as a realm of value and meaning." Niebuhr found questionable whether the supernaturalism against which Dewey inveighed, namely, "a realm of being separate from the natural world and interfering in its processes, is really the kind of supernature about which really profound religion speaks."[66] From Niebuhr's perspective Dewey represented one among many forms of modern thought that has "surreptitiously insinuated something of a Hebraic-Biblical view of life into their naturalism, thereby making nature the bearer and even the artificer of a meaningful history."[67] He chose to see Dewey as a religiously sensitive naturalist who, in the context of his humanistic naturalism, voiced a note that was congenial with the theistic vision of prophetic faith.

In *The Nature and Destiny of Man*, Niebuhr, stressing that "the problem of meaning" was "the basic problem of religion," wrote: "Implicit in the human situation of freedom and in man's capacity to transcend himself and his world is his inability to construct a world of meaning without finding a source and key to the structure of meaning which transcends the world beyond his own capacity to transcend it." This problem of meaning, in Niebuhr's estimation, "transcends the ordinary rational problem of tracing the relation of things to each other as the freedom of man's spirit transcends his rational faculties."[68]

While the question concerning the meaning of existence was, for Dewey as well as Niebuhr, central to the problem of religion, they divided sharply over the role the question of meaning had and how the problem of meaning was to be handled. For Niebuhr life overall is meaningless unless its ultimate meaning is seen in the power and providence of God who stands as both the basis and fulfillment of the world. He wrote, "We do not believe the human enterprise will have a tragic conclusion; but the ground of our hope lies not in human capacity but in divine power and mercy, in the character of the ultimate reality, which

[65] Ibid.
[66] Ibid.
[67] R. Niebuhr, *Nature and Destiny of Man-II: Human Destiny* (London: Nisbet and Co., 1943), p. 7.
[68] R. Niebuhr, *Nature and Destiny of Man-I*, pp. 175–6.

caries the human enterprise."[69] Dewey, however, setting himself against the heroic humanism of Bertrand Russell whose sense of the tragic in life portrayed man as "a weary and unyielding Atlas, who sustains for a moment the world which his own ideals have builded against the trampling march of unconscious power,"[70] rejected that the logic of experience without transcendental hope led inexorably into hopelessness and despair. Certainly Dewey recognized that our actions in this world are accompanied by no guarantees and grounded in nothing "approaching absolute certitude." Modes of action governed by intelligence provided "insurance but no assurance."[71] His position as a humanistic naturalist was:

The thing which concerns all of us as human beings is precisely the greatest attainable security of values in concrete existence. The thought that the values which are unstable and wavering in the world in which we live are eternally secure in a higher realm . . . that all the goods which are defeated here are triumphant there, may give consolation to the depressed. But it does not change the existential situation in the least.[72]

Both Dewey and Niebuhr understood something of the context of pathos and tragedy in which life and its problems occur. The important difference between them is that Niebuhr addressed that context and its impact upon the question of meaning on their own merits as *the* fundamental problem of all religion, and therefore, of human existence. Dewey, however, turned away from the problem of life's overall meaning as a futile, if not meaningless, venture and turned toward the kind of problems that life does permit us to constructively address. Pursuit of the question of "*the* meaning of life," as Dewey saw it, usually resulted in following one's private desires or abandoning the quest to a mood of despair. For Dewey, there was "no need of deciding between no meaning at all and one single, all-embracing meaning. There are many meanings and many purposes in the situations with which we are confronted – one, so to say, for each situation." Dewey was convinced that "belief in a single purpose distracts thought and wastes energy," and he saw "the future of religion [to be] connected with the possibility of developing a faith in the possibilities of human experience and human relationships." His position was that "such happiness as life is capable of comes from the full participation of all our powers in the endeavor to wrest from each changing situation of experience its own full and unique meaning."[73]

Niebuhr thought it "impossible to live at all without presupposing a meaningful existence, the life of every person is religious." Even those rare skeptics "have usually constructed a little cosmos in a world which they regard as chaos and derive vitality and direction from their faith in the organizing purpose of the

[69] R. Niebuhr, *Beyond Tragedy: Essays on the Christian Interpretation of History* (New York: Charles Scribner's Sons, 1937), p. 24.

[70] B. Russell, "A free man's worship" in *Why I Am Not a Christian and Other Essays on Religion and Related Subjects* (New York: Simon and Schuster, 1957), p. 116.

[71] J. Dewey, *The Quest for Certainty* (New York: G. P. Putnam's Sons, 1960 [1929]), p. 33: *L W* 4, 27.

[72] Ibid., 35; *L W* 4, 28.

[73] J. Dewey, "What I believe," *Forum* 83 (March, 1930), 179; *L W*, vol. 5, 272.

cosmos."[74] Although Dewey might well have agreed with Niebuhr that human beings generally presuppose a meaningful existence and derive both "vitality and direction" from faith, he would not have accepted Niebuhr's notion of the need, much less the availability, of some *ultimate* meaning and coherence. Dewey was quite content with particular meanings attached to life's moments. His understanding of the "religious" was strictly related to things of this world. The religious dimension for Dewey did not include any commitments to "ultimate" meaning, "ultimate" hope, or "ultimate" anything. Dewey's naturalism went *all the way down* and refrained from indulging in wholesale questions about the meaning of life.

THE LIBERAL TRADITION

In his 1932 book *Moral Man and Immoral Society*, Niebuhr launched an assault on the liberal tradition and, because Dewey was the most formidable and venerable spokesman of American liberal thought, Niebuhr targeted Dewey as the quintessential symbol of all that was wrong in that tradition. Niebuhr admitted that the book had a "polemical interest" aimed squarely at "the moralists, both religious and secular, who imagine that the egoism of individuals is being progressively checked by the development of rationality or the growth of a religious inspired goodwill and that nothing but the continuance of this process is necessary to establish social harmony between all the human societies and collectives."[75] Dewey was viewed by Niebuhr as the embodiment of that imagination and became the lightning rod for Niebuhr's broadside against the entire bastion of liberal idealism as expressed in its secular form. Repudiating what he saw as the love-perfectionism of the religious liberals and the rational-perfectionism of secular liberals such as Dewey, Niebuhr's book, as historian Arthur Schlesinger Jr. succinctly put it, "was a somber and powerful rejection of the Social-Gospel-Dewey amalgam, with its politics of love and reason."[76]

Niebuhr's thesis in *Moral Man and Immoral Society* was that there exists a substantive distinction between the moral behavior of individuals and that of collectives. Human communities, he contended, have far "less reason to guide and check impulse, less capacity for self-transcendence, less ability to comprehend the need of others and therefore more unrestrained egoism than the individuals who compose the group reveal in their personal relationships."[77] Tragically, both educators and moralists alike "underestimate the conflict of interest in political and economic relations, and attribute to disinterested

---

[74] R. Niebuhr, *Faith and History*, p. 57.
[75] R. Niebuhr, *Moral Man and Immoral Society*, p. x.
[76] A. Schlesinger Jr., "Reinhold Niebuhr's role in American political thought and life" in C. W. Kegley (ed.), *Reinhold Niebuhr: His Religious, Social and Political Thought* (New York: Pilgrim Press, 1984), p. 198.
[77] R. Niebuhr, *Moral Man and Immoral Society*, pp. xi–ii.

ignorance what ought usually to be attributed to interested intelligence."[78] Niebuhr lambasted that scion of "socially minded educators" who, following Dewey, sought to salvage society by using the school system as an agency for extending the social and political intelligence of the general community. The naïve hope that education will bring in its wake the achievement of justice in society belies the fact that "the interests of the powerful and dominant groups, who profit from the present system of society, are the real hindrance to the establishment of a rational and just society." Of course, Niebuhr chided, "It would be pleasant to believe that the intelligence of the general community could be raised to such a height that the irrational injustices of society would be eliminated. But unfortunately there is no such general community. There are many classes, all of them partially deriving their perspectives from, or suffering them to be limited by, their economic interest."[79]

What Niebuhr saw lacking in moralists, be they disciples of religion or reason, was "an understanding of the brutal character of the behavior of all human collectives, and the power of self interest and collective egoism in all inter-group relations" – realities that "make social conflict an inevitability in human history, probably to its very end.[80]

Dewey responded to Niebuhr's attack the year after the appearance of *Moral Man and Immoral Society*. The occasion was a series of articles published in *The World Tomorrow* that Niebuhr, who was on the editorial staff, might well have had a hand in organizing. The journal asked that contributors write an assessment of the American scene. On the first day of March, Niebuhr inaugurated the series with his "After Capitalism – What?" and Dewey's essay "Unity and Progress" followed one week later. Dewey replied to Niebuhr rather indirectly. He even stated that his intent was "not to write negatively, as would be the case if my article's main purpose was criticism of Dr. Niebuhr's view."[81] Yet Dewey proceeded to react to Niebuhr by name in all but two paragraphs of his essay.

Niebuhr obviously gained Dewey's attention because of the blistering attack that he had delivered against the entire edifice of the liberal tradition. And it is rather evident that barely beneath the surface of "Unity and Progress" lay a sharp repudiation of both Niebuhr's indictment of liberalism and his identification of Dewey as its leading proponent. Dewey took offense at being included among those who represent the type of sentimental liberalism which he himself deplored. His disclaimer was evident in his insistence that his method "is very different from that which Dr. Niebuhr criticizes under the name of 'liberalism.' It has nothing to do with the sentimentalism to which he gives that name. There has been and still is an immense amount of political immaturity and economic illiteracy in the American citizenship, and I am not questioning either the existence or the futility of what Dr. Niebuhr called liberalism. I am concerned

---

[78] Ibid., p. 215.
[79] Ibid., pp. 212–13.
[80] Ibid., p. xx.
[81] J. Dewey, "Unity and progress," *The World Tomorrow* (March 8, 1933), 232; *LW* vol. 9, 71.

only to point out the irrelevancy of his description and condemnation to the kind of procedure which I am proposing."[82]

All else paled before the burden of this crucial passage. Dewey sought to defend his liberal methods against Niebuhr's criticisms and to make it unmistakably evident that these methods were to be sharply distinguished from the stereotypical liberal errors by which Niebuhr was rightly disturbed. Dewey wanted it to be known that, in his estimation, Niebuhr's polemical salvos in no way applied to John Dewey's particular species of liberalism or to the methods of social reform and reconstruction derived from it. He felt that his position was exempt from the illusions of a facile liberalism which Niebuhr had otherwise quite rightly identified and targeted. Dewey, after all, had openly and deliberately separated his view of intelligence with the conception of "Reason" involved in absolutistic "Rationalism." As Dewey put it in 1948, he saw his view of intelligence as solidly grounded in empirical methodology – in those "ever-growing methods of observation, experiment and reflective reasoning which have in a very short time revolutionized the physical and, to a considerable degree, the physiological conditions of life."[83] Yet Niebuhr, both at the time of "Unity and Progress" and thereafter, was convinced that Dewey's use of intelligence, however modest and pragmatic in appearance, remained deeply embedded in romantically overoptimistic views of both science and society. He saw no reason to change his mind about Dewey's place among those whose liberalism was too rationalistic, too optimistic, and too far removed from the kind of realism so desperately needed in the arena of political reconstruction. Thus, Dewey's disclaimer notwithstanding, the actual applications and expectations of "experimental intelligence" in Dewey's sociopolitical thought had profound affiliations with broader motifs belonging to liberal culture as a whole.

Although Dewey only replied marginally to Niebuhr's attack in 1933, he responded openly and abruptly to Niebuhr in his article on "Intelligence and Power" published in *The New Republic* in April, 1934. With an indirect reference to the type of religious orientation Niebuhr represented, Dewey cited "habit, custom, and tradition" as examples of the difficulties intelligence have had making its way in the world. He was sarcastic in pointing out that "at critical times, widespread illusions, generated by intense emotions have played a role in comparison with which the influence of intelligence is negligible."[84] Dewey went on to deny that his conception and advocacy of social intelligence ignored the power and persistence of self-interest in human affairs. Rather, his aim was to bring the much needed critical-experimental intelligence of the natural sciences to bear against those debilitating forces of "habit, custom, and tradition" – forces that had reinforced vested interest and hindered intelligent social redirection.

According to Dewey, critics such as Niebuhr mistakenly believed that his advocacy of social intelligence was oblivious to the inertial forces of self-interest,

[82] J. Dewey, "Unity and progress," 233; *LW*, vol. 9, 71.
[83] J. Dewey, *Reconstruction in Philosophy* (Boston: Beacon Press, 1948 [1920]), pp. viii–ix.
[84] J. Dewey, "Intelligence and power," *The New Republic* (April 25, 1934); *LW*. vol. 9, 107.

constituting a prima facie case against an appeal to intelligence per se. Dewey resented the fact that "Mr. Niebuhr imputes to me middle-class prejudices in ignoring the role of class interest and conflict in social affairs!" Niebuhr, Dewey went on to say, charged him with "a great exaggeration of the possibilities of education in spite of the fact that I have spent a good deal of energy in urging that no genuine education is possible without active participation in actual conditions, and have pointed out that economic interests are the chief cause why this change in education is retarded and deflected."[85]

Dewey acknowledged the "power" of dominant, and often unjust, interest in society and knew that "intelligence becomes a *power* only when it is brought into the operation of other forces than itself." However, because in the context of social struggle the dominant force was never the exclusive force, "the real problem," as Dewey described it, "is whether there are strong interests now active which can best succeed by adopting the method of experimental intelligence into their struggles, or whether they too should rely upon the use of methods that may have brought the world to its present estate, only using them the other way around."[86] He felt it quite unjust to be represented as advocating a form of intelligence separate from or oblivious to the interplay of interests in the social arena. The issue as Dewey viewed it was only whether or not interests could be sufficiently enlightened so as to come to rely upon methods of experimental intelligence, rather than upon the traditional methods that had brought us to our present sorry state of affairs.

Niebuhr did not see himself as attacking reason or intelligence as such, only a misguided and misplaced estimate of its role in dealing with conflicting interests. The point he wished to make (as stated in a response to George A. Coe's criticism that Niebuhr simply dismissed the power of rational and moral force in *Moral Man and Immoral Society*) was that "I believe that once rational and religious idealists stop fooling themselves and recognize the basic fact of a social struggle in society they will be the more able to direct it morally and rationally."[87] Recognizing that there "has of course been a cumulation of social experience and intellectual discipline" in history, "by recognizing that men will remain selfish to the end we will be saved from the errors of both a liberalism which wants to achieve political ends by purely ethical means and a radicalism which hopes to achieve ethical ends by purely political means."[88]

Niebuhr's counsel was that once the brutalities of social conflict are acknowledged and accepted, then and only then was there "every possibility of introducing very important ethical elements into the struggle."[89] He did not consider moral and intellectual idealism as futile, because such idealism is essential for

---

[85] Ibid., 307; *LW*, vol. 9, 110.

[86] Ibid., 109.

[87] R. Niebuhr, "Two communications: Coe vs. Niebuhr," *The Christian Century* (March 15, 1933), 363.

[88] Ibid., 364.

[89] R. Niebuhr, "After capitalism – what?" *The World Tomorrow* (March 1, 1933), 205.

any measure of fairness and decency in society. Indeed, Niebuhr knew that "no basic reorganization of society will ever guarantee the preservation of humaneness if good men do not preserve it." However, what is crucial when assessing the relevance of education and moral suasion to the life of the dominant group in society is whether they can affect whether that group "will yield in time under pressure" or "defend its entrenched positions so uncompromisingly that an orderly retreat becomes impossible and a disorderly rout envelopes the whole of society in chaos." Niebuhr noted that "if such conclusions seem unduly cynical they will seem so only because the moral idealists of the past century, both religious and rational, have been unduly sentimental in their estimates of human nature."[90]

Because they began with a different set of assumptions about human beings, conflict, power, and self-interest, Dewey and Niebuhr diverged sharply on what constitutes a "rational" view of reason and the limit of its possibilities in the collective life. This, of course, defined the framework for their clash over liberalism itself. Dewey, reacting with frustration against the long-standing "domination of the methods of institutional force, custom and illusion," cast about for some other "method," and he saw a solution in the method of intelligence as yet never tried with any degree of seriousness. Niebuhr wanted a measure of realism that clearly recognizes the tendency of reason to serve ends other than purely rational ones – a tendency most evident in the fact that reason continually deceived itself into thinking that it was so engaged. The liberal tradition, in effect, had never taken seriously, in its grandiose view of intelligence, the stubborn fact that intelligence is always "interested intelligence."[91]

Niebuhr and Dewey both deplored the laissez-faire version of that tradition that had become the defining mark of American "conservatism." In the wake of the euphoria of New Era business idealism in the decade after World War I, this now dominant laissez- faire ideology had muted the force of social liberalism's efforts to humanize and democratize American industrial society. In association with its emergence as a creed of the business community, liberalism metamorphosed into the self-serving ideology of a powerful capitalistic class that set liberal values against the economically weak and disenfranchised. The issue, as Niebuhr told a predominately business audience during World War II, was one of recognizing that "where power is disproportionate, power dominates weakness and injustice results."[92] Unbridled self-interest had led to greater inequalities in the economic sphere and thus exacerbated the problem of justice. A balance between liberty and equality was required for any approximation of social justice.

With the collapse of that euphoria in the wake of the Depression, both Niebuhr and Dewey shared the widespread loss of confidence in democratic prospects. In *Reflections on the End of an Era*, published in 1934, during his

---

[90] Ibid., 203–4.
[91] R. Niebuhr, *Reflections on the End of an Era* (New York: Charles Scribner's Sons, 1934), p. 45.
[92] R. Niebuhr, "A faith for history's greatest crisis," *Fortune Magazine* (July, 1942), 125.

most radical phase, Niebuhr's despair over the onslaught of reactionary and radical forces found him suggesting that, with Roosevelt's efforts bound to fail, American politics will likely "disintegrate into a more obvious conservatism and radicalism."[93] Niebuhr's despondent mood was even echoed in the normally unflappable and less apocalyptic-minded Dewey, whose 1937 review of Stephen Spender's *Forward From Liberalism* warned that "the conclusion I personally draw from this sincere and courageous book is that unless there is organized assertion of economic and cultural democracy in this country, liberals here may find themselves in a position where they see only a choice between fascists and communists of the official stripe."[94]

During the 1930s, Dewey set about to rethink and to reformulate the entire liberal tradition. His role in this endeavor was monumental, coming to expression in a series of six essays on "Individualism: Old and New," published between January 22 and April 2, 1930, and then continuing with a profusion of articles defending an energetic and rational democratic liberalism. Many of these essays were published in *Social Frontier*, whose "John Dewey's Page" pleaded the case for radical democracy before an audience that was often far more radical than he.[95] All this led up to his most important book on the subject, *Liberalism and Social Action*, published in 1935. In both this book and Niebuhr's reply, all the old issues were joined once again. Niebuhr's response to Dewey's *Liberalism and Social Action* came in his article "The Pathos of Liberalism" published in 1935. Niebuhr acknowledged that "No one in America has a more generally conceded right to speak in the name of liberalism than John Dewey," and that Dewey "has been for many years not only the leading philosophical exponent of liberal doctrine but the fountain and source of liberal pedagogical theory and method." Niebuhr praised Dewey for his dedication and commitment to "a score of political and social movements," proving "not only his interest in the practical application of his theories but also a courageous willingness to extend both his theory and his practice beyond the limits set by traditional liberalism."[96]

Nonetheless, Niebuhr mixed praise with disillusionment regarding Dewey's effort in *Liberalism and Social Action*, concluding, however, that unfortunately the much needed support for liberal self-criticism would not be forthcoming from the single most important spokesman of the liberal community. Niebuhr applauded both Dewey's call for an extension of liberty to the economic situation confronting most individuals and his willingness to allow the state to curtail legal liberties that often simply rationalized harsh inequalities. He shared

---

[93] R. Niebuhr, *Reflections on the End of an Era*, 80.

[94] J. Dewey, "Review of *Forward From Liberalism* by Stephen Spender," *Common Sense* (May, 1937), 26; *LW* vol. 11, 498.

[95] The title of some of these essays include: "The crucial role of intelligence," *Social Frontier*-I (February, 1935), 9–10; "Liberalism and social control," *Social Frontier*-II (November, 1935), 41–2; "The meaning of liberalism," *Social Frontier*-II (December, 1935), 74–5; and "Liberalism and equality," *Social Frontier*-II (January, 1936), 105–6. See *LW*, vol. 11.

[96] R. Niebuhr, "The pathos of liberalism," *The Nation* (September 11, 1935), 303.

Dewey's realistic awareness that our abstract appeal to liberty obscures the fact that liberty often functions as an ideological refuge of power and privilege in capitalistic social systems.[97] In essence, Niebuhr agreed with Dewey's position as far as it went, even applauding Dewey for showing a greater measure of realism than was evident in so much social thinking coming out of the mouths of liberal voices.

For all the occasional insights into self-interest and social conflict shown in Dewey's assessment of historic liberalism, Niebuhr saw the prognosis for a "renascent liberalism," with which Dewey concluded his book, as tediously reiterating the naïve and exaggerated rational expectations so characteristic of liberalism. At the end, Niebuhr saw Dewey as persisting in trafficking off the more generalized illusions of liberal culture as a whole. Dewey's reconstructed liberalism simply failed to probe the core difficulties of the entire liberal creed or to subject them to the kind of rigorous self-criticism a genuinely reconstructed liberalism demanded. For Niebuhr, Dewey remained the quintessential liberal who, in his own words, was "committed to the organization of intelligent action as the chief method,"[98] and although Dewey paid lip service now and again to the fact that "coercive and violent force" must be directly and openly faced, such realistic moments were merely judged to be a temporary nuisance preliminary to grasping "the meaning of dependence upon intelligence as the alternative method of social direction."[99] On Niebuhr's view Dewey simply continued to see "violence only as a consequence of a social ignorance which a more perfect intelligence would be able to eliminate."[100] For Niebuhr, it was in Dewey's proposal to make "freed intelligence" socially effective [that] he simply fails to adequately perceive the ongoing, unavoidable presence of social and economic interest in all social conflict. This "ideal of a 'freed intelligence',," Niebuhr insisted, "expects a degree of rational freedom from the particular interests and perspectives of those who think about social problems which is incompatible with the very constitution of human nature."[101]

Niebuhr's sensitivity to the assault upon liberalism coming from the side of radical political thought led him, in 1936, to distinguish between the "creed" and the "spirit" of liberalism and proceed to characterize that "creed." He firmly

---

[97] Both Niebuhr and Dewey knew the changes that had taken place with respect to the term *liberalism* since it came into vogue in the nineteenth century. On one level, it is accurate to say that the liberal creed had remained constant and that massive changes in the economic environment occasioned by the industrial revolution had rendered the creed obsolete. On another level, the change was ideological, and thus altered the meaning of the creed itself. That is to say, what began as legitimate and just aspirations for individualism and liberty by an industrial and commercial class against undue restrictions against economic activity imposed by feudal aristocracies in Europe was later transformed into an inflexible and self-serving ideology of the highly expanded and concentrated propertied classes in capitalistic society.

[98] J. Dewey, *Liberalism and Social Action* (Carbondale, IL: Southern Illinois University Press, 1991 [1935]), pp. 62–3; *LW*, vol. 11, 45.

[99] Ibid., 64; *LW*, vol. 11, 46.

[100] R. Niebuhr, "The pathos of liberalism," 304.

[101] Ibid.

believed in the "spirit" of liberalism – the virtues of tolerance and fairness, as well as love, justice, and brotherhood – and scorned the lack of realism in liberalism's assessment of the conditions and possibilities relative to the ideals espoused, insisting that the liberalism's creed placed liberalism's spirit at great risk. He regarded the liberal creed as blind to "the perennial difference between human actions and aspirations, the perennial source of conflict between life and life, the inevitable tragedy of human existence, the irreducible irrationality of human behavior, and the tortuous character of human history."[102]

Without question Niebuhr was the enfant terrible inside the liberal household, yet politically he remained solidly inside that household. As William Lee Miller put it, "Niebuhr has always criticized the idealism of the liberals in politics, but, it should be noted, as a friend who remained identified with their purposes."[103] Niebuhr biographer Richard Fox claimed that Niebuhr's aim had always been "not so much to destroy liberalism as to transform it into a philosophy that was realistic ... about the role of power, self-interests, and political mobilization in the social arena."[104]

DEMOCRACY

Both Niebuhr and Dewey had attacked the liberalism of the "bourgeois world" – what Dewey called "pseudo-liberalism." As Niebuhr put it, the "bourgeois world" was a world that "in dreaming of achieving 'liberty, equality, and fraternity,' [had] developed such monstrous disproportions of social and economic power as to threaten not only the security of those who lacked power but the stability of society itself."[105] During the economic crisis of the 1930s, both men believed that democracy must find ways of remedying those injustices by democratizing America's economic life, in addition to what it had already achieved in its political life. Yet Niebuhr and Dewey had serious differences in their respective views of democracy. Some of these differences were substantive, while others were primarily a matter of emphasis.

Dewey's vision of democracy was an expansive one: for him, democracy was a way of life. He viewed democracy as a belief system involving a deeply held conviction that a rationally based associative life could give expression to a set of values which would lead to self-realization through individual growth. Democracy, for Dewey, was not merely one form of human association among others. He saw democracy as the idea of community itself – as the quintessential form of human association that allows for the expression of that very liberty that enables the development of inherent human capacities. The relationship between democracy and core liberal values was clearly a symbiotic one. On the one hand,

---

[102] R. Niebuhr, "The blindness of liberalism," *Radical Religion* (Autumn, 1936), 45.

[103] W. L. Miller, "The irony of Reinhold Niebuhr," *Reporter* (January 13, 1955), 13.

[104] R. W. Fox, "Reinhold Niebuhr and the emergence of the liberal realist faith, 1930–1945," *Review of Politics* (April, 1976), 246.

[105] R. Niebuhr, "The sickness of American culture," *The Nation* (March 6, 1948), 267.

the core values of the authentic liberal tradition brought about democracy – such values as "liberty, the development of the inherent capacities of individuals made possible through liberty, and the central role of free intelligence in inquiry, discussion and expression."[106] On the other hand, the converse is also true, namely that only democracy provides the context for generating and perpetuating those liberal values that allow for such self-realization.

Dewey clearly viewed democracy in religious terms. The real heart of Dewey's "common faith" was democracy itself seen as the set of conditions wherein the liberty and rationality so central to the values of the moral imagination could flourish and grow. For Dewey, the idea and ideal of democracy were the ultimate historical heritage and the basis of democracy's future prospects. The future of religion as he saw it "is connected with the possibility of developing a faith in the possibilities of human experience and human relationships that will create a vital sense of the solidarity of human interests and inspire action to make that sense a reality."[107] Consistent with Dewey's humanistic naturalism the conservation, expansion, and transmission of democracy and its core values contain "all the elements for a religious faith that shall not be confined to sect, class, or race" and "has always been implicitly the common faith of mankind. It remains to make it explicit and militant."[108]

Niebuhr perpetually cautioned against making democracy into a religion. Without a more inclusive religious faith, Niebuhr believed, we often idolatrize the nation by identifying "our particular brand of democracy with the ultimate values of life."[109] With respect to Dewey, however, Niebuhr knew that Dewey abhorred absolutes in the truth-telling activities of life, and that while Niebuhr regarded his vision of democracy as highly romantic, he knew that Dewey was not prone to idolatrizing the nation. Niebuhr's criticisms of Dewey's "religious" view of democracy centered on what Niebuhr regarded as his typically naturalistic myopia toward the deeper spiritual aspirations of human beings that Niebuhr felt no sociopolitical community could fully express or satisfy.

The expansive vision Dewey had when he wrote in defense of democracy was also evident in the fact that he saw the issues attending the crisis of liberalism and democracy in broad cultural terms. Dewey's emphasis on the social and communal aspects of democracy resulted in his treating democracy as having far broader vistas than its strictly political meaning as a system of government. Dewey insisted on the priority of the conditions for the achievement of democratic community over matters pertaining to political machinery. Robert Westbrook described Dewey's vision as one that seeks "opportunities and resources" by means of which "every individual [can] realize fully his or her particular capacities and powers through participation in political, social,

---

[106] J. Dewey, *Liberalism and Social Action in LW*, vol. 11, 25.
[107] J. Dewey, "What I believe," *Forum*, 83 (March, 1930), 180; *LW*, vol. 5, 273–4.
[108] J. Dewey, *A Common Faith*, p. 87; *LW*, vol. 9, 58.
[109] R. Niebuhr, "Democracy as a religion," *Christianity and Crisis* (August 4, 1947), 1.

and cultural life."[110] The road to creating conditions in which this vision is achievable is a difficult one. The problem as Dewey saw it was the urgent need to reconstitute local communities and achieve direct democracy in order to render democracy viable. The crisis facing this endeavor was nothing less than the difficulty in adapting the Jeffersonian ideal of democracy to the changed conditions of an industrial and technological age. The crisis of liberalism in the modern age was not merely that of readjusting liberty to the conditions and consequences of the industrial age, as important as this was. It cut into far wider and deeper channels. It was, for Dewey, "the problem of humanizing industrial civilization, of making it and its technology a servant of human life."[111] In spite of the difficulties, however, Dewey had an abiding optimism that what he called the "democratic convergence"[112] would bring about a current "set steadily in one direction: toward democratic forms."[113]

The disagreement Niebuhr had with Dewey's characterization of democracy was based on his attack on the liberal creed that Dewey represented. Niebuhr firmly believed that democracy itself was also put at risk by liberalism's creed. When writing about the "Ten Years That Shook My World," Niebuhr had insisted that "one of the real tragedies of our era is that the very democracy which is the great achievement of liberalism cannot be maintained if liberalism is not transcended as a culture."[114] A decade after both Niebuhr and Dewey had despaired of the future prospects for democracy, Niebuhr launched a vindication of democracy by engaging in a critique of its traditional defense. In his 1944 book *The Children of Light and the Children of Darkness*, Niebuhr insisted that democratic civilization had been built and defended by moralists and idealists who were consistent in underestimating the realities of power and self-interest in socio-political affairs. He distinguished between the "foolish children of light . . . who believe that self-interest should be brought under the discipline of a higher law" and the "children of darkness" whose moral cynicism knows "no law beyond their will and interest."[115] For Niebuhr, the democratic prospect required that the *democratic* "children of light" learn the wisdom of the "children of darkness" without yielding to its dangerous cynicism. In effect, Niebuhr wanted the "children of light" to "know the power of self-interest in human society without giving it moral justification," stating that this wisdom must be theirs "in order that they may beguile, deflect, harness, and restrain self-interest, individual and collective, for the sake of the community."[116]

---

[110] R. B. Westbrook, *John Dewey and American Democracy* (Ithaca, NY: Cornell University Press, 1991), p. xv.
[111] J. Dewey, "Individualism old and new: The crisis in culture," *The New Republic* (March 19, 1930), 126; *LW*, vol. 5, 108.
[112] J. Dewey, *Public and Its Problems in LW*, vol. 2, 287–8.
[113] Ibid., 327.
[114] R. Niebuhr, "Ten years that shook my world," *The Christian Century* (April 26, 1939), 545.
[115] R. Niebuhr, *The Children of Light and the Children of Darkness*, p. 9.
[116] Ibid., p. 41.

The realism so important in properly gauging political life, for Niebuhr, lay in the recognition that injustice is rooted in the destructive force of inordinate self-love that, along with human creativity, stems from the self's finite freedom. Niebuhr knew that, however it might be stated, the doctrine of "original sin" would always be offensive to the modern mind. Yet he insisted on the truth in it and maintained that the doctrine "is the only empirically verifiable doctrine of the Christian faith."[117] So obvious are the "force and danger of self interest in human affairs," Niebuhr insisted, that they cannot "remain long obscure to those who are not blinded by either theory or interest to see the obvious."[118] In *The Children of Light and the Children of Darkness*, he insisted that the doctrine helps confront us with the fact that "no matter how wide the perspectives which the human mind may reach, how broad the loyalties which the human imagination may conceive, how universal the community which human statecraft may organize, or how pure the aspirations of the saintliest idealists may be, there is no level of human moral or social achievement in which there is not some corruption of inordinate self-love.[119]

Although a measure of idealism is important for democracy, it is its realism that Niebuhr thought was important and was certainly *the* pressing problem of the day. He knew, however, that the much needed injection of realism in our reassessment of democracy must not obscure the fact that democracy as such rightly rejects an overly pessimistic view of human nature. Niebuhr was not oblivious to the fact that the self's indeterminate freedom includes an awareness of its indeterminate possibilities. He was fully aware that the self has some capacity for transcendence over self-interest. Indeed, if this were not the case, "any form of social harmony would be impossible; and certainly a democratic vision of such harmony would be quite unthinkable.[120] Niebuhr's wisdom here comes to expression in one of his most familiar aphorisms: "Man's capacity for justice makes democracy possible; but man's inclination to injustice makes democracy necessary."[121] The capacity of envisioning and pursuing justice that fuels democratic idealism is essential to the very possibility of democracy.

---

[117] R. Niebuhr, *Man's Nature and His Communities: Essays on the Dynamics and Enigmas of Man's Personal and Social Existence* (New York: Charles Scribner's Sons, 1965), p. 24. In the autobiographical section of this book Niebuhr, looking back on his Gifford Lectures, acknowledged what he described as the "unpardonable pedagogical error" in defining the persistence and universality of man's self-regard as 'original sin'" because of his own "theological preoccupation." The error, however, he believed owed to the inability of a thoroughly secular age to grasp the "realism" in the religious myth instead of stumbling over the mythic language. The most extensive discussion of this history and meaning of original sin, for Niebuhr, is found in *The Nature and Destiny of Man-I: Human Nature*, chapter 9, "Original sin and man's responsibilities." For a sense of Niebuhr's dialectical view of the self, this should be read in conjunction with chapter 10 of the same volume on "Justitia Originalis."

[118] R. Niebuhr, *The Irony of American History* (New York: Charles Scribner's Sons, 1952), p. 35.

[119] R. Niebuhr, *The Children of Light and the Children of Darkness*, pp. 16–17.

[120] Ibid., p. 39.

[121] Ibid., p. xiii.

However, because of the inclination to injustice, democracy is necessary as a system of checks and balances within society and within government itself.

Niebuhr's assessment of democracy led him to reject Dewey's notion that because democracy is essentially "a *personal* way of individual life" and "a moral ideal," we ought to "get rid of the habit of thinking of democracy as something institutional and external."[122] Niebuhr, on the other hand, believed that the governmental forms embedded in democracies aids in advancing human creativity and constraining human destructiveness. This led him to emphasize the importance of institutional structures for achieving both an effective balance of power in society and workable forms of democratic governance in which government itself is held in check.

Niebuhr's reflections on democracy rested upon two dominant anthropological motifs: first, an attempt to affirm both the indeterminate heights of the individual's self-transcending freedom and the inordinate depths of its corruption of that freedom; and, second, a lifelong effort to apply the norm of love (*agape*) to the historical and political task of achieving justice. In working through these motifs as against the backdrop of both cynical and romantic conceptions of democracy, Niebuhr cautioned against an overly grandiose vision of democracy's historical possibilities. He pointed instead to the irony that the very freedom so characteristic of viable democratic societies has made "for a fortunate confusion in defining the goal towards which history should move; and the distribution of power in a democracy prevents any group of world savers from grasping after a monopoly of power."[123] As an antidote to a tendency to idealize democracy, Niebuhr emphasized what he saw to be the pragmatic virtue of democracy as "a method of finding proximate solutions for insoluble problems."[124] He saw that the problems of adjudicating between the requirement of order and the need for justice in community were perennial ones, thus belying any permanent solutions. There is at least a modicum of irony in that Niebuhr was the one who stressed the pragmatic note of "proximate solutions for insoluble problems" while Dewey, the instrumentalist/pragmatist, would devote so much time and energy to providing a devotional rhetoric for democracy!

In the context of his effort to relate love and justice, however, Niebuhr consistently viewed the struggle of democracy to balance power in moral terms. In relation to a discussion of international problems in 1959, he urged that

The educational enterprise for this nation, in short, must include a thorough re-examination of the problems of political morality, which will help the new generation to understand that any consideration of power and interest in analyzing the peace within a

[122] J. Dewey, "Creative democracy – the task before us" in *The Philosophy of the Common Man: Essays in Honor of John Dewey to Celebrate His Eightieth Birthday* (New York: Greenwood Press, 1940), pp. 222 and 226.

[123] R. Niebuhr, *Irony of American History*, p. 11.

[124] R. Niebuhr, *The Children of Light and the Children of Darkness*, p. 118.

nation and among the nations need not be a cynical defiance of the moral order but can well be what responsible statesmanship has always been: an effort to coerce competitive and contradictory human aspirations and interests into some kind of tolerable order and justice. Such a task is a highly moral one.[125]

Although the anthropological basis of Niebuhr's analysis of democracy and power politics had profound moral implication, he did, indeed, focus his attention more narrowly on certain deficiencies within American liberal-democratic faith. From Niebuhr's standpoint the very last thing a defense of democracy required in its embattled position between internal bourgeois liberal illusions and external denunciations by cynical fascists, utopian Marxists, or disillusioned radicals was another ritual celebration and reassertion of the type of sentimental idealism that had been so thoroughly discredited by contemporary history. The pressing need, as Niebuhr saw it, was to launch a rigorous critique of those very creeds and illusions on which the traditional defense of democracy had come to rest and then provide a more realistic vindication of democracy against idealists and cynics alike.

Niebuhr knew fully well that "democracy in the West is both a political system and a way of life [requiring] a high degree of literacy among its citizens, a sense of the dignity of the individual but also a sense of his responsibility to a wider community than [the] family."[126] Along with Dewey, Niebuhr held that democracy embodies broad fundamental values that give fuller expression to the self's *humanitas* than alternative political systems. As he once put it, "ideally democracy is a permanently valid form of social and political organization which does justice to two dimensions of human existence: to man's spiritual stature and his social character; to the uniqueness and variety of life, as well as to the common necessities of all men."[127] As a form of social organization that maximizes liberty, the relative freedom of its social and political life corresponds to and allows for the endless elaboration of individual and collective vitalities that rise "in indeterminate degree over all social and communal concretions of life."[128] Along with Dewey, Niebuhr, too, believed that a free and open society such as democracy envisions is justified more than any other because it gives latitude to the creative expression of the vitalities of life – creative vitalities that such a society leaves open to ever-expanding opportunities. He saw democracy best reflecting and confirming to human beings' "essential nature": namely, to that freedom that is the self's "capacity for indeterminate transcendence over the processes and limitations of nature."[129]

In rethinking democracy's relations to liberal tradition, Niebuhr concluded that "democracy has a more compelling justification and requires a more realistic vindication than it is given by the liberal culture with which it has been

[125] R. Niebuhr, "Education and the world scene," *Daedalus* 88:1 (Winter, 1959), 116.
[126] R. Niebuhr, *Irony of American History*, pp. 123–4.
[127] R. Niebuhr, *The Children of Light and the Children of Darkness*, p. 3.
[128] Ibid., p. 49.
[129] R. Niebuhr, *The Children of Light and the Children of Darkness*, p. 3.

associated in modern history."[130] In short, "it has become important to save what is valuable in democratic life from the destruction of what is false in bourgeois civilization," and that requires "distinguishing what is false in democratic theory from what is true in democratic life."[131] The urgency of this task gave quite a different coloration to Niebuhr's and Dewey's respective agendas with regard to both what was involved in the reconstruction of liberalism and what was to have priority in addressing the nature and prospect of democracy. Because Dewey's and Niebuhr's understandings of human nature differed, their respective democratic accents would differ accordingly. The crisis within democracy as Niebuhr saw it came on the side of its political philosophy and not so much on the side of democracy as a "way of life."

What is clear is that the two individuals within the pantheon of American democratic theorists to whom Dewey and Niebuhr were drawn were Thomas Jefferson and James Madison – Dewey to Jefferson and Niebuhr to Madison.

For Dewey, Jefferson's vision of societal harmony was based on a presumption that human ambitions were moderate and conflicts amenable to rational accommodation. He also venerated the Jeffersonian combination of freedom, scientific enlightenment, education, and the practical experiment in self-government understood in broad cultural terms. Dewey identified with Jefferson's belief in "the will of the people as the moral basis of government," a trust he claimed "was temperamental" and "constitutional" with Jefferson. He believed that Jefferson's "deep-seated faith in the people and their responsiveness to enlightenment properly presented ... [as] the cardinal element bequeathed by [him] to the American tradition."[132]

For Niebuhr, it was James Madison who stood out as having "combined Christian realism in the interpretation of human nature and desires with Jefferson's passion for liberty."[133] Niebuhr saw Madison as "the only one of the founding fathers who made a realistic analysis of both power and interest from a political and democratic perspective." He was governed by a basic insight of political realism, namely the "intimate relation" between reason and self-love.[134] Niebuhr saw the pinnacle of Madison's political wisdom embodied in the understanding that "the highest achievement of democratic societies" rests in the fact "that they embody the principle of resistence to government within the principle of government itself."[135] The genius of democracy is in acknowledging

---

[130] Ibid., p. xii.
[131] Ibid., p. 40.
[132] J. Dewey, "Presenting Thomas Jefferson," *LW*, vol. 14, 214 and 216. Jefferson's confidence in the "will of the people as the moral basis of government" also had its counterpart in Niebuhr who periodically alluded to the "wisdom of common sense." But instead of lauding the capacity of the people for learning and enlightenment, Niebuhr praised "the native shrewdness of the common people who in small realism have had something of the same experience with human nature as the statesmen." Niebuhr, *Irony of American History*, p. 18.
[133] R. Niebuhr, *Irony of American History*, p. 96.
[134] R. Niebuhr, *Man's Mature and His Communities*, p. 66.
[135] R. Niebuhr, *Nature and Destiny of Man-II Human Destiny*, p. 278.

the need for sufficient power to cajole the anarchic forces of life's vitalities and the inordinate self-interest of individuals and groups while at the same time grasping the need to place restraint upon both governmental and social centers of power. Niebuhr's democratic realism was far more modest in its aims than Dewey's Jeffersonian idealism. It saw democracy, not in terms of a vast liberal vision of rational fraternity, but as a pluralistic, ever-contesting, problem-solving society, cajoled into a workable but free community of often divisive groups.

A FINAL WORD

For all the differences between Niebuhr and Dewey, occasionally generating levels of controversy bordering on acrimony, these differences masked a shared pragmatic heritage. Dewey succeeded William James as America's preeminent voice within the pragmatic tradition. Niebuhr, who bore the imprint of William James in the dissertations of his early years, continued to work within and creatively apply the pragmatic tradition throughout his life. We have seen that many of Dewey's secular and humanistic associates who understandably rejected Niebuhr's theology were particularly agitated because of their aware-ness of Niebuhr's pragmatic affinity with Dewey. Against their own instincts, men such as Sidney Hook were forced to take Niebuhr seriously in a way that was not the case with other religious voices. Niebuhr was resented and respected at the same time. His pragmatic bent and his political astuteness were recog-nized, and this awareness fueled both their repudiation of his theology and their resentment of his attacks on Dewey.

Professor James A. Martin's memory of Niebuhr's claiming that perhaps his criticisms of Dewey were too harsh and admitting that they might have had more in common than he realized at the time[136] brings to light two important facts. While it is true that Niebuhr targeted Dewey, he did so as the vehicle for attacking the misguided rationalism and excessive moralistic idealism he saw rampant throughout the religious and secular liberalism of that day. At the same time, Niebuhr not only shared many social and political causes with Dewey but also never abandoned the liberal tradition. His Christian realism, as Garry Dorrien describes it, remained a "neo-liberal realism" in both theology and politics.[137] What also remained and what Niebuhr shared with John Dewey was a pragmatic tradition that, in Niebuhr's case, found both theological expression and realistic political formulation.

[136] See note 8.
[137] G. Dorrien, "Christian realism: Reinhold Niebuhr's theology, ethics, and politics" in D. F. Rice (ed.), *Reinhold Niebuhr Revisited* (Grand Rapids, MI: Eerdmans, 2008), p. 26.

CHAPTER 3

Norman Thomas (1884–1968)

Reinhold Niebuhr met Norman Thomas when Niebuhr got involved in socialist politics after moving to New York City in 1928. His association with Thomas and *The World Tomorrow* staff began immediately by way of his joint appointment, financed by Sherwood Eddy, to a part-time teaching position at Union Theological Seminary and to an associate editing position at *The World Tomorrow*. As for what first prompted the social awareness resulting in his attraction to Thomas, Niebuhr informed us in his 1954 oral interview at Columbia University that his experiences as a pastor in Detroit with "raw politics" associated with Henry Ford are what sharpened his mind to "all the facts of life in regard to our industrial society."[1] He further recalled 1926 as the year when he "had come out with a socialistic answer to the problems of modern industrialism."[2]

Thomas had begun moving closer to accepting the general socialist critique of capitalism during the period of World War I. His embrace of socialism also grew out of experiences gained after graduating from Princeton University, first at the Spring Street Presbyterian Church in New York City in 1905, next as an assistant at Christ Church on West 36th Street in 1908, and then after his ordination in 1911 at the East Harlem Presbyterian Church. While a student at Union Theological Seminary, Thomas, like Niebuhr later, came under the influence of Walter Rauschenbusch, whose books *Christianity and the Social Crisis* and *Christianizing the Social Order* ignited social consciousness within Protestant religious circles. As Thomas recalled, however, his embrace of socialism came primarily as a matter of "events, not people and not books" – events relating to the "grotesque inequalities, conspicuous waste, gross exploitation, and unnecessary poverty all about me."[3]

---

[1] Interview with R. Niebuhr by H. B. Phillips on June 14, 1954. *The Reminiscences of Reinhold Niebuhr* (New York: Oral History Research Office, Columbia University, 1957), p. 89.

[2] Ibid., p. 90.

[3] Quoted in M. B. Seidler, *Norman Thomas: Respectable Rebel* (Syracuse, NY: Syracuse University Press, 1961), p. 29.

FIG. 3 Thomas
Courtesy of the Library of Congress

In spite of backing the Allies during World War I, both Thomas and Niebuhr eventually came to regret their support and allied themselves in different degrees with the pacifist movement. By 1916 Thomas had joined the Christian pacifist group, the Fellowship of Reconciliation – an organization Niebuhr also joined, serving on the executive council in 1929 and as chair in 1931. He also joined the National Civil Liberties Bureau, which later became the American Civil Liberties Union, and became increasingly outspoken against both the war and America's possible involvement in it. The May 26, 1917, issue of *The New Republic* found Thomas as the lead signatory among "Conscientious Objectors and Their Champions" who pled for toleration of "those humanists now in imminent danger of being bullied out of existence because their visions and their faiths extend beyond the time of bloody chaos." This group, above all others, looked forward to creating a more humane world in the reconstructive task ahead in the postwar world.[4]

Thomas became editor of the pacifist magazine *The World Tomorrow* in 1917, with its initial issue appearing in January, 1918. Niebuhr's first article published there, which was entitled "Religion's Limitations," appeared in the

---

[4] N. Thomas et.al., "The religion of free men," *The New Republic* (May 26, 1917), 110.

March, 1920, issue. Although his context was World War I, Niebuhr struck themes that were to become central to his thinking over his long career. He castigated the Christian church, not only for having abdicated its prophetic function in failing to "guide the conscience of the nations," but also for its failure to see its own moral limitations expressed in its arrogance in thinking itself to be sole agency in the struggle for moral progress. According to Niebuhr, Christianity's most grievous limitation was seen in the churches' preoccupation with matters of personal morality rendering them oblivious to the more complex issues facing social and political morality.[5] Meanwhile, as Thomas became more the social activist and advocate of radical causes, the Presbyterian Church which he served as an ordained minister became increasingly suspicious of him. He never held the traditional beliefs of his denomination.[6] The Presbyterians were much relieved when he resigned from Christ Church soon after the mayoralty election of 1917. There was mutual benefit in this, as Thomas's negative view of the church and its clergy was matched by the church's having all but blacklisted him for his political views.

Thomas, having felt the influence of the socialist leader Morris Hillquit, applied for membership in the Socialist Party in October, 1918. According to Murray Seidler, "Beginning with his formal Socialist affiliation, Norman Thomas became, in a real sense, a professional social reformer or radical. From that point on he devoted virtually all of his waking hours to organizing, speaking, and writing in behalf of a great number of organizations in the American radical and liberal worlds."[7] Richard W. Fox emphasized that it was "Norman Thomas's rapid rise in the Socialist ranks in the 1920s that made it possible for men like Niebuhr, [Paul] Douglas, John Dewey, and John Haynes Holmes to gravitate toward the Socialist cause and in some cases enter the Socialist Party."[8]

Norman Thomas's rise in the Socialist Party came at an inopportune time, when the party had entered a long period of decline. A strong desire for a third-party movement sprang out of the Conference for Progressive Political Action (CPPA), formed in 1922, and made up of socialists, railway men, union representatives, and members of the Farmer-Labor Party. In 1924, disillusioned with both mainstream political parties, the CPPA sought to find a candidate to run for president that year. Wisconsin's Robert La Follette was invited to be their candidate, but La Follette undermined their third-party aspirations by choosing to run as a candidate of his own Progressive Party. He, along with Democratic candidate John W. Davis, lost to Calvin Coolidge in a landslide. After La

[5] R. Niebuhr, "Religion's limitations," *The World Tomorrow* (March, 1920), 77.

[6] Gary Dorrien insists that Thomas "was not a traditional believer in any sense excepting moral seriousness," and he "had little conception of the church beyond its capacity to serve as an agent of social transformation." G. Dorrien, "Norman Thomas" in M. J. Buhle, P. Buhle, and H. Kaye (eds.), *The American Radical* (New York: Routledge, 1994), p. 214.

[7] M. B. Seidler, *Norman Thomas: Respectable Rebel*, p. 69.

[8] R. W. Fox, *Reinhold Niebuhr: A Biography* (New York: Pantheon, 1985), p. 116.

Follett's defeat, two things happened. The fragile alliance between socialists and labor dissolved as labor largely abandoned third-party politics, and many wrote the obituary for the Socialist Party, whose fortunes had precipitously declined since the early 1920s.[9] Thomas's official political career began during the La Follette campaign when, at age forty, he ran unsuccessfully for governor of New York as a candidate on both the Progressive and Socialist tickets. He lost again in a 1926 run for the State Senate in New York City's lower East Side's 14th District. Yet in spite of the disillusionment with third-party politics, the Party nominated Norman Thomas as its presidential candidate in 1928, following the death of longtime Socialist Party standard-bearer Eugene Debs two years earlier. Niebuhr was among those who supported Thomas.[10]

During his run for the presidency in 1928, Thomas prepared a statement "Why I Am a Socialist" which was published by the League for Industrial Democracy. While insisting that socialism is not an "infallible panacea," he nonetheless believed that it "affords our best hope of utilizing our immense resources of material and skill so as to abolish poverty and the terrible insecurity of the workers, reduce the menace of war, and increase the measure of freedom and fraternity in our world." Thomas saw poverty, the misery and insecurity of unemployment and old age, and the continual menace of war as built into the existing capitalist system because it was based on the power of private ownership designed for the profit of the owners. Countering the charge that socialism is the foe of liberty, he claimed that capitalism is the true enemy of freedom. In a capitalist system, "property is so much better defended than life," while "freedom is too generally the possession of man who is strong enough to take it for himself." Furthermore, freedom was then a "non-existent commodity" given the combination of the economic fear of workers and a press controlled by those holding power. With pointed sarcasm, Thomas concluded that "Diogenes might

---

[9] In 1932 Thomas gave his own take on this history as he sought to explain the Socialist Party's defeat in his first run for the presidency that year. He wrote that "my position [was not] weakened by reflection of the La Follette campaign of 1924 ... That year there was no such overwhelming anger against the party in power as this year, and there was resentment among farmers and workers against the Democrats, some of it because [Al] Smith was not nominated, some because [William G.] McAdoo lost. In this mood a temporary coalition was worked out which we fondly hoped might result in a labor party. The fact that after polling almost five million votes that coalition fell apart like a rope of sand is of itself proof that under exceptionally favorable circumstances the avoidance of the Socialist philosophy and the Socialist name got a large vote at the price of complete impermanence even of protest, to say nothing of constructive policy. After 1924 the Socialist movement had the courage to keep going. The Progressive movement quit the national field." N. Thomas, "Norman Thomas replies," *The Nation* (December 14, 1932), 585.

[10] Other notables who supported Thomas, according to Fleischman, were "geographer J. Russell Smith of Columbia University; theologian Reinhold Niebuhr of Union Theological Seminary, Robert Morss Lovett and Paul H. Douglas of the University of Chicago, Freda Kirchway of *The Nation*, Howard Brubaker of the *New Yorker*; Methodist Bishop Paul Jones, Rabbi M. S. Fisher; Rev. John Haynes Holmes of Community Church, and Harold E. Fey of the *Christian Century*." H. Fleischman, *Norman Thomas: A Biography* (New York: Norton, 1964), p. 116.

find an honest man with a lantern," but "he would have to look for a free man with a searchlight in our modern age."[11]

According to Richard W. Fox, Niebuhr at this time was not drawn to socialism's "Marxian heritage of social analysis or political action," finding this tradition too full of European dogmatism and violent undercurrents. "The appeal of the socialist movement for Niebuhr and other left-leaning liberals" was "the Socialist potential for gradualist reform."[12] Just prior to the election, Niebuhr published an article in *The World Tomorrow* on "Why We Need a New Economic Order." He saw injustice as the overriding problem with the capitalist system. He hoped that society might be able to modify the existing system but fully expected its eventual breakdown in the long run. Niebuhr had not yet become radicalized. He was content to maintain that "the widespread belief among radicals that a violent change is preferable because more thoroughgoing is not borne out by history." Nonetheless, Niebuhr did wonder if there was enough social intelligence to "modify the present system step by step as the need arises ... or whether through the stubbornness and blindness of the holders of power and privilege and through the ignorance of the masses the system will be permitted to disintegrate until change can come only through revolution and social convulsion."[13]

During the 1928 campaign, Thomas had called for various policies that could have blunted the worst of the impending economic crisis: "shortening the work day and week as technology increased labor productivity ... the adoption of a Constitutional amendment prohibiting child labor. ... federal old age pensions and unemployment insurance, to be financed by increased corporation taxes, [and] inheritance levies and taxes on large individual incomes."[14] All this proved of no avail. Herbert Hoover won the 1928 election in a landslide, with Thomas garnering only 267,000 votes. The Republicans' professed year of "prosperity" was but one year away from the onset of the Great Depression.

[11] N. Thomas, "Why I am a Socialist," Leaflet No. 4 (1928) published in *League for Industrial Democracy: A Documentary History*, compiled by B.K. Johnpoll and M.R. Yerburgh (1980), vol. I, pp. 725, 729, and 730. Thomas's article was reprinted from the *Princeton Alumni Weekly* of April 6, 1928. Two years earlier, in 1926, Niebuhr, who had refused to yield to business pressure preventing AFL members attending a Detroit convention from appearing in church pulpits, was not so confident about the courage or resolve of labor to take action on its own behalf. After attending sessions of the Federation of Labor convention, he remarked that labor leaders "impressed me as having about the same amount of daring and imagination as a group of village bankers." R. Niebuhr, *Leaves From the Notebook of a Tamed Cynic* (New York: Meridian Living Age, 1957), pp. 132–3.

[12] R.W. Fox, *Reinhold Niebuhr: A Biography*, p. 116. Fox wrote, "At first [Niebuhr] remained aloof from the Socialist Party itself. Instead he joined George Count's left-leaning New York Teachers' Union, the pacifist Fellowship of Reconciliation, Norman Thomas's educational organization (the League for Industrial Democracy), and University of Chicago economist Paul Douglas's League for Independent Political Action." Ibid., pp. 115–16.

[13] R. Niebuhr, "Why we need a new economic order," *The World Tomorrow* (October, 1928), 397.

[14] H. Fleischman, *Norman Thomas: A Biography*, p. 114.

Although Niebuhr had voted for Thomas in 1928, he was not yet a member of the Socialist Party. However, he did join at the end of the summer in 1929, soon before the stock market crash on October 29. That December, Niebuhr published an article on "Political Action and Social Change" in *The World Tomorrow*. He called for something more than a bipartisan or strike-based approach to economic inequalities in America. Both approaches assumed the soundness of the existing social and economic order. Instead, Niebuhr insisted that required social change could be brought about only by the kind of political action that transforms the system of private ownership. He questioned whether the Socialist Party could gain ascendency within the political system or whether a new party was required. As a member – along with John Dewey – of the League for Independent Political Action that Paul Douglas had organized in 1929, Niebuhr saw both major parties in lock-step with business interests. While he found nothing to disagree with in the 1928 Socialist platform, he did wonder – given "the general conservatism of a wealthy nation and the present political incompetence of the average worker" – whether "the political traditions of our people might not make the formation of a new party, including farmers and workers from the day of its organization, wise political strategy." At this point, Niebuhr believed that intelligent political action was preferable to the extremes of evolutionary change and revolutionary ardor. While acknowledging that "the stubbornness of reactionary forces and the blindness of men sometimes make social convulsions and catastrophes inevitable," he considered a violent approach "a wasteful method of change" and "no guarantee that the new order will be any more just than the old."[15]

As the impact of the market crash deepened, both Niebuhr and Thomas ramped up their pleas for fundamental social and economic reform. Niebuhr pressed for connecting property rights to human rights and for subsuming the former under the latter. While still alluding to the need to "develop ... intelligence quickly enough to readjust our social concepts and machinery to a changed environment," he urged greater action. Niebuhr feared that the preference for a socialism whose approach is only "parliamentary and evolutionary" is in "constant peril of letting its waters run into the sand of mere liberal reform." Niebuhr's burgeoning realism also led him to the ominous conclusion that if "the chronic weakness of our conventional 'idealism'" in failing "to deal realistically" with our traditional prejudices and assumptions "cannot be cured, the future of modern society will be determined by conflict and not by adjustment."[16]

When Thomas's book *America's Way Out* was published in 1931, he thought it important to list the three distinguishing characteristics of socialism: (1) socialism "believes in the public or social ownership and control of land, natural resources and the principal means of production and distribution of goods. This means the control of economic processes for human use rather than for

[15] R. Niebuhr, "Political action and social change," *The World Tomorrow* (December, 1929), 492–3.
[16] R. Niebuhr, "Property and the ethical life," *The World Tomorrow* (January, 1931), 20–1.

individual profit;" (2) "it believes in the use of the machinery of the existing state, or some modification of the existing state, as a means of achieving social control;" and (3) "socialism, theoretically, at least, insists on a comradeship of the worker which transcends racial or nationalist lines. It is therefore international in outlook."[17] In his article "Capitalism Will Not Plan" published that same year, Thomas insisted that the kind and degree of planning required for the transformation of America's now devastated economic order simply "could not occur within the framework of our capitalist society." In order to move away from a policy of private profit to one of general use, society "must own or at least control the vital economic enterprises for which it plans." Socialism, for Thomas, was necessary as "the essential condition of successful planning," just as planning was "the essential tool of successful socialism."[18]

Niebuhr acknowledged in 1931 that the lengthy depression had not yet moved a "politically and socially lethargic people to the kind of social realism which many had hoped for and longed for." Now his hope was that the election campaign of 1932 would bring to light political realities that would prompt the loyalty of American workers to join the ranks of socialism. The chief thing Niebuhr wanted the workers to learn was just "how much political realities are the expression of economic class interest." He also hoped they would "discover that the chief root of economic and social inequality in the present social order is the unqualified right of private property" that has been "sanctified by law and custom and made irrelevant by the facts of contemporary civilization." To this end he turned to his religious constituency, setting about to examine the relationship between Christianity and socialism in order to answer doubts his progressive Christian friends might have that would inhibit taking prompt action.

While Niebuhr knew that progressive Christians valued the aim of equal justice, he wondered just how church organizations and institutions would respond to the harsh reality of class conflict – a reality that "smells of hatred and warfare and seems incompatible with the ideal of love." However, he was convinced that if the Christian church "should stand for something that is less than justice in the name of the ideal of love" it professed, it could no longer "maintain any moral prestige whatsoever." Niebuhr sought to remind the church that the class struggle was a fact of history and not an invention of the socialists and that if this reality was ignored, it would result in an ethical betrayal of the very classes of people the Christian ethic of love should serve. Moreover, he wanted to convince his fellow Christians of the subtlety and complexity involved in the realities of violence – of how conservative forces use it and how non-violent force is employed against social change unethically by economic power and the prestige of the courts.[19]

[17] N. Thomas, *America's Way Out: A Program for Democracy* (New York: Macmillan, 1931), p. 54.
[18] N. Thomas, "Capitalism will not plan," *The New Republic* (August 12, 1931), 339–40.
[19] R. Niebuhr, "Socialism and Christianity," *The Christian Century* (August 19, 1931), 1038–40.

Two years into the Great Depression, and on the eve of a second run for the presidency in 1932, Thomas urgently claimed that in "this hour of crisis to reject socialism is to accept years of bitter strife and unimaginable catastrophe." He was certain that the ills American society was experiencing were symptomatic of a dying capitalism, and that the only prospect facing the foreseeable future was total disaster followed by the rise of either fascism, socialism, or communism. Capitalism was doomed because of its abysmal failure to provide security and plenty, its lack of ethical and intellectual standards, and its need for – or impotence to avoid – war. Thomas was horrified by the magnitude of the catastrophe he saw coming – abhorring the Mussolini-style fascism that he envisioned as a possibility for America and also recoiling from the rigorous dictatorship that communism would likely impose. For Thomas, only socialism that valued democracy and sought to preserve it could stave off the impending catastrophe. He was proposing socialism as a "philosophy, a social vision" and "a loyalty" that alone was "adequate to the realities of the interdependent world which the machine age has imposed upon us."[20]

Thomas accepted the reality of class division and class conflict that Marxism identified, but, unlike the Marxists, he did not believe that class struggle ruled out democracy in a country such as America that had an established democratic tradition. Nonetheless, he did question whether revolution in American would remain peaceful because, although he "did not think that the *desire* for violence" had increased in the world, he was "fully persuaded that an *acceptance* of the inevitability of violence [was] steadily on the increase." The real danger, for Thomas, was that the procrastination and compromise endemic to political action in parliamentary/democratic politics are "too enervating for ... firm and stern resolution."[21] He did not believe that the impending catastrophe had gone so far that it could not be averted. What he desperately wanted was to teach American workers the reality of class conflict and organization – the latter being an area, he insisted, wherein the socialists showed the greatest weakness. Thomas maintained that the need to organize efficiently would definitely require both a "challenge to social engineering" and a willingness to experiment – both of which were new to socialist planning.[22]

Looking ahead to the election, Thomas advocated immediate action on several fronts, including direct federal relief of the unemployed, using the taxing powers of government to provide employment through a program of public works, the five-day work week, unemployment insurance, public employment exchanges, a reduction of farm debt, and the reduction of national and international public and non-productive debts. In order to promote increased international cooperation, he recommended recognition of the Soviet Union and an end

---

[20] N. Thomas, *The Socialist Cure for a Sick Society* (New York: The Stratford Press for The John Day Company, Pamphlet No. 13, 1932), pp. 28 and 13.

[21] N. Thomas, "Is peaceful revolution possible?" *The World Tomorrow* (September 14, 1932), 251.

[22] N. Thomas, *The Socialist Cure for a Sick Society*, pp. 21 and 25.

to both real and planned embargos on Russian products,[23] a cancellation of war reparations and debts contingent on progress toward disarmament, the end of using military force to collect debts in weak nations, an end to imperialist adventures, an agreement with other nations to prohibit the sale or shipment of arms to aggressor nations, tariff reductions, and a world conference aimed at establishing a fiscal system and allocating raw materials.

As Thomas prepared for the upcoming election, he was convinced that the two major parties in America were largely fraudulent in promoting progressive action, and there were still many forces organizing in order to establish a new party. He summarily dismissed all options among those forces except for the Socialist Party whose fortunes he was attempting to promote. Thomas described the situation: the Communist Party opted for violence instead of making a serious effort at political action, the Socialist Labor Party was both numerically small and committed to a pure Marxist ideology, and the League for Independent Political Action was "not a party but a league." That, according to Thomas, left only the Socialist Party which, although weak in organization, he believed was "on the up grade" since its lowest level during the mid 1920s. With Paul Douglas saying that the Democratic Party was standing in the way of a much needed third party and John Dewey believing it suicidal to back Roosevelt as the lesser of two evils, the League for Independent Political Action finally voted to endorse Thomas at its Cleveland meeting in July.

According to Arthur Schlesinger Jr., whereas Eugene Debs "had Americanized Socialism for the working class, Thomas Americanized Socialism for the middle class,"[24] and in 1932 his "real impact" was "on the educated middle class – more than on the working classes."[25] Thomas's concern was whether the workers and their unions would "move in the direction of socialist philosophy" or "in the direction of AFL's trade-union capitalism and hostility toward Russia." With great optimism, he thought that eventually men and women in America "will come together in a socialist party, by whatever name it may be called." Thomas believed that if the movement was to be successful, it must be comprised of farmers' organizations and the more

---

[23] Niebuhr, too, was concerned with America's relationship to Russia at this time, believing that among all problems jeopardizing world peace, the most pressing was "the question of achieving and maintaining amicable relations with Russia and the other nations of the world." Niebuhr realized that fear caused by Russia's "bold departure from the generally accepted political and social organization of the rest of the world" was an unsettling factor. So, too, was Russia's combination of "aggressive zeal and defensive valor" and "the fanatic devotion of the communists to their cause, coupled with their unshaken conviction that the world is plotting the destruction of their state." Niebuhr believed that Russia's aggressive expansionist objectives would, in the immediate future, yield to her "preoccupation with her industrialization program" and her need to justify "communism first of all by a successful program at home." See R. Niebuhr, "Making peace with Russia," *The World Tomorrow* (November, 1931), 354.

[24] Arthur Schlesinger Jr., *The Politics of Upheaval* (Boston: Mariner Books/Houghton Mifflin, 2003), p. 177.

[25] Arthur Schlesinger Jr., *The Age of Roosevelt* (Boston: Mariner Books/Houghton Mifflin, 2003), p. 435.

progressive unions. His hope was that the movement would not come under the control of the unions, but rather that "the present Socialist Party will have earned the right and power to be the leader and teacher."[26]

Niebuhr came out in strong support of Thomas's presidential bid in 1932. He was no doubt the figure behind the editorial "Thomas for President" in *The World Tomorrow* that announced the journal's choice of a presidential candidate. Nevertheless, the editorial was "frank to say" that the journal was "first of all supporting socialism as socialism." In spite of being "rather enamored of Norman Thomas's stature," the editorial emphasized knowing "very well that his real stature depends upon his ability to call into being, and to lead, a powerful socialist movement." *The World Tomorrow* also wanted to make clear to its readers that, given its belief that "nothing is quite so dead in America as the liberal tradition," its aim was to explicitly draw "a sharper line" than ever before "of demarcation between its policy and that of the so-called 'liberal journals' with which it is associated in the popular mind."[27] At the same time, Niebuhr, as Chairman of the Organization Committee of the Committee of Five Thousand, was also busy appealing for support for Thomas and the socialist program in such publications as *The Nation* and *The New Republic*, urging their readers not to "be neutral in this crisis," but rather "to support a fundamental program and a man of outstanding ability for President." He stressed the need to "organize [the prevailing] discontent in the nation into a propelling force behind a program and a genuine leader."[28]

As the election drew ever closer, Niebuhr wrote a letter to the editor of *The Christian Century* blasting its recent editorial on "The Stakes in the Election." While crediting *The Christian Century* with having "done so much to clarify the social and political thought of American Protestantism," he was appalled that they thought Hoover was "educable" and "represented 'sound capitalism' as against Mr. Roosevelt's 'uncertain capitalism'" – a claim that was supportable only if "soundness" was defined "in terms of consistent and intransigent conservatism." Niebuhr then characterized the editor's recommendation of a "disinterested party" whose ideals might help show the major parties a way out of present difficulties as the "pure moonshine" of "middle class intellectualism." He indicted the editors of *The Christian Century* for ignoring the "economic basis of politics" and for their "non-partisan" stance when it was obvious that both major parties generally represent the commercial and financial classes. Niebuhr argued that it was the workers and farmers who "have been excluded from the charmed circle of American prosperity" and who must find a way of

[26] N. Thomas, *America's Way Out*, pp. 284–5 and pp. 289–90.
[27] R. Niebuhr, "Thomas for president," *The World Tomorrow* (July, 1932), 195. Thomas, writing "hastily in the midst of an absorbing and very crowded political campaign," welcomed "*The World Tomorrow* into the weekly field" adding "a double welcome because *The World Tomorrow* is categorically and avowedly Socialist." Thomas, "Is Peaceful Revolution Possible?" *The World Tomorrow* (September 14, 1932), 251.
[28] See both "Thomas for president" letters in *The New Republic* (August 17, 1932), 22, and *The Nation* (August 17, 1932), 147.

developing sufficient political strength to counter the combined forces that perpetuated injustice because of disproportions of power. Clearly, power must be set against power if any justice was to be attained.[29]

The year 1932 also saw the appearance of one of Niebuhr's most powerful and influential books, *Moral Man and Immoral Society*. Thomas was of mixed opinion regarding its value. In his review of the book, he credited Niebuhr with possessing "one of the most stimulating minds and one of the purest purposes in America," and he saw the book "filled with the learning, and lightened by the brilliance, and inspired by the insight which his friends have learned to expect from him." However, such accolades aside, Thomas felt compelled to attack what he deemed Niebuhr's "degree of defeatism, which I do not believe the author intends." No doubt Thomas's view of human nature was far more idealistic than that of Niebuhr. While agreeing that the harsh facts of political life must be recognized in contrast to the "sentimentalists, the romanticists, and the believers in panacea," Thomas felt that Niebuhr had overstated the case. Most importantly, Thomas was unwilling to accept Niebuhr's judgment that democracies cannot achieve major progress in social justice without illusion and that the perfect society in the vision of socialists or communists is equally illusory.[30]

Thomas's review appeared in *The World Tomorrow* in mid-December, 1932. Niebuhr, in the February, 1933, issue of the same journal, responded to a multitude of critics who had reviewed *Moral Man and Immoral Society*. In his rejoinder to Thomas, Niebuhr first chose to respond to Thomas's charge that he had oversimplified the issue of pacifism by claiming that "subsequent reviews have rather justified me in believing that the entire middle-class world, whether avowedly pacifistic or not, is confused about the relation of coercion to moral idealism" being "shocked by insistence that coercion is an inevitability in man's collective life." Indeed, Niebuhr contended that "failure to recognize the coercive character of economic and political life, when coercion expresses itself in covert forms, is the very root of the moral confusion from which our dominant social classes suffer."[31] Niebuhr consistently placed Thomas in close proximity to those utopian romantics of whom he was most critical. Thomas always denied such interpretations, viewing himself as preaching a "realistic socialism" while insisting that "Utopia had better be a private or a party hope rather than a party dogma of the future."[32] Nonetheless, Niebuhr saw at the basis of the utopian

---

[29] R. Niebuhr, "A communication: the stakes in the election," *The Christian Century* (November 9, 1932), 1379–80.

[30] N. Thomas, "Moral man and immoral society: a review," *The World Tomorrow* (December 14, 1932), 565, 567. Thomas also identified what he felt were a few omissions in Niebuhr's book; namely, his having paid scant attention to our having overcome scarcity, yet our inability to bring about shared abundance; his failure to deal adequately with the problem of wholesale violence in his attack on pacifism; and, while convinced that Niebuhr's chapters on the class struggle were among the best, Thomas believed his treatment of the proletariat in America was oversimplified.

[31] R. Niebuhr, "Optimism and utopianism," *The World Tomorrow* (February 22, 1933), 179.

[32] N. Thomas, *America's Way Out*, pp. 150 and 146.

expectations of all Marxists and liberals – Thomas included – a "romantic conception of human nature and its perfectibility." The point he was intent on making against those who indicted him for the sharp limits he placed on what reason could accomplish was that "every force of reason and intelligence will fail to create that anarchistic millennium which is the implied hope of all liberals." Perhaps a society that is socialistic might be expected to be "more just and sufferable than our capitalistic one," but he considered it "foolish to assume that it will completely socialize human beings and create the perfect society."[33]

The election of Roosevelt in 1932 led to the nadir of socialist influence among progressives in America. Roosevelt had received considerable support from many socialist sympathizers and some Socialist Party members, not so much because they had abandoned their socialist principles but because of a fear of Republican policies. Thomas's somewhat embittered postmortem on the election was summed up in a response to an open letter to him from the well-known radio broadcaster Gabriel Heatter. With undisguised resentment, he remarked that "progressives come very cheap in America. All they wanted to know this year was that Governor Roosevelt was not President Hoover."[34] As the course of events unfolded, Thomas did concede that Roosevelt's programs such as the National Industrial Recovery Act (NIRA) and the Agricultural Adjustment Act (AAA) were likely to get the country out of the depression. However, he considered them merely Band-Aids on American capitalism. Thomas begrudgingly admitted an admiration for Roosevelt's "energy and directness of purpose" but saw "no miracles" regarding substantive accomplishments in reversing the abysmal business conditions. He voiced fear that, because of the "semi-dictatorial powers" given to the president, whatever minimal success could be accomplished would be achieved "at the price of a definite transition to a fascist stage of capitalism."[35] Whatever else he believed, Thomas failed to see in Roosevelt's administration any serious movement in the direction toward socialism. What he did see was only an effort to establish state capitalism, whereby a measure of government ownership and government regulation combine to shore up the profit system.

However, in his 1933 article "New Deal or New Day" published in *The World Tomorrow*, Thomas did introduce a new note that would become his mantra with respect to both Roosevelt's administration and subsequent American administrations – a mantra that would reach its ultimate expression in his 1948 article "Republicans and Democrats are Stealing from my Socialist Platform," published in *Look*.[36] In 1933, he insisted that whatever successful policies Roosevelt was using to get the country out of the Depression were essentially an acceptance of many of Thomas's own views and those of the

[33] R. Niebuhr, "Optimism and utopianism," 180.

[34] N. Thomas, "Norman Thomas replies," *The Nation* (December 14, 1932), 585.

[35] N. Thomas, "What has Roosevelt accomplished?" *The Nation* (April 12, 1933), 399.

[36] N. Thomas, "Republicans & Democrats are stealing from my Socialist platform," *Look Magazine* (August 17, 1948), 34, 36, and 38.

Socialist Party. Policies such as "great-scale public works, federal unemployment relief, federal action to abolish child labor [and] the 30-hr week," Thomas insisted, "have been affected by the demands of Socialist teaching" more than seemed "at all probable."[37]

Thomas nonetheless persisted in maintaining that America would either "move forward to some sort of socialism or make the terrible plunge to fascism" – a prognostication he sardonically repeated in 1936 when, in "answer to the question: After the New Deal – What?" Thomas concluded that "the probable answer is this: After the New Deal: Fascism."[38] In his treatise written for the League for Industrial Democracy Thomas had concluded that "there are no adequate countervailing forces to Fascism which are not essentially Socialist."[39] This fear that America, like much of Europe during the 1930s, would become fascist became somewhat of an obsession with both Thomas and Niebuhr – a fear that gained plausibility at a time when progressive movements were being crushed by fascism in Europe. While Niebuhr was at work on his book *The End of an Era* during 1933, he published his article "After Capitalism – What?" The article expressed what he believed to be both the inevitability and desirability of capitalism's death, and he could only speculate whether that would "give way to a new order created by the political power of those who have been disinherited" or "destroyed by a revolution." Whatever that outcome, Niebuhr was absolutely convinced that political liberalism was a "spent force" and that capitalism could not "reform itself from within." That left him seeing "the inevitability of fascism as a practical certainty in every Western nation," however long capitalism might succeed in avoiding disintegration.[40] Niebuhr's 1934 book *The End of an Era* – a book Arthur Schlesinger Jr. said "throbbed with urgency and foreboding"[41] – witnessed the zenith of Niebuhr's radicalism and the zeal with which he predicted the rise of fascism amid the demise of capitalism.[42]

---

[37] N. Thomas, "New Deal or new day," *The World Tomorrow* (January 31, 1933), 488.

[38] N. Thomas, *After the New Deal, What?* (New York: Macmillan, 1936), p. 142.

[39] N. Thomas, "A Socialist looks at the New Deal" (1933), 1307. In his article "New Deal or new day?" he set forth his view as to the differences between fascism and true socialism. He deemed the inner spirit of fascism to be "undemocratic and ruthlessly dictatorial" while "socialism is international in outlook and democratic in spirit and, so far as possible, in method." Demanding blind obedience to the totalitarian state, fascism espouses the economics of state capitalism. Socialism seeks "as its goal a confederation of cooperative commonwealths in which our great resources, our public services, including banking, and our immense aggregations of machinery will be socially owned and managed for use instead of for private profit. N. Thomas, "New Deal or new day," 488.

[40] R. Niebuhr, "After capitalism – what?" *The World Tomorrow* (March 1, 1933), 203–4.

[41] Arthur M. Schlesinger Jr., "Reinhold Niebuhr's role in American political thought and life" in C. W. Kegley (ed.), *Reinhold Niebuhr: His Religious, Social and Political Thought* (New York: Pilgrim Press, 1984), p. 201.

[42] This book was a strident and welcoming obituary for capitalism that drew on Marxism's vision of impending catastrophe. In a chapter entitled "Prophecy of doom," he judged the sickness of

In sequential issues of the *The World Tomorrow* appearing in the early months of 1934, Thomas resumed his analysis of the New Deal and sought to define the immediate task of the Socialist Party in the wake of his defeat. In spite of "Mr. Roosevelt's strength" in managing "to be one jump ahead of each crisis," Thomas judged as totally unsatisfactory Roosevelt's programs in agriculture, the National Recovery Administration (NRA), unemployment relief, and debt control. He insisted the fundamental fact was that "we live in a disintegrating capitalism" whose pump is "rapidly wearing out" and cannot be primed.[43] Thomas did claim that Roosevelt's leadership fell "short of true dictatorship" and gave him faint praise for giving "us at least modest grounds for hope in the possibilities of democracy." Expecting the worst, however, he took this interlude as an opportunity to concentrate on both the urgent task and the pressing organizational issues facing the Socialist Party.[44] The most urgent task was to "propagandize" the core truth of socialism – to unmistakably state the meaning of the cooperative commonwealth as "a fellowship of free men," requiring central planning aimed at changing the American economic system, prior to being fulfilled in a "federation of cooperative commonwealths." Identifying the lack of organization as the weakest problem within American socialism, Thomas focused on organizing farmers and industrial labor; establishing consumer cooperatives, and organizing "workers with hand and brain in a political party."[45] His hope was to "keep our struggle on the plane of economic and political, rather than military, conflict." However, given the tragedy of Austria falling to the Nazis, he encouraged the tactic of making "Socialists, especially younger Socialists, keen to organize in military fashion so as to resist similar Fascist tyranny as it may arise in America."[46]

The high point of American socialism under Norman Thomas came in the period between the beginning of the Great Depression in 1929 and the election of Roosevelt in 1932. However, everything for Thomas and the socialist cause began to unravel as a result of the combination of the ever-increasing popularity of Roosevelt's New Deal and the splintering effects of the dissention internal to socialism itself. As to the latter, Daniel Bell stated it best when he wrote that "factional discord, like the curse on the House of Atreus, was an ineradicable

---

modern Western civilization to be "organic and constitutional" because of a vastly "unequal distribution of social power" leading "automatically to inequality and injustice." Niebuhr expected that during its death throes capitalism would seek to abolish or circumscribe democracy, "not only to deprive its foes of a weapon, but to save itself from anarchy." It will aim at resolving class antagonisms during the process of disintegration "partly by nationalistic hysteria and partly by the use of force" against revolutionary groups seeking to overturn the existing order. The end of capitalism will thus be "bloody rather than peaceful." Niebuhr saw "nothing in the unique character of American life which can prevent a social struggle, inherent in the nature of modern society, from working itself out to its logical conclusion." R. Niebuhr, *Reflections on the End of an Era* (New York: Charles Scribner's Sons, 1943), p. 24, p. 56–7, p. 59, and p. 82.

[43] N. Thomas, "Surveying the New Deal," *The World Tomorrow* (January 18, 1934), 37–8.
[44] N. Thomas, "Our immediate task," *The World Tomorrow* (February 15, 1934), 83.
[45] N. Thomas, "American socialism's weakest link," *The World Tomorrow* (April 12, 1934), 180.
[46] N. Thomas, "Hastening the day," *The World Tomorrow* (March 15, 1934), 135.

heritage, and in the next eight years the savage fratricide ripped the party to shreds."[47]

The "Old Guard" socialists were comprised of older European immigrants who saw the party as a workers' party. Those opposing the Old Guard in large part reflected a generational shift. They were, as Bell described them, "of middle-class parentage, college educated, ministerial, pacifist," with their primary strength coming "from such institutions as the League for Industrial Democracy and the magazine *The World Tomorrow*," whose editors included Norman Thomas. He, "having been the party's standard-bearer in 1928, sought to become, in fact as well as in name, the spokesman of the party."[48] These self-described "Militants," who opposed gradual reform, actively strove for political power and were supportive of the revolutionary trends in the Soviet Union. They became the faction with which both Thomas and Niebuhr identified. The seriousness of the split began in the May prior to the 1932 election when the militant faction sought unsuccessfully to unseat Morris Hillquit as national chairman of the party. In addition, other splintering events were occurring: a more radical third-party movement was sought by those socialists who, in May, 1933, organized a Continental Congress of Workers and Farmers; key socialists defected to the La Guardia New York City mayoral campaign; and Upton Sinclair, after initiating successful reforms in California, joined the Democratic Party, much to the dismay of Socialist Party loyalists.

A more radical stance taken by an emerging revolutionary wing among socialists gained momentum due to events abroad. Hitler's destruction of a timid and divided socialism in Germany and the Nazi conquest of Austria resulted in America's revolutionary-minded socialists identifying with the communist movement in Russia. In the April 12, 1934, issue of *The World Tomorrow*, there appeared "An Appeal to the Socialist Party" signed by forty-seven members representing a group that Niebuhr, in his subsequent commentary, identified as the "Revolutionary Policy Committee." While sympathetic to the radical agenda of making "an honest effort to redirect Socialist policy to the Left and disavow the reformist tendencies" so prevalent among American socialists, Niebuhr faulted the "Appeal" for espousing a form of revolutionary socialism "which follows the Communist pattern so exactly, even to the point of pledging itself to 'defend the victories for socialism which have been achieved in the U.S.S.R.'" So intent were advocates of the "Appeal" to flee "from the errors of reformism" that they failed to define "a revolutionary policy which would be at once politically realistic and relevant to the American scene." Niebuhr knew that America and the West were not Russia and that the "Russian pattern will not be repeated in any Western nation."[49]

[47] D. Bell, "The background and development of Marxian socialism in the United States" in D.D. Egbert and S. Pearson (eds.), *Socialism and American Life* (Princeton, NJ: Princeton University Press, 1952), vol. I, p. 369.

[48] Ibid., p. 370.

[49] R. Niebuhr, "Comment by Reinhold Niebuhr," *The World Tomorrow* (April 12, 1934), 185.

The height of the fratricidal warfare came at the convention of the Socialist Party held in Detroit on May 31, 1934. Thomas had published "Proposals for Action at Detroit" on April 26, citing as the major problems "a compact and vigorous state of the Socialist position," the need to address as "the relation of the Party to organized labor," and the possibility of forming "a Farmer-Labor Party."[50] With Thomas declaring his intention to support the militant position, the stage was set for internecine battle.[51] The battle centered on the radical "Declaration of Principles" – a declaration calling unequivocally for the overthrow of the capitalist system. The convention itself was merely the start of a bitter and prolonged struggle for control within the Socialist party. As Daniel Bell saw it, "the passage of the Detroit declaration unloosed a civil war in the Socialist party and many members welcomed the party strife."[52] So intense did the internecine warfare become, according to Harry Fleischman, that "after the *New Leader* became the virtual house organ of the Old Guard, the national executive committee withdrew official party endorsement and the Militants and Centrists started a new paper, the *Socialist Call*," to which Thomas transferred his weekly column. Thomas was vilified from both directions with Old Guard leader Louis Waldman "saying publicly that Thomas was 'the conscious or unconscious tool of the Communist Party' while the communists continued to maintain that Thomas had sold out to American reactionary and imperialist interests."[53]

Thomas, who sought to minimize the severity of the conflict, published his own thoughts on the convention. He played down the strident, revolutionary tone of the Declaration of Principles finding that "war and violence are neither blessed nor accepted as inevitable." Thomas emphasized instead "socialist allegiance to peaceful and orderly methods of struggle and to democracy in industry and politics." However, he did warn that, while "socialism and democracy each requires the other for the perfection of either," if fascist tendencies accompanying capitalism's demise do not yield to a Socialist majority at the polls, then "we will use the solidarity of the workers to crush antidemocratic forces." In an attempt to explain the virulent attacks on the Declaration within party circles, Thomas attributed them to two factors: "the bitter disappointment of the Right-wing Old Guard at losing to a large degree its control over party machinery," and "the obsession some Socialists have lest any departure from liberal parliamentarianism [will] mean a drift to communism."[54]

While not attending the June, 1934, Socialist Party convention in Detroit where the fracturing of the Party occurred, Niebuhr reflected a year later on both of Thomas's judgments. It was his opinion that the right wing of the Socialist

---

[50] N. Thomas, "Proposals for action at Detroit," *The World Tomorrow* (April 26, 1934), 206–8.
[51] For an account of the Detroit convention and its aftermath, see M. B. Seidler, "Fratricidal warfare" in *Norman Thomas: Respectable Rebel*, pp. 125–70.
[52] D. Bell, "The background and development of Marxian socialism in the United States," p. 379.
[53] H. Fleischman, *Norman Thomas: A Biography*, pp. 165–6.
[54] N. Thomas, "What happened at Detroit," *The World Tomorrow* (June 28, 1934), 321.

Party had failed to learn any lessons from what had happened in Germany, Spain, and Austria. He scorned the conservative wing for simply mouthing platitudes about democracy and saw "its insistence that socialists must always remain within the bounds of legality" as "a perfect revelation of the spiritual decay in socialism."[55] At the same time Niebuhr also saw weaknesses on the left-wing side, especially in its abstract revolutionary romanticism used to encourage workers to engage in "armed insurrection." He urged the radicals to avoid undue reverence as well as undue recklessness with regard to constitutional approaches to achieving revolutionary aims. Niebuhr still preferred "a wise socialism" to "save democracy by adapting it to the realities of an industrial civilization and to prove to a confused nation that only by such an adaptation can democracy be saved."[56]

The year 1936 brought another presidential election. According to Harry Fleischman, "Thomas actually did not want to run for President." He fully expected an increased loss of support for the Socialist Party coming, not from right-wing defection, but from an additional shift of voters in the direction of Roosevelt.[57] Recognizing that this move to support Roosevelt was based on a fear of returning to Hoover-like policies, Thomas caustically characterized the upcoming contest between Democrats and Republicans by stating "what an uninspiring contest it promises to be between 'statesmen' to see how few crusts and how cheap circuses will prevent riots." In spite of his awareness that there would be "no automatic rush to vote the socialist ticket" and that even the very identity of socialism might be at stake, Thomas, with faint heart, claimed that, given the crucial nature of the issues, the Socialist Party "shall have to work for what we get."[58] In this campaign, his attack on Roosevelt was widening out beyond that of merely criticizing the inadequacies of New Deal programs. As Arthur Schlesinger Jr. put it, Thomas now emphasized fear of "the militarism of the Roosevelt administration," harshly "criticized its indifference to the plight of tenant farmers and sharecroppers," and "raised his voice courageously and insistently on questions of civil liberties and of civil rights" – issues of "ethical urgency badly needed in politics."[59]

Niebuhr supported Thomas in his 1936 election bid, but he did so knowing that Thomas was "forced to conduct a rather disheartening campaign," one "with little prospect of a vote which will give any indication of the growing sentiment for a genuine realignment of politics in this country." It was becoming clear that, while Niebuhr continued to find himself at home with Norman Thomas, he was fast losing faith in the ability of the Socialist Party to find the cohesive magic that would bring together the farmers, workers, and sympathetic

---

[55] R. Niebuhr, "The revolutionary moment," *American Socialist Quarterly* (June, 1935), 9.
[56] R. Niebuhr, "Our romantic radicals," *The Christian Century* (April 10, 1935), 474.
[57] H. Fleischman, *Norman Thomas: A Biography*, 171.
[58] N. Thomas, "Roosevelt faces re-election," *American Socialist Monthly* (March, 1936), 4–5, 7.
[59] Arthur Schlesinger Jr., *The Politics of Upheaval*, p. 179.

elements of the middle class essential for building a viable political force. His continuing support of Thomas did not mask his view that Roosevelt was "preferable to the Republican candidate" and, while "no real ground has been gained for social justice in his administration," certain social services had been "established which no administration will dare to destroy" even when the time came to raise taxes to support them.[60]

Thomas fully expected his defeat, but he was surprised that Roosevelt's numbers were so high and his so low. Because he was convinced Roosevelt had committed himself to nothing of substance, Thomas could not avoid the sarcasm of suggesting that, as Roosevelt was headed into office, he was as much "to be trusted with such a blank check as any candidate of a capitalist party." What Thomas wanted for the future was a renewed effort to encourage a farmer-labor party but one that would not take the place of the Socialist Party – a party definitely loyal "to Socialism" but so well organized that it could "permit a certain flexibility to meet local requirements."[61] Niebuhr was also again angling for a third-party movement. Like Thomas, he was aware of the havoc reactionary forces in the Democratic Party were creating for Roosevelt's New Deal programs. By the fall of 1937, Niebuhr saw the defeat of the Wages and Hours Bill by those forces as a stark failure of the Roosevelt coalition that pointed to a "serious break" in the Democratic Party. Crediting Roosevelt with "having carried the party much further to the left than anyone imagined possible," he saw the faltering alignment as a possibility for "a party more solidly based upon the support of workers and farmers" even if it failed "to stand for a complete socialist program."[62]

By the end of 1937, with the crisis in Europe worsened by the triumph of fascist movements in Spain, Italy, and Germany, Thomas explored ways war could be avoided. He rejected the notion of American participation in collective security in spite of many who had gravitated toward Roosevelt's desire for a "concerted action to quarantine aggressors." Offended by those who called him an isolationist, Thomas did insist that, given the country's geographic position, "it is more practicable to keep the United States government out of war than to use it in war for ideal ends." On a personal level he was proud that those like himself, who worked diligently to keep America out of war, would garner a "better hearing from the potential builders of a new social order than those who must assume responsibility for another war." Thomas was adamant that "a collective security of democratic states in our crazy, capitalist-nationalist world" was nothing less than "a utopian dream." At the very best, he believed that only national and imperial interests stood to benefit from nations such as the United States or Great Britain going to war against those perpetrating the fascist threat. America's focus should be on the long-range prospect for peace

---

[60] R. Niebuhr, "The political campaign," *Radical Religion* (Autumn, 1936), 7, 6.

[61] N. Thomas, "The election of 1936 and the prospects of a farm-labor party," *American Socialist Monthly* (December, 1936), 8, 13.

[62] R. Niebuhr, "A new party?" *Radical Religion* (Autumn, 1937), 7.

and that, Thomas insisted, would require "an active struggle for a new social and international order impossible under capitalist nationalism."[63]

Niebuhr's reflections on "The Coming Presidential Election" in the autumn of 1939 showed him moving ever closer in the direction of openly supporting Roosevelt. Niebuhr agreed with Thomas, that it was "necessary for all progressive forces to point beyond" what Roosevelt had achieved. Yet with the Republicans moving toward "ignorant and dangerous reaction" – seeking "to destroy the Wagner act, the social security legislation," as well as "the freedom of labor to organize and the relief of the unemployed" – he admonished "Socialist Christians" not to "be beguiled by simple panaceas" as they "call attention to the basic defects in our social order which cause its discontents." On the Democratic side, Niebuhr, convinced that there was "no one of sufficient stature" among prospective candidates "to bear the mantle of Roosevelt and gain the election," went so far as to claim that "Roosevelt, despite anti-third-term traditions, [was] the only hope of maintaining the real gains which have been made in the past years of the depression."[64]

Niebuhr made two momentous choices in 1940. He voted for Roosevelt and he resigned from the Socialist Party. In his article "An End to Illusions," Niebuhr reported that among the mail received that day, the "first is a letter from the Socialist party informing me that my views on foreign affairs violate the party platform and asking me to give account of my nonconformity. The party position is that this war is a clash of rival imperialism in which nothing significant is at stake." Niebuhr's response: "I answer the Socialist communication by a quick resignation from the party."[65] Niebuhr had begun the process of deserting socialist orthodoxy in the late 1930s. His decision involved several factors: a growing sympathy for FDR and the New Deal, an ever-increasing disillusionment with the Socialist Party, and an open break with Socialists over the decision to enter World War II – all resulting in a rupture in his relationship with Norman Thomas.

In the fall 1940 issue of *Radical Religion*, Niebuhr claimed "it was clear that, whatever reservations some of us have about some aspects of the Roosevelt administration, we will have to vote for Roosevelt" in spite of the continuing loyalty many readers of the journal have "to the Socialist party" in their intention to vote for Norman Thomas. Niebuhr was adamant in his conviction that Roosevelt must be "supported on grounds of both his foreign and domestic policies." On domestic issues, no matter how liberal-sounding the Republican candidate Wendell Willkie seemed, the forces behind him represented policies that had plunged the United States into depression in 1929 and were firmly committed to undoing Roosevelt's progressive gains. Niebuhr saw Roosevelt's "one big mistake" in foreign policy to be his having caved to Roman Catholic

---

[63] N. Thomas, "How can we escape war?" *The Nation* (December 25, 1937), 707–9.

[64] R. Niebuhr, "The coming presidential election," *Radical Religion* (Fall, 1939), 4.

[65] Niebuhr, "An end to illusions" in *Christianity and Power Politics* (New York: Charles Scribner's Sons, 1940), pp. 167–8. This article first appeared in *The Nation* (June 29, 1940), 778–9.

pressure during the Spanish Civil War. He also admonished Roosevelt for "two much cuteness" in preparing the nation United States for war. In spite of his criticisms, Niebuhr claimed that "the charge made by socialists and other radicals that big business is trying to drag us into the war is a foolish piece of dogmatic fiction" and that the truly pathetic thing is that with the pressing need to confront "the fascist peril in Europe" our pure idealists inadvertently cooperate with predatory interests "in weakening the defenses of democracy." Tragically, "bourgeois complacency and utopian idealism march hand in hand."[66] In December, greatly relieved by Roosevelt's successful bid for a third term, Niebuhr concluded that "despite the ambiguities of Rooseveltian liberalism the reelection of the president was a heartening revelation of the right ability of democracy to arrive at a right decision in a crisis."[67] Niebuhr's resignation from the Socialist Party and his support of Roosevelt did not mean he had abandoned all hopes for the emergence of a viable third-party movement in America. In his article on "The Socialist Campaign," published in the summer of 1940, for example, he still held that "a genuine farmer-labor party of national scope" was part of "the inevitabilities of American politics," expecting that it would be realized within an eight-year period at most. Niebuhr persisted in this hope until March, 1947, when he helped found Americans for Democratic Action (ADA).

Niebuhr's appreciation for Roosevelt's New Deal policies came gradually and was given begrudgingly at first. Only later did Niebuhr come to the conviction that there was an inherent danger in compounding economic and political power as required by State Socialism. He increasingly came to value the need in a viable democracy for balances of power running throughout society on all levels, political and economic – a need that placing political and economic control in the same hands would jeopardize. In the end Niebuhr believed that a democratic society could be successful in finding solutions to problems of economic injustice. His view of society was not a static one, so he never thought any complete or final justice was achievable. The struggle to balance power against power was endless, although some of his critics contended that he became too complacent about the status of economic justice in the 1950s.

Niebuhr, disillusioned with the course of events following World War I, had rejected war by the early 1920s, declaring himself a pacifist in his December, 1927, article "Why I am not a Christian."[68] However, seeing a new war in Europe only a short time away with a resurgent Germany under the Nazis in the 1930s, his views changed drastically. While maintaining respect for the pure pacifist, Niebuhr came to disagree sharply with those who saw pacifism as a political strategy rather than a pure moral stance. By January, 1934, he had resigned from the pacifist organization the Fellowship of Reconciliation, of

---

[66] R. Niebuhr, "Willkie and Roosevelt," *Radical Religion* (Fall, 1940), 5.
[67] R. Niebuhr, "Roosevelt's Election," *Radical Religion* (Winter, 1940), 4.
[68] R. Niebuhr, "Why I am not a Christian," *The Christian Century* (December 15, 1927), 1482.

which he had once served as chairman.[69] Nazism, as Charles Brown put it, was a threat that Niebuhr believed to be "an evil worse than war itself."[70]

With American entry into the war coming ever closer and Niebuhr's decisive break from the isolationism of socialists and liberals intensifying, he launched a new journal – *Christianity and Crisis* – the first issue of which appeared on February 10, 1941. He sounded the alarm that Nazism struck at "the very fabric of our Western civilization," seeking "to annul the liberties and legal standards which are the priceless heritage of ages of Christian and humanistic culture."[71] While still hoping American participation in the European war could be averted, Niebuhr urged that Congress pass Lend-Lease, Roosevelt's bill for providing immediate aid to Great Britain and its allies. In the journal's next issue, Niebuhr, confronting those who conflated the faults of the warring nations into variations on the same theme, spelled out his answer in posing the question "What Is At Stake?" While admitting the ambiguity of the term "democracy" as applied to Great Britain, what was clearly unambiguous was that the reality of an "open society" was at stake in "the British Commonwealth" as it was "in the democracies which have [since] lost their freedom" throughout Europe.[72]

Niebuhr's support of American intervention in World War II put him at irreconcilable odds with Thomas. Niebuhr was a signatory with others who wanted a hearing in front of the House Foreign Affairs Committee to oppose Thomas's testimony against Roosevelt's Lend-Lease Bill.[73] As for Thomas, 1941 brought a litany of charges against Roosevelt's international policies. He voiced sharp anger at the impending disaster he saw coming as a result of the deceit with which Roosevelt was manipulating the American public into complicity with his war aims. In March, Thomas accused the administration of using hysteria and lies to sway the public, and he represented the likely conflict as resting on nothing less that a "theory of the sanctity of Anglo-American imperialism as against German imperialism."[74] In July, anticipating that both Hitler and Stalin would

[69] R. Niebuhr, "Why I leave the F.O.R.," *The Christian Century* (January 3, 1934), 17–19. Reprinted in D. B. Robertson (ed.), *Love and Justice: Selections from the Shorter Writings of Reinhold Niebuhr* (Philadelphia: Westminster Press, 1957), 254–9.

[70] C. C. Brown, *Niebuhr and His Age*, 53. For an overall view of Niebuhr's pacifism, see C. McKeogh, "Niebuhr's critique of pacifism" in D. F. Rice (ed.), *Reinhold Niebuhr Revisited: Engagements with an American Original*, pp. 201–21.

[71] R. Niebuhr, "Christian faith and the world crisis," *Christianity and Crisis* (February 10, 1941), 6. Niebuhr wrote that "It is our purpose to devote this modest journal to an exposition of our Christian faith in its relation to world events" and that "we intend this journal to be both polemic and irenic, as far as human frailty will permit the combination of these two qualities," 4.

[72] R. Niebuhr, "What is at stake?" *Christianity and Crisis* (May 19, 1941), 1.

[73] See the article "Socialist group hits Thomas view," *The New York Times* (Thursday, January 23, 1941), 8.

[74] Niebuhr saw the charge by Thomas and other socialists that World War II was solely a conflict between rival empires as a dangerous legacy of Marxist ideology that had continued to infect socialism, thus blinding it to the seriousness of the dangers of Nazism. He reiterated that criticism during the West's conflict with Russia in the postwar era. In 1952 Niebuhr wrote: "The Marxist

end up imposing tyranny on Europe, he claimed that "for America to rush into the war as it has now developed would be, as never before, an act of unnecessary, inexcusable madness" – bringing in its wake "our own fascism born of interventionism."

By August, Thomas used *The Call* to post a letter he "might have written" to Roosevelt admonishing him for falsely stating the present danger facing us in order to extend the draft of young soldiers. In addition, he posted a hypothetical letter to "Mr. and Mrs. Average American" blaming them for passively acquiescing in the drift to war and imploring them to take pen in hand and write the congress and the president. In August, Thomas repeated his prediction that this "will be an imperialist war in which victory would make Stalin rather than either Roosevelt or Churchill overlord of most of Europe and Asia, including China." By November, he resolutely opposed the repeal of the Neutrality Act, cited an increasing fatalism among the public, and accused Roosevelt of a demagogic performance in his Navy Day speech. On December 20 – two weeks after the attack on Pearl Harbor – Thomas, admitting his "long struggle against war has ended" and, although he expected that "we shall be fully involved in Europe as well as Asia," he pleaded that we "limit our involvement as much as possible, and to avoid great expeditionary forces in Europe, Asia and Africa." In February, 1942, Thomas posed the question "Will the War Bring Socialism?" His pessimistic answer was that the direction of events would "be toward fascism rather than toward democratic socialism."[75]

Thomas had decided to run for president again in 1944, and in the years preceding the campaign he kept up a barrage of criticism against Roosevelt and the New Deal – often publishing in *Socialist Call*, a newspaper founded by the group identified as the Militants back in February, 1935. In the November 6, 1942, issue Thomas went so far as to suggest that American democracy had been "reduced to the cult of trust in Roosevelt as if he were some earthly god, enthroned in Washington."[76] With the war gradually winding down, however, his dominant focus was on the postwar environment, and he then accused Roosevelt of both lacking a "peace offensive" and permitting an excessively punitive policy toward Germany.

As the election approached, the conflict between Niebuhr and Thomas over the war intensified, reaching very personal levels during the campaign. Things started out reasonably well. In a letter Niebuhr wrote to Thomas late in 1943, responding to Thomas's invitation that he return to the Socialist Party, Niebuhr

dogma of 'imperialism' is as great a hazard today in our fight against Communism as it was in the days of our fight with Nazism, because it denies the possibility of making ethical choices between the supposedly common 'imperialistic' ends of various 'capitalist' states." R. Niebuhr, "The anomaly of European socialism," *Yale Review* (December 1952), 164.

[75] N. Thomas, "Saviors of imperialism," *The Call* (March 1, 1941), 5; "Predictions and conclusions," *The Call* (July 19, 1941), 5; "Open letter to the President," *The Call* (August 2, 1941), 5; "Imperialism rampant," *The Call* (August 16, 1941), 5; "Neutrality repeal means war," *The Call* (November 15, 1941), 5; "The war and democracy," *The Call* (December 20, 1941), 5; and "Will the war bring socialism?" *The Call* (February 21, 1942), 5.

[76] N. Thomas, "It is indeed later than we think," *The Call* (November 6, 1942), 1.

expressed "continued respect for all of [Thomas's] splendid qualities of mind and heart." He politely declined the offer, stating that he read Thomas's "letter with good feeling because it revealed how near and yet how far men of similar convictions may be from each other." While also acknowledging that his and Thomas's differences over the war were "honest ones," Niebuhr shuddered "to think that the policy of the socialist party, if universalized, would have meant the present triumph of Hitler." As for Thomas's view that there was no difference between the two major parties, Niebuhr admitted that Thomas's accusation that he would be voting for "what I don't want" might well "be a possibility and necessity for the rest of my life in the sense that I can imagine no political program which will not incorporate some elements which I do not accept." Niebuhr informed Thomas, however, that he no longer saw the Socialist Party as playing a major role and that he and many of his friends could not "afford the luxury of a gesture toward a perfect program, while real issues are being decided on a much lower level" – issues that "are real despite your effort to equate the two programs" of the major parties. With what he deemed real political power at stake, Niebuhr said that he intended "to vote to avert a bad alternative in favor of a slightly better one; just as we went to war for the same purpose."

Niebuhr also criticized what he saw as socialism's misguided idealism on the most pressing international issue. He admitted that he did "not know how the world is going to be organized but [am] quite sure that if we wait for an ideal constitutional world order, we will soon be involved in another world war." Niebuhr believed that peace would require the need for the very thing Thomas abhorred, namely, "the necessity of working out some kind of agreement between the great powers" that would, as Niebuhr hoped, be inclusive rather than exclusive. While suspecting that Thomas "would call almost anything short of a real constitutional world order 'phony internationalism,'" Niebuhr insisted that any "ideal plans lack relevance because there are no adequate social forces to implement them." In the end, Niebuhr confessed that "as I read history I simply find escape from its ambiguities and tragedies more difficult than my perfectionist brethren. For all I know, we may have to spend all of our energy staying out of a hell-on-earth in the next century and have little chance to build a heaven-on-earth."[77]

On January 4, 1944, Niebuhr responded to a second letter he had received from Thomas about issues surrounding World War II. His response involved both a reprimand and advice, and it is of sufficient importance to quote in full:

Dear Norman:

I have no quarrel with your statement of the problem in your second letter to me. I do not believe that we ought ever to accept the forces and destinies of history without seeking to form the stuff of history into a higher justice.

[77] R. Niebuhr to N. Thomas, nd (likely late 1943 or early 1944), Norman Thomas Papers – Reinhold Niebuhr Correspondence, New York Public Library.

There are nevertheless very powerful forces in history which we may be able to deflect but not suppress.

No good purpose is served if people of your persuasion try to approach us with an "I told you so." The world which will come out of this war will not be very lovely. The "I told you so" would only apply in any event to those who prophesied that a utopia would emerge from it. We are at a disadvantage in argument with you because we will defeat the Nazis and therefore it will not be apparent what kind of a world would have emerged if we had allowed the Nazis to defeat us, which would certainly have happened if the pacifist and isolationist argument had prevailed.

But that's about the past. About the future my concern is that liberals should not hail the cooperation of the united nations are [sic] guaranteeing justice. It will be better to have that cooperation than not to have it; for without it we will continue in international anarchy. With it we may face a period of super-imperialism. We can not escape the fact that three of four nations of the world will have the effective power. That is an inexorable fact of history and no amount of wishing can put us into a position where the power of the nations will be equal.

For me the important point is to distrust power, even though we know we have to use it. Most liberals distrust American power; but even when they are not fellow-travelers they seem to believe that Russia stands for some absolute justice in the world. There is thus a lack of realism in all the analyses of the Moscow and Teheran conferences.

This business of achieving a decent world community is about the most difficult which has ever faced mankind. We may fail in it completely. We may partly succeed and partly fail. As far as I can see all decent government has been the consequence of using power for the sake of maintaining order provided there has been some contrite recognition of the fact that yours is never just and must never be trusted without qualification.

Yours,
Reinie[78]

What affected Thomas most personally was the increasing defection of former liberals from the Socialist Party. As W. A. Swanberg put it, "the transfer of Socialists and unionists either into the Democratic Party or some 'independent' but pro-Roosevelt group like Niebuhr's Union for Democratic Action (UDA) had sounded in his ears like the thunder of an army marching to join forces with the enemy."[79] The poignancy of his attitude is clearly evident in an open letter he sent to Niebuhr, who, at that time, was chairman of the Union for Democratic

---

[78] R. Niebuhr to N. Thomas (January 5, 1944), Norman Thomas Papers – Reinhold Niebuhr Correspondence, NYPL.

[79] W. A. Swanberg, *Norman Thomas: The Last Idealist* (New York: Charles Scribner's Sons, 1976), p. 283.

Action. In his letter dated July 25, 1944,[80] Thomas asked Niebuhr why he and those within the UDA who are "by conviction ... democratic socialists" were supporting Roosevelt and the Democratic ticket. Thomas saw the platforms of both major parties as basically interchangeable, and he insisted that Roosevelt had all but abandoned any "major progressive legislation since 1937." He acknowledged that Niebuhr's departure from the Socialist Party in 1940 was "because of honest differences over an interventionist policy before Pearl Harbor." But Thomas now posed the question: "HOW ABOUT WINNING THE PEACE?" and he pleaded for Niebuhr to return to the Socialist Party because it, alone, is demanding that "unconditional surrender be replaced by terms which may hasten a constructive people's revolution in Germany." He challenged Niebuhr directly:

How often have you yourself argued that there can neither be full employment nor abundance without plan and without the social control of the commanding heights of our economic order! You have shared my conviction that such control CAN be democratic and can indeed increase the amount of true freedom in the world. Have you changed your mind now that the undesirability and impossibility of restoring the dominance of the profit system has been proved by depression and war and the miracle of war time production under planning?[81]

Niebuhr penned a sharp reply to Thomas on September 8 in which he cited the irony in the "spectacle of American Socialists talking of the necessity of 'winning the peace'" when, in fact, if we had heeded the Socialists' "telling us that our capitalist society was not pure enough in heart to take up arms against fascist aggression, Hitler would be making the peace today." While acknowledging the lack of earlier New Deal fervor in bringing about social legislation, Niebuhr preferred efforts to "make the Democratic Party the liberal party" rather than having "American progressives ... cast in their lot with the Socialists." What Niebuhr chose to remind Thomas of was the irresponsibility of the Socialists' purist views. He wrote:

Indeed, although you profess many progressive ideals and support many progressive measures, there is an exasperating quality of irresponsibility about the whole Socialist position, and it is difficult to take seriously your criticisms. This irresponsibility, which led to the folly of our pre-Pearl Harbor isolationism, stems from your inability to conceive of politics as the art of choosing among possible alternatives. This blindness makes it impossible for you to correctly gauge the political climate of the country.

While having no illusions about the internal machinations of the Roosevelt administration, Niebuhr saw signs of hope for reform within the Democratic Party and wanted to work from within by pushing "it forward along the paths of domestic reform and of genuine international organization." The point he wanted to make to Thomas was that "the battles ahead will not be contests

---

[80] The complete letter that Thomas wrote to Niebuhr along with Niebuhr's reply can be found in M. B. Seidler, *Norman Thomas, Respectable Rebel*, pp. 217–24.

[81] N. Thomas to R. Niebuhr, in Seidler, pp. 217, 219, 220, and 218.

between unmitigated evil and absolute good, and that a true perspective of the struggles of our time cannot be had from the Olympian heights of Socialist dogma." In short, he suggested to Thomas that insofar as "you shun the daily skirmishes and belittle the modest gains which are the staff of politics, then you – not we – are 'throwing away your vote' on those decisions affecting the course of the war and the nature of the peace."[82]

Norman Thomas made his final run for the presidency of the United States in 1948, claiming that he "was literally drafted into campaigning."[83] Niebuhr wrote an article in the November 1, 1948, issue of *Christianity and Crisis* on "The Presidential Campaign." While sharing the common expectation that Truman would go down in defeat, he never mentioned Thomas's name while discussing the candidates in the contest – Truman, Thomas Dewey, and Henry Wallace. He could only hope that in what he thought would be "its years in the wilderness" the Democratic Party would "be refashioned into a more genuine instrument of liberalism."[84] Niebuhr's neglect of Thomas revealed just how marginalized and irrelevant Thomas's presidential bid had become.

As he neared the end of campaigning for the presidency,[85] Thomas spent time reflecting on the fate of socialism in America. He took some solace in knowing that much of what he and his party had advocated were taken up by both major political parties – for example, when early in 1948, while assessing "Socialism's Impact upon America," Thomas pointed out that "it is generally admitted, even by the sharpest critics of Socialism, that its influence in America is far greater than its direct power" – socialism having been the source of "all important social legislation, including that of the New Deal" and "to a very great extent [furnishing] the impetus and the leadership of the progressive wing of American labor."[86] Yet, because Roosevelt had established "state capitalism" rather than socialism, Thomas was quite ambivalent in paying homage to the New Deal legacy, having once claimed that "Roosevelt did not carry out the Socialist platform unless he carried it out on a stretcher."[87] Nevertheless, he often gave voice to his mantra that was best captured in the title of his *Look* article – "Republicans & Democrats are stealing from my Socialist Platform."[88]

---

[82] Ibid., 221–24. For Swanberg's take on this controversy between Niebuhr and Thomas, see his *Norman Thomas: The Last Idealist*, 286–90.

[83] N. Thomas, "Republicans & Democrats are stealing from my Socialist platform," 36.

[84] R. Niebuhr, "The presidential campaign," *Christianity and Crisis* (November l, 1948), 138.

[85] Eugene Debs received some 900,000 votes – about 6 percent of votes cast in 1912. Four years later, Allan Benson received less that 600,000. In 1920, Debs, from prison, garnered 919,000 votes, but by this time the electorate had doubled through the granting of women's suffrage, so that the percentage was only half of what it had been in 1912. In 1928, when Norman Thomas first ran (after La Follete's defeat in 1924 as a Progressive Party candidate), his vote total was only 267,000. He received 903,286 votes in 1932; 187,342 in 1936; 116,796 in 1940; 80,518 in 1944; and 140,260 in 1948.

[86] N. Thomas, "Socialism's impact upon America," *Modern Review* (January, 1948), 22.

[87] Quotation taken from Arthur Schlesinger Jr., *The Politics of Upheaval*, p. 562.

[88] N. Thomas, "Republicans & Democrats are stealing from my Socialist platform," pp. 34, 36, and 38.

When he turned to the question as to why the socialist movement had been so weak in capitalistic America, he saw the weaknesses as having economic, sociological, and political causes: (1) Thomas identified the major *economic* factor as relating to conditions in America that provided young workers and laborers with "a better chance to rise out of their class than to rise with it." America's undeveloped and unsettled country, combined with educational opportunity, enabled the ambitious young to move up in society. He also pointed out that "the development of mass production," which required "mass consumption to keep it going," provided incentive to American capitalists "to raise wages well above a subsistence level in order to provide markets for their goods." (2) As for *sociological* factors, Thomas identified the "rise of a sociological middle class, not truly self-employed, yet not sympathetic to wage workers." This factor, which allowed the upwardly mobile to see themselves "as members of the general community rather than of the working class," undercut the sense of working class identity so central to the success of socialism. (3) Finally, the *political* situation in America contained multiple aspects that made it extremely difficult for any third-party movement, including Socialism, to gain the traction necessary to become a major player in the political arena.[89]

Will Herberg, the former Marxist turned Burkean conservative, captured both the sociological and political factors in his observation that "Socialism in America 'never was really a workers' movement'" – that "in its days of greatest vitality and promise American Socialism was essentially Populism gone Marxist." The democratic reforms sought by socialists in Europe were largely a part of the fabric of life in America. American workers, Herberg pointed out, "had the ballot ... their political rights ... and their recognized, legitimate place as 'free and equal' American citizens," and they certainly "did not consider themselves to be a disfranchised, unprivileged class."[90] The problem, according to Daniel Bell, was that "the Militants and the young intellectuals around Norman Thomas had no eye for the American scene. ... Their attention was riveted on Europe, because, as Marxist theory foretold, the fate of capitalism there foreshadowed the course of capitalism here."[91] And the philosopher Sidney Hook was convinced that "the spectacle of the Soviet Union, a police state based on total cultural terror which boasted that its economy was socialist, had an enormous influence in prejudicing American workers against anything that was labeled socialist that involved centralized planning on a grand scale."[92]

Niebuhr concurred in this interpretation, having noted that "the fluid class structure of the American society failed to provide the class resentments which

[89] N. Thomas, "Socialism's impact upon America," pp. 25–6.
[90] W. Herberg, "What Happened to American Socialism?" *Commentary* (October, 1951), 336–8.
[91] D. Bell, "The background and development of Marxian socialism in the United States," 374.
[92] S. Hook, "The philosophical basis of Marxian socialism in the U.S." in D. D. Egbert and S. Persons (eds.), *Socialism and American Life* (Princeton, NJ: Princeton University Press, 1952), vol. I, p. 451.

furnish the socialist cause with its primary motive power."[93] Yet he probed more deeply in pointing out that socialists, along with communists, shared a cynicism that prevented them from seeing the persistence of a variety of national sentiments, including loyalty to country. This scorn for "cultural traditions and inheritances, including religion" had simply alienated "the middle classes in which these traditions still have power."[94] As early as 1934, Niebuhr insisted that "if socialism is to make real inroads into the middle classes, it will have to revise some of its dogmas which set it against the cultural inheritances of those groups."[95]

Niebuhr consistently emphasized the inability of communism and Marxist-leaning socialism to "deal adequately with the cultural and psychological factors of a complex Western civilization," most evident in their "intransigent attitude toward all forms of culture which have any organic relations to the capitalist social system." This total lack of any sense or appreciation of the organic relations of life antagonizes the middle classes, among whom those organic and personal social relations are still considered important. This is especially the case with the deep loyalties rural people have to many established middle-class traditions. Niebuhr emphasized that many of the "bourgeois" factors that communists and socialists both detest and wish to eradicate are "in fact merely human."[96]

Niebuhr and Thomas continued their involvement and cooperation during the years following Thomas's defeat in his last run for the presidency in 1948, as is evident in the Norman Thomas Papers at the New York Public Library which includes numerous letters of Niebuhr that Thomas had received during the decade of the 1950s.[97] By far the most important letters between them coming

---

[93] R. Niebuhr, "Farewell," *Christianity and Society* (Summer, 1956), 3.

[94] R. Niebuhr, "A new strategy for socialists," pp. 490–1.

[95] R. Niebuhr, "Comment by Reinhold Niebuhr," *The World Tomorrow* (April 2, 1934), 186.

[96] R. Niebuhr, "Making radicalism effective," 683. In his article on "The revival of feudalism," Niebuhr contrasted the organic aspects of society characteristic of feudalism with the mechanical aspects that dominate modern day views and showed how little radicals comprehend of the existence or appeal of the organic factors. See "The revival of feudalism," *Harper's Monthly Magazine* (March, 1935), 483–8.

[97] These letters include a letter from Niebuhr thanking Thomas for intervening in support of the Resettlement Campaign for Exiled Professionals (October 17, 1950), and another again thanking him and providing him with encouraging financial information (October 27, 1950); letters in which Niebuhr asked for material pertaining to an article *Atlantic Monthly* had requested Niebuhr write on the anti-Communist J. B. Matthews (August 7, 1953) – a request Niebuhr turned down with confirmatory advice from Thomas as to Matthews' dishonesty (August 20, 1953); a letter in which Niebuhr apologized that his words in a *Christianity and Society* article gave the mistaken impression he had attributed to Thomas a "sweeping repudiation of social ownership"(September 16, 1953); a letter stating that Niebuhr would sign a statement that Thomas requested on behalf of his group Citizens for Reason assuming he obtained a larger number of signatories (March 30, 1955); a letter declining to sign, but agreeing with Thomas's intention to send a letter to the Secretary of the Socialist International (April 4, 1956); letters dealing with the situation in Israel (November 14, 1956) and plans to meet in New York near the end of December for further discussion of the issues (December 7, 1956); a letter from Niebuhr asking Thomas to sign a petition to President Eisenhower regarding the Smith Act (November 25,

from this era (housed in the Niebuhr Papers at the Library of Congress), were written on December 4–6, 1956, related to the Anglo-French "Suez Crisis" during which time Israel had attacked the Egyptian-occupied Sinai in response to Nasser's pan-Arab militancy. The intensity of the exchange between Niebuhr and Thomas on the Arab–Israeli issue is important enough to warrant extensive quotation.[98] Thomas wrote Niebuhr on December 4:

Dear Reinie:

Various pressures, internal and external, compel me to examine the Arab-Israel aspect of the continuing Middle East crisis. For a long time, I have wanted to be a pretty whole-hearted supporter of Israel partly because I share, as I ought, the guilt complex of the Christian world because of anti-semitism, and more largely because so many of my warm friends in Jewish organizations and in liberal organizations are Jews who, if not Zionists, are such strong supporters of Israel that they almost define desirable American foreign policy in terms of Israel's support. And Zionist intolerance leads to actual social and economic persecution of many dissenters.

Nevertheless, I have never been able to change my original position to Zionism, as a matter of principle. It is to my mind a very great loss that intelligent Jews, leaders in liberal causes since the enlightenment have in such large numbers become so nationalistic. There is a quality of Greek tragedy in the fact that homeless Jews have found a most insecure home by processes which rendered an equal number of Arabs homeless.

What gave political excuse, perhaps even necessity, for some sort of Jewish homeland wasn't Arab or Moslem anti-semitism but Christian anti-semitism culminating, of course, in Hitler's horrors. ... What happened was that Christian or Western anti-semitism was in the Arab experience paid for at Arab expense. ... Jews, who originally went to Canaan as conquerors, returned as conquerors. ...

What troubles me is the extraordinary partisanship for Israel which some liberals, especially liberal churchmen, yourself included, have shown. To me it doesn't help in the education either of Jews or Arabs to a necessary reconciliation. I say this of course, with respect for positive achievements along democratic and hopeful lines in little Israel. I am fully aware of the

1957); a refusal to sign a letter Thomas was sending about Russian anti-Semitism when, according to Niebuhr, "what they have done in Hungary is so much worse" (June, 1959); and a letter stating his unwillingness to sign an open statement to President Kennedy that Thomas was planning to send dealing with the possibility of military intervention in Cuba. Niebuhr agreed that the administration made "a colossal blunder" but did not think there was either a direct or indirect intent to invade (May 2, 1961).

[98] Thomas to Niebuhr (December 4, 1956); Niebuhr to Thomas (December 5, 1956); and Thomas to Niebuhr (December 6, 1956), Reinhold Niebuhr Papers, General Correspondence, Box 12, Library of Congress.

social backwardness of most of the Arab nations yet I see very little hope for Israel in the long run in terms of the unquestioned bravery of her own soldiers and the support she can muster from the Western world. Hope that Israel will be a blessing certainly depends on beginning the slow process of reconciliation. How do you propose that be done?

I write to you because I am not sure who else would have the patience to read this. Which, if any, of my facts is wrong? Which of my deductions from those facts? I do not write to that Christian Committee on Palestine from which I often hear because, frankly, they seem to be high grade Saboth Goyim. Until I am otherwise persuaded I shall have to agree with the Arab who said to me in effect: "You Christians and Westerners, not we, persecuted the Jews and you make us pay the price."

As ever, yours,
Norman Thomas

Niebuhr replied the next day:

Dear Norman:

I thank you for your letter. It raises some interesting and searching questions which I am afraid I can't answer adequately in a mere letter. I take a fundamentally different position on the Israeli–Arab dispute than you do, and have done so ever since I wrote the article for the *Nation* entitled "Jews After the War." At the same time I see the validity of your position. It doesn't disturb me, however, that liberal Jews have become Zionist, for the Jewish nation is the only nation without a homeland. Nor am I disturbed by the fact that what you call liberal Churchmen, are on the side of the Jews, because the great weight of Christian opinion is pro-Arab.

It may shock you to know that I think that the Israeli venture on the Sinai desert put the Egyptians to flight and uncovered a cache of Russian weapons for an Army of 250,000, was a necessary stroke and that it might have felled Nasser if the United Nations hadn't been so prompt to back him up. Nevertheless the problem is as serious as you state it. But it is serious partly because the Islamic world is thoroughly moribund, and it is prompted not only by ancient hatreds but by present fears of a highly technical and democratic society with which the leaders of the Arab world are unable to deal, while they hold their masses in abject poverty. But I have been rather uneasy about Jewish nationalism, nevertheless. After sharing the platform with Rabbi Silver, and being horrified by Realpolitic, I refuse to address any more Zionist meetings. I have maintained my membership with the American Christian Palestine Committee but I refused to sign almost all their statements. This is probably not a consistent record, but the inconsistency proves my confusion.

I would say that generally I agree with you but lean more to the Israeli side than to the Arab side than you do, and of course I have very definite convictions about the position of our nation, not only with reference to Israel but with reference to the whole complex of international problems. I feel that Eisenhower is becoming the Chamberlain of our day, and I am afraid you won't agree with me on this.

I so wish we could have a talk about all these things some time, for I value your judgment and always respect your integrity and wisdom with extravagant respect.

Yours cordially,
Reinhold Niebuhr

On December 6, this exchange of views on the Arab–Israeli conflict ended with Thomas suggesting a meeting in New York before December 20 for the purpose of continuing a discussion of the issues.

After he gave up running for the presidency in 1948 to his death in 1968, Thomas remained steadfast in his conviction that socialism, however muted in tone, was the best course for America. In his 1951 article "Restating Socialism's Ideals for Our Time," Thomas identified himself with those "Democratic socialists" who acknowledge "that American capitalism has been profoundly, not superficially, affected by various reforms," and "believe firmly in the reality of democracy in our American system," even while justifiably attacking those imperfections inherent in the nature of capitalism. Nonetheless, while acknowledging "Keynesian devices may avoid a spectacular breakup [of capitalist society] without achieving the socialist ideal," he remained a firm defender of the need to find a way "to persuade our fellow-citizens that socialism has a central idea, a driving power and potentially a program for more vital than Keynesianism or any rule-of-thumb reformism followed by politicians and labor leaders."[99] Thomas would go on to write in defense of his version of socialism in America – especially in his books *A Socialist's Faith* (1951) and *Socialism Re-examined* (1963).

Niebuhr had seen democratic socialism's self image – as a "third force" attempt to find a middle way between capitalism and communism in Europe – severely diminished by the ideological baggage from Marxism that it still carried. Unfortunately, he also saw much of that baggage also afflicting socialism in America. While rightly recognizing the existence of a class struggle, it failed to see that "class forces in modern society are much more complex than Marxism understood." Moreover, its strategy to socialize property "still bore a halo of redemption ... which made it difficult for socialist parties to deal pragmatically with the institution of property." And while its "materialistic conception of human nature" underestimated the spiritual depth in the human freedom and dignity it purported to proclaim, democratic socialism also "still held to the Marxist belief that human egoism is caused by a social institution and would

---

[99] N. Thomas, "Restating socialism's ideals for our time," *The Socialist Call* (June 22, 1951), 2, 5.

therefore be eliminated by getting rid of that institution," rather than seeing egoism as a perennial aspect of human nature.[100]

Niebuhr never abandoned the passion for social justice he had learned from his socialist days. He consistently supported the gains achieved through America's "mixed economy," and he came to consider the greatest achievements of progressive politics as the "establishment of the basic policies of the 'welfare state' which [had] become the standard of justice in every modern nation." In this development, according to Niebuhr, "experience and pragmatic wisdom had triumphed everywhere in Western civilization over doctrinaire positions."[101] Of utmost importance, Niebuhr always expected the never-ending need for balancing power against power as the sine qua non of any justice in society. Although Niebuhr never failed to criticize the absurdities of laissez-faire and its use as an ideology by conservatives, he did come to reject the socialists' core conviction as to the need for public ownership of productive property. His pragmatic instincts and his view of the "triumph of experience over dogma" led him to see the dangers of a combined economic and political bureaucracy and to appreciate the value of diverse centers of power in society. Niebuhr knew that the automatic harmony of social and economic interests that laissez-faire theory expected was utter nonsense. Yet he found elements of truth in classical economics, "which remain a permanent treasure of a free society" and became convinced that "some forms of a 'free market' are essential to democracy." He was convinced that if the socialist alternative of regulating the economic process through bureaucratic-political decisions was "too consistently applied," the "the final peril of combining political and economic power" would be the result.[102] As Niebuhr put it three years later, in 1955, socialism "failed to anticipate all the various strategies and forces in a developing society by which undue power would be checked, neutralized and made responsible by the political dialogue and conflict which is possible in a free society."[103]

Fortunately, the intense conflict between Niebuhr and Thomas over World War II and Niebuhr's departure from the Socialist Party did not reach a level of acrimony sufficient to destroy their friendship. Late in his career, when the event-filled years they shared together were over, Niebuhr reflected the friends he had had over a lifetime. In a series of interviews conducted in the mid-1950s Niebuhr mentioned that "Norman Thomas [had been his] good friend all through the years." What truly impressed Niebuhr was that "Norman Thomas" possessed "integrity" and that there was "a real moral quality in his life."[104] He credited Thomas with having "acquired the status of an elder statesman in our nation in

[100] R. Niebuhr, "The spiritual weakness of the third force," *Christianity and Society* (Summer, 1949), 6.

[101] R. Niebuhr, "The fate of European socialism," *New Leader* (June 20, 1955), 7.

[102] R. Niebuhr, *The Irony of American History* (New York: Charles Scribner's Sons, 1952), p. 93.

[103] Niebuhr, "The fate of European socialism," 8.

[104] Interview with R. Niebuhr by H. B. Phillips on June 14, 1954. *The Reminiscences of Reinhold Niebuhr*, pp. 94–5.

spite of his being the leader of an essentially irrelevant and dying political movement." Noting that a cynic might question the honor if "the movement behind him were more formidable," the cynic would be incorrect. For Niebuhr, Thomas clearly had "a shining integrity which appeals to the people beyond all party loyalties."

A decade later in 1965, Niebuhr wrote a piece in *Christianity and Crisis* commemorating Thomas's eightieth birthday, at which more than 1,000 people were in attendance. Niebuhr referred to Thomas's "enormous integrity" and his being "a monument to the value of complete courage." He labeled Thomas as our "incarnate conscience" – crediting the honor bestowed upon him, "not for his creed but because he had become a symbol to the whole nation of an incorruptible spirit of justice."[105] In his *Reminiscences*, Niebuhr had expressed the wish that Thomas's "leadership could have been made effective more directly, and that he could have led an effective political movement."[106] With sadness, Thomas had come to accept the label of "idealistic failure" that had been attached to him by many. Yet he had indeed been lionized, largely because of what Gary Dorrien described as "his unsurpassed dedication, compassion, and eloquence, and through his insistent appeal to the vision of a good society."[107]

[105] R. Niebuhr, "Norman Thomas: incarnate conscience," *Christianity and Crisis* (January 11, 1965), 271–2.
[106] R. Niebuhr, "Norman Thomas," 5–6.
[107] G. Dorrien, "Norman Thomas" in *The American Radical*, p. 219.

CHAPTER 4

Arthur Schlesinger Jr. (1917–2007)

Reinhold Niebuhr's impact on influential individuals outside the domain of theology included the notable historian and political activist Arthur Schlesinger Jr. Schlesinger's association with Niebuhr began in late 1940 or early 1941 and continued until Niebuhr's death in 1971. Schlesinger appeared as a prominent figure in Niebuhr's life at a time when Niebuhr was making the transition from his earlier socialism to his eventual embrace of a pragmatic realism that found its expression in a position eventually described as "Christian realism."

Arthur Schlesinger Jr. was a unique historian. He was a historian of the first rank, a strenuous advocate and defender of liberal democracy, a partisan activist in American political life, and, eventually, a presidential assistant and speechwriter in the administration of Democratic President John F. Kennedy. In other words, Schlesinger was both a scholar and a polemicist. This fact led the economist John Kenneth Galbraith to contend that "no one else in our time and Republic quite enjoys such prestige as both an ally and an opponent, and, no doubt, especially the former."[1]

Schlesinger's writings were extensive and diverse. His major historical writings include his 1946 Pulitzer Prize-winning *Age of Jackson* and his three-volume *Age of Roosevelt* (1957–60); he authored biographies on the Kennedys – *A Thousand Days* (1965) on President Kennedy and one on his brother entitled *Robert Kennedy and His Times* (1978); his interpretive-polemical books included *The Vital Center* (1949), *The Imperial Presidency* (1973), *Cycles of American History* (1986), and *The Disuniting of America* (1991); and he wrote two autobiographies – *A Life in the 20th Century: 1917–1950* (2000), and *Journals: 1952–2000*, the latter completed by his son and published in 2007.

---

[1] J. K. Galbraith, "The lessons of an historian" in J. P. Diggins (ed.), *The Liberal Persuasion: Arthur Schlesinger, Jr., and the Challenge of the American Past* (Princeton, NJ: Princeton University Press, 1997), p. 62.

FIG. 4 Schlesinger
Courtesy of the Graduate Center, City University of New York

In the first volume of his memoirs, Schlesinger reported that "it was from [Perry] Miller that I first heard about Reinhold Niebuhr."[2] Later in this volume Schlesinger gives us a rather humorous account of his first view of Niebuhr:

The war was everywhere. It lay behind everything you said or did. One snowy Sunday morning in the winter of 1940–41 [my wife] Marian insisted that I accompany her to Memorial Church in Harvard Yard to listen to a professor at the Union Theological Seminary named Reinhold Niebuhr. After Coeur d'Alene, the last thing I felt I needed was a dose of evangelical religion, and I abandoned the Sunday papers and the fireside under protest.

The pews were packed long before the tower bells chimed eleven. A tall, rangy man with a massive bald head came to the pulpit. Establishing instant command over the congregation, he spoke, without notes, in rushes of jagged eloquence. His eyes flashed; his voice rose to a roar and sank to a whisper; outstretched arms gave emphasis to his points; but underneath the dramatics, the argument was cool, rigorous and powerful. Man was flawed and sinful, he told the hushed but initially dubious audience. Yet even sinful man had the duty of acting against evil in the world. Our sins, real as they were, could not justify our standing apart from the European struggle.[3]

Over the long period of time that Schlesinger knew Niebuhr, he came to definite conclusions about him as a person. In a 1992 *The New York Times* article commemorating the centennial of Niebuhr's birth, Schlesinger remarked that

[2] A. Schlesinger, *A Life in the Twentieth Century: Innocent Beginnings, 1917–1950* (New York: Houghton Mifflin, 2000), p. 163.

[3] Ibid., p. 249.

Niebuhr "was high-spirited, great-hearted, devoid of pomposity and pretense, endlessly curious about ideas and personalities, vigorous in his enthusiasms and criticisms, filled with practical wisdom and, for all his robust ego, a man of endearing humility."[4]

Schlesinger, twenty-five years Niebuhr's junior, was soon drawn to Niebuhr's social and political writings. Early on, he read Niebuhr's groundbreaking book *Moral Man and Immoral Society* and, in a publication based on his memorial address for Niebuhr given in 1972, claimed that some years after first seeing Niebuhr preach, he "came to read *The Nature and Destiny of Man* [and] found there an interpretation of human nature and history that gave a coherent frame to my own groping sense of the frailty of man and the inscrutability of events."[5] Nonetheless, like many among those the philosopher Morton White derisively labeled "atheists for Niebuhr,"[6] Schlesinger remained at arm's length from Niebuhr's theological convictions and was among those who pondered how it was that Niebuhr, "this passionate, profound and humble believer should have had so penetrating an influence on so many nonbelievers."[7]

Niebuhr, in turn, had reviewed Schlesinger's *The Age of Jackson* in 1945. He regarded the book "more than mere history" because "Schlesinger is a political philosopher as well as historian and withal a genuine believer in democracy." Niebuhr saw Schlesinger's book as "a perfect refutation of the idea that history must be written 'objectively,' or that the alternative is partisan propaganda." The young Arthur Schlesinger appealed to Niebuhr as a "skilled historian" because Schlesinger was able to illuminate the past for us in a way that held out hope that "we may," in light of the "perplexities which confront democracy in this age of technics," find a way of "facing the new problems of late capitalism" as well as "the Jacksonian era did in facing those of early capitalism."[8]

---

[4] A. Schlesinger, "Reinhold Niebuhr's long shadow," *The New York Times* (June 22, 1992), A17. In a book review published 43 years earlier, Schlesinger remarked: "Unlike other religious teachers who content themselves with obeisances toward humility, Niebuhr has the essential humility to regard himself as subject to general human limitations and frailties. He possesses himself to a remarkable degree what he somewhere calls 'a wisdom which recognizes the limits of human knowledge and a humility which knows the limits of all human powers.'" A. Schlesinger, review of R. Niebuhr's *Faith and History* in *Christianity and Society* (Summer, 1949), 27.

[5] A. Schlesinger, "Prophet for a secular age," *The New Leader* (January 24, 1972), 12.

[6] The context in which Morton White's reference to "Atheists for Niebuhr" appears is as follows: "The answers to the question 'What is religion?' have come trippingly in the twentieth century. It is a species of poetry (Santayana); it is variety of shared experience (Dewey); it is ethical culture; it is insight into man's nature. (The last is the view of a group that might be called 'Atheists for Niebuhr.')." Morton White "Religion, politics, and the higher learning," *Confluence* 3:4 (1954), 404. Schlesinger placed himself within close range of White's description when he wrote: "Many of us understood original sin as a metaphor, Niebuhr's distinction between taking the Bible seriously and taking it literally invited symbolic interpretation and made it easy for seculars to join the club. Morton White, the philosopher, spoke satirically of Atheists for Niebuhr." A. Schlesinger, "Forgetting Reinhold Niebuhr," *The New York Times* (September 18, 2005).

[7] A. Schlesinger, "Prophet for a secular age," *New Leader* (January 24, 1972), 11.

[8] R. Niebuhr, review of *The Age of Jackson* in *Christianity and Society* (Spring, 1946), 38–9.

Close to the time Schlesinger first encountered Niebuhr in Harvard's Memorial Church, several changes occurred in Niebuhr's life. He had resigned from the Socialist Party (June, 1940); came, however reluctantly, to the support of Roosevelt (endorsing him in the election of 1940); founded the journal *Christianity and Crisis* (February, 1941), and served as chairman of the Union for Democratic Action (UDA) (May, 1941) – an organization that left-liberals and disillusioned socialists founded as an antidote to both pacifists and isolationists leading up to America's entry into World War II. Schlesinger became actively involved in both the UDA and later Americans for Democratic Action (ADA) which was founded in early 1947 and eventually absorbed the Union for Democratic Action. Schlesinger served as ADA Chairman in 1953–4.[9]

Schlesinger's book *The Vital Center*, published in 1949, had made an immediate and enduring impact. Niebuhr's influence was evident throughout the book. In the preface to the original edition Schlesinger, referring to the "false optimism of the nineteenth century," cited Niebuhr as having "brilliantly suggested, that we were simply rediscovering ancient truths which we should never have forgotten." Later, in the introduction to the 1998 edition, Schlesinger stressed that "Reinhold Niebuhr revived for my contemporaries the historic Christian insights into the mixed nature of human being."[10] Indeed, Alonzo L. Hamby had claimed in 1973 that "*The Vital Center* displayed not only Schlesinger's own thought but to a large extent popularized the political ideas of Schlesinger's friend and philosophical mentor, Reinhold Niebuhr." Hamby goes further when he suggested that "the publication of *The Vital Center* probably represented the point at which Niebuhr's ideas, as well as his personality, began to have a significant impact upon the liberal community."[11]

Schlesinger's thesis has often been either misunderstood or misrepresented as advocating a tepid, middle-of-the-road politics that would avoid the excesses of

[9] The ADA was founded by anti-Soviet liberals who broke with those who identified with Henry Wallace's sympathetic views of Stalinist Russia. Because of ill-health, Niebuhr's involvement with the ADA lessened over time, disappointing friends like Jim Loeb and Schlesinger. By 1958 Niebuhr had concluded that the ADA was more involved in day-to-day politics rather than in formulating ideas. When he learned that Schlesinger, on May 21 of that year, had expressed disappointment in liberal organizations, Niebuhr wrote Schlesinger stating that "I was relieved to have you say that about liberal organizations, because I have the same lack of enthusiasm for them. As I see it there is no liberal foreign policy – there is only a realistic foreign policy."[R. Niebuhr to A. Schlesinger, May 21, 1958, in the Schlesinger Papers, New York Public Library.]

[10] A. Schlesinger, *The Vital Center: The Politics of Freedom* (New Brunswick, NJ: Transaction Publishers, 1998), pp. xxi and xii. It is also clear that Schlesinger had read Niebuhr's 1944 book *The Children of Light and the Children of Darkness*. After citing Niebuhr as among the "moderate pessimists," he remarked that "consistent pessimism about man, far from promoting authoritarianism, alone can inoculate the democratic faith against it. 'Man's capacity for justice makes democracy possible' Niebuhr has written in his remarkable book on democratic theory; 'but man's inclination to injustice makes democracy necessary.'" [Ibid., pp. 166 and 170.] Niebuhr's quote comes from *The Children of Light and the Children of Darkness* (New York: Charles Scribner's Sons, 1944), p. xiii.

[11] A.L. Hamby, *Beyond the New Deal: Harry S. Truman and American Liberalism* (New York: Columbia University Press, 1971), pp. 279–80.

both conservatives and liberals. This was not what Schlesinger had in mind. Schlesinger was speaking to the mood of the time – a mood in which the demise of liberal democracy was fearfully anticipated by many amid the apparent tide of communism on one side and fascism on the other. In his introduction to the 1998 reissue of the book, Schlesinger reminded us that his "vital center was in a global context – liberal democracy as against its mortal enemies, fascism to the right, communism to the left" and that "*The Vital Center* was an attempt to strengthen the liberal case against the renewed totalitarian impulse" of that time.[12] He reiterated that "'Vital center' refers to the contest *between* democracy and totalitarianism, not to contests *within* democracy between liberalism and conservatism, not at all to the so-called 'middle of the road' preferred by cautious politicians of our own time." So far as Schlesinger was concerned, "The middle of the road is definitely not the vital center: it is the dead center." He stressed that "within democracy the argument adheres to FDR's injunction to move always 'a little to the left of center.'"[13]

Niebuhr was certainly in agreement with Schlesinger's emphasis on strengthening democracy against totalitarianism. He knew that Schlesinger was not advocating a tepid, middle-of-the-road politics. Nonetheless, in an unpublished, undated paper, Niebuhr voiced his own concerns about the notion of a "vital center." He insisted that our liberties are imperiled by all of us and not just by anti-democratic extremists: "We all contribute to the perils of a free society by either indulging in, or entertaining, indiscriminate judgments which are meant to identify our foe or competitor in one enterprise as a foe of some other of our cherished values." For Niebuhr the "vital center" must be extended "against the inroads of the extremism of the right and the left" both of which "agree only in being intolerant of opinions and purposes other than their own, and in their ambitions to annul the freedom to express or seek them." What is required is that we realize a healthy democracy involves "a decent regard for justice and freedom beyond the particular ends and interests which lie close to [our] heart; and a measure of tolerance for purposes and convictions, other than [our] own."[14]

In the summer of 1949, Schlesinger reviewed Niebuhr's book *Faith and History*, published that year. Once again we find the balancing point on which Schlesinger stood with regard to his profound appreciation of Niebuhr on the one hand, and the position he occupied with respect to Niebuhr's religious commitments on the other. Schlesinger considered *Faith and History* to be "the most profound and penetrating critique of modern culture which our time has

---

[12] A. Schlesinger, *The Vital Center: The Politics of Freedom* (New Brunswick, NJ: Transaction Publishers, 1998), p. x.

[13] Ibid., p. xiii. Niebuhr once commented that "Arthur Schlesinger uses the phrase 'the vital center.' That's a good phrase. Democracy is on the whole the vital center, but it must be worked so that it doesn't go to dead center." *The Reminiscences of Reinhold Niebuhr* (Oral History Research Office, Columbia University, 1957), pp. 78–80.

[14] R. Niebuhr, "Balanced Judgment and the Democratic Security," nd. Box 15, Reinhold Niebuhr Papers, Manuscript Division, Library of Congress.

produced" – indeed, "in the context of the failure of liberalism, [Niebuhr] has constructed the most comprehensive restatement of the Christian interpretation of man."[15] He made the point of emphasizing that "the distinction of [Niebuhr's] analysis is his success in restating Christian insights with such irresistible relevance to contemporary experience that even those who have no decisive faith in the supernatural find their own reading of experience and of history given new and significant dimensions."[16] Schlesinger was willing to concede that "from a secular viewpoint Niebuhr's affirmation of divine sovereignty in history may be less instructive than his consequent conception of history as 'filled with man's proud and pretentious efforts to defy the divine sovereignty, to establish himself as god by his power or virtue, his wisdom or foresight.'" Nonetheless, Schlesinger was willing to say that "without passing upon the final significance of this statement, one can accept it as a profoundly illuminating insight into human experience."[17] Niebuhr's theological commitments aside, his reading of the religious tradition was seen by Schlesinger as a basis for his insights into human nature and experience.

In Schlesinger's review of *Faith and History*, he harkened back to *The Nature and Destiny of Man*, in which he claimed that Niebuhr "revived the traditional insights of Christianity with a wisdom and cogency which vindicated the Christian analysis of human experience even for many for whom Christian ontology had no reality." He also cited Niebuhr's *The Children of Light and the Children of Darkness* for having "demonstrated that the Christian conception of human nature with its complexity and ambiguity provided a far more solid foundation for democracy than the simple optimism about man with which democracy has been conventionally associated."[18] In *Faith and History*, Schlesinger applauded Niebuhr's indictment of modern culture for its belief in the redemptive character of history within history itself, promising that increased knowledge and technical expertise would guarantee human mastery of history. Certainly one element of Niebuhr's "Christian" analysis Schlesinger could accept was that, contrary to modern history which locates the source of evil everywhere and in everything other than man, Niebuhr's Pascalian sensibility finds it in man himself.

---

[15] A. Schlesinger, review of Niebuhr's *Faith and History* in *Christianity and Society* (Summer, 1949), 26.

[16] The philosopher Sidney Hook, both an admirer and critic of Niebuhr, sharply disagreed with Schlesinger. Hook was adamant that "not one of the positions that Niebuhr takes on the momentous issues of social and political life is dependent on his theology." (Sidney Hook, "The new failure of nerve," *Partisan Review* [January–February, 1943], 13). While Hook was willing to admit that Niebuhr offered penetrating analyses of social and political issues, he considered Niebuhr all the more dangerous because his analyses were couched in theological categories – the danger being that he was being well-received by otherwise rational and respected secular thinkers. For an overall treatment of the relationship between Niebuhr and Hook, see my article "Reinhold Niebuhr and the philosophers, part 2: Sidney Hook," *Union Seminary Quarterly Review* 62:1–2 (2009), 17–45.

[17] A. Schlesinger, review of R. Niebuhr's *Faith and History*, 27.

[18] Ibid., 26.

In the fall of that year, Niebuhr was sent to Paris as an American delegate to the Fourth Conference of UNESCO where, according to Richard W. Fox, "he delivered a speech urging the organization to stick to the realm of culture, rather than imagine it could contribute directly to conflict resolution."[19] A month after his return from Paris, Niebuhr had the occasion to travel to Washington once again, this time to attend a conference convened by Dean Acheson, who was then serving as Secretary of State. Niebuhr wrote Schlesinger on November 13, telling him that he was "spending Thursday, Friday and Saturday at the State Department in a conference called by Acheson to consider "various plans for strengthening the non-communist world without impairing the UN" – adding: "It may be interesting."[20] Niebuhr was also in on a meeting with the president. In his autobiography *A Life in the Twentieth Century*, Schlesinger recorded: "On May 21, 1951, Reinhold Niebuhr, Francis Biddle, Joseph Rauh, Hubert Humphrey and I had a private meeting with President Truman. 'The worst thing I ever did,' Truman told us, 'was to give the order which killed all those people over there [Hiroshima]. It was terrible; but I had no alternative; and I would give such an order again if it ever became necessary.'"[21] Sadly, Niebuhr's direct participation in and involvement with the active political policy makers would diminish sharply in the aftermath of the strokes he would suffer starting in 1952.

One of Niebuhr's most influential books, *The Irony of American History*, was published in 1952. On September 11 of the preceding year, Niebuhr wrote to Schlesinger informing him that he had spent much of the summer "working on a little book on the role of irony in American history." He added that "since I am treading on ground which you know so much better than I, I am almost tempted to send you the manuscript if you have any time to read it, in the hope that you will save me from some bad errors."[22] Niebuhr overcame his reticence and on November 10, after having read the material, Schlesinger airmailed his reactions to Niebuhr. He suggested that Niebuhr include the abysmal treatment of the Negro in this country as one of many ironies of American democracy deserving attention. Schlesinger was also troubled by Niebuhr's "use of the phrase 'our traditional theory' or 'the Whig-Republican theory,'" pointing out that "the Jackson-Populist-Progressive-New Deal tradition calls for a considerable measure of state intervention and control."[23] Four days later, Niebuhr thanked Schlesinger and stated that he would "incorporate and take heed of all your criticisms." He did tell Schlesinger that he knew very well that his "phrase 'our traditional theory' ... is primarily the theory of the business community" but

---

[19] R. W. Fox, *Reinhold Niebuhr: A Biography* (New York: Pantheon Books, 1985), p. 239.

[20] R. Niebuhr to A. Schlesinger, November 13, 1949. Schlesinger Papers, New York Public Library. Henceforth cited as Schlesinger Papers, NYPL.

[21] A. Schlesinger, *A Life in the Twentieth Century: Innocent Beginnings, 1917–1950*, pp. 351–2.

[22] R. Niebuhr to A. Schlesinger, September 11, 1951. Schlesinger Papers, NYPL.

[23] A. Schlesinger to R. Niebuhr, November 10, 1951. Niebuhr Papers, Box 10, Library of Congress.

that it was also used by "a New Deal or Fair Deal Administration in its voice of America." Niebuhr also informed Schlesinger that he purposely got off the committee that wrote "the recent Freedom House Statement" because it, too, used the phrase, and "didn't seem to know what my criticisms meant – particularly my criticism of the assumption in the document that justice would flow inevitably from freedom."[24]

When it came time for Schlesinger to review *The Irony of American History*, he did so in the journal *Christianity and Society* – the same journal in which he had reviewed *Faith and History* three years earlier. He regarded Niebuhr's most recent book to be "a brilliant and penetrating discourse on the American experience in terms of the dilemmas and ambiguities of American power." Nonetheless, being the astute historian that he was, Schlesinger's take on the situation was that, "many of the ironies which [Niebuhr] detects in the American scene are less peculiarities of our American past than they are incidents of the historical process itself, displayed, perhaps with special sharpness of outline against the backdrop of American innocence and idealism."[25] He then pointed to a change in Niebuhr, whose previous degree of pessimism seemed somewhat reduced. It was now Niebuhr's view that America's recent triumph of experience over dogma – both with respect to the economic complexities of our industrial society and to some of our foreign policies – held out the possibility that the United States could, indeed, relate itself in a mature and creative way to the post–World World II world community. Schlesinger also highlighted Niebuhr's concept of "irony" – a concept Niebuhr saw as the distinctive mark of a Christian interpretation of history. Distinguished from pathos and tragedy, Niebuhr saw an ironic predicament or situation was open to being dissolved insofar as the person becomes aware of his involvement in it. This awareness of U.S. complicity in the predicament in which it finds itself, he believed, could alone serve to help America in overcoming the ironic elements in its history. How clear was the likelihood of such awareness on the part of the United States remained an open question.

More than half of Schlesinger's review of *The Irony of American History* was given over to confronting other reviewers' assessments. One such critic, Anthony West, consigned Niebuhr's view to a fatalism in which destiny is both determined by God and sinful for us to resist. Schlesinger found this barely worthy of comment. What he did give attention to was what he felt to be the unjust view of the young philosopher Morton White who, it will be remembered, authored the phrase "atheists for Niebuhr." So put off was White with Niebuhr's use of the term "sin" that he missed Niebuhr's conviction that "man invites disaster when he seeks to play the role of God in history, and that the self, whether individual or collective, must have a 'modest awareness of the limits of its own knowledge and power,'" – a position, Schlesinger rightly insisted, "was by no means a call

---

[24] R. Niebuhr to A. Schlesinger, November 14, 1951. Schlesinger Papers, NYPL.
[25] A. Schlesinger, "Niebuhr and some critics," *Christianity and Society* (Autumn, 1952), 25.

for quietism or resignation, or a rejection of human purpose and reason and experiment."[26]

Schlesinger did give credence to what he called "a portent in the reaction which Morton White typifies," convinced that White might well have been reacting to "felt pressures in the intellectual atmosphere."[27] Citing Justice Jackson's recent concern about a trend toward "compulsive godliness" and pointing to the theocratic impulses of men such as Whittaker Chambers and William F. Buckley Jr., Schlesinger argued that these "are real and dangerous tendencies," but the "'irony' of trying to impute them to Niebuhr is self-evident to any one who has ever read Niebuhr's warnings about the covert idolatries concealed in the worship of God." As Schlesinger saw it, the line Niebuhr sought to hold between pragmatism and religion in order to keep the absolute out of the relative – especially when confronting followers of John Dewey – might need to be reversed. "In the future," Schlesinger wrote, "it may be more important to hold this line against the simplistic believers in religion, who wish to swallow up the relative in the absolute."[28]

In 1952, Niebuhr suffered the first of a series of debilitating strokes. Arthur Schlesinger Jr., along with their friend and former executive secretary of Americans for Democratic Action, James Loeb, solicited contributions from other ADA friends for the purpose of providing Niebuhr with a television set so that he could view the presidential campaign coverage while he convalesced. Niebuhr, somewhat embarrassed by this act of kindness, wrote Schlesinger on May 29, thanking him for his role in initiating that generous gift, adding that he had "been deeply touched by the loyalty of [his] friends during [his] illness."[29]

In the same letter, Niebuhr expressed his appreciation for Schlesinger's review of Whittaker Chambers' book *Witness* that had been published in 1952. Chambers' testimony on August 4, 1949, before the House Un-American Activities Committee had been crucial in sending Alger Hiss to trial as a traitor. It also fueled the tragic carnival sideshow featuring Senator Joseph McCarthy of Wisconsin's wild accusations of communists lodged throughout the government and even the military. Schlesinger's review "Whittaker Chambers and His *Witness*" appeared in the May 24 issue of *Saturday Review*. He considered Chambers' book an invaluable account of the Communist conspiracy in the

---

[26] Ibid., 26. In her book, *Remembering Reinhold Niebuhr*, Ursula Niebuhr made available the long letter Niebuhr had written to Morton White on May 17, 1956, thanking him for his *Partisan Review* article and attempting to respond to White's criticism. Mrs. Niebuhr also included the letter Niebuhr wrote to Schlesinger about his debate with White – a letter in which Niebuhr also enclosed his letter to White. See U. M. Niebuhr, *Remembering Reinhold Niebuhr* (New York: Harper, 1991), pp. 378–81.

[27] Ibid.

[28] Ibid., p. 27. Sidney Hook, along with other supporters of John Dewey, had castigated Niebuhr for playing into the hands of the religious obscurantism of the early 1940s. See Hook's articles "Theological tom-tom and metaphysical bagpipes" in *The Humanist* 11:1 (March, 1942), 96–102; and "The new failure of nerve" in *Partisan Review* 10:1 (January–February, 1943), 2–23.

[29] R. Niebuhr to A. Schlesinger, May 29, 1952. Schlesinger Papers, NYPL.

United States, one that was quite likely to have an enduring interest as an impressive and searching personal testament. What Schlesinger hoped was that Chambers' political and philosophical dogmatisms would recede over time. In his letter to Schlesinger, Niebuhr reported that he read the review "with great enthusiasm because of the shrewdness and fairness of all of your estimates," hoping that his enthusiasm "was not prompted by your generous reference to me." Schlesinger, whose reference to Niebuhr was both pointed and germane, had written:

Mr. Chambers admires Reinhold Niebuhr; but he seems to have forgotten Niebuhr's repeated warnings that no human being – nor human church – is safe from the flux and relativity of human existence and that religion confronts fallible and prideful man with some of his gravest temptations. ... When Mr. Chambers demands belief in God as the first credential, he is surely skating near the edge of an arrogance of his own. He has forgotten the Grand Inquisitor; he has forgotten his reading in Dr. Niebuhr. For Niebuhr's conception of history involves no herding of mankind into worshipers and rejecters. His conception allows, as Mr. Chambers' does not, for the fanatical believer. It allows non-worshipers or rejecters to be tentative and experimental in history and humble and contrite before the mystery which lies beyond history. It is aware that the vanity of belief may be as corrupting as the vanity of atheism.[30]

Schlesinger and Niebuhr were both involved with the presidential campaigns of Adlai Stevenson, who would lose decisively in 1952 and again in 1956 to the World War II hero General Dwight Eisenhower. By 1946, Stevenson was already beginning to gain national attention. On December 18, 1946, Niebuhr wrote to Stevenson inviting him to "come to Washington on Saturday, January 4, 1947, to meet with a limited group of prominent American liberals in a completely off-the-record and informal session to make a real effort to re-chart a desperately-needed path for the months and years ahead" – Niebuhr's plea centered on finding "ways and means ... to create a climate of liberal opinion which is explicitly and uncompromisingly democratic in purpose."[31] Niebuhr's letter was sent out on the stationery of the Union for Democratic Action, and the meeting turned out to be the founding meeting of Americans for Democratic Action. Stevenson, according to his biographer John Bartlow Martin, "did not attend that founding meeting of ADA."[32]

Dwight Eisenhower was being courted as a presidential prospect by both the Republicans and the Democrats in the 1952 election. Niebuhr had expressed ambivalence regarding Eisenhower to his friend James Loeb when it was still unclear as to which party's presidential candidacy Eisenhower would accept. In

---

[30] A. Schlesinger, "Whittaker Chambers and his *Witness*" in *The Politics of Hope* (Princeton, NJ: Princeton University Press, 2008), pp. 241 and 243–4.

[31] R. Niebuhr to A. Stevenson, December 18, 1946. Adlai E. Stevenson Papers: Box 60, Folder 9, Seeley G. Mudd Manuscript Library, Princeton, NJ.

[32] J. B. Martin, *Adlai Stevenson of Illinois* (Garden City, NY: Doubleday, 1977), p. 56. Martin writes that "thereafter [Stevenson] was 'very careful' about his relationship with ADA, as Jim Loeb has said, 'to the point where some of us were quite angry.'" Ibid.

one letter Niebuhr claimed that he was "dead set against this Eisenhower boon among liberals. I just don't get it. It's foolish not only because Eisenhower probably will refuse and leave everyone on a limb but also because no one knows where he stands on a dozen important issues; and there is no possibility of finding out in the circumstances."[33] In a subsequent letter Niebuhr said, "I quite agree with you about Eisenhower. I thought it dangerous to go all out for a general. But we are sunk now and Eisenhower is the only possible candidate who could defeat the Republicans."[34] Later on, however, during the 1952 campaign between the now-declared Republican Eisenhower and Democrat Stevenson, Niebuhr, in a remark to Schlesinger, stated that while taking "Eisenhower's measure on television" he had concluded that "he is quite empty of everything but clichés."[35]

Niebuhr soon became an avid supporter of Adlai Stevenson as the Democratic candidate in that election. As the 1952 campaign approached, Niebuhr responded to a letter Stevenson had written to him. According to Niebuhr, Stevenson had displayed "a certain reluctance to take the fateful step" of declaring himself a candidate for the presidency. Niebuhr urged Stevenson "to give this matter further consideration." Stevenson was informed that the group on behalf of which Niebuhr was speaking "urged me to invite myself to Springfield or Chicago, if you would receive me, in order to impress upon you what many of the 'best' people in the country think about the wonderful possibilities of your candidacy."[36]

By mid-July, Niebuhr's physical condition left him terribly weakened. He wrote Schlesinger expressing envy for his "participation in the coming political events," adding that Niebuhr's own son Christopher "left for [the Democratic convention in] Chicago this morning and for what is to him the greatest adventure of his young life." Niebuhr went on to say that "I sincerely wish that Harriman, who would certainly make an excellent President, would be a little bit more available as a winning candidate. He simply can't put it across in his public utterances." At this point Niebuhr, who was somewhat put off by what he considered Stevenson's coyness, added, "I am beginning to lose confidence in the availability of Stevenson, so I am wondering what will happen at Chicago. It is bound to be an exciting show."[37] Certainly ever since April, when President Truman made it clear that he would not be seeking a second term, Schlesinger had been aware of Stevenson's ambivalence and equivocation about seeking the nomination.[38] Writing on the "Election of 1952," J. B. Bernstein put this in stark terms: "Prior to the nomination Stevenson emerges as a man of self-doubt,

[33] R. Niebuhr to J. Loeb, nd., ADA, File, Box 74, Folder 1, Reinhold Niebuhr Papers, Library of Congress.

[34] R. Niebuhr to J. Loeb, June 28, nd. ADA, Box 74, Folder 2, Ibid.

[35] R. Niebuhr to A. Schlesinger, July 3, 1952.

[36] R. Niebuhr to A. Stevenson, February 10, 1952. Stevenson Papers, Box 60, Folder 9, Seeley G. Mudd Manuscript Library, Princeton, NJ.

[37] R. Niebuhr to A. Schlesinger, July 14, 1952. Schlesinger Papers, NYPL.

[38] See J. B. Martin, *Adlai Stevenson of Illinois*, p. 566.

uneasy modesty, indecision, ambivalence: he would not seek the office nor would he refuse it. He sought power, prestige, and responsibility, but he also felt unworthy, inadequate, unsure. By late June he acknowledged that he would accept a genuine draft, yet he pleaded not to be drafted."[39]

By late July, Stevenson had accepted the nomination. Niebuhr told Schlesinger that all his "misgivings about [Stevenson's] coyness were overcome by gratitude for such a candidate," and that he was deeply appreciative of having an individual with "a quality of urbanity and sophistication ... which we have not had for a long time in public debate." Niebuhr did express concern regarding the political machinations at the convention by telling Schlesinger that he did not "fully understand the desire of our crowd to throw the South out nor Stevenson's willingness to risk some northern states in order to keep the South loyal."[40] Meanwhile, Schlesinger informed Niebuhr that he planned to work full-time for Stevenson until the college term at Harvard resumed in the fall. He ended up becoming a major speechwriter in Stevenson's run for the presidency. Stevenson's biographer John Bartlow Martin described Schlesinger's multiple talents and indefatigable energy, pointing out that Schlesinger "carried on an astonishing correspondence and telephone dialogue. He could, seemingly, simultaneously hold a telephone conversation, write a speech, read source materials, and talk to somebody across the desk. He wrote rapidly and well. He wrote basic drafts on major speeches, did heavy rewrite on other peoples' drafts, and, from his friends across the country, obtained dozens of drafts."[41]

In the same letter in which Schlesinger told Niebuhr he would work for Stevenson, he provided Niebuhr with his judgment regarding Stevenson and a detailed account of his reactions to the convention and its subsequent nomination of Stevenson:

I think there are great possibilities in the Stevenson nomination. He is the one person in either party who speaks with an authentically new voice. Where Eisenhower, for example, utters the clichés of the right, and [former ambassador W. Averell] Harriman the clichés of the left, Stevenson speaks with his own fresh voice. One has the sense of a personal vision which may lift us above and beyond the increasingly sterile party debates of the past generation and move us into a new political climate. I believe that Stevenson bears the imprint of an original political personality and has great creative possibilities.[42]

Stevenson, of course, lost the election to Eisenhower in November. In the aftermath of that defeat, Niebuhr wrote to Stevenson on November 11, 1952, stating that "all I can do is to thank you personally for the quality of sincerity and candor which you put into the campaign. ... Whatever the future you will have the goodwill of millions of your fellow-citizens, who will count on you for

[39] J. B. Bernstein, "Election of 1952" in A. Schlesinger (ed.), *The Coming to Power: Critical Elections in American History* (New York: Chelsea House/McGraw-Hill, 1971), p. 408.

[40] R. Niebuhr to A. Schlesinger, July 27, 1952. Schlesinger Papers, NYPL.

[41] J. B. Martin, *Adlai Stevenson of Illinois*, p. 631.

[42] A. Schlesinger to U. and R. Niebuhr, August 6, 1952, in U. M. Niebuhr (ed.), *Remembering Reinhold Niebuhr* (New York: Harper, 1991), pp. 375–6.

leadership."[43] Stevenson replied on December 15, claiming that he "could not be more grateful" for Niebuhr's letter. After expressing his being "honored to be included as an irreverent member of [the] chorus," praying for Niebuhr's speedy recovery, Stevenson ended by saying: "You have paid me a great compliment and I am your debtor."[44]

On May 28, 1953, Niebuhr wrote to Schlesinger, stating that he "was thrilled to hear and read that you had accepted the co-Chairmanship of the ADA [a position Schlesinger would hold during the year 1953–4]. Your leadership is going to be very important even as the services of the ADA to the country will become more and more significant. I confess that I shudder when I see how things are developing, and feel a little frustrated that I can do so little."[45] In part, what was developing was increased frustration on the part of some ADA members that progress in United States relations with Russia had stalled. Schlesinger saw frustration coming from both sides of the political spectrum with Republican conservatives advocating a "showdown" while more strident Democratic voices, including elements within the ADA, wanting "a final and comprehensive settlement." Schlesinger wrote one of the ADA's impatient voices, Ed Hollander, citing with approval an article on "Reconstruction of Policy" in *The Economist* which referred to both views as "daydreams of the impatient." Concurring with the judgment of *The Economist*, Schlesinger insisted that no genuine settlement was possible until an adequate degree of mutual confidence had been achieved, but this would require a lengthy period in which both the United States and the Soviet Union refrained from both overt and covert aggression against each other.

Schlesinger and Niebuhr had both valued the original wisdom in George Kennan's broad, non-militaristic version of what became known as the "containment policy" – a policy articulated by Kennan in the article "The Sources of Soviet Conflict," published under the name "X" in the July, 1947, issue of *Foreign Affairs*. In the present circumstances, Schlesinger saw no alternative to maintaining a flexible containment policy. He lamented the current state of affairs whereby "Republican pressure and Democratic fear drove that policy into a state of inflexibility which was not inherent in it." Stating his strong opposition to the ADA's encouraging belief in either the single-stroke solution or in the easy solubility of the present crisis, Schlesinger concluded: "In short, my feeling is that there is no dramatic 'new' answer to this. I think we must keep plugging along, maintaining our armed strength, helping keep our friends strong, working toward free world unity, and keeping the door open for negotiation. I do not believe that any final settlement will be possible with a totalitarian Russia – at least not until a generation or more of armed truce finally convinces each side that co-existence is possible."[46]

[43] R. Niebuhr to A. Stevenson, November 11, 1952. Stevenson Papers, Box 60, Folder 9. Seeley G. Mudd Manuscript Library, Princeton, NJ.

[44] A. Stevenson to R. Niebuhr, December 15, 1952. Ibid.

[45] R. Niebuhr to A. Schlesinger, May 28, 1953. Schlesinger Papers, NYPL.

[46] A. Schlesinger to E. Hollander, July 22, 1953. ADA File, Box 72, Folder 9, Reinhold Niebuhr Papers, Library of Congress.

Two weeks later, on August 4, Niebuhr wrote Hollander thanking him for sending the plans for reexamination of American foreign policy. While finding it worthwhile "making a re-examination of our foreign policy and assessing the virtues of the old 'containment' and the dangers of the new 'liberation' policy," Niebuhr agreed with Schlesinger that "we ought not propose a new overall settlement." Niebuhr's view was that "rather we ought to analyze the chances of 'coexistence' over a long pull, showing that there must be constant willingness for conference on points of friction on the one hand and yet a constant moral and political pressure on the other hand which may hasten the disintegration of the Soviet empire." And he added that "we ought I think commend Eisenhower for revealing so clearly that war is not our intent."[47] A week later Niebuhr wrote to Schlesinger informing him that "Ed Hollander sent me his proposals for a reexamination of foreign policy together with your reaction, with which as usual I was in full agreement" and adding, "I am surprised that Hollander thought an overall settlement could be feasible."[48]

On May 9, 1956, Schlesinger wrote Niebuhr to remind him, "As you know, I have been working for some time on a multi-volume history to be entitled *The Age of Roosevelt*. The first volume is due to come out in the fall. If you do not mind, I would like to dedicate this volume to you. The reasons for this are self-evident; and I can only add that friendship with you and Ursula has meant more for Marian and me that I can easily say, or than this inadequate gesture can express."[49] Niebuhr wrote back on May 14, 1956, graciously accepting the honor:

Ursula and I were deeply touched by your letter saying that you wanted to dedicate the first volume of your magnum opus, "The Age of Roosevelt" to me. I don't think the reasons are self-evident, at least they are not so self-evident to me that I am amazed of the honor you wish to do me. Ursula and I have always been grateful, more than we could express, for the friendship with you and Marian. I gratefully accept the dedication as a witness to that friendship, even thought I am conscious of the fact that you have many friends to whom you might, as an academic kudo, more fittingly dedicate such a book.[50]

The friendship between Schlesinger and Niebuhr did not prevent Schlesinger from pointing out what he considered to be a grievous flaw in Niebuhr's political vision during the mid to late 1930s. That flaw was in what Schlesinger deemed to be Niebuhr's belated appreciation of Franklin D. Roosevelt's pragmatic role in helping to steer democracy through the shoals of confusion and self-doubt during the turbulent era when fascism was considered all but inevitable in America's future. Before dealing with the background and substance of Schlesinger's criticism, two important facts should be kept in mind. First of all, Schlesinger's criticism of Niebuhr was made in the 1950s at a time when both he

[47] R. Niebuhr to E. Hollander, August 4, 1953. ADA File, Box 72, Folder 9, Ibid.

[48] R. Niebuhr to A. Schlesinger, August 11, 1953. Schlesinger Papers, NYPL.

[49] A. Schlesinger to R. Niebuhr, May 9, 1956, Reinhold Niebuhr Papers, Box 10, Library of Congress.

[50] R. Niebuhr to A. Schlesinger, May 14, 1956. Schlesinger Papers, NYPL.

and Niebuhr had become instrumental in advancing the kind of pragmatic realism that had gained prominence in post–World War II Democratic liberal circles. Secondly, it should be noted that Schlesinger was only eighteen years old when in 1935 Niebuhr reached the pinnacle of his despondency regarding the prospects of democratic reforms' succeeding in America.

Niebuhr's mood in the mid-1930s was definitely despairing and apocalyptic, influenced as it was by Marxism's catastrophic views of the inevitable demise of capitalistic societies. These views appeared most forcefully in his 1934 book *Reflections on the End of an Era* – a book that Schlesinger, writing in 1956, rightly said "throbbed with urgency and foreboding."[51] What Niebuhr expected as a likely political outcome was the self-destruction of capitalism, the demise of democracy, and the inevitable drift toward fascism. During this period he was a staunch supporter of Norman Thomas's presidential aspirations and in basic agreement with Thomas's socialist agenda. The only hope Niebuhr saw lay in the socialization of property. He saw no middle course that could save capitalism or fend off the seeming inevitability of fascism. In 1935, Niebuhr attacked the right wing of the Socialist Party in the United States for failing to acknowledge the need for revolutionary action and lamented that its "touching devotion . . . to legality and the constitution is proof either of inability or unwillingness to profit from the clear lessons of recent history or it is merely a convenient ideological tool for suppressing new life in the party."[52]

Even in his most radical phase, however, Niebuhr was never uncritical of Marxism, judging it to contain utopian expectations more extreme than that of the liberals. Schlesinger viewed Marxism's appeal to Niebuhr as "a measure of his recoil from the optimism and moralism of Christian liberalism" – the very weaknesses he had vehemently attacked Dewey for perpetuating as the leading voice of America's secular liberalism. For Niebuhr, both religious and secular liberals trafficked in the same illusions. It was Schlesinger's judgment, looking back from the vantage point of the mid-1950s, that "rebounding from the liberal belief in the inevitability of progress, Niebuhr was all too susceptible to an equally extreme belief in the inevitability of catastrophe. The recurrence of the 'end of an era' formula in his writings of the thirties suggests his shocked fascination with the possibility of some basic turn, some drastic judgment in history."[53] As Schlesinger saw it,

as Marxist catastophism countered liberal optimism, so Marxist cynicism about the power of self-interests countered liberal sentimentalism and idealism; so Marxist collectivism, with its understanding of the need for community, countered liberal individualism; so Marxist determinism, with its sense of the implacability of history, countered the naïve liberal faith in the perfect plasticity of man and society; so the Marxist commitment to the

[51] A. Schlesinger, "Reinhold Niebuhr's role in American political thought and life," C. W. Kegley (ed.), *Reinhold Niebuhr: His Religious, Social and Political Thought* (New York: Pilgrim Press, 1984), p. 201.

[52] R. Niebuhr, "The revolutionary moment," *American Socialist Quarterly* 4:2 (June, 1935), 9.

[53] A. Schlesinger, "Reinhold Niebuhr's role in American political thought and life," 202.

working class countered the self-righteous complacency of the middle class. Above all, the historical and economic analysis of Marxism seemed to make increasing sense in what appeared to be an era of disintegrating capitalism.[54]

At the beginning of Roosevelt's presidency in 1933, Niebuhr judged liberalism to be a "spent force."[55] As late as the presidential election of 1936, Niebuhr was still supporting the candidacy of his friend Norman Thomas and, while recognizing the lack of support for Thomas, he held out hopes that there were still opportunities "for convinced socialists to ... point to the futility and superficiality of all the panaceas offered by capitalistic liberals and to spread the gospel of socialism."[56] What Niebuhr watched with a sense of pathos were "all the soul stirring appeals on behalf of Roosevelt by labor leaders, church leaders and tired radicals." And while he considered it obvious that "Mr. Roosevelt is preferable to the Republican candidate [Kansas Governor Alf Landon]," he regarded it "just as obvious that no real ground has been gained for social justice in his administration."[57]

Schlesinger was astounded that Niebuhr, "who was realistic about man and who wanted to equilibrate power in society," persisted in clinging to a total "commitment to socialization" that ended up being "both the price of indifference to the achievements of piecemeal reform and a symptom of despair."[58] He saw Niebuhr as unrealistically persisting in seeing the New Deal "as an image of incoherent and aimless triviality." Schlesinger saw it as paradoxical that, while Niebuhr was making this judgment, "the imperiled oligarchy was being forced by effective democratic government to accept measures of regulation and reform which would avert fascism and lead to recovery." Instead, "blinkered by doctrine," Niebuhr "scornfully rejected in practice the very pragmatism he called for in theory."[59]

Schlesinger saw the turning point for Niebuhr as occurring between 1939, when Niebuhr equivocated on his commitment to socialism, and 1940, when Niebuhr resigned from the Socialist Party in June and voted for Roosevelt in November. Schlesinger maintained that it was foreign rather than domestic policy that played the dominant role in Niebuhr's approval of Roosevelt and rejection of the Socialist Party. Schlesinger's opinion was that the continuing commitment of Socialists to pacifism amid the gathering storm of Nazi aggression is what led Niebuhr to an appreciation of Roosevelt. In sharp contrast to "the consequences of moralized politics," Niebuhr came to appreciate and respect "the canny and opportunistic political realism of Roosevelt," who "now seemed to have the dimensions of a great democratic leader."[60]

[54] Ibid., 202–3.
[55] R. Niebuhr, "After capitalism – what?" *The World Tomorrow* (March 1, 1933), 203.
[56] R. Niebuhr, "The political campaign," *Radical Religion* 1:4 (Autumn, 1936), 7.
[57] Ibid., 6.
[58] A. Schlesinger, "Reinhold Niebuhr's role in American political thought and life," 205.
[59] Ibid., 205–6.
[60] Ibid., 208.

The venue in which Schlesinger expressed his views of Niebuhr's flaw was in his analysis of Niebuhr's thought in the 1956 Kegley-Bretall volume on Niebuhr – the second volume in a series devoted to living theologians, following one on Paul Tillich published in 1952. Schlesinger's essay was entitled "Reinhold Niebuhr's Role in American Political Thought and Life" and appeared as Chapter 7 in the book *Reinhold Niebuhr: His Religious, Social and Political Thought.* In spite of his retrospective contention that Niebuhr misjudged FDR, Schlesinger's treatment of Niebuhr was profoundly appreciative. He saw Niebuhr as having successfully challenged the excessive optimism about human nature and the resulting political naiveté of both religious and secular liberalism, exemplified in the Social Gospel on the one hand and John Dewey on the other. He also praised the mature Niebuhr for his reformulation of the defense of democracy and for his mature political realism.

For all their differences, Niebuhr and Dewey were pragmatists. Yet, in spite of their pragmatic instincts, Schlesinger saw both Niebuhr and Dewey as being doctrinaire in their economic views. Reiterating his views of Roosevelt, Schlesinger's criticism of both these self-professed "pragmatists" was scathing:

For all their rejection of closed abstract systems, each saw the contemporary American problem in closed and abstract terms. The passionate champions of experiment, both flatly condemned the most massive and brilliant period of political and economic experimentation in American history. With a supreme political pragmatist as President, and with the most resourceful and creative economic and legal pragmatists of the time seeking patiently and tirelessly to work out a middle way between *laissez-faire* and collectivism, neither the secular pragmatist nor the Christian pragmatist managed to work up much interest. The pragmatic philosophers, abandoning pragmatism to Franklin D. Roosevelt, retreated precipitately to their own crypto-utopias.[61]

An interesting question presents itself: just how did Niebuhr react to Schlesinger's criticism – a criticism that began ten pages into a twenty-four page article and ran eight pages, or one-third of the total? Niebuhr had an immediate chance to respond, because the Kegley-Bretall volume contained a section for the featured theologian to reply to his critics. Even about two years before the publication of that book, Niebuhr had received the essay Schlesinger was preparing for the volume on Niebuhr. Niebuhr's response was unequivocally a "mea culpa" – a profession of guilt regarding what he was reading. On April 15, 1954, Niebuhr wrote to Schlesinger expressing appreciation for the "wonderful essay" Ursula had shown him, adding, "I'm not surprised, but nevertheless amazed that you should have taken time to go through all of my inconsequential writings to get your material. Outside of the fact that you are too generous toward me, the essay is superb. I find the record of my travels, however, embarrassing, and if you had not given chapter and verse I would

---

[61] Ibid., 204. For a treatment of Niebuhr's views on pacifism, see C. McKeogh, "Niebuhr's Critique of Pacifism" in D. F. Rice (ed.), *Reinhold Niebuhr Revisited: Engagements with an American Original* (Grand Rapids: Eerdmans, 2009), pp. 201–21.

not have believed that it took me so long to draw the conclusions from my presuppositions." After stating that he thought (mistakenly as it turned out) he had left the Socialist Party in either 1936 or 1937, Niebuhr was nonetheless bewildered that even after he had "rejected the main features of Socialism" he "still hung on to Marxist catastrophism." He ended his letter by confessing that his "negative attitude toward Roosevelt is really a scandal considering that he elaborated a pragmatic approach which I should have appreciated long before I did."[62]

At the time Schlesinger made his criticism and Niebuhr confessed his agreement, Niebuhr was busy giving form and substance to his theologically based pragmatic realism. From the time of his book *The Children of Light and the Children of Darkness* in 1944 through his affinity with the political realism of Hans Morgenthau and his service on Kennan's Policy Planning Committee in 1949 to the appearance of *The Irony of American History* in 1952, he and Schlesinger shared both a common outlook and an active political agenda. The very same year that Niebuhr was invited as an outside adviser to Kennan's State Department committee, Schlesinger's book *The Vital Center* appeared – a book, as we have observed, that was replete with an indebtedness to Niebuhr. Finally, in the mid-1950s, as he voiced his criticism of the 1930s Niebuhr, Schlesinger was also involved in a reassessment of the 1930s by way of his *The Age of Roosevelt*, the first volume of which appeared in 1956 with a dedication to Niebuhr.

1956 also brought Adlai Stevenson's second run for the presidency against the ever-popular Eisenhower. Two years earlier, on September 11, 1954, Niebuhr had written Schlesinger hoping that Stevenson wouldn't "continue his coy attitude but come out definitely as the leader of liberal democracy, looking to 1956."[63] On November 21, 1955, however, Niebuhr wrote to Stevenson, telling him,

I have hesitated for some time to write to you because I know how hard pressed you are from correspondence from all over the country, and I am writing you now with the distinct understanding that you must not answer my letter. I wanted to tell you how glad many of us are that you have entered the Presidential race and that the prospects for your nomination and election seem at the moment to be quite overwhelming. We heard you on Saturday night and felt the same thrill about your statesman-like approach to the problems of our day. This is merely to express my admiring affection for your person and for your stature as a statesman.[64]

Once 1956 arrived, Niebuhr found himself joining forces with Schlesinger in support of Stevenson. In a letter dated July 16, Schlesinger informed Niebuhr that he was "going to Chicago in a few days more or less for the duration" and asked Niebuhr "if you have any thought about things that might be said and

---

[62] R. Niebuhr to A. Schlesinger, April 15, 1954. Schlesinger Papers, NYPL.
[63] R. Niebuhr to A. Schlesinger, September 11, 1954. Schlesinger Papers, NYPL.
[64] R. Niebuhr to A. Stevenson, November 21, 1955. Stevenson Papers, Box 60, Folder 9. Seeley G. Mudd Manuscript Library, Princeton, NJ.

done, I would hope you will let me know. Perhaps governor Stevenson has already written you about the acceptance speech; but, if not, we would all very much appreciate your thoughts as to what might be in the speech – indeed, as to what the main issues of the campaign are as you see them."[65] On July 22 Niebuhr replied: "I am so glad that you are going to Chicago to help Adlai as four years ago. His nomination seems assured, despite Harriman's rather frantic gesture which I am inclined to judge rather more severely than others because I do not believe that they are motivated by basic policy differences." In response to Schlesinger's request that he make some suggestions, Niebuhr stated that he would make only two – one about civil rights and the other about foreign policy. He recommended lifting civil rights to the "plane of principle," thus vindicating "both the principle of the Bill of Rights in our Constitution and the right of the Supreme Court to implement the liberties guaranteed in the Constitution." On foreign policy, Niebuhr believed that the "central problem is obviously to score the administration for its complacency in the face of the new communist flexibility." Here, Niebuhr saw the issue to be "the uncommitted world of Asia and Africa" where the problem was "how to encourage the rightful aspirations for independence of the colonial and ex-colonial peoples and yet prove that there must be some preparation for independent nationhood."[66]

Schlesinger, who was working in the trenches for Stevenson, wrote back on July 31 thanking Niebuhr for his suggestions but admitting what a hard sell it is "to achieve a formulation on civil rights which can be at once politically, morally and intellectually adequate" and asking Niebuhr to "let us know if you have any further thought on this or on anything else."[67] After expressing gratitude for Schlesinger's letter, Niebuhr replied wondering what could possibly "be done on the foreign issues in such a way that the nation will not be unduly alarmed but at the same [time] be made conscious of the fact that the issues are more complex than the simple contrast between communism and democracy; and that the Administration's complacent moralism is absolutely inadequate for the issues of the day."[68] Niebuhr's charge of "complacent moralism" leveled against the Eisenhower administration related in large part to the policies of John Foster Dulles, whose pieties ill-served his obligations as secretary of state. Niebuhr was intensely critical of the kinds of facile moral judgments typically made by Dulles. As Schlesinger remarked, "Niebuhr had demonstrated [that] most secular questions intermingle good and evil in problematic proportions and are more usefully handled in other than moralistic categories."[69]

As the election approached, Niebuhr mentioned to Schlesinger that he had not "written Adlai Stevenson since Stevenson's nomination. He is always so

[65] A. Schlesinger to R. Niebuhr, July 16, 1956, Schlesinger Papers, NYPL.

[66] R. Niebuhr to A. Schlesinger, July 22, 1956. Schlesinger Papers, NYPL.

[67] A. Schlesinger to R. Niebuhr, July 31, 1956. Schlesinger Papers, NYPL.

[68] R. Niebuhr to A. Schlesinger, August 10, 1956. Schlesinger Papers, NYPL.

[69] A. Schlesinger, *The Crisis of Confidence: Ideas, Power and Violence in America* (Boston: Houghton Mifflin, 1967), p. 89.

thoughtful in answering letters that I felt it pretentious to bother him with a letter which he thought would have to be answered since he obviously has a press of so many duties." That Niebuhr's hopes had been fulfilled was evident when he added: "I was thrilled by the turn of events at the Convention, and equally thrilled and hopeful by the turn of events ever since." Niebuhr's advice was that in the campaign the Democrat should spell out the claim that America is losing the Cold War. In the process, he recommended that a "sharp distinction ought to be made between the actual mistakes of the Administration, such as trying to contain the social revolution in Asia by military pacts, and the developments for which the Administration is not directly responsible, which are due to the new flexibility of Russian policy, about which it is so complacent, and tries to persuade the American people to be complacent. I think if a sharp distinction could be made between these two points both points would be more effective."[70]

Niebuhr did write Stevenson on October 31, just before the election, thanking him "for undertaking a very significant job" and expressing the judgment that he had "successfully challenged the Eisenhower myth." That myth, as Niebuhr saw it, was "composed ... of the ingredients of an amiable man, the virtual acceptance of the foreign policy of the previous Administrations, and the packaging so expertly done by the Madison Avenue craftsmen," adding that "the nation has been very glad to accept this myth because it is its only way of remaining complacent in a perilous world."[71] Niebuhr, of course, was fully aware of the appeal of the Eisenhower myth, and when Stevenson lost the election, he and Stevenson exchanged letters. Niebuhr wrote:

Dear Adlai:

I write to you with some hesitation because I know that you will be inundated by letters and most of the letters will say the obvious. But I do want to say that again and again my thoughts have come back to you with deep regret that you should become the victim of what is the most fantastic political myth of the century, and that the very mistakes of the Administration in foreign policy should have in the last days contributed to its overwhelming victory. There is a deep irony in these developments which one cannot quite comprehend. I was talking with the Editor of the London Sunday Times, who came to visit me just before the election, and who predicted the result after touring America. We both lamented the fact that we did not have a parliamentary government that would give full scope to a man of your great talent. Our Presidential elections are a great "all or nothing" gamble. I sincerely hope that despite these constitutional difficulties you will be able to assert a creative influence in our political life, which

---

[70] R. Niebuhr to A. Schlesinger, September 17, 1956. Schlesinger Papers, NYPL.
[71] R. Niebuhr to A. Stevenson, October 31, 1956. Stevenson Papers, Box 60 Folder 9. Seeley G. Mudd Manuscript Library, Princeton, NJ.

the two splendid campaigns which you have waged have made possible and necessary.

With great admiration and affection

Sincerely yours,
Signed "Reinhold"[72]

In the aftermath of Stevenson's defeat, Niebuhr expressed to Schlesinger how "overwhelmed" he was "by the fact that the Eisenhower myth was so great that nothing that Stevenson or all the rest of you could have done would have changed the results."[73] Three days later on November 19, 1956, Niebuhr told Schlesinger that he had received "a nice letter from Adlai." Reiterating his view regarding the advantage of a parliamentary system that he voiced to Stevenson on November 9, he told Schlesinger, "I really regard his defeat as rather tragic because, without a parliamentary government this simply eliminates him from the scene, and we have no leadership but of Lyndon Johnson. So God help us!"[74]

By the end of November, Niebuhr was informing Schlesinger of the reason the latter was not being asked to sign a statement that a group comprised of university people and members of the Council of Foreign Relations was about to release regarding the Suez Canal crisis, in which the seizure of the Canal by Egypt's Nasser prompted a military intervention by both England and France – an action that brought the United States into open conflict with its allies.[75] The reason Niebuhr gave for Schlesinger's exclusion related to his close involvement in the recent election. "The Committee," Niebuhr wrote,

decided, to my embarrassment, that your father and not you should be asked. They exclude [the economist John Kenneth] Galbraith also on the ground that you were both too close to Stevenson and they are anxious to have this document, which is very critical of

---

[72] R. Niebuhr to A. Stevenson, November 9, 1956. Ibid.
[73] R. Niebuhr to A. Schlesinger, November 16, 1956. Schlesinger Papers, NYPL.
[74] R. Niebuhr to A. Schlesinger, November 19, 1956. Schlesinger Papers, NYPL.
[75] In the space of a week (November 19–27, 1956), Niebuhr voiced his own views on this crisis to Schlesinger. He saw the situation as a very serious one in which, in the "name of freedom from 'colonialism,'" the Soviet Union is threatening "to get their hand upon the whole European economy via the Suez Canal." Seeing the initial mistake as our own in not realizing "how serious this threat of Nasser was," and how desperate this made the British and French, they "have played into Nasser's hands just at a time when it was important for the Russians to obscure the brutalities in which they were engaged in Hungary." Niebuhr regarded one aspect of the tragedy the fact that "Britain, which has always been so united, should be so deeply divided on this issue" because "it faces a conflict between economic survival on the one hand, and its moral scruples on the other hand" (R. Niebuhr to A. Schlesinger, November 19, 1956. Schlesinger Papers, NYPL). A week later Niebuhr noted that "the spectacle of the English being torn apart because all the 'good people' find their conscience outraged by this act of aggression, is a rather sad and tragic one.... I am inclined to believe that we committed all the original errors, and that the British, French and Israelis have compounded them." Niebuhr then concluded by saying that "the complacency of this nation is really more terrible to bear than the act of aggression which disturbs the British people of conscience so much." (R. Niebuhr to A. Schlesinger, November 27, 1956. Schlesinger Papers, NYPL).

the Administration, not seem to be influenced by Party political considerations. You might not agree with it, and at any rate there is no particular honor in signing it, but I thought I would let you know why some of the members of the Harvard faculty are being asked and you are not.[76]

On January 10, 1957, Stevenson wrote a letter telling Niebuhr that he wanted to discuss a speech he was considering making "before 'Christian Action' in London late this Spring." Stevenson wanted "to talk about the implications of the failures of the West since Potsdam, or something calculated to shed some light on our real hazards and our failures to understand the revolution that has taken place since the atom bomb."[77] A week later Niebuhr wrote that he "would love to talk to [Stevenson] about the whole situation and about 'Christian Action.'"[78] In his next letter to Niebuhr, written on January 23, Stevenson said that what he had in mind

was that since the explosion of the bomb nothing could ever be the same again. The old Europe was gone forever. The heir to the Western empire which had for so long disposed of the destinies of far away peoples was now starkly exposed and a center of weakness. None of the old terms of reference made sense. But, of course, we went on using words like France, Germany, Europe, as if we still knew what they meant. But they had lost their former meaning and we had little knowledge of what their new meaning would be.

After declaring how imperative new ideas are on these issues, Stevenson confessed that

While, like many of us, I am a better diagnostician than physician, I am not without some remedies for the Western patient. But it is yours that interest me far more. And your view as to whether or not this is even a theme worthy of development or too highbrow for what I gather might be a massive London audience will be very welcome.[79]

Niebuhr and Schlesinger met in New York City to discuss these issues. Niebuhr wrote to Stevenson on February 5 and, as promised, enclosed "the lecture I gave for our Columbia University Seminar on Foreign Policy." He suggested that the second part of that lecture would have some bearing on the topic of Stevenson's upcoming talk in London. Niebuhr's Columbia lecture on "Power and Ideology in National and International Affairs"[80] assessed the comparisons between the West and the Soviet Union in their respective appeals to Asia and Africa and discussed the dangers posed by Soviet power in the Middle East. In the copy of the lecture filed in Stevenson's papers at the New York Public Library, we find that Stevenson had actually underlined Niebuhr's analysis of American foreign policy failures under Secretary of State John Foster Dulles during the Suez Crisis. He also underlined several of Niebuhr's other claims, including his criticisms of

---

[76] R. Niebuhr to A. Schlesinger, November 30, 1956. Schlesinger Papers, NYPL.

[77] A. Stevenson to R. Niebuhr, January 10, 1957. Ibid.

[78] R. Niebuhr to A. Stevenson, January 17, 1957. Ibid.

[79] A. Stevenson to R. Niebuhr, January 23, 1957. Ibid.

[80] A copy of Niebuhr's lecture can be found in the Stevenson Papers, Box 60, Folder 9 at the Seeley G. Mudd Manuscript Library, Princeton, NJ.

America's mistake in assuming its democratic creed is obviously available to the recently emancipated feudal or pastoral cultures of Asia and Africa and its error in indiscriminately viewing all European powers as "colonial" – thus giving support to the communist ideological claims – instead of carefully discriminating between persistent colonial powers and those powers that have extricated themselves from colonialism and helped tutor former colonies for independence.

On May 4, 1957, Schlesinger informed Niebuhr that "[J. Robert] Oppenheimer is here and speaks with great enthusiasm about your descent on Princeton next year" – Niebuhr was then preparing for his upcoming year at Princeton Institute for Advanced Study of which Oppenheimer was the head. Schlesinger observed that "I find him much more likeable than I expected – curiously sweet and gentle; also awfully idealistic and highbrow. He makes me feel even more impure, worldly, philistine, and corrupt than usual."[81] Niebuhr responded by agreeing that Oppenheimer "is certainly sweet and gentle and rather other-worldly" but that, in his mind, this only confirms how much more "worldly-wise" Schlesinger was. Niebuhr concluded that, when he spoke to Oppenheimer about "Einstein's childlike naivete in all political matters," Oppenheimer "said very simply, 'actually I think that kind of naiveté is a resource for physical scientists. It gives them a very pure vision.' I thought that remark was very revealing."[82]

Three years earlier, in the October, 1954, issue of *The Atlantic Monthly*, Schlesinger had written an article on "The Oppenheimer Case." Oppenheimer, who had such a profound role in the atomic bomb project at Los Alamos, was now judged wanting in matters of loyalty and was deemed a security risk. His superb wartime and postwar records failed to offset his damaging prewar patterns of political association.[83] And, as Schlesinger noted, although his formal opposition to the development of "Super" – the thermonuclear, hydrogen bomb – "was not to be formally held against him" by the Atomic Energy Commission, "few who read the record are likely to doubt that, if Oppenheimer had not opposed Super in 1949, he would not have had to stand trial in 1954."[84] Schlesinger found bogus the two main allegations of "imprudent and dangerous associations" and "substantial defects of character" that the AEC majority based its decision.

In 1958, Niebuhr took up residence at the Princeton Institute for Advanced Studies, working on a manuscript that would be published as *The Structure of*

---

[81] A. Schlesinger to U. and R. Niebuhr, May 4, 1957. U. M. Niebuhr (ed.), *Remembering Reinhold Niebuhr* (San Francisco: Harper, 1991), pp. 383–4.

[82] R. Niebuhr to A. Schlesinger, May 7, 1957. Schlesinger Papers, NYPL.

[83] On the issue of political association, Schlesinger cited George Kennan's reasonable remark: "I suppose most of us have had friends or associates whom we have come to regard as misguided with the course of time, and I don't like to think that people in senior capacity in the Government should not be permitted or conceded maturity of judgment when they can't." Kennan added, "I myself say it is a personal view on the part of Christian charity to try to be at least as decent as you can to them." A. Schlesinger, *The Politics of Hope*, pp. 260–1.

[84] A. Schlesinger, "The Oppenheimer case" in *The Politics of Hope*, 259.

Nations and Empires. In the course of writing this book, Niebuhr would often approach Schlesinger for advice, criticism, and even detailed corrections. Hard at work at his new summer home in Stockbridge, Massachusetts, Niebuhr was catching up on political and historical works needed in writing his own book. In addition to approaching Schlesinger about historical matters, he gave evidence of his well-documented insecurity about undertaking a work of more traditional scholarship than was his usual style of writing. On April 16, 1958, he wrote Schlesinger that while he has "been very happy in doing my work ... I must confess that putting all one's time on one particular project without distraction is rather rigorous for a person like myself with no more scholarly instincts than I have."[85] In July, he queried Schlesinger, again confessing doubt about his ability to follow through with this book:

I wanted to tell you how anxious I am to see you, not only to talk over my things, but to tell you about the project in which I have been engaged. I need some help on one chapter from some young historian. As I see it, the chapter would be entitled: The Anti-imperialist Ideologies of American Democracies and the Imperialist Realities. This chapter would be just before the concluding one, which I am doing now. I don't feel I have enough historical knowledge for the chapter I mentioned. As a matter of fact, I don't have enough historical knowledge for any of the chapters that I have written. I got into a depression worrying about having bitten off a bigger piece than I can chew.[86]

Again on August 24, Niebuhr wrote Schlesinger in a pensive mood reflecting the deepening depression he was experiencing. After expressing his gratitude for Schlesinger's recent visit, Niebuhr remarked that his depression was "partly due to overwork, partly to anxiety for daring to write a book for which I know too little; and partly because my thesis prompts a direct challenge to the two communities with which I have been intimately related: the Christian community and the liberal community" – Niebuhr having challenged their claims that "Christianity or Democracy would guarantee a just foreign policy." He ended his letter with profound sadness, asking himself "why I should have been fool-hardy enough to write such a book with such a thesis at the end of my days and with my physical powers, and perhaps my intellectual powers, on the wane."[87]

In early 1959, after the publication of *The Coming of the New Deal: 1933–1935*, the second volume of Schlesinger's *The Age of Roosevelt*, Niebuhr informed Schlesinger that he "was especially pleased to have a copy ... which I read in place of all the Christmas books which I received." Praising Schlesinger for the high standard of his writing, Niebuhr went on to say that he admired "the way that you combine descriptions of basic political and social trends with biographical sketches of the actors and agents in the political scene. Both of the little and the big ones. I enjoy particularly of course your analysis of the character of the great man."[88] Once the third volume – *The Politics of Upheaval:*

[85] R. Niebuhr to A. Schlesinger, April 16, 1958. Schlesinger Papers, NYPL.
[86] R. Niebuhr to A. Schlesinger, July 30, 1958. Schlesinger Papers, NYPL.
[87] R. Niebuhr to A. Schlesinger, August 24, 1958. Schlesinger Papers, NYPL.
[88] Ibid.

1935–1936 – was published in 1960, Niebuhr wrote Schlesinger: "I don't have to tell you that each of your volumes improves the already high standard of the 'Age of Roosevelt.' Your third volume has this in common with a good novel that it makes me disobey doctors' orders and stay up long after my bedtime. Perhaps the vignettes of the personalities of the age, Coughlin, Long, LaGuardia, Ickes, Hopkins, the members of the court etc., also establishes the comparison with creative fiction. You are in short an artist as I always knew."[89]

Niebuhr retired in 1960 after teaching at Union Theological Seminary since 1927. His retirement occurred the year of a presidential election and Niebuhr, at that point, strenuously resisted efforts made by Schlesinger, among others, to garner his support for the candidacy of John F. Kennedy. In June, 1960, the Niebuhrs moved to Santa Barbara, California, to spend the summer at the Center for the Study of Democratic Institutions. They resided there during the time the Democratic Convention was being held at Los Angeles. For Niebuhr, there was a definite pathos about the Democratic nominating process that year. He wrote Schlesinger stating that Stevenson once again "was rather pathetic in explaining his ambiguous attitude toward the nomination."[90] Niebuhr did not hesitate voicing his harsh views of Kennedy to Schlesinger even after the Massachusetts senator had secured the nomination. He stated:

I am also grateful that you will not be too active in the campaign, for the Kennedy machine is more ruthless than the bosses and I dread the prominence which young Bob will have in the campaign ... Bill Shannon visited us and declared that in his lifetime he had never seen such a consistently shrewd and also unscrupulous drive for political power. Nevertheless he was of the opinion that there were touches of FDR in the candidate.

I told him that in the naïveté of my youth I took a snooty attitude toward FDR's first campaign, but there were two distinctions between the great man and Kennedy. FDR had a heart; and he never bought primaries. I nevertheless expect him to be a good president certainly better than Eisenhower (which is saying nothing) and better than Nixon whom he partly resembles as an operator.[91]

Schlesinger, for his part, chose to make his apologia to Niebuhr by saying that, although had he known "a strong draft-Stevenson movement" was in the offing, he would have stayed with the former Illinois governor. At the same time he thought it exposed "Stevenson himself in his worst posture – the posture of indecision," concluding that while Stevenson "has a dimension that all these other fellows lack," he simply "lacks the will to command and the will to victory." Schlesinger told Niebuhr that he thought Kennedy possessed those "qualities in abundance" and deserved the nomination. He did admit, however, that his "liking for him and confidence in him declined in the course of the convention." While believing that the nomination of Lyndon Johnson for

---

[89] R. Niebuhr to A. Schlesinger, Saturday, nd. (but written sometime after September 9, 1960, and the November presidential election). Schlesinger Papers, NYPL.

[90] R. Niebuhr to A. Schlesinger, nd. Santa Barbara, CA. Schlesinger Papers, NYPL.

[91] Ibid. R. Niebuhr to A. Schlesinger, September 3, 1960. Schlesinger Papers, NYPL.

vice-president was both wise and politically sound, Schlesinger felt "the dissimulation and deceit with which Kennedy brought Johnson out were depressing." Because he always considered himself "a member of the Stevenson club," Schlesinger concluded that he did "not think Kennedy will ask me to work for him during the campaign; and, after L.A., I really don't care."[92]

In early September before the election, Niebuhr responded to Schlesinger's letter, confessing that he took some solace in the fact that "Kennedy has even converted Marian," thus revealing his trust in both "her judgment and the intuitions of her sex." Reminding Schlesinger that "I've only seen him once, at your party two years ago," he added: "My prejudices are due to the excessive use of money in the primaries and to his brother Bob." Niebuhr ended by saying that he recognized "the cool intelligence of the young Senator" and that "I know he will be a good President, if not a great one, but even the latter is a possibility."[93]

As the election between Kennedy and Nixon drew near, Niebuhr became embroiled in a situation wherein, within accidental earshot of Union Theological Seminary's President Henry Pitt Van Dusen, he was overhead making critical comments about Kennedy's sex life. Niebuhr replied to concerns that Schlesinger voiced by telling him that his colleague John Bennett was trying to deter Van Dusen from going public with the Kennedy scandal, and he assured Schlesinger that he, Niebuhr, had never talked directly to Van Dusen about Kennedy on this subject. The point Niebuhr wanted to make clear to Schlesinger was that, while he did not "like promiscuity and particularly what seems to be compulsive promiscuity," the real issue for him was the fact that "the church is already so trivial in its approach to politics that if this issue is raised, together with the 'Roman peril,' it will lose its last dignity." After commenting on the inane views of Norman Vincent Peale and the blend of piety with Goldwater Republicanism on the part of Sun Oil Company's Mr. Pew, Niebuhr concluded his letter to Schlesinger by saying: "If these pious people keep on bringing up fake religious issues they will succeed in making me an ardent Kennedy supporter, which I have not been."[94] In his September 3 letter to Schlesinger, Niebuhr, referring to his young friend and former editor of the Catholic journal *Commonweal*, John Cogley, Niebuhr had cautioned what little Cogley was likely to achieve in the way of overcoming the bias against Kennedy's Catholicism by suggesting that "most of the arguments will be phony, Texas oil using Baptist bigotry as a shield."[95]

Niebuhr finally endorsed Kennedy. He then spotlighted economic reasons as the actual basis for the support popular religious voices such as Norman Vincent Peale and Dan Poling were giving to Nixon. Schlesinger wrote Niebuhr: "I thought your statement on Peale-Poling excellent. I think also that it has had

[92] A. Schlesinger to U. and R. Niebuhr, July 21, 1960. Ursula Niebuhr, *Remembering Reinhold Niebuhr*, 385.

[93] R. Niebuhr to A. Schlesinger, September 3, 1960. Schlesinger Papers, NYPL.

[94] R. Niebuhr to A. Schlesinger, September 9, 1960. Schlesinger Papers, NYPL.

[95] R. Niebuhr to A. Schlesinger, September 3, 1960. Schlesinger Papers, NYPL.

considerable effect." He then went on to ask: "Do you think that more could be done to put Nixon on the spot? At present he is enjoying all the benefit of Peale-Policy without suffering any of the obloquy. Why should he not be challenged to make an explicit repudiation of the Peale movement? Of course, he might do so; but any repudiation coming so long after the fact and in response to challenge would not be very effective. Certainly he should not be permitted to avoid direct comment on Peale, as he has done up to this point."[96]

Soon after the election, Niebuhr wrote President-elect Kennedy to congratulate him on his victory and to implore him to consider Stevenson for the post of secretary of state. He suggested to Kennedy that "Stevenson's very considerable gifts will not only enhance our prestige in the world but will assure you of wise and prudent counsel in the affairs of the State Department." He then reminded Kennedy that, given his own record, he did "not have to worry about a two-time [presidential] nominee being in any way a threat to your authority," and that the appointment of Stevenson as Secretary of State would "not only enhance our prestige in the world but will assure you of wise and prudent counsel in the affairs of the State Department."[97]

On January 2, 1961, Niebuhr wrote Schlesinger, letting him know that he would be accepting the autumn invitation for a joint appointment at Harvard teaching a course on democracy and communism. He teased Schlesinger that the reason the Kennedy administration had "made a brilliant start" was partly a result of "moving the Harvard faculty to Washington." He also let Schlesinger know that he was hearing "various rumors about [Schlesinger's] acceptance of this or that position in the administration," confessing that he had "mixed feelings about that, as about every brilliant teacher and scholar who is put on an executive grindstone."[98] Schlesinger, of course, would indeed join the Kennedy administration as special assistant to the president – a position in which he served Kennedy between 1961 and 1963, staying over for a brief period after Lyndon Johnson became president.[99]

When President Kennedy was assassinated, Schlesinger was left devastated and demoralized. He once again decided to become active in the presidential election of 1968, vigorously supporting Robert Kennedy's late entry into the campaign. In the aftermath of the younger Kennedy's death, Schlesinger wrote Niebuhr:

What a sad year this has been! The murder of Robert Kennedy terminated my interest in the campaign, and perhaps in American politics for some time to come. Hubert

---

[96] A. Schlesinger to R. Niebuhr, September 10, 1960. Ursula Niebuhr, *Remembering Reinhold Niebuhr*, 387.

[97] R. Niebuhr to J. F. Kennedy, November 16, 1960. Schlesinger Papers, NYPL.

[98] R. Niebuhr to A. Schlesinger, January 2, 1961. Schlesinger Papers, NYPL.

[99] It was economist John Kenneth Galbraith's opinion that Schlesinger, who "was one of the first of the academic community to align himself with John F. Kennedy," served in the "administration as a voice of quiet restraint among the many of more adventurous mood." J. K. Galbraith, "The lessons of an historian" in John Patrick Diggins (ed.), *The Liberal Persuasion* (Princeton, NJ: Princeton University Press, 1997), pp. 65–6.

[Humphrey] seems to me a burnt-out case, emasculated and destroyed by L.B.J. and unlikely ever to become a man again. [Eugene] McCarthy an ungenerous, self-pitying man who has no concern for the other America and no belief in the presidency. When George McGovern became a candidate, I rallied round; as you may remember, George is a very close friend of mine, and he seemed to me better qualified to be president than the other two. But of course his candidacy was never realistic.

Schlesinger was a man adrift, and in a self-reflective mood he concluded his letter to Niebuhr by asking,

What do we do now? I have always supposed that anyone would be better than Nixon. But, if Hubert and Nixon have pretty much the same Vietnam policy, might it not be better to have Nixon on the ground that it will be easier to block further escalation if the Democratic party is opposing a Republican president than it would be if half the Democratic party feels it must go along out of loyalty to a Democratic president? Certainly Goldwater, had he been elected in '64 and pursued the identical policy pursued by L.B.J., could never have got so far with it because the entire Democratic party would have been mobilized against it.[100]

By the time Nixon was elected to the presidency in 1968, Niebuhr's health had declined to such an extent that he was sidelined from involvement in the ebb and flow of current politics. The tumultuous events occurring during this era of national turmoil did elicit comment from an increasingly ailing Niebuhr. In May, 1969, he wrote Schlesinger, whom he thanked for sending greetings from all his friends in the ADA who had lifted "the spirits of a senile old soul, when you attribute virtues to my leadership in the old days which I do not deserve." Niebuhr then mounted some of his old vitality, urging that we now "face a new crisis. Our old friend Hubert, has been defeated by that old scoundrel Nixon," who, promising to end the war has extended it into Cambodia. The resulting hysteria and violence among the young led Niebuhr to conclude by claiming that "my trivial sentiment that both LBJ and Nixon are S.O.B.s is thereby justified."[101]

The late 1960s saw the rise of student radicalism in the wake of an escalating war in Vietnam and the assassinations of President Kennedy, his brother, and Martin Luther King. In his book *Violence: America in the Sixties*, published in 1968, Schlesinger addressed the history of violence in America and its recent recurrence in American life. Echoing the British historian Herbert Butterfield's warning that civilization is a perilously thin veneer, he tells us that we "must begin to realize how fragile the membranes of our civilization are, stretched so thin over a nation so disparate in its composition" and laments how "little is more dismaying than the way in which some, a few, in the intellectual community have rejected the process of reason" and "have succumbed to the national

[100] A. Schlesinger to R. Niebuhr, September 8, 1968. U. M. Niebuhr, *Remembering Reinhold Niebuhr*, 389.
[101] R. Niebuhr to A. Schlesinger, May, 1969 (exact date unclear). Schlesinger Papers, NYPL.

susceptibility for hatred and violence" as they came to despair constitutional processes.[102]

Schlesinger was unwilling to condemn wholesale the student uprisings on America's campuses, although he was distraught that some among their numbers were willing to abandon political liberalism. While admitting that the rebellions had, on occasion, led to excess, Schlesinger contended that "on balance the nation stands to gain from student protest."[103] Schlesinger's concern was with the disjunction he saw between the Old Left and the New Left. What distinguished the New Left of the 1960s from earlier expressions of American radicalism was its "refusal to state revolutionary goals except in the most abstract and empty language ... its unwillingness to define what it aims for after the revolution" as well as "its belief that such mystification is a virtue.[104] Schlesinger abhorred the irrationalism of the New Left and its advocacy of a creed, traceable to the French syndicalist Georges Sorel, in which the revolutionary deed is paramount while the goal is quite irrelevant. He saw this creed containing "so much in the way of fakery and fallacy – to put it bluntly, it is so preposterous and so depraved – that I do not see how it can be long entertained by any serious democrat."[105] What is assuredly the case for Schlesinger is that "little is more pathetic than the view that in American society violence will benefit the left." And "if the left, through the cult of the deed, helps create an atmosphere which destroys the process of democracy itself, the only winners will be those who use violence best, and they will be on the right."[106]

In one of his last publications, Niebuhr managed to react publically to the student protests. His article entitled "Indicting Two Generations" was published in *The New Leader* late in 1970. While lauding the revolutionary generation of the 1930s for its quest for justice in modern industrial society, Niebuhr pointed out its naiveté regarding Marxist ideology and its inability to recognize liberal democracy's ability to correct the worst injustices of early American industrialism. And while recognizing the legitimacy of the student-led movement of the 1960s in its reaction against the Vietnam War and racial injustice in America, Niebuhr pointed out how lacking this new radicalism was in support from the working class that fueled the earlier movement. Moreover, he saw it more as dissatisfaction with the status quo – with things as they are – than as an attack upon the "system," in spite of the widespread use of anti-Establishment language. Niebuhr's view was that "while the young express an abundance of seemingly disjoined grievances, their attitude might best be described as a general moral uneasiness – a lack of respect to a culture that boasts of affluence and technical efficiency, but has failed to achieve ethical integrity and

---

[102] A. Schlesinger, *Violence: America in the Sixties* (New York: Signet Books, 1968), pp. 64–5.
[103] Ibid., pp. 62–3.
[104] Ibid., p. 74.
[105] Ibid., p. 77.
[106] Ibid., p. 82.

humanness."[107] When it came to indict this youthful revolt for its violence, Niebuhr pointed out that, contrary to the disavowal of terror by the radicals of the 1930s, this new radicalism was willing to "engage in violence of every kind from the occupation of college buildings to arson against ROTC headquarters to battles with policemen," concluding that "rock throwing and lead-pipe fusillades seem to be their standard revolutionary response." Yet Niebuhr did not see this recent streak of violence as either an extension of the American frontier or as something peculiar to America. Rather he saw it as "a universal phenomenon, induced by a combination of self-righteous perfectionism and a sense of impotence characteristic of the young." Niebuhr ended with a double-indictment:

It is surely one of the ironies of our times that a segment of our youth has resorted to terror tactics because it has been confronted with the moral and human inadequacy of an affluent technological culture. And since this situation has been bequeathed to them by their elders, our second revolution indicts both generations. The violence resulting from the desperation of the young over American society's sterility, however, will certainly complicate rather than cure the problem which prompted it.[108]

Schlesinger responded in a letter telling Niebuhr, "Your piece in the *New Leader* is excellent."[109] Five days later, on October 19, 1970, Niebuhr replied thanking Schlesinger for his "kind words" and expressing the wish that "the title had suggested my abhorrence of the violence engaged in by the current revolutionaries." He told Schlesinger that he noted "from the morning papers that young girls were involved in the bombing of the library and the robbery of a bank." Labeling those engaged in violence "murderous young revolutionaries," Niebuhr angrily concluded by saying "they create a crisis of confidence in our nation even if a fool Ohio grand jury indicts the rock throwing students [at Kent State] and absolves the murderous national guardsmen who killed 4 students."[110]

   Less than two months before Niebuhr died in 1971, Schlesinger wrote to tell him that he "should know that Jim Loeb, as toastmaster at the ADA Roosevelt Day dinner on March 11, surpassed himself in the grace and eloquence of his opening remarks. He reminisced for a moment about the beginning of ADA and concluded with a superb tribute to you. The audience was deeply stirred and moved." Then Schlesinger let Niebuhr know that he had gotten involved in George McGovern's presidential campaign in spite of his desire to quit politics. He claimed that McGovern "grows steadily; he is right on nearly every issue; and, the more impact he has, the more likely the Democratic party is to end up with a reasonably liberal candidate and program, even if it may not be McGovern himself."[111] He then asked Niebuhr if he would consider joining

[107] R. Niebuhr, "Indicting two generations," *The New Leader* (October 5, 1970), 14.
[108] Ibid.
[109] A. Schlesinger to R. Niebuhr, October 13, 1970. Schlesinger Papers, NYPL.
[110] R. Niebuhr to A. Schlesinger, October 19, 1970. Schlesinger Papers, NYPL.
[111] A. Schlesinger to R. Niebuhr, March 15, 1971. Schlesinger Papers, NYPL.

a committee on behalf of a McGovern candidacy that Schlesinger was helping to form.

Such was not to be the case. Three days later, on March 18, Ursula Niebuhr wrote to Schlesinger thanking him for his nice letter and informing him that "I read it to Reinhold, who is in hospital at Pittsfield, following pneumonia, and an embolus in the other lung. He has been quite wretched but is now a little improved but still not much himself." She added: "I know he will want to write to you when he is better. Although I read your letter to him, I doubt that he was able to take much of it in. He has been quite confused during the last few days with this sickness and all they are doing to him. I was very glad to hear from you, however, about George McGovern."[112]

Reinhold Niebuhr died on June 1, 1971, in Stockbridge, Massachusetts. On that very day Schlesinger had written him a letter in which he reminded Niebuhr:

You have probably forgotten that in 1950 you gave the baccalaureate address and I the commencement address at Muhlenberg College in Allentown, Pennsylvania. I only remember because I have just returned from giving the commencement address there again, 21 years later. I am appalled by that statistic – 21 years! – but it does recall the high pleasure of the occasion nearly a quarter century ago.

I suppose we were more hopeful then. . . . I find myself still a long-term optimist (i.e. I think we will blunder through) but something of a short-term pessimist, at least about America. I attach a copy of the 1971 talk – you will note, I think with a number of Niebuhrian points, which suggests how penetrating, and fortunate your influence was on my generation, and how that influence endures.

I reread *Moral Man and Immoral Society* the other day in preparing a lecture on that old chestnut, Morality and International Politics. Your analysis applies to so many of our contemporary confusions; but why is it that we have to go through the same argument anew every generation? Who could have predicted the rebirth of utopianism – or really of antinomianism – among the young?[113]

A day later, having learned of Niebuhr's death, Schlesinger wrote to Ursula enclosing the letter he had written the day before. He told her:

On Sunday I gave a commencement talk at Muhlenburg College where, 21 years ago, Reinhold gave the baccalaureate and I the commencement address and we both received degrees. The occasion suddenly filled my heart with memories of the past; and, on my return, I dictated – too late – alas – a letter to Reinhold. I attach a copy now.

I don't think I need to say to you how much Reinhold meant to me through the years. He has more intellectual influence on me than anyone I have ever known; and, even more important, his combination of penetrating and realistic intelligence with total sweetness and unlimited generosity proved to a hopeless agnostic what a truly Christian man can be. We all loved him so much, learned so much from him, and will be in his debt for the rest of our lives. And in your debt too – I can imagine how difficult the last years have been for

[112] U. M. Niebuhr to A. Schlesinger, March 18, 1971. Schlesinger Papers, NYPL.
[113] A. Schlesinger to R. Niebuhr, June 1, 1971. U. M. Niebuhr, *Remembering Reinhold Niebuhr*, 390–1.

you, and I know how marvelous you have been and how indispensably you recreated a life for him.

I mourn with you the death of a great and beloved man and send all love to Elisabeth and Christopher.[114]

On November 1, 1971, Schlesinger delivered an address at a memorial service held at Riverside Church adjacent to Union Theological Seminary. The address, "Prophet for a Secular Age," was published a few months later in *The New Leader*. He recounted the personal qualities he found in Niebuhr. In spite of possessing genuine humility, he claimed Niebuhr never lacked "clarity and force of expression." Keenly aware of the "moral precariousness of human striving," he never permitted such realism to devolve into a cynicism that would "sever the nerve of action." Schlesinger saw in Niebuhr a "temperament" and a "faith" that were "mutually reinforcing in producing his remarkable personal combination of modesty and strength." Focusing on the man himself, Schlesinger saw "the sparkling play of [Niebuhr's] marvelous human qualities – the trenchancy, the humor, the inexhaustible curiosity, the passion, the generosity, the sweetness, the grandeur, all contained in an energy so overpowering that he seemed never to be able to sit still." Schlesinger remembered Niebuhr "above all restlessly pacing the floor, throwing out ideas, jokes and challenges."[115]

Schlesinger also focused on what he believed was a central paradox in Niebuhr's life and influence, namely, "why this passionate, profound and humble believer should have had so penetrating an influence on so many nonbelievers."[116] Schlesinger could not "but feel that part of Niebuhr's influence on [this highly secular] age was a product of his capacity to show how the most piercing contemporary insights had their precedents in historical Christianity – or, to put it in an opposite way – in his capacity to restate historical Christianity in terms that corresponded to our most searching modern themes and anxieties."[117] For many, Niebuhr's understanding of "historical Christianity" – or "biblical faith," to incorporate the wider prophetic tradition that Niebuhr valued so highly – was compelling as a cultural resource of wisdom but not as a resource of religious belief. Schlesinger was content to stress that Niebuhr "was simply one of those men who, whatever their ontological beliefs, had to a rare degree the gift of political diagnosis."[118]

---

[114] A. Schlesinger to U. M. Niebuhr, June 2, 1971. Ibid., 391.
[115] A. Schlesinger, "Prophet for a secular age," *The New Leader* (January 24, 1972), 14.
[116] Ibid., 11.
[117] Ibid., 12.
[118] Ibid., 13.

CHAPTER 5

Hans Morgenthau (1904–1980)

Hans Morgenthau immigrated to the United States from Germany in 1937. A major voice among political realists, he soon became the leading figure in international political theory in America in the wake of the impact of his 1948 book *Politics Among Nations*. Niebuhr and Morgenthau met at the University of Chicago in 1944 and rapidly developed a lasting friendship.

In 1962, Morgenthau referred to Niebuhr as "perhaps the greatest living political philosopher in America,"[1] with Niebuhr returning the compliment in 1965 by calling Morgenthau "the most brilliant and authoritative political realist."[2]

The extent and direction of the influence Niebuhr and Morgenthau had on each other have been much debated. Christoph Frie's 2001 book on Morgenthau played down any influence Niebuhr might have had on Morgenthau, contending that Morgenthau simply "used Niebuhr's language to introduce his German intellectual heritage in an unobjectionable manner in America."[3] Yet the one thing underestimated by Frei is the likely effect of the new American culture – both in language and ideas – on Morgenthau as a recent émigré.[4] It might well be that, quite aside from any direct intellectual influences,

---

Portions of this chapter first appeared in my article "Reinhold Niebuhr and Hans Morgenthau: A friendship with contrasting shades of realism," *Journal of American Studies* 42:2 (2008), 255–91.

[1] H. Morgenthau, "The influence of Reinhold Niebuhr in American political life and thought" in H. R. Landon (ed.), *Reinhold Niebuhr: A Prophetic Voice in Our Time* (Greenwich, CT: Seabury Press, 1962), p. 109.

[2] R. Niebuhr, *Man's Nature and His Communities* (New York: Charles Scribner's Sons, 1965), p. 71.

[3] C. Frei, *Hans J. Morgenthau: An Intellectual Biography* (Baton Rouge, LA: Louisiana State University Press, 2001), p. 111.

[4] H. Stuart Hughes in his book *The Sea Change: The Migration of Social Thought, 1930–1965* (New York: Harper & Row, 1975) provided this interesting perspective in the context of commenting on the difficulty Americans had understanding Paul Tillich: "The other intellectual émigrés with concerns extending beyond the boundary of a single discipline had encountered a similar half-understanding in the lands of English speech. Readers thinking exclusively in the English language almost never succeeded in entering fully into the idea world of men whose deepest reflections continued to go on in the other language they had spoken as children." Ibid., p. 268.

FIG. 5 Morgenthau
Courtesy of the University of Chicago

Niebuhr's writings and friendship on occasion helped the German-speaking, German-thinking Morgenthau in entering more fully into the world of an America relatively new to him.

G. O. Mazur, who has edited two books on Morgenthau, claims that both Niebuhr and the jurist Hans Kelsen were among "the most direct influences upon Morgenthau"[5] and that, in the United States "Niebuhr would in many ways assume the place of collegiality and support which Kelsen had provided to Morgenthau during his European years."[6] In terms of intellectual influence, the proper question for Martin Halliwell is "who influenced whom the most."[7] Michael J. Smith goes so far as to insist that Morgenthau "sought to incorporate Niebuhr's insights (in the process, of course, secularizing them) into a general theory of international politics."[8] And Morgenthau's protégé Kenneth

[5] G. O. Mazur, "Introduction" in G. O. Mazur (ed.), *One Hundred Year Commemoration to the Life of Hans Morgenthau: 1904–2004* (New York: Semenenko Foundation, 2004), p. 5.

[6] G. O. Mazur, "Introduction" in G. O. Mazur (ed.), *Twenty-Five Year Memorial Commemoration to the Life of Hans Morgenthau: 1904–2005* (New York: Semenenko Foundation, 2006), p. iii.

[7] M. Halliwell, *The Constant Dialogue: Reinhold Niebuhr and American Intellectual Culture* (Rowman and Littlefield, 2005), p. 210.

[8] M. J. Smith, *Realist Thought from Weber to Kissinger* (Baton Rouge, LA: Louisiana State University Press, 1986), p. 134.

Thompson insisted that Niebuhr's "formative influence on thinkers such as Hans J. Morgenthau in the United States and E. H. Carr in Britain was early, direct, and unquestioned."[9] What is undeniable is that Niebuhr and Morgenthau both acknowledged and expressed reliance on each other's contributions. The fact that they recognized the seriousness of their interdependence is evident when an ailing Niebuhr in October, 1970, wrote to Morgenthau, "I am forced to ask whether all my insights are not borrowed from Hans Morgenthau,"[10] only to receive a reply two weeks later stating, "I have asked myself the same question with reference to you, and I am sure I have by far the better of the argument."[11] It appears reasonable to conclude that in finding a profound intellectual kinship with this older American – also of German heritage and conversant with the German language – at the very least Niebuhr proved to be one of Morgenthau's main sources in America for thinking and writing in American terms in an American context for an American audience.

NIEBUHR'S INTERACTION WITH MORGENTHAU

Niebuhr was on the lecture circuit when he first met Morgenthau in 1944 at the University of Chicago. Morgenthau had immigrated to America in 1937 and had been teaching there since 1943. Their meeting came soon after the publication of Niebuhr's prestigious Gifford Lectures (1941–3) – a time when his reputation was approaching its zenith. The year 1944 was also when Niebuhr, working from themes set forth in *The Nature and Destiny of Man*, published his vindication of democracy in *The Children of Light and the Children of Darkness*. Morgenthau, of course, was familiar with Niebuhr's writings and had read *The Nature and Destiny of Man* as well as *Moral Man and Immoral Society*. It was soon after this, in 1946, that Morgenthau published his first important book since coming to America, *Scientific Man Versus Power Politics*, which clearly echoed one of the major themes Niebuhr had attacked, namely, "scientism." Morgenthau had defined scientism as "the belief that the problems of social life are in essence similar to the problems of physical nature and that, in the same way in which one can understand the laws of nature and, by using this knowledge, dominate nature and harness it to one's own ends, one can understand the facts of society and, through this knowledge, create a gigantic social mechanism which is at the command of the scientific master."[12]

---

[9] K. W. Thompson, "Niebuhr and the foreign policy realists" in D. F. Rice (ed.), *Reinhold Niebuhr Revisited: Engagements with an American Original* (Grand Rapids, MI: Eerdmans, 2009), p. 139.

[10] R. Niebuhr to H. Morgenthau, October 29, 1970, Hans Morgenthau Papers, Container 44, Library of Congress.

[11] H. Morgenthau to R. Niebuhr, November 13, 1970, Hans Morgenthau Papers, Container 44, Library of Congress. A copy of this letter is also in the Niebuhr Papers, Container 64, Library of Congress.

[12] H. Morgenthau, "The escape from power" in *Politics in the Twentieth Century* (Chicago, IL: University of Chicago Press, 1962), vol. I, p. 312. First published in Lyman Bryson et al., (eds.), *Conflicts of Power in Modern Culture*, Seventh Symposium of the Conference on Science, Philosophy and Religion (New York: Harper & Brothers, 1947), pp. 1–10.

It is not that Morgenthau and Niebuhr were denigrating science. Rather, they opposed what they believed to be the misapplication of scientific method. While seeing no problem in scientific descriptions and interpretations of the natural world, Niebuhr saw the usefulness of the scientific method in the domain of human affairs as severely limited by both the complexity of history and the fact that human beings are not disinterested observers relative to the phenomena they are studying. Human beings are creatures of nature to be sure. However, in their freedom they are creators of history rendering historical and political events radically different from events in nature. Morgenthau pointed out that Niebuhr was quite correct in having "time and again made emphatically the point that the historic area – the social scene – is essentially different from nature, and that the intellectual methods which are capable of understanding politics and society in general are bound to be different from the methods which apply to the discovery of the secret of nature."[13] Writing in 1960 for the journal *Christianity and Crisis*, Morgenthau stated the issue in this way:

In the world of nature, which he faces ready-made ... man proves himself a master of understanding, initiation and control. How different, how frustrating and humiliating is the role he plays in understanding and controlling the social world, a world that is properly his own, which would not exist if he had not created it, and which exists the way it does only because he has given it the imprint of his nature. ... [The] social world, being but a projection of human nature onto the collective plane, being but man writ large, man can understand and maintain control of society no more than he can of himself. Thus the very intimacy of his involvement impedes both understanding and control.[14]

Niebuhr had reviewed Morgenthau's *Scientific Man Versus Power Politics* and lamented that "this very important little book has been, so far as I know, completely ignored by the journalists of opinion, probably because the prejudices and idolatries of a scientific age, which it attacks, are still dominant in most of our intellectual centers."[15] In a letter expressing gratitude for Niebuhr's review and disappointment that his book had not been reviewed in *The Nation*, Morgenthau wrote: "The theological responses to the book have generally been very gratifying. The philosophic ones have been mixed, but at least understanding ... The reactions of the political scientists are mostly disastrous; the review for *The American Political Science Review* calls me 'often dogmatic,

---

[13] H. Morgenthau, "The influence of Reinhold Niebuhr in American political life and thought," p. 101.

[14] H. Morgenthau, "The intellectual and moral dilemma of history," *Christianity and Crisis* (February. 8, 1960), 3.

[15] R. Niebuhr, review of *Scientific Man Versus Power Politics* in the journal *Christianity and Society* (Spring, 1947), 33–4. Five years later Niebuhr wrote, "It is worth noting here that, when political science is severed from its ancient rootage in the humanities and 'enriched' by the wisdom of sociologists, psychologists and anthropologists, the result is frequently a preoccupation with minutia which obscures the grand and tragic outlines of contemporary history, and offers vapid solutions for profound problems." R. Niebuhr, *The Irony of American History* (New York: Charles Scribner's Sons, 1952), p. 60.

at times supercilious, and not infrequently sneering and flippant.' A review by a former president of the American Political Science Association ... is in a similar vein."[16] Of course, *Scientific Man Versus Power Politics* would, in due course, be seen as a watershed book. But Niebuhr, at the time of its publication, had put his finger on the problem when he wrote back to Morgenthau that when "you challenge the credos of our day so basically ... I can imagine what the reviews are like."[17]

Throughout the years, Niebuhr and Morgenthau continued to cite each other on a variety of matters, both substantive and peripheral. In praising the realist E. H. Carr, for example, Morgenthau held, "No other thinker, with the exception of Reinhold Niebuhr, has seen more clearly and exposed with more acute brilliance the essential defects of Western political thought."[18] In the same volume, first published in 1948, Morgenthau criticized Walter Lippmann, claiming that "Herbert Butterfield, Reinhold Niebuhr, myself, and others have tried to show how much more ambiguous and involved the relations between reason and politics are than is suggested by [Lippmann's] simple rationalistic faith."[19] In addition, in 1951 Morgenthau had Niebuhr contribute an article entitled "Germany and Western Civilization" to a book Morgenthau edited on postwar Germany.[20] One of their most interesting exchanges occurred in 1965, when Morgenthau wrote Niebuhr telling him, "I want you to know that I have been following your writings with very great interest, as usual, and am particularly gratified to learn you have recently paid some attention to my writings as well."[21] A few days later Niebuhr wrote back:

Dear Hans. Excuse me for addressing you in the familiar form when you address me as Professor Niebuhr. I only do this in order to underscore your misunderstanding when you say [you are pleased to learn that I] "have recently paid some attention to my writings as well." My dear friend, Hans, I have not just recently paid attention to them, I have read all your writings avidly and have been particularly impressed by what you said about Vietnam.[22]

[16] H. Morgenthau to R. Niebuhr, May 16, 1947, Hans Morgenthau Papers, Container 44, Library of Congress.

[17] R. Niebuhr to H. Morgenthau, May 20, 1947, Hans Morgenthau Papers, Container 44, Library of Congress.

[18] H. Morgenthau, "The surrender to the immanence of power: E. H. Carr" in *Politics in the Twentieth Century* (Chicago, IL: University of Chicago Press, 1962), vol. I, p. 42. This tribute to Carr first appeared in *Foundations for World Order* (Denver, CO: Social Science Foundation, University of Denver, 1948).

[19] H. Morgenthau, Ibid., 66.

[20] H. Morgenthau (ed.), *Germany and the Future of Europe* (Chicago, IL: University of Chicago Press, 1951), pp. 1–11.

[21] H. Morgenthau to R. Niebuhr, April 23, 1965, Hans Morgenthau Papers, Container 44, Library of Congress.

[22] R. Niebuhr to H. Morgenthau, April 27, 1965, Hans Morgenthau Papers, Container 44, Library of Congress.

Late in his career, Niebuhr was invited by J. Robert Oppenheimer to take up residence at the Princeton Institute for Advanced Study, where he would write *The Structure of Nations and Empires*. The year was 1958, and Niebuhr, after his first series of strokes in 1952, suffered from diminished abilities and had a much curtailed schedule of activities as the decade progressed. Although suffering from intermittent depression, Niebuhr looked forward to writing a book in which he hoped to prove to both himself and others that he could write in the academic vein of more traditional scholarly works. In a sense this was a shame, because Niebuhr's forte was the powerful, incisive, and often polemical kind of writing in which he excelled throughout this long career. Among Niebuhr's friends who labored with him and for him during the writing of the book were George Kennan, Kenneth Thompson, and Hans Morgenthau – three of his compatriots in the camp of political realists. Kennan, according to Richard W. Fox, "sensed . . . a certain fatigue in Niebuhr's work," claiming that all three friends, while offering "some reassurance with their prepublication plaudits . . . mixed some misgivings with glowing sentiments."[23] Many years later near the end of his life, Niebuhr remembered the help Morgenthau had given him back in 1959. In a letter written on January 13, 1970, Niebuhr wrote: "I cease to do any significant work, on account of various failures of the flesh. Hence I am the more dependent upon old friends like you. I have often reported to my friends what an honest and helpful critic you were of the manuscript that I produced at the Institute."[24]

Niebuhr's and Morgenthau's most direct practical influence came in the decade between 1949 and 1959 when they participated in meetings of the Policy Planning Staff of the Department of State, which was founded on May 5, 1947, by Secretary of State George Marshall for the purpose of formulating, developing, and advising on America's long-range foreign policy problems. George Kennan was its director and brought realists such as Niebuhr, Morgenthau, and Arnold Wolfers in for various sessions, along with many others. Niebuhr was there for two sessions in June, 1949. What Kennan found attractive, according to Richard Fox's interview with him, was Niebuhr's "philosophical perspective" more than his "political judgments and foreign-policy views." Niebuhr returned many times and, according to Fox, "continued to give voice to his modestly idealistic realism."[25] Niebuhr's trips to Washington grew less frequent as his physical capacities declined. Kenneth Thompson, in recalling Niebuhr's 1959 trip – his first since the stroke he suffered in 1952 – told of a conversation on foreign policy at which he was present along with, among others, Morgenthau, Kennan, Wolfers, Lippmann, *The New York Times* correspondent James Reston, and Dean Rusk. The notes Thompson jotted down

---

[23] R. W. Fox, *Reinhold Niebuhr: A Biography* (New York: Pantheon Books, 1985), p. 269. Fox's assessment is quite harsh, but his sketch of the Princeton episode in Niebuhr's life is worth looking into for its details. See pp. 267–9.

[24] R. Niebuhr to H. Morgenthau, January. 13, 1970, Hans Morgenthau Papers, Container 44, Library of Congress.

[25] R. W. Fox, *Reinhold Niebuhr: A Biography*, 238.

showed a far more favorable portrait of Niebuhr than we find in Fox's account. Thompson's notes read:

Niebuhr had the historian's command of the facts [and while having] little time for the more simple-minded moralists [these] contemporary policymakers were not impatient with Niebuhr; surely one reason [being] his mastery of political realities and the facts. [Niebuhr] was at home in the theoretical world of the philosopher, the theologian, and the philosopher of science [and] recognized this was not the world of the politician or states-man. [Finally] it was Niebuhr, conspicuous as a lone theologian among the theorists who met in Washington, who was the first to insist that no single overarching norm in international politics provided the basis for evaluating and judging all other norms. This viewpoint set him apart from those who saw freedom or security or justice as the controlling objective of American foreign policy. He concurred with Justice Holmes' phrase: "People are always extolling the man of principle but the superior man is the one who knows he must find his way in a maze of principles."[26]

Two of the most prominent and outstanding exchanges between Niebuhr and Morgenthau came five years apart in the 1960s – first, a 1962 tribute to Niebuhr, and second, an exchange on "The Ethics of War and Peace in the Nuclear Age" published in 1967.[27] Specific aspects of these rare direct exchanges of views will come into play later in the appropriate context.

By the time Morgenthau had moved from Chicago to New York in 1968, Niebuhr was in a state of seriously declining health. They no doubt saw more of each other than before and were involved in discussions regarding both the nuclear stalemate between the United States and the Soviet Union and the evolving quagmire of the Vietnam War. Both Niebuhr and Morgenthau ended up opposing American intervention, although Morgenthau arrived at that posi-tion earlier than Niebuhr, who wanted to believe that the rationale given by the Johnson administration was valid. Finally, however, he awakened to the erro-neous assumptions on which United States intervention had been based and attacked that intervention. Niebuhr finally came to admit that he had supported the war for far too long and for bad reasons. Based on his chapter "To Intervene or Not to Intervene" from the book *A New Foreign Policy for the United States* (which itself had appeared in an earlier form in the April, 1967, issue of *Foreign Affairs*), Morgenthau argued that "the policies the United States is pursuing in Vietnam are open to criticism on three grounds: they do not serve the interests of the United States, they even run counter to these interests, and the objectives we have set ourselves are not attainable, if they are attainable at all, without unreasonable moral liabilities and military risks."[28]

---

[26] K. W. Thompson, "The political philosophy of Reinhold Niebuhr" in C. W. Kegley (ed.) *Reinhold Niebuhr: His Religious, Social and Political Thought* (New York: Pilgrim Press, 1984), pp. 247–9.

[27] H. Morgenthau, "The influence of Reinhold Niebuhr," pp. 99–109, with Niebuhr's response to Morgenthau coming at pp. 120–3, and in "The ethics of war and peace in the nuclear age," *War/ Peace Report* 7:2 (February, 1967), 3–8.

[28] H. Morgenthau, *A New Foreign Policy for the United States* (New York: Praeger, 1969), p. 129.

For many "realists," including Morgenthau's one-time friend Henry Kissinger, opposition to the war was an act of heresy. In an interview for his 1977 tribute, Morgenthau stated that he had, since 1961, "warned against our military involvement in Vietnam. When we got involved in 1965 I opposed the involvement. I simply applied certain basic principles of foreign policy which I had formulated almost twenty years earlier to the situation in Vietnam." He went on to say that "since I had been previously regarded as a hard-liner in foreign policy, people jumped to the conclusion that I was bound to support any hard line even if it was unsound." When people asked Morgenthau how he reconciled his opposition to the war in Vietnam with his core position on foreign policy, he would refer "the questioner to one of the basic principles I developed in the first edition of *Politics Among Nations* (1948) concerning the correct conduct of foreign policy: Never put yourself in a position from which you cannot retreat without loss of face and from which you cannot advance without undue risk."[29]

Denying any risk-taking on his part in opposing the war (largely because he did not anticipate the firestorm of criticism he would later receive from both the administration and his academic colleagues),[30] Morgenthau wrote that he

had pointed out that the war in South Vietnam was primarily a civil war, not a war of foreign aggression; that the domino theory was a literary invention with no correspondence in historic experience; that counterinsurgency was not a military tactic which could be applied indiscriminately and with any chance of success in a situation in which large masses of indigenous people took to arms for deeply felt national and social objectives. [and finally] that the Saigon government could not keep itself in power for any length of time without the massive military support supplied by the United States, and that to speak here of the defense of freedom and democracy against its enemies was stretching terms beyond endurance.[31]

In May, 1970, Morgenthau wrote Niebuhr a letter in which he mentioned that he had "just written an article on the Cambodian adventure, of which I shall send you a copy," informing Niebuhr that he had "just finished a collection of essays which will be published this summer under the title TRUTH AND

[29] H. Morgenthau, "Postscript to the transaction edition: Bernard Johnson's interview with Hans J. Morgenthau" in K. W. Thompson and R. J. Myers (eds.), *Truth and Tragedy: A Tribute to Hans J. Morgenthau* (New Brunswick and London: Transaction Books, 1984; first published in 1977 by the New Republic Book Company), p. 382.

[30] G. O. Mazur reminds us that "it was Niebuhr who eventually joined with Morgenthau, when Morgenthau made his early position of dissent against Vietnam (as early as the Kennedy and Johnson administrations where he was an advisor then) and at the time that Morgenthau became largely disenfranchised by these administrations." (G. O. Mazur, "Introduction" in G. O. Mazur [ed.], *Twenty-Five Year Memorial Commemoration to the Life of Hans Morgenthau: 1904–2005*, p. iii.] Mazur also informs us that "in the third and last period of his life in New York City … Morgenthau would spend much effort in correcting the distortions to his reputation and image which his vocal dissent of Vietnam had brought upon him by two successive presidential administrations (Johnson in 1964–8, and Nixon in 1968–76)." Ibid., pp. 9–10.

[31] H. Morgenthau, *A New Foreign Policy for the United States*, pp. 383–4.

POWER," and confessing that Niebuhr's "departure from New York has created a painful void for your friends. I wish there was something I could do to make life a little bit easier for you and to show you my affection."[32]

Morgenthau and Kenneth Thompson were welcome guests at the home in Stockbridge, Massachusetts, where Niebuhr spent his last year. Morgenthau wrote to Niebuhr on August 24, 1970, recalling a recent visit. "Just a line," he wrote, "to tell you how great an experience it was to talk to you again and, more particularly, to listen to you after so long an interval. I only am sorry that I delayed that experience for so long, for no good reason except lack of initiative."[33] Niebuhr replied three days later in a brief note thanking him for his letter and saying that "yours and Kenneth's visit were a boon to all of us. I need not tell you how much your thought has influenced me, so your visit was doubly welcome."[34] On March 17, 1971, just short of three months prior to Niebuhr's death, Morgenthau wrote to Niebuhr telling him that the previous day he had been "at a dinner celebrating the thirtieth anniversary of *Christianity and Crisis*. Your name was mentioned so often and with such enthusiasm and admiration that the evening in good measure became a celebration of your stewardship."[35] After Niebuhr's death, Morgenthau continued to correspond with Niebuhr's wife, Ursula, and, in a letter to Morgenthau, she remarked that she was "so glad to remember that Reinhold had that visit from you and Kenneth Thompson last year."[36]

NIEBUHR'S THEOLOGICAL "DISPOSITION"

The common ground Niebuhr and Morgenthau shared was considerable in that they were both rightfully classified as "realists" and, as such, agreed upon a broad range of convictions pertaining to power politics. They both held that all politics, including international politics, is grounded in and must always be

---

[32] H. Morgenthau to R. Niebuhr, May 12, 1970, Hans Morgenthau Papers, Container 44, Library of Congress. The "Cambodian adventure" to which Morgenthau refers here is President Nixon's expansion of the Vietnam War into Cambodia. This occurred on Thursday, April 30, 1970, and on this day Morgenthau was delivering an address on "A New Foreign Policy for the United States" at a symposium on United States Foreign Policy in Asia that I had organized at Appalachian State University in Boone, North Carolina, where I first taught. Morgenthau joined Edwin Reischauer, former U.S. ambassador to Japan, to speak in opposition to American involvement in Vietnam. That very day the announcement came of the bombing of Cambodia. When the group reconvened for the evening session, all participants were called upon to respond spontaneously to this most recent event.

[33] H. Morgenthau to R. Niebuhr, August 24, 1970, Reinhold Niebuhr Papers, Container 64, Library of Congress.

[34] R. Niebuhr to H. Morgenthau, August 27, 1970, Hans Morgenthau Papers, Container 44, Library of Congress.

[35] H. Morgenthau to R. Niebuhr, March 17, 1971, Hans Morgenthau Papers, Container 44, Library of Congress.

[36] U. M. Niebuhr to H. Morgenthau, January 8, 1972, Reinhold Niebuhr Papers, Container 64, Library of Congress.

related to an adequate understanding of human nature. Borrowing Kenneth Waltz's imagery, Niebuhr and Morgenthau shared the view that the nature of man rather than either the nature of the state or the nature of the international system was the basis for political conflict.[37] They viewed "political man" as self-interested and self-loving, resulting in a conflict-ridden life. They both saw that conflict and power were related and that power manifested itself as a drive for domination. Certainly they shared the view that the national interest and how it worked itself out in relation between nations was the sine qua non of any serious understanding of international politics. Consequently, they knew that any stability in domestic and international politics depended on both a balance of power and an accommodation of conflicting interests. And both Niebuhr and Morgenthau were "realists" in understanding politics as a sphere apart, requiring analyses separate from even though related to other spheres, particularly that of ethics and morality.

In spite of this broad range of agreement, there are important aspects of the Niebuhr–Morgenthau dialogue that reveal differences between Niebuhr's "Christian realism" and the realism of Morgenthau. This chapter does not aim to provide a comprehensive, detailed treatment of either Niebuhr's or Morgenthau's rich analyses of politics. An effort of that magnitude would be monumental, requiring a book-length digression. The aim here is simply to isolate and highlight areas where these two men reveal different accents or depart ways.

Niebuhr and Morgenthau tended to play down the degree and importance of their differences. Certainly this was the case when Niebuhr responded to a question raised during their 1967 discussion on "The Ethics of War and Peace in the Nuclear Age." Niebuhr remarked that "I wouldn't say that the views of Morgenthau and myself are 'somewhat different.' We basically have common ideas with certain peripheral differences."[38] Although Niebuhr's statement was made in the restricted context of a discussion of ethical considerations in war and peace, it is in basic agreement with a position Morgenthau had back in his early days in Chicago when he said that he and Niebuhr had "come out pretty much the same on politics."[39] Yet the source that differentiates them is made strikingly evident in a crucial amendment Morgenthau made to his admission that they "came out pretty much the same on politics." Morgenthau quickly added the qualifier, "but I do not need all his metaphysics to get where we both get."[40] It is precisely Morgenthau's admission that he came to essentially the same place as Niebuhr but without dragging along the religious/metaphysical baggage that

---

[37] See K. Waltz, *Man, the State and War* (New York: Columbia University Press, 1959).

[38] R. Niebuhr, "The ethics of war and peace in the nuclear age" in *War/Peace Report* 7:2 (February, 1967), 3.

[39] M. E. Marty, "The lost worlds of Reinhold Niebuhr," *American Scholar* (Autumn, 1976), p. 569.

[40] Ibid. In an email Professor Marty elaborated on this account by saying, "I was a young prof not in the Morgenthau prestige circle, but my reference was to a faculty-club conversation, where he talked about not needing all the 'metaphysical' stuff Reinie needed to come to a point similar to his own." M. E. Marty to D. F. Rice, April 26, 2005.

suggests something more than merely "peripheral differences" in their respective views of "realism."

The basis for the differences between Niebuhr and Morgenthau is to be found precisely in what Morgenthau chose to label Niebuhr's "metaphysics," namely, with the theological orientation that gave Niebuhr what James Gustafson called a "disposition" to see the world in a certain way. Indeed, virtually all of Niebuhr's disagreements with his realist friends derived from this "disposition" – this theological frame of reference from which Niebuhr drew so consistently and so well. Niebuhr's was a "Christian realism" and it was this version of realism that provided the vantage point from which he found reason to criticize his friend Hans Morgenthau.

What separated Niebuhr from Morgenthau was the way in which Niebuhr applied his view of man's radical freedom to the social and political world. For Niebuhr this radical freedom is the source of both human dignity and human misery. Niebuhr's own formulation of the Pascalian conundrum at the outset of his Gifford Lectures is legendary and defines the parameters for his view of humankind's intractable condition. Niebuhr wrote that

Man has always been his most vexing problem. How shall he think of himself? Every affirmation which he may make about his stature, virtue, or place in the cosmos becomes involved in contradictions when fully analyzed. ... If man insists that he is a child of nature and that he ought not to pretend to be more than the animal which he obviously is, he tacitly admits that he is, at any rate, a curious kind of animal who has both the inclination and the capacity to make such pretensions. If on the other hand he insists upon his unique and distinctive place in nature and points to his rational faculties as proof of his special eminence, there is usually an anxious note in his avowals of uniqueness which betrays his unconscious sense of kinship with the brutes.[41]

On both sides of the issue, Niebuhr's view of the "nature of man" set him apart from the political realists. With respect to the dignity of man, the fact that the self is defined by the law of love stretched the meaning of justice far beyond the bounds of its usual political meaning. With respect to the misery of man, the fact of sin – that the self in its self-love is in violation of the law of love – gave Niebuhr a broader, deeper, and more subtle sense of human propensities for evil than was found in political realists such as Morgenthau. Both realities – human dignity and misery – arising out of the self's freedom, revealed a highly complex and nuanced understanding of the self's creative and destructive capabilities. It is this understanding that had direct bearing on Niebuhr's formulation of political realism. Indeed, his analysis and appreciation of democracy, of domestic politics, and his understanding of what was possible in international politics derived from this theological "disposition."

For Niebuhr, sin was understood essentially as pride, the pride of the spirit that expresses itself in three forms: through power, through knowledge, and through virtue. There is, therefore, the lust for power (so basic to all political

---

[41] R. Niebuhr, *The Nature and Destiny of Man* (London: Nisbet, 1941), vol. I, p. 1.

realists), intellectual pride (a spiritual sublimation of man's pride of power), and moral pride (the pride of self-righteousness). This latter was the most insidious form of pride for Niebuhr because, as the quintessential spiritual form of pride, it finds expression as religious arrogance – "arrogance in the very name of Christ." Such arrogance results in "the worst form of intolerance" – a "religious intolerance, in which the particular interests of the contestants hide behind religious absolutes. The worst form of self-assertion is religious self-assertion in which, under the guise of contrition before God, He is claimed as the exclusive ally of our contingent self."[42]

It was also Niebuhr's view of the Christian view of grace that spared him from the degree of pessimism that one detects in Morgenthau's tragic sense of life. There was, for Niebuhr, a "beyond tragedy" – a perspective of hope, of faith, of love, and of forgiveness that rendered pessimism penultimate rather than ultimate. Given the frustrations of historical existence in general and political life in particular, Niebuhr found that the swing between sentimentality and despair could be avoided only in the serenity and nonchalance that faith allows. This attitude was not, as some have said, a capitulation to cynicism or fatalism. Rather, it was an expression of a trust in God that releases us into a life of responsible action in spite of the failures, contradictions and penultimate tragedy of history. This relationship between divine grace and serenity had an immediate and ongoing role in Niebuhr's political thought that was lacking in other realists. As James Gustafson put it, for Niebuhr the "revelation of God's grace" provided a "stance or basic disposition toward the world" in which "one can be realistic and hopeful at once ... pragmatic without illusions about fulfilling the ultimate good in his relative and temporal efforts."[43] Although this "disposition," rooted in Niebuhr's view of Christian faith, might allow Christians to be ultimately hopeful, Niebuhr's religious viewpoint, as Michael J. Smith put it, would "not attract the skeptically minded."[44] And, of course, the list of the skeptics included the quintessential realist Hans Morgenthau, who, according to Martin Marty, "was the most eloquent among those who could take Niebuhr without his religion."[45]

Curiously enough, however, we find Morgenthau crediting Niebuhr with being our "greatest living political philosopher" precisely because he was a theologian and not simply a statesman, a practical politician, or a professor of political science. The curiosity is that this is not, as it might seem, a contradiction. For the reason Morgenthau made this judgment is not because he was convinced that theology (i.e. "metaphysical beliefs") was crucial for interpreting political man but rather because his theology provided Niebuhr with a

[42] Ibid., pp. 213–14. See his entire discussion of the three forms of pride at pp. 198–216.
[43] J. M. Gustafson, *Christ and the Moral Life* (New York: Harper & Row, 1968), p. 142. Gustafson's section on "Freedom to be realistic and pragmatic" (pp. 137–46) remains one of the best and most succinct treatments of Niebuhr's social ethics.
[44] M. J. Smith, *Realist Thought from Weber to Kissinger*, p. 110.
[45] M. E. Marty, "The lost worlds of Reinhold Niebuhr," p. 569.

perspective "from the outside – *sub specie aeternitatis* – to develop such a political philosophy." Morgenthau was convinced that statesmen, political practitioners, and professors of political science take our institutions for granted without standing back, as it were, and looking afresh. Niebuhr's outside approach allows that fresh perspective. He was willing to grant that Niebuhr's theological travels contributed to his insights into political man, but Morgenthau did not require that journey to arrive at a similar destination. Quite late in his book *Science: Servant or Master?* published in 1972, Morgenthau made the remark that "religion in its proper sense operates on the same functional level as metaphysical philosophy. Both open human consciousness ... to the mysteries within which the empirical world is confined, and both in this respect supplement empirical science." Whatever this might have meant for the sympathy Morgenthau gained for religion as providing a palliative for the harsh realities of life, it did not mean that he changed his understanding of either political man or demanded a reinterpretation of his theory of international politics. Morgenthau never changed his view of having never "needed all [Niebuhr's] metaphysics to get where we both get."

Niebuhr's view of human nature was, of course, theologically grounded. He not only believed that his approach was the best one for adequately interpreting human nature, but that it was also highly relevant to understanding political life. Christian realism, for Niebuhr, was a fundamental reorientation growing out of a reaction against excessive idealism and utopianism – a reorientation that relied in part on Niebuhr's discernment of historical precedents within the Christian tradition. Yet in Niebuhr's hands, as Kenneth Thompson observed, "what emerged was a philosophic position that was uniquely and distinctly his own."[46]

DIVERGENT SHADES OF REALISM

One element that defines realism for realists such as Niebuhr and Morgenthau is their historically based reaction to and rejection of excessive liberal moralism, idealism, and utopianism. This historical context underpins Morgenthau's 1962 tribute to Niebuhr, when he credited Niebuhr with "the rediscovery of Political Man." Morgenthau listed five things he believed were implied in that rediscovery: (1) "the autonomy of the political sphere," (2) "the intellectual dilemma of understanding politics and acting within the political sphere," (3) "the moral dilemma of political action," (4) "the organic relationship between political thought and political action," and (5) "the tragedy which is inherent in the political act."[47]

It was this "rediscovery of Political Man" that allowed Niebuhr to define political realism as the disposition to "take all factors in a political situation, which offer resistance to established norms, into account, particularly the factors

---

[46] K. W. Thompson, *Masters of International Thought*, p. 27.
[47] H. J. Morgenthau, "The influence of Reinhold Niebuhr," p. 99.

of self-interest and power."[48] This disposition led Colm McKeogh to observe that "constraint is thus the core of political realism" – constraints, for example, that with Niebuhr and other realists are "founded on their view of human nature."[49] Niebuhr, as we have seen, shared this starting point with Morgenthau. However, as we noted it was also Niebuhr's view of human nature, framed by the uniquely powerful analyses of his Christian realism, which gave unique shading to his understanding of political realism. The different shadings given to political realism by Niebuhr and Morgenthau can be clearly observed in their respective views of power and national self-interest.

Power

According to Stanley Hoffmann, Morgenthau tied his "sweeping analyses to two masts, the concept of power and the notion of the national interest."[50] Morgenthau had claimed that the very first lesson Niebuhr provided us with was the fact that the all-pervasive "lust for power" persists as "an intrinsic quality of human nature itself," and therefore "cannot be reformed out of existence."[51] Niebuhr knew that the problem of power was an important one and that it had significant bearing on domestic as well as international politics. He had acknowledged that "there has never been a scheme of justice in history which did not have a balance of power at its foundation."[52] As Kenneth Thompson emphatically stated, Niebuhr had "declared war on the most fateful illusion of all, the liberal view of power, according to which power was an archaism, the last remnant of the barbaric pre-industrialized, feudal age."[53]

Niebuhr certainly acknowledged that the lust for power was a "universal" element in human affairs. But he did not view it as definitive of what human nature is like. It was because of such interpretive tendencies that Niebuhr rejected those he viewed as too pessimistic – as "cynical" realists. Niebuhr indicted realists such as Thomas Hobbes and Martin Luther for not being sufficiently realistic – for being so fearful of anarchy that they had not been realistic enough to see the dangers of tyranny. As forceful a critic of idealism as Niebuhr was, he nonetheless found the voices of historic realists far too cynical about human nature. Even Niebuhr's beloved St. Augustine, whom he heartily

---

[48] R. Niebuhr, *Christian Realism and Political Problems* (New York: Charles Scribner's Sons, 1953), p. 119. Niebuhr goes on to say that "definitions of 'realists' and 'idealists' emphasize dispositions, rather than doctrines; and they are therefore bound to be inexact. It must remain a matter of opinion whether or not a man takes adequate account of all the various factors and forces in a social situation." Ibid., p. 120.

[49] C. McKeogh, *The Political Realism of Reinhold Niebuhr: A Pragmatic Approach to Just War* (Basingstoke, UK: St. Martin's Press, 1997), p. 12.

[50] S. Hoffmann, "An American Social Science: International Relations," *Daedalus* I (Summer, 1977), 44.

[51] H. Morgenthau, "The influence of Reinhold Niebuhr," p. 100.

[52] R. Niebuhr, *Christianity and Power Politics* (New York: Charles Scribner's Sons, 1952), p. 104.

[53] K. W. Thompson, *Political Realism and the Crisis of World Politics*, p. 24.

recommended to his realist friends, came in for criticism here. Niebuhr insisted that "an analysis of Augustine's and Luther's dualism and consequent 'realism' affecting political communities must yield the negative conclusion that the realism was too consistent to give a true picture of either human nature or the human community, even before the advent of free governments, and was certainly irrelevant to modern democratic governments."[54]

Niebuhr spared his friend Hans Morgenthau the indictment of being a "cynical realist," but he did believe that Morgenthau's mistake was in misunderstanding the relation between the will to power and the impulse of love in human nature. Morgenthau saw power and love to be "organically connected, growing as they do from the same root of loneliness." Thus it is the "striving to escape loneliness [that] gives the impetus to both the lust for power and the longing for love."[55] Niebuhr saw the relationship between the lust for power and love quite differently and thought that "in Morgenthau's realistic rigor to isolate the dominant motives of the nations [the lust for power] from the pretended higher one [the hypocritical pretense of a deeper loyalty to higher values], he may have made the mistake of obscuring the important residual creative factor in human rationality."[56]

Michael Smith rightly pointed out that whereas "for Morgenthau the will-to-power is the starting point of analysis; for Niebuhr it is an aspect of the sin of pride which itself is part of a larger analysis."[57] Unlike Morgenthau, Niebuhr did not view the "lust for power" as a "law of nature." Moreover, Niebuhr cast the "lust for power" in a broader and deeper channel than did Morgenthau. While Niebuhr held that what he called the "will to power" was an undeniable fact of experience as well as a perennial feature in human affairs, he discerned "spiritual" depths in the will to power that extended its meaning. Niebuhr saw the "will to power" as a spiritualized modification of the mere survival impulse. Power as such in the human being is a neutral phenomenon that is paradoxically subject to a double transmutation. On the one hand, it becomes the will to "self-realization" whose highest form is "self-giving." Following the biblical paradox that "he who gains himself shall lose himself, while he who loses himself shall gain himself," Niebuhr insisted that the law of love (*agape*) means that only in self-giving can the self achieve fulfillment. It is love that defines our "essential nature" for Niebuhr and not the "lust for power" or unbridled self-interest. On the other hand, because the self is anxious in its finite freedom, the self, through the sinful pride of self-love, violates the law of love. Consequently, the power that inheres in the survival impulse is spiritually transmuted into the will to power understood as the desire for power and glory.[58]

---

[54] R. Niebuhr, *Man's Nature and His Communities*, p. 46.
[55] H. Morgenthau, "Love and power," *Commentary* (March, 1962), 247.
[56] R. Niebuhr, *Man's Nature and His Communities*, 75.
[57] M. J. Smith, *Realist Thought from Weber to Kissinger*, pp. 136–7.
[58] This outline of Niebuhr's position comes from *Children of Light and Children of Darkness* (New York: Charles Scribner's Sons, 1944), pp. 19–20.

Undoubtedly, self-love – in which the self falsely makes itself the center of existence – plays havoc in all areas of life and constantly threatens the very fabric of community. But for Niebuhr, egotism, or self-love, "is 'natural' [only] in the sense that it is universal, it is not natural in the sense that it does not conform to man's nature who transcends himself indeterminately and can only have God rather than self for its end."[59] The imperialistic impulse in every person that St. Augustine knew so well, though all-pervasive, is a corruption of human nature and not, as Michael Smith claimed is the case with Morgenthau, central to self-identity. Niebuhr, as we noted above, thought that because Morgenthau viewed the self as inevitably turning to power to achieve what it found unachievable through love, he might well have underplayed a residual creative element in human rationality. Indeed, Niebuhr's aphorism that "man's capacity for justice makes democracy possible; but man's inclination to injustice makes democracy necessary"[60] captures the degree to which this residual creativity plays a role in Niebuhr's understanding. Because Morgenthau saw the desire for power arising from the "logic of competition" and from a universal *animus dominandi* that overwhelms the former, he gave us, in Smith's words, "a form of original sin which, unlike Niebuhr's, is both necessary and inevitable."[61]

Niebuhr's concern with power in the political arena – even in the international scene – was driven by his interest in issues of justice and injustice. For Morgenthau, the struggle for power was all-pervasive and inescapable, setting the stage for seeming endless conflict between nations. Niebuhr saw the struggle for power, though constant, as open to some modification and occasionally able to be transcended in the quest for justice. Justice, for Niebuhr, was both the adjudication of conflicts of self-interest by the balancing of power and a hoped-for approximation of love in the fabric of social life. Because it is the law of love that defines the self for Niebuhr, it is love that enables the self to discern and meet the needs of others in ways that the discriminate adjustments of interests and balancing of power against power cannot know or achieve. Niebuhr understood justice as love making its way in the world, prompting "us to seek ever wider and more inclusive structures of justice."

Niebuhr's focus was primarily on the quest for justice within a stable enough community to make that quest for justice viable. Morgenthau's focus was on the international scene, where anarchy usually reigns between states. However difficult it might be, Niebuhr felt that the residual creative element in human rationality was evident even in the domain of international life. Given his conviction that the power impulse was a corruption of love, Niebuhr insisted that even the "strength of the modern nation's self-regard and power impulse has not eliminated the residual capacity of peoples and nations for loyalty to values, cultures, and civilizations of wider and higher scope than the interests of the nation." Being ever the realist himself, however, Niebuhr insisted that "the

[59] R. Niebuhr, *Christian Realism and Political Problems*, pp. 129–30.
[60] R. Niebuhr, *Children of Light and Children of Darkness*, p. xiii.
[61] M. J. Smith, *Realist Thought from Weber to Kissinger*, p. 135.

proportionate strength of the 'lower' and the 'higher' motives and ends is seriously altered in collective morality." He fully realized that "the power impulse of the nation is, in fact, so strong, and its sense of a higher loyalty so weak, that only an irrelevant idealism would speculate about the possibility of the nation subordinating its national interest to that of an overarching culture." What Niebuhr was interested in was that realists such as Morgenthau acknowledge "the possibility that even a residual loyalty to values, transcending national existence, may change radically the nation's conception of the breadth and quality of its 'national interest.'"[62]

National Interest

The theological basis for Niebuhr's analysis of power also led to key differences with Morgenthau over the nature and place of self-interest in the life of nations. Niebuhr recognized the relevance national interest has for policy decisions in international politics but, as Kenneth Thompson noted, he also "concluded that focusing too narrowly on the national imperative was almost as hazardous as viewing the world through idealistic prisms."[63] In Niebuhr's convictions that love is the law of the self and that self-love is a violation of that law, we find the wellsprings for his critique of the political realist's assessment of self-interest in political affairs. He insisted that in their reaction to extreme idealism some realists go too far in claiming that the nation should only act on its own self-interest. Because "collective self-interest is so consistent," Niebuhr thought it was "superfluous to advise it." His point was that "a consistent self-interest on the part of a nation will work against its interests because it will fail to do justice to the broader and longer interests, which are involved with the interests of other nations."[64]

The problem for Niebuhr was that the way in which Morgenthau stated his analysis of self-interest, and particularly the "national interest," seemed to leave his view bereft of moral substance in spite of Morgenthau's obvious moral concerns. Morgenthau, in his 1962 tribute to Niebuhr, contended that there was an "inescapable discrepancy between the commands of Christian teaching, of Christian ethics, and the requirement of political success," concluding that "it is impossible, if I may put it in somewhat extreme and striking terms, to be a successful politician and a good Christian."[65] After cautioning that Morgenthau might have conceded "too much to the perfectionist versions of Christianity," Niebuhr chided Morgenthau by saying, "I do not think we will sacrifice any value in the 'realist' approach to the political order, of which Morgenthau is such an eminent and acknowledged exponent, and to which I am personally deeply

[62] R. Niebuhr, *Man's Nature and His Communities*, p. 77.
[63] K. W. Thompson, "Niebuhr and the foreign policy realists" in D. F. Rice (ed.), *Reinhold Niebuhr Revisited: Engagements with an American Original*, p. 140.
[64] R. Niebuhr, *Christian Realism and Political Problems*, p. 136.
[65] H. Morgenthau, "The influence of Reinhold Niebuhr," p. 102.

indebted, if we define the moral ambiguity of the political realm in terms which do not rob it of moral content."[66]

Niebuhr, in effect, saw the corrective for such extreme realism resting with "the Augustinian formula for the leavening of a higher upon a lower loyalty or love" – as being "effective in preventing the lower loyalty from involving itself in self-defeat."[67] He was convinced that viewing self-interest devoid of moral content inclined a nation to define its interests too narrowly, thus sacrificing those mutual interests it has with other nations. Niebuhr's theological approach, as Gordon Harland noted, aimed at "showing how the Christian understanding could widen the vision of realists and thus provide a sounder and more humane basis for American policy."[68] In his relationships with his fellow realists, Niebuhr was more concerned with stressing the need to find areas where values transcending self-interest intersect than with the national interest itself. He felt very strongly that the responsible view "must know the power of self-interest in human society without giving it moral justification."[69] Niebuhr was adamant in his claim that "realism becomes morally cynical or nihilistic when it assumes that the universal characteristic in human behavior must also be regarded as normative."[70] He was convinced that "a preoccupation with our own interests must lead to an illegitimate indifference toward the interests of others, even when modesty prompts the preoccupation." Niebuhr insisted that egotism was not the cure for pretentious idealism. Rather, the cure lies in "a concern for both the self and the other in which the self, whether individual or collective, preserves a "decent" respect for the opinions of mankind derived from a modest awareness of the limits of its own knowledge and power."[71]

What Niebuhr wanted was for Morgenthau to entertain the question of whether there is "anything in the anatomy of man, as a 'rational' and 'moral' creature, which prompts his embarrassment about the consistent self-regard of his parochial community and the consequent hypocrisy of claiming a higher motive than the obvious one."[72] He knew that Morgenthau sometimes had suggested that nations possess loyalties and values beyond their own interest, but he knew also that Morgenthau considered appeals to such loyalties and values as fraudulent and any invocation "of moral principles for the support of national policies . . . always and of necessity a pretense."[73]

[66] R. Niebuhr, "The response of Reinhold Niebuhr" in H. R. Landon (ed.), *Reinhold Niebuhr*, pp. 121–2.
[67] R. Niebuhr, *Christian Realism and Political Problems*, p. 136.
[68] G. Harland, "The theological foundations of Reinhold Niebuhr's social thought" in G. A. Gaudin and D. J. Hall (eds.), *Reinhold Niebuhr: 1892–1971: A Centenary Appraisal* (Atlanta, GA: Scholars Press, 1994), p. 118.
[69] R. Niebuhr, *The Children of Light and the Children of Darkness*, p. 41.
[70] R. Niebuhr, *Christian Realism and Political Problems*, p. 130.
[71] R. Niebuhr, *The Irony of American History*, p. 148.
[72] R. Niebuhr, *Man's Nature and His Communities*, p. 73.
[73] H. Morgenthau, "National interest and moral principles in foreign policy: The primacy of the national interest," *American Scholar*, 18 (Spring, 1949), 207.

As for Morgenthau, in his review of Niebuhr's *Structure of Nations and Empires*, he had credited Niebuhr with having lain "bare the mechanisms by which morality clothes politics with underserved dignity and politics transforms morality into an instrument of political domination."[74] Niebuhr had written extensively on such pretense and largely agreed with Morgenthau. Yet he had a slightly different take on the matter, stating that while "on the whole I think [Morgenthau] rightly [maintained] that moral reasons given by nations for their actions are pretenses to justify their national self-interests," the point Niebuhr wanted to make "is that people, even nations, engage in this pretense because they are moral. This pretense is not engaged in to aid the ally or defeat the enemy, but to convince the people themselves that they are behaving morally."[75]

Because Morgenthau was so focused on the pretension and hypocrisy of nations' hiding their self-interests behind the mask of some "higher virtue," he strongly advised that we emphasize only the national interest in the conduct of foreign affairs. This exchange between Niebuhr and Morgenthau appeared in the pages of *The War/Peace Report* and was based on a gathering in New York at which Niebuhr was too ill to attend.[76] Niebuhr, while having acknowledged self-interest in all political action, and knowing nations never "sacrifice themselves for other nations," wanted nonetheless to insist (and get Morgenthau to agree) that "the Marshall Plan, which might be defined as an act of wise self-interest, really [did] include interests other than our own."[77] It is the wisdom of statesmanship, he urged, to use self-interest for moral ends, both domestically and internationally. Morgenthau remained a bit more suspicious, noting that in speaking "of nations and moral acts of nations" we are talking about "an abstraction." Moreover, while moral considerations obviously entered into the president's actions, whenever "we are dealing with a principle of abstract justice on the one hand and a consideration of national self-interest on the other, the latter wins over the former every time."[78]

In essence, Niebuhr considered Morgenthau's appeal to realism as having missed something important. He believed that in too narrowly spotlighting the dominant motive of the nations, the "important residual creative factor in human rationality" was overlooked. In arguing for the superiority of Augustine as a "more reliable guide than any known thinker," Niebuhr insisted that while

Modern "realists" know the power of collective self-interest as Augustine did ... they do not understand its blindness. Modern pragmatists understood the irrelevance of fixed and

---

[74] H. Morgenthau, "The intellectual and moral dilemma of history," 7.
[75] R. Niebuhr, "The ethics of war and peace in the nuclear age," 5.
[76] "The ethics of war and peace in the nuclear age," 2. The editor tells us that "the talk was held around Rev. Niebuhr's desk in his apartment on Riverside Drive in Manhattan, over-looking the beautiful but then very cold Hudson River. The discussion took place in two sessions, on Dec. 16 and 29, since Rev. Niebuhr is under doctor's orders to limit his exertions. This will explain why it may seem to the reader that Prof Morgenthau fell silent for a while; WPR editor Richard Hudson and the Rev. Niebuhr began the second session a few minutes before Morgenthau's arrival."
[77] Ibid., 3.
[78] Ibid.

detailed norms; but they do not understand that love must take the place as the final norm of these inadequate norms. Modern liberal Christians know that love is the final norm for man; but they fall into sentimentality because they fail to measure the power and persistence of self-love.[79]

Niebuhr's unwavering conviction was that the norms of justice, which can and must be instruments of the love commandment, are relevant to international as well as domestic life. Indeed, he believed that a Christian realism does not sacrifice anything in the way of a "realist" approach to the political order. Rather, it deepens and enhances such an approach.

INTERNATIONAL POLITICS AND WORLD VISION

For the political realists, the problems of power and national interest in the international scene were central to any serious discussion of the potential for world organization. Kenneth Thompson wrote that "perhaps Niebuhr's chief contribution to the realm of international politics can be found in his bold and fearless attacks on the most widely held illusions, such as the misconception that institutions in and of themselves would reshape international society."[80] According to Ronald Stone, when Niebuhr was in attendance at sessions of Kennan's Policy Planning Staff, Niebuhr "played the role of critic when world government proposals were discussed. His position was to promote all possible international cooperation and organization, but not to allow utopian visions of world government to interfere with the complicated task of securing the precarious order and justice that were available within the existing system."[81]

Living only up to the Cold War era, Niebuhr held out little expectation for the establishment of a viable transnational organization that could effectively maintain world order. Although he valued the United Nations, he did not, according to Kenneth Thompson, see it "as the source of much hope, although he was more optimistic about its economic and social activities than its role as a peace and security agency in the Cold War."[82] Even technological achievements that one might think helpful in this regard had actually exacerbated the perennial problems in achieving a supranational organization by having "established a rudimentary world community" but not having "integrated it organically, morally or politically."[83] Most important of all, the difficulties facing international cooperation for Niebuhr were accentuated by his convictions about the Cold War – namely, that both the revolutionary stage and ideological fervor of Russian communism had a long way to go before they would dissipate and

[79] R. Niebuhr, *Christian Realism and Political Problems*, p. 146.
[80] K. W. Thompson, *Political Realism and the Crisis of World Politics*, p. 24.
[81] R. H. Stone, *Professor Reinhold Niebuhr: A Mentor to the Twentieth Century* (Louisville, KY: Westminster/John Knox Press, 1992), p. 158.
[82] K. W. Thompson, "Postscript" in C. W. Kegley, *Reinhold Niebuhr*, p. 251.
[83] R. Niebuhr, "The illusion of world government" in *Christian Realism and Political Problems*, p. 15. This article first appeared in the April, 1949, issue of *Foreign Affairs*.

allow for genuine accommodation between Russia and the West. At the most, he felt that if each side in the bipolar balance of power (between the United States and the Soviet Union) could temper the ideological fanaticism that demonized the opposition and prevented compromise and cooperation, the chances for international stability could improve.

In 1955, he deplored the fact that we now "face the problem of integrating the world community under unanticipated hazards" – Communism's attempt to "organize the whole world upon the basis of its utopian vision" and "the development of atomic weapons."[84] In this situation, Niebuhr reluctantly saw nuclear deterrence as the only viable option for preventing mutual annihilation. Morgenthau had no such confidence in the deterrent policy. Yet while he did believe that the advent of the nuclear age had rendered the traditional nation-state obsolete and that nuclear weaponry had ushered in the "first qualitative change in the history of international relations," Morgenthau found no viable organizational substitute on the immediate horizon. He could only lament that the spiritual longing for a supranational organization, has, in the nuclear age, "been greatly strengthened by the desire innate in all men, for self-preservation."[85]

Both Morgenthau and Niebuhr clearly recognized international politics to be essentially anarchical, however much regulated by mankind's desire for self-preservation. As Niebuhr put it, "beyond the national (and in a few cases the imperial) community lies international chaos, slightly qualified by minimal forms of international cooperation." However, he agreed with Morgenthau in noting that "the problem of overcoming this chaos and of extending the principle of community to world-wide terms has become the most urgent of all the issues which face our epoch."[86] While at the time a clear outcome in World War II was still an open question, Niebuhr was thinking ahead to the postwar world. He much preferred the approach of those he called "historical realists" over that of the "rationalists and idealists" when it came to notions of the feasibility of world government. Having had a long track record of playing down the likelihood of establishing anything like a "world government," Niebuhr consistently attacked a variety of views that espoused just such a possibility. His point was that, as sad as it is to admit, the possibility of achieving a workable world government bore no relation to the desire for or urgent need of one.

Whereas the idealists thought in abstract moral terms and pointed to the pressing need of finding a global solution to world government, the historical realists understood the "perennial problems of politics" that resisted such a simple solution. With respect to the realists whose wisdom he favored,

[84] R. Niebuhr, *The Self and the Dramas of History* (New York: Charles Scribner's Sons, 1955), pp. 203 and 202.

[85] H. Morgenthau, "International relations," *Politics in the Twentieth Century* 1:169, 174. I am indebted here to M. Benjamin Mollov's book *Power and Transcendence: Hans J. Morgenthau and the Jewish Experience* (New York: Lexington Books, 2002), p. 20.

[86] R. Niebuhr, *Children of Light and Children of Darkness*, p. 153.

Niebuhr made a distinction. On the one hand, there were those realists who, wholly cynical as to the likelihood of moving beyond the anarchy of international life, saw a balance of power as the only solution to international chaos. This, for Niebuhr, was no solution at all, but rather at best a holding action – one that was destined to break down and degenerate into future conflicts. On the other hand, there were those he labeled "imperial realists" who at least knew that in order to achieve a workable balance of power there must be an organizational center. Because world government was illusory, this group advocated that a coalition or hegemony of postwar powers assume the mantle. The major flaw here, as Niebuhr saw it, was that such a solution did not take very seriously the problem of global justice and ignored the issue of tyranny in the hegemonic order that was to be achieved via the imperial process.[87] For Niebuhr, it was axiomatic that "the less a community is held together by cohesive forces in the texture of its life the more it must be held together by power." This fact led him "to the dismal conclusion that the international community, lacking these inner cohesive forces, must find its first unity through coercive force to a larger degree than is compatible with the necessities of justice."[88]

Niebuhr, of course, scorned any naïve proposal calling for "a world constitutional convention which would set up the machinery of a global constitutional order and would then call upon the nations to abrogate or abridge their sovereignty in order that this new created universal sovereignty could have unchallenged sway. No such explicit abnegation," he insisted, "has ever taken place in the history of the world."[89] In reaction to the patent absurdity of such a hope, Niebuhr called upon Augustine, who, in the context of Stoic euphoria over the prospect of a cosmopolis in the form of a benign Pax Romana, cautioned that a world community "is fuller of dangers as the greater sea is more dangerous."[90]

The problem went deeper, however. Niebuhr argued that beyond the fact that governments cannot be created by fiat, governments themselves have only "limited efficacy in integrating a community." Communities, as Niebuhr never tired of emphasizing, emerge out of organic factors – meaning by this elements such as geographic boundaries, ethnic homogeneity, common language, unique cultural forces, and some common experience and tradition – namely, a historic process and not an artificial contrivance.[91] He pointed out that communities were not created by government: "The authority of government is not primarily the authority of law nor the authority of force, but the authority of the community itself. Laws are obeyed because the authority of the community accepts them as corresponding, on the whole, to its conception of justice."[92] In their

---

[87] R. Niebuhr, "Plans for world organization," *Christianity and Crisis*, October 19, 1942. Reproduced in D. B. Robertson (ed.), *Love and Justice: Selections from the Shorter Writings of Reinhold Niebuhr* (Philadelphia: Westminster Press, 1957), pp. 206–13.

[88] R. Niebuhr, *The Children of Light and the Children of Darkness*, p. 168.

[89] R. Niebuhr, *Christian Realism and Political Problems*, p. 18.

[90] Ibid., p. 125. Augustine's remark comes in *Civitas Dei* 19:17.

[91] R. Niebuhr, *The Children of Light and the Children of Darkness*, p. 157; see also p. 165.

[92] R. Niebuhr, *Christian Realism and Political Problems*, p. 22.

1967 interview, Morgenthau and Niebuhr were in accord on the point of the organic basis of community. Niebuhr, speaking of the prospects of world government, claimed, "I don't see any immediate solution. ... The difficulty with the constitutional convention idea is that it presupposes that law can create a community. I think it is the other way around – the community creates law." Morgenthau agreed, saying, "I think you are absolutely right in saying that without a social integration capable of exerting pressure toward the creation of legal institutions, we cannot have a local order, a national order, or a world order."[93]

Niebuhr, criticizing Gerhart Niemeyer's *Law Without Force*, wrote that men such as Niemeyer imagine that the reason we "insist upon absolute sovereignty [is] only because we have had a 'natural law' which justified such sovereignty; and that therefore a new definition of international law, which denied the principle of absolute sovereignty of nations, would serve to annul the fact." In thinking that "we lack an international government only because no one has conceived a proper blueprint of it," these "pure constitutionalists" reveal "a touching faith in the power of a formula over the raw stuff of history."[94] Niebuhr pointedly remarked in 1953 that life "is a better unifier than law. Law can only define and perfect what life has established."[95]

In the 1967 interview, Morgenthau, speaking in "theoretical terms," pointed out that "a stable order requires three elements: first, a central power that cannot be challenged by any sub-power within the community; secondly, loyalties that transcend parochial loyalties, and thirdly, a common expectation of justice, which at least will promise all important segments of the population a modicum of satisfaction for their aspirations." Niebuhr replied:

In the history of democracies, there is always sovereign power at the center which operates by the consent of the governed. Now this consent permits the sovereign power to use armed might to quell dissent. I think there is no possibility of getting on the world level a sovereign power that has sufficient consent of the governed from all over the world so that it can use military power to put down dissent. So I would say real world order is probably impossible for decades to come. First there must be integration on all levels.[96]

Niebuhr held out hope that over time expanded loyalties and trusts (increased economic interdependences, fear of mutual annihilation, and perhaps the moral one – that enlightened people perceive some obligation to their fellow human beings beyond the limits of the nation state) would occur. To the extent this occurs, more adequate institutional arrangements would emerge. However, Niebuhr was not sanguine about the overall prospect of such a scenario. Economic interdependence might instead lead to the strong outmaneuvering or outvoting the weak. And the prospect of nuclear annihilation seemed too

---

[93] R. Niebuhr, "The ethics of war and peace in the nuclear age," 6–7.
[94] R. Niebuhr, *The Children of Light and the Children of Darkness*, pp. 163–4.
[95] R. Niebuhr, "Can we organize the world?" *Christianity and Crisis* (February 2, 1953), 1.
[96] R. Niebuhr, "The ethics of war and peace in the nuclear age," 7.

abstract as compared to threats from tangible foes. Finally, for Niebuhr, the "inchoate sense of obligation to the inchoate community of mankind," however, important, "did not have as much immediate political relevance as is sometimes supposed."[97]

Overall, Niebuhr and Morgenthau remained sadly pessimistic as to any realistic hope for a solution to this most pressing problem. Niebuhr's judgment, given in *The War/Peace Report*, was that there could not be a "world peace" without a "world army," and that is unlikely for two reasons: first, because the nations that comprise the United Nations are a long way from integrating their armies, and, second, because there is little prospect that member nations will submit their power to a world government. As Niebuhr viewed it there is simply "no prospect of averting disaster in the next decades through a constitutional convention. A constitutional convention would not solve the problem of order so long as the world itself has not become integrated, as the national community has been integrated."[98] Morgenthau, returning to the view that we are stuck with the nation-state system for the foreseeable future, held out the hope that "the anarchic tendencies of that nation-state system can be mitigated and developed toward world integration by intelligent diplomacy. Common interests can be created and antagonistic interests can be reconciled. All kinds of things can be done to oil the machinery that keeps peace and order among sovereign nations. That is the immediate hope."[99]

ETHICS AND POLITICAL REALISM

Roger Shinn claimed that "the most striking paradox in [Morgenthau's] paradoxical character concerned the place of morality in human life and especially in politics."[100] That Morgenthau concerned himself with moral issues is certainly correct and yet contradicts the dominant view that he was simply a modern-day Hobbsean. In his 1980 memorial to Morgenthau, Kenneth Thompson cites an incident involving the journalist Walter Lippmann. As Thompson recalled it, "At the close of a conference in the 1960s Walter Lippmann turned to Hans Morgenthau and said: 'How curious you are misunderstood. You are the most moral thinker I know.' To that we would add, yes, and forever the example of a courageous and compassionate friend."[101]

However, there is an element of confusion with respect to Morgenthau's view of ethics and its place in politics. In his book *In Defense of the National Interest*, Morgenthau rather stridently claimed, "The United States flatters itself that in its

[97] See R. Niebuhr's discussion in *The Children of Light and the Children of Darkness*, pp. 26–31.
[98] R. Niebuhr, "The ethics of war and peace in the nuclear age," 6.
[99] Ibid., 7.
[100] R. L. Shinn, "The continuing conversation between Hans Morgenthau and Reinhold Niebuhr" in G. O. Mazur (ed.), *One Hundred Year Commemoration to the Life of Hans Morgenthau: 1904–2004*, p. 65.
[101] K. W. Thompson, "Hans J. Morgenthau (1904–1980)," *Worldview* (September 1, 1980), 17.

dealing with other countries it seeks no selfish advantage but is inspired by universal moral principles."[102] Over his career he had continually ridiculed the pretentiousness of nations, yet, ironically, later came to see America in highly moral terms. In 1970, Shinn, after dealing with Morgenthau's having come to view America as being a "moral example" for the world, posed the question: "What I must ask is whether his famed realism does not require some criticism of a romanticized conception of America's origins."[103] This Wilsonian turn seemed out of character for Morgenthau who was not only rightly suspicious of all national pretensions but also knew extremely well how prone America was to seeing itself with a moral halo. Shinn went on to say: "What might not have been expected is the intimate connection [Morgenthau] draws between American identity and moral purpose, a connection so close that one might ask whether Morgenthau the realist may not have some unsettling criticisms to make of Morgenthau the idealist."[104]

Aside from this peculiar and uncharacteristic nod to American virtue, it is quite true that Morgenthau was never without a moral compass in seeking always to relate morality and politics. We find it in his very first major American publication he called for a renewal of "those intellectual and moral faculties of man to which alone the problems of the social world will yield."[105] Morgenthau's biographer Christoph Frei obviously agreed when he maintained that Morgenthau

never was nor could he ever be solely a realist. Such was his nature that two sides were always present: the lucid, dispassionate observer of reality and the deeply passionate moralist. Which side of his nature was more strongly manifested at any given time depended largely on his surroundings. "I might have become a great idealist if I had lived in a realistic environment," he wrote many years later without a trace of irony. Fate, however, had cast him adrift in America – in an intellectual environment where the lessons of the realist were bound to create a greater stir than his basic liberal values.[106]

No doubt because of Morgenthau's having lived as a realist in the highly idealistic United States, his critics, as Kenneth Thompson put it, "overlooked Morgenthau's early emphasis on the limitations and proper use of power, its integral relations to natural purpose and the constraints of national interest. They also overlooked his extended analysis of international morality and the role of ethics, mores, and laws."[107]

---

[102] H. Morgenthau, *In Defense of the National Interest* (New York: Alfred Knopf, 1951), p. 93.
[103] R. L. Shinn, "Hans Morgenthau: Realist and moralist," *Worldview* 13:1 (January, 1970), 12.
[104] Ibid., 11.
[105] H. Morgenthau, *Scientific Man Versus Power Politics*, p. vi.
[106] C. Frei, *Hans J. Morgenthau: An Intellectual Biography*, p. 177. The Morgenthau quote comes from his manuscript "The realist and the idealist views of international relations: A realist's interpretation," lecture at the U.S. Army War College at Carlisle Barracks, PA, September 28, 1959, HJM-B 170, 15.
[107] K. W. Thompson, *Masters of International Thought*, p. 85.

In his discussion with Niebuhr, Morgenthau responded to Niebuhr's question, "Has ethics anything whatsoever to do with foreign policy in the practical sense?" by replying, "Of course it has. This is one of the old chestnuts that there are two compartments: one is foreign policy and the other is ethics. Neither I, nor you, nor anybody else can act without considerations of morality. Neither can a statesman. Surely the making of foreign policy, as a human act, is involved with moral decision. This is inevitable because man is a moral being – the statesman, too."[108] Yet in the domain of politics, Morgenthau seemed willing to see good and evil as bearing only on the issue of lesser or greater evils. Politics was always "the ethics of doing evil" in which choices between greater or lesser evils are the essence of ethical consideration. In the context of talking about Christian ethics, he wrote that the moral strategy of the "lesser evil" looks for that particular action at one's disposal "which is likely to do the least violence to the commands of Christian ethics."[109] Morgenthau's famous statement is apropos:

To know with despair that the political act is inevitably evil, and to act, nevertheless, is moral courage. To choose among several expedient actions the least evil one is moral judgment. In the combination of political wisdom, moral courage and moral judgment, man reconciles his political nature with his moral destiny.[110]

So far as "political man" is concerned, the statesman must concern himself "with human nature as it actually is,"[111] and, in doing so, seek out the most effective and least evil of whatever realistic actions are open to him. How the statesman is to being together what is an effective course of action with what is of lesser evil is not spelled out other than to suggest it depends entirely on the wisdom and ability of the particular statesman. In this process, one seeks out the individual with a sense of moral responsibility to so equip himself with the requisite statesmanlike wisdom and ability.

To a large extent, both Morgenthau and George Kennan are left with the skilled, morally inclined statesman and "prudence" as the ethical guidelines for international power politics. When Kennan advanced prudence as the proper disposition for the statesman, he seemed to be restricting it as a procedure for acting strictly within the boundaries of national self-interest – actions in which one is guided by the circumstances one faces, and not by anything extraneous to that. On the other hand, he and Morgenthau both seemed to see prudence in terms fraught with moral considerations. Robert C. Good insisted that "in denying the application of any criteria for directing or judging state behavior other than those derived from state necessity, the realist must end up the cynic. But Kennan and Morgenthau are anything but cynics. Indeed, their views of

---

[108] R. Niebuhr, "The ethics of war and peace in the nuclear age," 4.

[109] H. Morgenthau, "The demands of prudence" in *The Restoration of Politics*, p. 16. This article first appeared in *Worldview*, June, 1960.

[110] H. Morgenthau, *Scientific Man Versus Power Politics*, pp. 202–3.

[111] H. Morgenthau, *Politics Among Nations: The Struggle for Power and Peace*, 4th ed. (New York: Alfred A. Knopf, 1967), p. 4.

policy and international politics are replete with norms that serve to direct and judge interest."[112]

On the matter of "prudence" Niebuhr saw limitation. "Considerations of prudence ... inevitably arrest the impulse toward, and concern for, the life of the other."[113] Yet under the prompting of criticism from Kenneth Thompson, Niebuhr seemed to accept the charge that he came "rather late in arriving at the idea that prudence as well as justice must be a norm of statesmanship."[114] While Niebuhr never denied the importance of prudence in politics, he did think that when seeking to find a meeting point between parochial interests and the general interest in the art of statecraft, prudence alone would lead the statesman to define interest too narrowly. "It is necessary, therefore," Niebuhr wrote, "to draw upon another moral and spiritual resource to widen the conception of interest." And that resource is the "sense of justice" that can "prevent prudence from becoming too prudential in defining [the parochial] interest."[115]

What Roger Shinn found most striking of all was Morgenthau's explicit religious references made in his book *Science: Servant or Master?* published in 1972 – a book dedicated to "the memory of Reinhold Niebuhr" (Niebuhr having died the year before). In this book Morgenthau, confronting the terrible dilemma of nuclear destruction, insisted that nothing less was required than a radical transformation of human nature (something wholly inconsistent with his views of the nature of man). He went on to say that while we humans inevitably suffer, God cannot, and introduced something akin to the Christian view of the suffering God-man who identifies with human suffering. Shinn did not know quite what to make of this but was unwilling to "ascribe it to the musings of an aged man" because Morgenthau claimed that he had written these reflections in the 1930s. Expressing an unfulfilled desire to have conversed with Morgenthau about his use of religious language, Shinn let the matter drop.[116]

Benjamin Mollov has insisted that only recently has "the existence of moral and even spiritual sensitivities among modern political realists" been "accorded greater recognition."[117] The attempt to bring these elements to the fore, specifically in the case of Hans Morgenthau, has been his major objective. Viewing traditional treatments of Morgenthau as "one-dimensional," Mollov argued that this one-dimensional view has ignored "many aspects of his writings

[112] R. C. Good, "National interest and moral theory: The 'debate' among contemporary political realists" in R. Hilsman and R. C. Good (eds.), *Foreign Policy in the Sixties: The Issues and Instruments* (Baltimore: Johns Hopkins University Press, 1965), p. 281.

[113] R. Niebuhr, *The Nature and Destiny of Man* (London: Nisbet, 1943), vol. II, p. 86.

[114] R. Niebuhr, "Reply to interpretation and criticism" in C. W. Kegley, *Reinhold Niebuhr*, p. 512.

[115] R. Niebuhr, "Our moral and spiritual resources for international cooperation," *Social Action* 22 (February, 1956), 18–19.

[116] R. L. Shinn, "The continuing conversation between Hans Morgenthau and Reinhold Niebuhr," pp. 86–7.

[117] M. B. Mollov, *Power and Transcendence: Hans J. Morgenthau and the Jewish Experience* (New York: Lexington Books, 2002), p. 5. Morgenthau's relation to moral issues is at pp. 31–5 and to spirituality at pp. 55–61.

which show deep concern for morality and even transcendent spiritual issues."[118] Mollov employed a typology in which he included among "three pillars of analysis" the contention that the thought of "realist expositors" (including Niebuhr and Morgenthau), "despite 'realist assumptions' concerning conflict and power, [strove] to transcend, either morally, intellectually, or spiritually, the limitations of political life in order to infuse transformation, purpose, or at least meaning into an otherwise bleak social and political landscape."[119] I would certainly agree that there are indisputable moral and spiritual aspects in Morgenthau that Mollov has helped bring into focus. However, Niebuhr moved back and forth between both morality and politics and religion and politics in a way Morgenthau did not.

There is no doubt that Morgenthau believed in moral principles that had universal scope. He insisted that he had "always maintained that the actions of states are subject to universal moral principles."[120] He knew, of course, that political life did not conform to the transcendent moral norms he espoused. However, Morgenthau did not attempt to relate these admittedly abstract formulations to political life in the comprehensive and detailed way Niebuhr's did with his "impossible possibility" – the law of love. Morgenthau's vision remained compartmentalized between the realities of actual life rooted in a thoroughgoing anthropological pessimism and a transcendental realm of "ought" in which the ethical norms are recognized but dismissed as inapplicable to actual life. The best morality can do is to seek out the "lesser evils" in mediating the possible, the "is," and the desirable, the "ought" and attempt to close the gap between the two. The fact that he recognized a tension between the two is both moral and important. Nevertheless, for Morgenthau it is a tension that lingers, devoid of any creative connection.

While bringing to our attention the moral and spiritual side of Hans Morgenthau, Mollov does not make a convincing case that Morgenthau's moral and spiritual concerns significantly altered or were even genuinely related to his assessment of political realities. Morgenthau certainly was not propelled by such concerns to recast or reinterpret his fundamental views of either political man or international politics. Kenneth Thompson and Robert Good seem correct in their assessments: Thompson observing that "in the realm of normative political thought, Niebuhr moved beyond some of the political realists with whom he was otherwise in accord,"[121] and Good insisting that "one difference between these realists and Niebuhr is that while Niebuhr openly acknowledges his transcendental norms, Kennan and Morgenthau tend to conceal them."[122]

---

[118] Ibid., p. 15.

[119] Ibid., p. 5.

[120] H. Morgenthau, "The problem of the national interest," *Politics in the Twentieth Century*, vol. I, p. 106.

[121] K. W. Thompson, "Niebuhr and the foreign policy realists," p. 159.

[122] R. C. Good, "National interest and moral theory: The 'debate' among contemporary political realists," p. 281.

We have seen that Niebuhr's analysis of political reality grew out of a theological position whereas Morgenthau clearly did not. This made Niebuhr a unique moral and political philosopher among his fellow political realists. Niebuhr was, indeed, highly creative in attempting to relate transcendent norms to the proximate norms of politics. His analysis of the absolute norm of love and its corruption into self-love were brought to bear on political realities in a unique way and brought specific issues of justice to the foreground of both national and international politics.

CHAPTER 6

George Kennan (1904–2005)

George Kennan ranks high on the list of America's most respected diplomats – a man whom the historian Arthur Schlesinger Jr. praised as holding "our American democracy to the highest standards of responsible public and historical discourse" and who was "the conscience of the republic."[1] Although Reinhold Niebuhr did not have the close relationship with Kennan that he had with Hans Morgenthau, Niebuhr and Kennan had a sufficient degree and quality of contact to warrant special attention. All three men were political realists who shared an interest in international relations and had a measurable impact on foreign policy thinking in post–World War II America. Although they had little personal contact, Niebuhr and Kennan influenced each other, worked together on occasion, and voiced mutual admiration and respect.

An appropriate starting point for understanding the Niebuhr/Kennan relationship can be found in the familiar story of Kennan's having cited Niebuhr as being the "father of all of us" – referring to Niebuhr's having been a major influence on the group of political realists that included Kennan. Niebuhr biographer Richard W. Fox questioned the veracity of that story.[2] However, Morgenthau's former student, political theorist Kenneth W. Thompson, insisted that when Kennan was called to discuss the memorial tribute to Niebuhr that he was to deliver before the American Academy of Arts and Letters, "he used the words 'Niebuhr is the father of us all.'"[3]

---

[1] A. Schlesinger to G. Kennan, February 20, 1999. George F. Kennan Papers, Box 43 Folder 10, Seeley G. Mudd Manuscript Library, Department of Rare Books and Special Collections, Princeton University Library. Henceforth referred to as "George F. Kennan Papers," Princeton, NJ.

[2] See R. W. Fox, *Reinhold Niebuhr: A Biography* (Ithaca, NY: Cornell University Press, 1996), p. 238.

[3] K. W. Thompson, "Niebuhr and the foreign policy realists" in D. F. Rice (ed.), *Reinhold Niebuhr Revisited: Engagements with an American Original*, p. 139.

FIG. 6 Kennan
Courtesy of the Library of Congress

In the opening section of that memorial tribute given on December 10, 1971 (a draft of which Kennan sent to Thompson to look over),[4] Kennan spoke in a manner that gave credibility to Thompson's view of the story. Kennan wrote that "it is not without reason that I should be asked to speak to [Niebuhr's] memory today. For I regarded him during his lifetime, and continue to do so, as the greatest of my own teachers – as the man whose thought and example have exerted the greatest influence on my own view of life; and it is not unjust that a pupil conscious of such a debt should be asked to speak to the qualities of his teacher."[5] Or as he

[4] In his letter to Kenneth Thompson, Kennan wrote: "On December 10 I am to read, at the annual meeting of the American Academy of Arts and Letters, a tribute to Reinhold Niebuhr. It will be published later in the Proceedings of the Academy. I have drafted a statement for this purpose and enclose a copy. Knowing how close you were to Niebuhr, I would be grateful if you would look it over, tell me if you see any inaccuracies, and let me have any other critical comments that may occur to you." Kennan to Thompson, November 29, 1971. George F. Kennan Papers, Box 43, Folder 10, Princeton, NJ. Thompson wrote back thanking Kennan for having given him "the opportunity to read your tribute to Reinhold Niebuhr. It is superb. You have captured what was essential and at the heart of Niebuhr's philosophy, and examined both what he was and was not. ... I think this is an outstanding tatement, and I feel that RN would have been moved and touched. It is striking that someone both you and I saw only a few times could have had so deep and profound an effect." Thompson to Kennan, December 2, 1972. Ibid.

[5] G. Kennan, "Tribute to the Rev. Reinhold Niebuhr" (December 10, 1971), 1. George F. Kennan Papers, Box 43, Folder 10, Princeton, NJ. A copy of this tribute published by the American

phrased it in the fragmentary notes that he wrote as he was organizing his speech: "On talking about this man, I am talking about the man whom I regard as the greatest of my own teachers – the man who taught me more fundamental, more basic things than any man I know."[6] Kennan, twelve years younger than Niebuhr, wrote a very personal letter to the older man in 1966 saying, "I am not sure whether you know how greatly indebted I feel myself to you for all that I have learned from you. I don't think I ever learned from anyone things more important to the understanding of our predicament, as individuals and as a society, than those that I have learned, so to speak, at your feet."[7]

Niebuhr, in return, considered Kennan to be "one of most eminent specialists in foreign policy."[8] Voicing Niebuhr's feelings toward Kennan in a letter written to Kennan soon after Niebuhr's death in 1971, Ursula Niebuhr wrote Kennan: "I must tell you that Reinhold's enormous respect for you and your knowledge was combined with very warm personal regard for you." She then reported that after "a delightful evening" in Kennan's house on Cleveland Circle, Reinhold "said to me 'There is no one I feel more compatible with,' and he echoed this several times."[9]

Richard Fox claimed that "it was Niebuhr's philosophical perspective that [Kennan] found personally attractive."[10] Kenneth Thompson saw this "philosophical perspective" in terms of Niebuhr's having given shape to "an intellectual tradition that Kennan and others have continued."[11] That "intellectual tradition" involved a firm realism about human nature and political power that Niebuhr set over against the prevailing naïve idealism and inordinate optimism in both America's religious and secular thought. In addition, Richard L. Russell remarked that "the similarity of Kennan's views with those of Niebuhr is too striking to be a coincidence."[12]

Kennan valued "the power and consistency and the immense moral earnestness of [Niebuhr's] thought," and he claimed that his "greatest contribution was made in a quality that I can describe only as that of a religious philosopher and spiritual anthropologist." By that, Kennan meant that Niebuhr was "a profound student ... of the moral nature, and the moral dilemmas, of the human

Academy of Arts and Sciences as "Reinhold Niebuhr: 1892–1972" can be found in the Reinhold Niebuhr Papers, Box 49 Folder 20, Library of Congress.

[6] G. Kennan, "Fragments on Niebuhr," George F. Kennan Papers, Princeton, NJ.

[7] G. Kennan to R. Niebuhr, April 12, 1966. Reinhold Niebuhr Papers, Box 49 Folder 20, Library of Congress.

[8] R. Niebuhr, *The Irony of American History* (New York: Charles Scribner's Sons, 1952), p. 147.

[9] U. M. Niebuhr to G. Kennan, December 2, 1971. Professional File of Ursula Niebuhr, Reinhold Niebuhr Papers, Box 63 Folder 2.2, Library of Congress.

[10] R. W. Fox, *Reinhold Niebuhr: A Biography* (Ithaca, NY: Cornell University Press, 1996), p. 238.

[11] Quoted in C. W. Brown, *Niebuhr and His Age: Reinhold Niebuhr's Prophetic Role and Legacy* (Harrisburg, PA: Trinity Press International, 2002), p. 243. In note 49 on page 304 Brown wrote: "Kennan's phrase, more often quoted as 'the father of us all,' was circulating by the late 1950s and appears in an article by Thompson in *The Journal of Politics* 20 (August 1958): 447."

[12] R. L. Russell, *George F. Kennan's Strategic Thought: The Making of an American Political Realist* (Westport, CT: Praeger, 1999), p. 24.

individual and human communities."[13] In the fragments he had written out in preparation for his 1971 memorial address, Kennan wrote: "Niebuhr's service was to make men aware of the impossibility for me and societies of divesting themselves entirely from the insidious sins of self-love and pride, and to remind them of the element of corruption introduced by these sins into all human impulses and undertakings."[14] When it came time to deliver his memorial address, he honed his thoughts and wrote:

At the heart of [Niebuhr's] philosophy there lay the uncompromising recognition of the essential ambivalence of man's nature – of the extent, that is, to which all of man's behavior, even his most noble undertakings, even his most exalted flights of rational insight – tended to be corrupted and distorted by the insidious impulses of self-love: vanity, pride, self-congratulation, thirst for admiration and praise, love of power.

Kennan went on the say that Niebuhr rightly recognized evil, not as something external to ourselves, but rather something "internal to ourselves, as something built into our imperfect nature, something not fully eradicable by our own insight or effort, and therefore a real and permanent force in human affairs."[15] He saw that Niebuhr focused on the relevance of the biblical notion of original sin because of his understanding of the tragic aspect of human nature, in spite of later lamenting the use of the biblical language and imagery in our secular age. Kennan also shared Niebuhr's notion of the "nonchalance of faith" – the serenity that allows us to avoid both the illusion of perfectionist expectations and the cynicism and despair in the wake of disillusionments. In a commencement address at Radcliffe College in 1954, Kennan advised that "the first criterion of a healthy spirit is the ability to walk cheerfully and sensibly amid the congenital uncertainties of existence, to recognize as natural the inevitable precariousness of the human condition, to accept this without being disoriented by it, and to live effectively and usefully in its shadow."[16]

In his tribute, Kennan expressed appreciation for "Niebuhr's passionate rejection of all that was extravagant and vainglorious in the pretensions of nations and political movements as well as of individual men." He also valued Niebuhr's rejection of "all utopian and messianic political movement" and other tendencies "which professed to see in the process of popular enlightenment or in the workings of modern science some sort of total redemption of humanity from the miseries and failures that had beset it in the past."[17] As an astute and experienced statesman, Kennan especially prized Niebuhr's judgment that "no statesman ... was capable of foreseeing entirely the historical consequences of

---

[13] G. Kennan, "Tribute to the Rev. Reinhold Niebuhr," 2. Page 80 in the copy in Reinhold Niebuhr Papers.

[14] G. Kennan, "Fragments on Niebuhr," George F. Kennan Papers, Princeton, NJ.

[15] G. Kennan, "Tribute to the Rev. Reinhold Niebuhr," 2–3. Page 80 in the copy in Reinhold Niebuhr Papers.

[16] G. Kennan, "The illusion of security," *The Atlantic* (August, 1954), 34.

[17] G. Kennan, "Tribute to the Rev. Reinhold Niebuhr," 3–4. Pages 81 and 82 in the copy in Reinhold Niebuhr Papers, op. cit.

his acts; and it was because of the tendency of statesmen to ignore this fact, and to claim for their behavior a prescience and a power they did not possess, that the relationship between their proclaimed intentions and their actual achievements was frequently so ironic."[18]

The prominence of Kennan in governmental circles was guaranteed by his having authored two influential documents during the period 1946–7. On February 22, 1946, while serving in Moscow, he sent home a lengthy telegram detailing what became known as the "containment policy." This was soon followed by his famous "X" article, which was published in the July, 1947, issue of *Foreign Affairs*, under the title "The Sources of Soviet Conduct."[19] Kennan claimed that the American people, in accord with President Roosevelt, were mistaken in believing that Joseph Stalin would be amenable to a spirit of cooperation in the post–World War II environment. Kennan insisted that Russian policy, fueled by its Communist ideology, remained as intractable as ever. Yet, given Russia's belief in the inevitability of the triumph of communism, he also judged that it felt no urgency to achieve victory over the West. In light of this, Kennan advocated restraint rather than bellicose actions toward Russia. He also contrasted the Soviet regime with the character of the Russian people who had endured the harsh rule of Russian rulers since Ivan the Terrible and, he believed, would outlast the present government.

On the basis of his assessment, Kennan advised that "the main element of any United States policy toward the Soviet Union must be that of a long-term, patient but firm and vigilant containment of Russian expansive tendencies." Kennan believed that the Soviet leaders would not be conciliatory toward the West, as they needed outside enemies to justify harsh internal control of their people. What the United States ought not to do is force Russian leaders into unnecessary and dangerous belligerence by engaging in "outward histrionics: with threats or blustering or superfluous gestures of outward 'toughness.'" Kennan knew that the Russians wanted to get the United States out of Europe. They wanted to gain control of Germany's industrial areas and to undermine both economic recovery and political confidence throughout Western Europe. At the same time, he saw no real danger of a Soviet military attack on the West. He wanted the United States policymakers to realize that "the Soviet pressure against the free institutions of the western world is something that can be contained by the

---

[18] Ibid. Page 81 in the copy in Reinhold Niebuhr Papers, op. cit.

[19] G. Kennan's "The sources of Soviet conduct" appeared under the authorship cited as "By X" under the title of the article on page one. The article was published in *Foreign Affairs* 25:4 (1947), 566–82. In commenting on a 1973 interview with Kennan, *The New York Times* journalist Arthur Krock stated that "when I read the Mr. 'X' article in *Foreign Affairs*, its similarities with the Kennan paper of 1946 were so striking that I had no doubt of its authorship, a deduction that [Secretary of the Navy James] Forrestal confirmed when I told him of it, a deduction I published as a fact." A. Krock, "Three comments on the 'X' article" in R. W. Tucker and W. Watts (eds.), *Beyond Containment: U.S. Foreign Policy in Transition* (Washington, DC: Potomac Associates, 1973), p. 18.

adroit and vigilant application of counter-force at a series of constantly shifting geographical and political points" corresponding to shifts in Soviet policy.[20]

Kennan was far more prescient than others concerning the prospects for the eventual weakening of Soviet communism. As early as 1947 he observed that "the future of Soviet power may not be by any means as secure as Russian capacity for self-delusion would make it appear to the men of the Kremlin. . . . Soviet society may well contain deficiencies which will eventually weaken its own total potential." For Kennan, this meant that the United States should enter "with reasonable confidence upon a policy of firm containment, designed to confront the Russians with unalterable counter-force at every point where they show signs of encroaching upon the interests of a peaceful and stable world."[21] He wanted a firm but restrained policy of containment in anticipation of an eventual lessening of tensions that would lead to a process of negotiation. However, a policy that Kennan understood in political and economic terms was soon transformed into a predominantly military strategy. He regretted this all his life, and on several occasions he reflected on the impact that his "X" article had made. In his 1983 memoirs, Kennan acknowledged that his "X" article was deficient in clarity, lending itself to misinterpretation – most especially in his failure "to make clear that what I was talking about when I mentioned the containment of Soviet power was not the containment by military means of a military threat, but the political containment of a political threat."[22] In a 1975 interview with CBS commentator Eric Sevareid, Kennan reminded Sevareid he was convinced the Russians were not intent on expanding any farther by force of arms, and that when he "talked about containment, what [he] had in mind was an effort on our part to stiffen the hope, the confidence, of European Nations in themselves, and to persuade them that they didn't need to yield to one great power or another, that they could resume life. We would help them to do it. That was all that was involved." He also told Sevareid that, finding that the "the British and the Benelux people" were focused on the NATO pact, "I was quite surprised. I said, 'Why are you giving your attention to this? We're just getting the Marshall Plan through. For goodness sake, concentrate on your economic recovery. Nobody's going to attack you.' But I found that all of

---

[20] G. Kennan, "The sources of Soviet conduct," *Foreign Affairs* 25:4 (1947), 575–6. In his introduction to the book *Interviews with George F. Kennan*, T. Christopher Jespersen claimed that "even though what [Kennan] wrote did more to crystallize, rather than influence, the growing mood amongst American policy makers, its impact was substantial just the same." He goes on to suggest that the reason policymakers were finally willing to listen to Kennan in 1946–7 was because Truman, after becoming president in April, 1945, "began changing course from Franklin D. Roosevelt . . . in the nation's dealings with the Soviet Union. The wartime cooperation" and other "collaborative" efforts "for postwar engagement and cooperation stressed by FDR, gave way to increasing wariness and even hostility in viewing Soviet actions in Eastern Europe and Iran toward the end of 1945 and into 1946." T. C. Jespersen (ed.), *Interviews with George F. Kennan* (Jackson, MS: University Press of Mississippi, 2002), p. xi.

[21] Ibid., pp. 580–1.

[22] G. Kennan, *Memoirs, 1925–1950* (Boston: Little, Brown, 1967), p. 358.

Western Europe had what the French call 'la nanie d'invasion' – the mania of invasion."[23]

There were few personal contacts between Niebuhr and Kennan. In his memorial address Kennan noted that "I did not know [Niebuhr] really well. I could count on the fingers of one hand, I suppose, the times I have talked with him in anything more than a casual way."[24] There were, however, brief contacts that involved matters of state – contacts that grew out of Niebuhr's increased prominence in political circles after his return from Germany in 1946 as part of the United States Government Commission to Investigate the Occupied Territories. The most significant contact came in 1949 when Niebuhr was invited, along with several other individuals outside of the government, to participate in a planning committee headed by Kennan.

President Truman had appointed General George C. Marshall as Secretary of State, with Marshall taking office on January 21, 1947. On April 29, the day after returning from Russia to the United States, Marshall ordered Under Secretary of State Dean Acheson to organize the Policy Planning Staff. Marshall, disillusioned with the foreign ministers' conference in Moscow, recalled Kennan from his position at the National War College and assigned him to head the State Department group that was officially established on May 7. The task of the Policy Planning Staff was to assess the issue of Europe's near future and provide advice regarding long-range problems facing the United States as it formulated policy in both Europe and Asia. In the aftermath of World War II, the United States had been propelled into the prominent position of leader of the free world. Not wanting America to withdraw from global responsibility as it had done after World War I, Marshall and Kennan sought to forge a way that the U.S. role as a world power could be exercised responsibly.[25]

The urgency was in finding a way to thwart Russia from gaining control over Europe. Kennan, intimately familiar with the Stalinist regime, was convinced that "Russia was unfit as an ally for the United States." He was intent on getting

---

[23] E. Sevareid, "Conversation with George Kennan" in T. C. Jespersen (ed.), *Interviews with George F. Kennan* (Jackson, MS: University Press of Mississippi, 2002), pp. 145–6.

[24] Ibid.

[25] Writing about the Policy Planning Staff in 1983, Kennan maintained that "there was no other place in the [State Department] where papers on such a wide variety of questions were produced, over an extensive span of time, from a single point of view." Indeed, he insisted that "there was no place in the realms of government or of academe that lent itself better to an exercise of this sort than General Marshall's newly created Policy Planning Staff. Other divisions of the State Department, geographic and functional, could express themselves, as a rule, only on subjects that fell within the areas of their respective competencies, and then only within the framework of established general policy. For us in the Planning Staff, the world was our oyster; there was no problem of American foreign policy to which we could not address ourselves – indeed, to which it was not our duty to address ourselves – if we found the problem serious enough and significant enough to warrant the effort. In this respect, our efforts were unique." G. Kennan, "Foreword" to *The State Department Policy Planning Staff Papers: 1947–1949* (New York: Garland Publishing, 1983), p. vii.

policymakers in the United States to understand the situation clearly so that the country might then be able to cope adequately with the range of problems facing the postwar world. The first paper to come out of the Policy Planning Staff in 1947, PPS/1, bore the title "Policy With Respect to American Aid to Western Europe." Eventually leading to what was called the Marshall Plan, the paper dealt with European economic recovery. Kennan, who was essentially the paper's author, emphasized that the core problem was the vulnerability of Europe to despotism in the wake of its devastating economic malady caused by the war. Determination by the United States to undertake dramatic action to reverse this situation was seen as crucial to European hope both as a psychological boost and as assurance that America was actively supportive of their recovery efforts. The fourth paper "was the most complete articulation of the principles behind the Marshall Plan" and "the first to illustrate the kind of planning that seemed to be envisioned in the staff's mandate."[26]

The 1947 Marshall Plan clearly reinforced the view of containment that Kennan had proposed. Niebuhr was in enthusiastic agreement with Kennan's approach. Publishing an editorial in *Christianity and Crisis* in July of that year, Niebuhr saw the Marshall Plan as offering the opportunity to embark "upon a more positive and less military program in Europe" and to brighten "the prospect of European recovery, without materially increasing the prospect of war." Niebuhr considered the Marshall Plan to be "of the greatest moment in present world politics. It did what the Truman doctrine failed to do. It gave western Europe new hope in the possibility of economic recovery, without which military resistance to communism (as envisaged in the Truman plan) is in vain."[27] In the next edition of the journal, he claimed that it had become clear that the Marshall Plan was a postwar turning point insofar as it revealed we were "intent upon strategic" and not merely military problems. Niebuhr ended by suggesting that the United States "offer to help in a comprehensive scheme of European rehabilitation proved a nexus between European and American interests."[28]

The year 1948 began to see a shift of emphasis toward increased military preparedness rather than political and economic solutions to the situation in Europe. The framework of the Marshall Plan that Kennan had so much to do with did not receive final congressional approval until March, 1948. In the meantime, 1948 saw Czechoslovakia recede behind the Iron Curtain and Czech Foreign Minister Jan Masaryk, a strong advocate of Czech nationalism,

---

[26] A. K. Nelson, "Introduction" to *The State Department Planning Staff Papers: 1947–1949*, p. xvi. I have relied on Nelson's account of events involved in this period for my summation.

[27] R. Niebuhr, "Editorial notes," *Christianity and Crisis* (July 21, 1947), 2.

[28] R. Niebuhr, "Editorial notes," *Christianity and Crisis* (August 4, 1947), 2. In a 1955 review of books by former members of the State Department's Policy Planning Staff, Niebuhr focused on the fact that all three – C. B. Marshall, Louis J. Halle, and Dorothy Fosdick – sought "to impress the nation with the limits of power, particularly military power, which even so great a nation as ours must observe. They all counsel patience amidst the tortuous processes of modern history." R. Niebuhr, "Editorial notes," *Christianity and Crisis* (January 10, 1955), 178–9.

died from either assassination or suicide. Then on June 24, the escalating conflict between Russian and the West resulted in the Soviet blockade of all routes into West Berlin – an act to which American and British forces responded with massive airlifts of supplies into the city, forcing the Soviets to suspend its blockade by May, 1949. By June 11, the Senate passed the Vandenberg Resolution, which proposed the outlines of a regional defense pact that eventually led to U.S. participation in a North Atlantic defense alliance. This would eventually result in the ratification of the North Atlantic Treaty in late July, 1949, put into effect on August 24, thus creating NATO.

In 1948, Niebuhr wrote an article in the aftermath of the capitulation of Czechoslovakia and the probable suicide of Masaryk, noting how these events "revealed the relentlessness of the communist will-to-power and the vanity of confidence in so-called 'bridges' between Russia and the West." He saw the tragic consequence in all of this to be that "leaders in Washington were no longer confident that a political and economic program for the containment of communism could be relied upon to stem the communist tide." Niebuhr posed the question as to whether this shift represented "a justified alertness to imminent military peril, or whether we are involved in the stupidity of meeting political peril by military threats." His answer to the question he posed was mixed. On the one hand, Niebuhr acknowledged that "insofar as communist strategy avails itself of both military and political pressure it must be countered by both types of defense." Yet on the other hand – and here he quotes Justice William O. Douglas – if the gloom encircling us by recent events encourages us "to fashion our policy merely in terms of anti-communism – we will end by railing and ranting at the specter of communism but do nothing to eliminate the conditions upon which communism thrives. If we follow that course war will soon appear as the only alternative and this time war could be an Armageddon."[29]

Anna Kasten Nelson claimed that as events shifted attention toward military solutions to Soviet aggression, the Policy Planning Staff paper on "Considerations Affecting the Conclusion of a North Atlantic Security Pact" (PPS/43) gave Kennan the opportunity of going on record against the shift. Realizing that the preponderance of voices within the State Department were moving in the direction of a military alliance, "Kennan recognized that his own views diverged too far to be effective." He nonetheless reminded "the secretary of state that the 'basic Russian intent still runs to the conquest of Western Europe by political means.' A North Atlantic Security Pact would be useful to 'stiffen the self-confidence of the western Europeans.'" However, as Nelson reported, Kennan concluded that there was a definite danger "that the pact will encourage the preoccupation with military affairs rather than economic recovery and the necessity for a political solution to the problems in Europe."[30] Kennan in his

[29] R. Niebuhr, "Amid encircling gloom," *Christianity and Crisis* (April 12, 1948), 41.
[30] A. K. Nelson, "Introduction to volume II," in *The State Department Policy Staff Papers-1948* (New York: Garland Publishing, 1983), p. ix.

November 23, 1949, report to Secretary of State Marshall (PPS/43) strove to make the point that NATO should not be allowed to undermine the need for the unification of Europe and ought not to supersede the Marshall Plan. He warned that "a general pre-occupation with military affairs to the detriment of economic recovery" would cause an economic disaster resulting in a resumption of the political struggle far more dangerous to the security in Western Europe than any likely threat of Soviet military aggression.

Niebuhr found himself in somewhat of a quandary a year later that was expressed in an article published for *Christianity and Crisis* in advance of the Senate's approval of the North Atlantic Pact. On the one hand, he identified NATO as the "capstone of a policy which has been developing ever since we emerged from the Second World War as the world's most powerful nation." It confirmed the fact that the United States, unlike a generation earlier, had finally accepted the idea that "the frontiers of our interests and responsibilities lie far beyond our geographic boundaries." On the other hand, he qualified his approval by entertaining key objections – among which was his recognition of the validity of those who emphasized that the peril of communism was essentially moral and political rather than military and "ought, therefore, be countered primarily by such policies as are incorporated in the European Recovery Program and not by military alliances." Niebuhr concurred with the judgment that "western European nations require assistance in achieving economic recovery more than military help," and that "if they can achieve economic aid and political health, there is little danger of military attack upon them" – a point that Kennan made over and over again.

Niebuhr nonetheless conceded that the military pact was "necessary" largely because "the European nations desire it"[31] – a desire based on their distrust of United States commitments due to our previous isolationist tendencies. He thought that by failing to ratify the pact, America would end up sowing distrust throughout Europe. At the same time, he feared an "undue emphasis upon military cooperation" at the expense of a "fully political alliance" that would "have served the purposes of strengthening the West better." What the situation required, according to Niebuhr, was "a complete political federation of the West" and that "cannot be achieved quickly enough to serve the purpose of allaying present European fears."[32]

Kennan, too, while believing that from a political standpoint European Union was urgently needed subsequent to achieving economic stability, questioned whether union was possible or even desirable in light of current dangers. Given the circumstances in 1949 of a "split Europe, security of western nations and prospects for future progress in integration of various sovereignties," Kennan was reluctantly willing to recommend that America's "position toward projects of European union should rest squarely on continued firm military commitment of United States and United Kingdom within Atlantic Pact framework right up to the

[31] R. Niebuhr, "The North Atlantic Pact," *Christianity and Crisis* (May 30, 1949), 65.
[32] Ibid., 66.

iron curtain."[33] Yet while Niebuhr and Kennan recognized that "the North Atlantic Treaty encouraged freedom by extending a sense of security to Western Europe," they insisted that "military security was not an end it itself, but rather a prop for economic recovery."[34] And while Kennan assumed that a military shield might indeed be necessary, he feared it would likely exceed all rational requirements. In the end, the increasing militarization of the containment policy, brought to a head in 1950 by the NSC-68 document advocating both the program of increased nuclear weapons production and the policy of nuclear "first use," sealed Kennan's departure from governmental service in 1953.

In heading the Policy Planning Staff, Kennan desired "not only to have extensive consultations with officials within the administration but also to bring in distinguished outside consultants to benefit from their perspectives."[35] By 1949, when Niebuhr briefly attended meetings, Kennan's view of containment had lost favor and his overall influence on policy was on the wane.[36] During the time in June when Niebuhr was in attendance, the Staff, according to Michael Hogan, was focused on helping "to launch the State Department's first full-blown effort to hammer out a policy on European unification."[37] Kennan's focus was on devising the best possible federal structure for the noncommunist part of Europe. Historian John Lewis Gaddis reports that it was Niebuhr's recollection that when Kennan prompted his staff to proceed in its deliberations "as if there was no Russian threat" Kennan's suggestion "struck Niebuhr like saying: 'Let us proceed as though there was not sex in the world' – but [it] did at least stimulate discussion."[38]

[33] G. Kennan, "Outline: Study of U.S. stance toward question of European union" (PPS/55) in *The State Department Policy Planning Staff Papers, 1947–1949* (New York: Garland Publishing, 1983), vol. III, p. 99.

[34] A. L. Hamby, *Beyond the New Deal: Harry S. Truman and American Liberalism* (New York: Columbia University Press, 1973), p. 359.

[35] W. D. Miscamble, *George F. Kennan and the Making of American Foreign Policy, 1947–1950* (Princeton, NJ: Princeton University Press, 1992), p. 282.

[36] Steven Rearden has pointed out that "it was against [the] background of unrelenting tensions with the Soviet Union, fiscal restraint, and growing reliance on nuclear weapons that Paul H. Nitze became deputy director of the Policy Planning Staff in the summer of 1949, officially succeeding Kennan as head of the organization on January 1, 1950." By that time Kennan's approach was reversed, and Kennan became increasingly disillusioned, retiring from the foreign service in 1953. Under Nitze's direction, the focus on military containment, at the expense of Kennan's political and economic conception, took ascendancy. Steven L. Rearden, "Paul H. Nitze and NSC 68" in A. K. Nelson (ed.), *The Policy Makers: Shaping American Foreign Policy from 1947 to the Present* (Lanham, MD: Rowman & Littlefield, 2009), p. 7 and p. 9.

[37] M. J. Hogan, *The Marshall Plan: America, Britain, and the Reconstruction of Western Europe, 1947–1952* (Cambridge: Cambridge University Press, 1987), p. 258.

[38] J. L. Gaddis, *George F. Kennan: An American Life* (New York: Penguin, 2011), p. 360. Gaddis' biography of Kennan is superb and thoroughly researched. Several chapters provide a much more detailed and comprehensive view of certain aspects of Kennan's life and thought than are touched upon in my chapter on Niebuhr and Kennan. See chapters 12 ("Mr. X: 1947"), pp. 249–75; 13 ("Policy planner: 1947–1948"), pp. 276–308; 14 ("Policy dissenter: 1948"), pp. 309–36; 15 ("Reprieve: 1949"), pp. 337–70; and 16 ("Disengagement: 1950"), pp. 371–403.

Niebuhr biographer Richard W. Fox reported that in an interview Kennan recalled "that Niebuhr had no discernible impact on the proceedings." Niebuhr confirmed that estimate in a 1969 interview with Ronald Stone when he said: "I was only on an advisory committee of the Policy Planning Staff of the State Department, and didn't play any significant part."[39] Nonetheless, Niebuhr was conversant with the issues involved in the deliberations leading up to the first Policy Planning Staff paper devoted to European problems (PPS/55) dated July 7, 1949 – a paper, according to Anna Nelson, that "represented the culmination of two months of consultation and thought." In PPS/55 on the "Study of U.S. Stance Toward Question of European Union," Kennan had written to the Secretary of State that "the Policy Planning Staff, as you know has spent some time, with the assistance of a number of outside consultants, in the study of the problems connected with projects of further European union." He made clear that "we feel that some form of union is needed in Europe if industrially advanced portions of the continent are to have plausible chance of permanently withstanding pressures from Russia."[40]

Among Kennan's studied opinions – many of which were at odds with those of official American foreign policy – is one that both focused on the "German 'problem.'" In the context of a divided Germany, Kennan sought a way in which, over the long haul, states in Central Europe could move out of the orbit of Soviet control. Above all else, he held "that the aim of United States policy should be a form of continental union that could absorb Germany and also provide a framework for the membership of the Central and Eastern European countries when the time was ripe – a time he recognized as in the distant future."[41] Kennan knew that the prospects for a unified Germany were quixotic, given the fact that countries in Europe were as, or more, afraid of Germany than they were of Russia. What was of immediate concern to Kennan and his group was the fact that they saw "no answer to the German problem within the sovereign-national framework." He felt that that framework would only lead to a "repetition of post-Versailles sequence of development" including increased frustration particularly among German youth, inadequate resources in an ever-crowded national confinement, "escape into extremist ideas; eventual crushing of modern elements by extremists; and finally new attempts at forceful outbreak and domination of the continent." As Kennan saw it, the sole answer was "some form of European union which would give young Germans wider horizon and remove introverted, explosive, neurotic quality of German political thought."[42]

---

[39] R. Niebuhr in R. H. Stone, "An interview with Reinhold Niebuhr," *Christianity and Crisis* (March 17, 1969), 48.

[40] G. Kennan, "Outline: Study of U.S. stance toward question of European union" (PPS/55) in *The State Department Policy Planning Staff Papers, 1947–1949*, vol. III, p. 82 and p. 84.

[41] A. K. Nelson, "Introduction to volume III" in *The State Department Policy Staff Papers-1949*, p. vii.

[42] G. Kennan, "Outline: Study of U.S. stance toward question of European union," p. 85. A decade later in 1958 Kennan reiterated this point of view in "The problem of Eastern and Central Europe," the third chapter in his book *Russia, the Atom and the West* (New York: Harper & Brothers, 1957), pp. 32–49.

Both Niebuhr and Kennan had focused on the German problem as key to the wider arena of Western Europe at the end of World War II. Whatever contribution Niebuhr may or may not have made at the Policy Planning Staff meetings, his views on the German situation preceded and conformed to those Kennan expressed in his July 7, 1949, Staff report. In his article "The Fight for Germany," published in the October, 1946, issue of *Life*, Niebuhr related how a recent trip to Germany had reinforced his belief that "the Russians ... are seeking to extend their power over the whole of Europe." In addition to political firmness, he saw the need for an economic strategy as being "most obvious in the case of Germany, a nation which our policy thus far ... has permitted to become an economic shambles and morass of wholly unnecessary human misery."[43] Niebuhr believed urgent economic help from the West was crucial and appealed to his audience to understand how important it was to back moderate anti-Communist Germans – whether they be Social Democrats or Christian Democrats – whose strength and voice in Germany depended on U.S. support. He sought a way around those military government policies in occupied Germany that opposed economic aid; he called for a reexamination of America's entire position, including its policies on reparations and the Trading with the Enemy Act aimed at opening up ordinary channels of trade between Germany and the West; and he even advocated priming the pump by means of assisting in the reconstruction of German industry. Niebuhr, in effect, was calling for "a policy of strategic firmness and affirmative reconstruction for Western Europe." At the same time he thought this "might well be supplemented by a policy toward the present Russian sphere which recognizes where the limits of our power are, and makes no demands in words that cannot be carried out short of war."[44]

In an article on "Europe, Russia, and America," published a month earlier in *The Nation*, Niebuhr was adamant in insisting that "the effort to keep Russian power in bounds must not be primarily military. The way to save Western Europe is to give it a sound economic basis for a sound political life." In the final analysis, he stressed that "America must recognize that the West will have to develop a positive social strategy and not merely a military and negative one. If western Germany remains an economic desert and Western Europe an economic chaos, communism will spread despite the present unpopularity of Communist parties."[45]

In 1957, Kennan delivered a series of lectures for the BBC while in London in the BBC's ongoing "Reith Lectures" – lectures that later appeared in book form as *Russia, the Atom and the West*. Kennan saw a real danger in the inability of the Soviet Union to accurately assess world realities because of the distorting effect of its Marxist-Leninist ideology. This left Kennan with the "comfortless message" that all "those devices to which the minds of people here in the West

[43] R. Niebuhr, "The fight for Germany," *Life* (October 21, 1946), 66.
[44] Ibid., 70 and 72.
[45] R. Niebuhr, "Europe, Russia, and America," *The Nation* (September 14, 1946), 289.

have most hopefully turned in these recent years: summit meetings, global solutions, coalition diplomacy, the United Nations, disarmament" have proven ineffective. In their place, he was able to suggest "only the unglamorous devices of an informational war of indefinite duration, and a quiet old-fashioned diplomatic attack on certain of the individual political problems that divide us from the Soviet world."[46]

Regarding the "Problem of Eastern and Central Europe," Kennan held that further violent efforts on the part of the people there to achieve independence would either increase, or adjustment to the realities of Soviet domination would occur. The only solution he saw was the removal of the entire area as a potential battleground between the major powers and that hinged on solving the "German problem" – an extremely complex problem that he insisted required the eventual reunification of Germany.

For Kennan, the most immediate and pressing danger was the atomic weapons race – a development that had unfortunately sidelined all major political differences between the United States and the Soviet Union. The nuclear arms race altered everything.[47] While both Kennan and Niebuhr held the view that the policy of nuclear deterrence restrained the likelihood of nuclear war, they knew very well that the stabilizing effect of deterrence was too fragile to last forever. Kennan was amazed "that there are people who still see the escape from [our present danger] in the continued multiplication by us of the destructiveness and speed of delivery of the major atomic weapons." Such people "seem unable to wean themselves from the belief that it is relative changes in the power of these weapons that are going to determine everything."[48] The only solution he saw to this bleak situation was "the possibility of separating geographically the forces of the great nuclear powers, of excluding them as direct factors in the future development of political relationship on the Continent, and of inducing the continental peoples ... to accept a higher level of responsibility for the defense of the Continent than they have recently borne."[49] In the meantime, both Kennan and Niebuhr urged pursuing negotiations toward achieving a reduction of nuclear arms until more permanent political solutions could be found. Both men had read Henry Kissinger's 1957 book *Nuclear Weapons and Foreign Policy* and found its advocacy of a policy of continued reliance on nuclear weapons disturbing. John L. Gaddis found in Kennan's reading notes in his 1958 diary at the time he "was reading Henry Kissinger and Reinhold Niebuhr

---

[46] G. Kennan, *Russia, the Atom and the West* (New York: Harper & Brothers, 1957), pp. 20–1 and p. 30.

[47] Responding to a question posed by Ronald Stone in 1969, Niebuhr claimed that "we've all followed [Kennan] in shifting subtly from the containment of Communism to the partnership of two superpowers for the prevention of nuclear war. This is the change that history has wrought, so that Kennan would be the first one now to disavow any simple containment of Communism." R. Niebuhr in R. H. Stone, "An interview with Reinhold Niebuhr," 48.

[48] G. Kennan, *Russia, the Atom and the West*, p. 51.

[49] Ibid., pp. 60–1.

on nuclear weapons, [that he] found the former unconvincing and the latter prophetic."[50]

Returning to his long-standing dispute over NATO, Kennan sought once again to show the fallacy of seeing the military as the solution to what were essentially political problems demanding political solutions. He deplored those who saw strengthening NATO as a means for unleashing a preventive war; those who, believing war to be inevitable, viewed NATO as a means of assuring survival; and those who saw NATO as being able to cultivate the necessary military strength to guarantee the success of a political settlement. What Kennan wanted was to de-emphasize NATO and return to the original plans and intentions of the European Recovery Program. As Kennan looked back, he saw nothing to invalidate the original concept on which both the Marshall Plan and NATO was based. He saw NATO as only a means to an end and not an end in itself. Its strengthening ought not to be considered a substitute for negotiations. U.S. policies must not be based on the assumption that war is inevitable, that absolute security is possible, or that the military power of NATO or NATO's political entities is the solution to America's problems. Indeed, for Kennan, "NATO must not be strengthened in such a way as to prejudice the chances for an eventual reduction, by peaceful negotiation, of the danger of an all-out war."[51]

In early 1958, when Niebuhr was at Princeton, he corresponded with Kennan after having read Kennan's Reith Lectures in book form. Niebuhr, writing on behalf of several people at the Institute, informed Kennan "how much we all appreciated the breath of fresh air which you brought into the stale atmosphere of the cold war" and cited one of his friends saying "that he had a sense of almost physical relief in reading your words because the urbanity, charity, and circumspection with which you dealt with our contest with the Russians was so clearly in line with what we were all thinking and yet so different from all the stale arguments prompted by the nuclear stalemate."[52]

---

[50] J. L. Gaddis, *George Kennan: An American Life*, p. 543.

[51] G. Kennan, *Russia, the Atom and the West*, p. 94. In a letter written to Hans Morgenthau in 1966, Kennan felt that Morgenthau had over-rated Soviet military strength in Europe. He reminded Morgenthau of his long-standing "differences with the standard assumptions of NATO policy" and wondered "if today, in particular, these assumptions should not be re-examined" in light of the drastic reductions in Soviet forces in Europe since 1957 when he had delivered his Reith Lectures. Given these "tremendous changes: a halving of the forces attributed to the adversary and a doubling of one's own ... I have failed to detect the slightest effect of these changes on official NATO thinking about the problems of conventional defense in Western Europe. This seems to me to confirm what I have long suspected: namely, that NATO calculations about the problem to which the alliance is ostensibly addressed are based not really on any serious examination of the nature or dimensions of the threat itself but rather on the subjective sense of insecurity of the western European peoples, for which careless, sweeping assumptions about Soviet superiority merely serve as a convenient rationalization." Kennan to Hans Morgenthau, September 21, 1966. George F. Kennan Papers, Box 32 Folder 3. Princeton, NJ.

[52] R. Niebuhr to G. Kennan, February 25, 1958. George F. Kennan Papers, Princeton, NJ.

Kennan answered three days later saying that "no opinion about the Reith Lectures could have meant more to me. I never dreamed they would have this impact, and have a tendency, I fear, to cringe with remorse every time I think of them – out of a feeling that no person like myself ought ever to have made so much noise" adding that "your opinion goes far to reassure me that perhaps, on balance, it was not a bad thing that I did what I did."[53]

In the late 1950s, Kennan became involved in Niebuhr's invitation to spend a year at the Princeton Institute for Advanced Study. On December 21, 1956, Niebuhr sent Kennan a copy of a letter he was sending to J. Robert Oppenheimer. Oppenheimer had extended the invitation to Niebuhr and the question was raised concerning the opportune time for Niebuhr to come to Princeton. Because of scheduling issues at Union Theological Seminary, Niebuhr asked if it would be acceptable to take his leave from February, 1958, to February, 1959. His primary concern was whether Kennan would be available during that period. He wrote Oppenheimer: "I would like very much to know whether Mr. Kennan agrees with this new plan. I must say that one of the advantages of it for me would be that I would have a chance to consult him at the latter states of my work."[54] In his letter to Kennan, he thanked him for the interest he had shown in Niebuhr's coming to the institute, adding that he "found advantages in [the delay] because I thought it would give me a chance to confer with you occasionally in the latter part of my work [after you] return from your Professorship at Oxford." In the meantime, Niebuhr expressed the hope that he would have the chance to see Kennan before he left for Oxford in order to get his "guidance on the best plan for my project."[55]

Beginning in late February of that year, Niebuhr began outlining his research plan to Kennan and suggesting a possible meeting. After extended letters sorting out their schedules, Kennan agreed to a meeting with Niebuhr in Princeton in April, prior to his departure for Oxford. Niebuhr had sent Kennan a "sketchy outline" of his proposed study on February 26, 1957. He said he would first "like to study the relationship of the concept of the universal community to particular communities, and the whole history of the West." Second, he hoped to analyze "the concept of natural law" that has been "overwhelmed by the fact of historical contingency" so as to address the question "whether, and in what sense we can speak at all of norms, particularly in the field of international relations." And, third, Niebuhr wanted "to deal with the whole question of power in international relations, and ask why there is such a persistent tendency ... to hide the fact that even the most ideal values of justice and order must deal with power realities."[56] Replying a week later, Kennan said that he had read Niebuhr's letter "with great interest," assuring him that he had

---

[53] G. Kennan to R. Niebuhr, February 28, 1958. Ibid.
[54] R. Niebuhr to J. R. Oppenheimer, December 21, 1956. George F. Kennan Papers, Box 34 Folder 3, Princeton, NJ.
[55] R. Niebuhr to G. Kennan, December 21, 1956. Ibid.
[56] R. Niebuhr to G. Kennan, February 26, 1957. Ibid.

"no doubts whatsoever as to the suitability of the Institute as a place for the pursuit of these inquiries" adding that he "would be very happy to talk [to Niebuhr] about it."[57]

Niebuhr and Kennan continued corresponding during the year Niebuhr was in residence at the Institute and Kennan was at Oxford. In his third week at the Institute Niebuhr informed Kennan, who was then in Oxford, that he felt Kennan's "presence constantly as I live in your office and make use of the services of your very efficient secretary."[58] Kennan replied by saying: "I was delighted to know that you are installed in my room and have Dorothy's help. I do hope that you will find the whole arrangement, with the sight of the quiet field and woods in the distance, as restful and helpful for your purposes as I did for mine."[59]

In the fall of 1958, Niebuhr was at home in New York having to postpone his return to Princeton for a semester's teaching obligation. On September 25, 1958, he wrote Kennan, who had returned to Princeton, that he "was so looking forward to getting your advice and criticisms this fall on the volume on which I have been working and I still hope to get them." Stating that he had completed thirteen chapters, he told Kennan, "I will bring the crucial final three chapters with me when I come to Princeton. They deal with subjects which are beyond my competence and I feel rather squeamish about them. . . . If you should have any chance to look at the chapters that are available I would be deeply appreciative."[60] Kennan had Niebuhr's manuscript in his possession for two weeks. He replied to Niebuhr that, while having time thus far to only read "most of it fleetingly" he did "welcome the opportunity to tell [Niebuhr] with what excitement and what admiration I went through the chapters [he] sent down and what pride that all this should have emanated from our own institutional midst." After that accolade, Kennan added:

There are, as is inevitable in any treatise so wide in focus, questions of organization of material, and at times I thought I detected signs of the author's weariness with his own work which goes with the exposition of any long and complicated body of thought and which I know only too well myself. But all this is secondary. The discussion seems to me replete with insights of power and importance; and the whole will stand, I am sure, as one of the truly great works of American political philosophy.

If there is any way I can help with the ordering and the final editing of the material, it will be a privilege for me to do so.[61]

On December 22, 1959, Niebuhr wrote Kennan expressing the desire on the part of the Editorial Board of *Christianity and Crisis* to have Kennan become a contributing editor. He told Kennan that he believed "our Journal follows a general line in international relations with which you would be in thorough

[57] G. Kennan to R. Niebuhr, March 5, 1957. Ibid.
[58] R. Niebuhr to G. Kennan, February 25, 1958. Ibid.
[59] G. Kennan to R. Niebuhr, February 28, 1958. Ibid.
[60] R. Niebuhr to G. Kennan, September 25, 1958. Ibid.
[61] G. Kennan to R. Niebuhr, September 29, 1958. Ibid.

agreement," and he tried to assure Kennan that "to be a contributing editor does not mean any particular chore but only that we would like to have an article from you whenever you feel prompted to give us such an article."[62] Unfortunately, two weeks later Kennan replied that "with a heavy heart I must tell you that I think I would be doing no one a favor if I attempted to add anything to what now looms up ahead of me as a series of writing commitments monstrous enough to absorb most of my remaining active life. . . . I say this with sadness. How hard it is in life to have to forego the worthwhile things."[63]

In January, 1960, *Foreign Affairs* published Kennan's article "Peaceful Coexistence: A Western View." The term "peaceful coexistence" was being trumpeted by then Soviet Premier Khrushchev. Kennan stressed the duplicity involved in both Khrushchev's insistence that peaceful coexistence had always been a part of Soviet history, and in Soviet unwillingness to be open to actual conditions operating in the West. Pointing out the expansion of Soviet power in Europe by the advance of its armies in 1945, achieved at the expense of the freedom of other peoples it came to occupy, Kennan indicted the Soviets for casting "the question of coexistence . . . in terms which take no account of this situation and which ask us, by implication, either to ignore it or to pretend that it does not exist."[64] He then recited a litany of difficulties that prevent any genuine allowance for "peaceful" coexistence, concluding:

If Moscow is sincere in the quest for peaceful coexistence, and if to this end it is prepared to envisage *general* revision, on both sides, of the attitudes and practices that have produced, or have been produced by, this dangerous state of world affairs known as the cold war, there will then be no lack of people in the countries outside the Communist orbit prepared to lend their influence to this process, and if need be, at considerable cost; for it is not in Russia alone that the extent of the danger is apparent. But if it is conceived in Moscow that the adjustment has all to be made on the Western side, there will be little that anyone on this side of the line can usefully do to advance coexistence beyond its present uncertain status.

Kennan ended his article with the hope that "the pretense of total righteousness" be abandoned, and that we together "admit to a measure of responsibility for the tangled processes of history that have brought the world to its present dangerous state." Only in this way could we "address ourselves at long last, earnestly and without recrimination, to the elimination of the central and most intolerable elements of the danger."[65]

In his December 22, 1959, letter inviting Kennan to join the editorial board of *Christianity and Crisis*, Niebuhr told Kennan "how thrilled I am by your leading article in *Foreign Affairs* on 'Coexistence.'" Niebuhr considered it "so well balanced and yet keeps the future open in a way that many realistic analysts of

[62] R. Niebuhr to G. Kennan, December 22, 1959. Ibid.
[63] G. Kennan to R. Niebuhr, January 6, 1960. Ibid.
[64] G. Kennan, "Peaceful coexistence," *Foreign Affairs* (January, 1960), 178.
[65] Ibid., 190.

the Russian scene do not do. I was very much heartened, inspired and instructed by what you had to say."

Niebuhr wrote Kennan on April 1, 1966, expressing appreciation for three items Kennan had sent him: Kennan's testimony before the Foreign Relations Committee, Marvin Kalb's article about Kennan in *The New York Times*, and *The New Republic*'s supplement on his testimony. It was the turning point in the Vietnam War. Appearing before the Committee chaired by Senator J. William Fulbright of Arkansas on February 10, Kennan contended that "Vietnam is not a region of major military, industrial importance" and, "if we were not already involved as we are today," with "considerations of prestige" to consider, Vietnam "would not, in my opinion, present dangers great enough to justify our direct military intervention." His position was that "our military involvement in Vietnam has to be recognized as unfortunate, as something we would not choose deliberately, if the choice were ours to make all over again today." Kennan urged that "it should be our government's aim to liquidate this involvement just as soon as this can be done without inordinate damage to our own prestige or to the stability of conditions in that area."[66]

Kennan also rejected the notion of the "so-called domino effect," reminding the Committee of the historic distrust that the North Vietnamese had for China. He insisted that only if the U.S. posed a threat to China by pressing too close to that nation's borders would the Chinese enter Vietnam militarily. Kennan further considered the internal situation in Vietnam as being far more a struggle within one country rather than the alleged military invasion of one nation-state by another. Of equal importance for Kennan was the damage the distraction of the Vietnam War was doing to other, more important, U.S. interests. Negative Japanese feeling about American destruction of Asian lives had resulted in both "the sacrifice by us of the confidence and goodwill of the Japanese people" and a reduction of "the prospects generally of peace and stability in East Asia."[67] Meanwhile, ever-fragile hopes of achieving progress on key issues in U.S. relations with the Soviet Union had been severely diminished – issues such as disarmament, restraining the proliferation of nuclear weapons, and the problems of both German and European stability.

Kennan questioned what U.S. policymakers understood as a commitment to the government in South Vietnam. He feared that America's stated obligation was not only to "defend the frontiers of a certain political entity against outside attack" but also included a promise "to assure the internal security of its government in circumstances where that government is unable to assure that security by its own means." Kennan found such a policy bewildering and abhorrent – going far beyond "normal obligations of a military alliance." He was dismayed by the damage being done to America's global image by its use of its immense power against a poor and powerless people of a race different than its own. It was Kennan's view that "our county should not be asked, and should not ask of itself,

---

[66] G. Kennan in "Kennan on Vietnam," *The New Republic Supplement* (February 26, 1966), 20.
[67] Ibid., 21.

to shoulder the main burden of determining the political realities in any other country, and particularly not in one remote from our shores, from our culture, and from the experience of our people. This is not only not our business, but I don't think we can do it successfully."[68] He held firmly to the notion that America's influence in the world was essentially a matter of what it is at home in its own civilization. Kennan appealed to the view of John Quincy Adams who in 1821 stated that "while America stood as 'the well-wisher to the freedom and independence of all, she should be the champion and vindicator only of her own.'"[69]

In Niebuhr's letter thanking him for his remarks before the Foreign Relations Committee, he also informed Kennan of his own critical article "Vietnam and the Imperial Conflict" published in *The New Leader*. Although early on Niebuhr had supported the war, he became increasingly critical of American involvement and of the policies that fueled it. In the article that he recommended to Kennan, Niebuhr argued that the Vietnam War had brought home what he called an awareness of "a triangular imperial conflict" in which China, as well as the U.S. and the USSR, was now involved. Niebuhr used the term "imperial" in a non-traditional sense, referring to those nations "which have enough power to extend their control or even merely influence beyond their boundaries and which profess a supra-national ideology – religious, moral, or economic – that justifies to themselves and their allies the extent of their dominion." While he continued to hope that "a way will be found for us to 'save face,' or more exactly, to prevent the Communist takeover of a small nation, after we have spent so much money and blood trying to prevent this eventuality," Niebuhr's article was primarily concerned with America's need to understand the dynamics of the imperialist and ideological dimensions of the conflict. It was his view that the United States had failed to understand the relationship between Russia and China, the character of Chinese imperialism, the reasons for Ho Chi Minh's reliance on but distrust of China, and, most especially, its own self-righteous dogmas. At this point in 1966, Niebuhr still maintained that America's own "imperial position makes it important not to yield to Vietcong terror and abandon Vietnam."[70]

POINTS OF DIFFERENCE

In Niebuhr's relations with Kennan over the years, certain issues of special interest surfaced that deserve attention: the national interest, morality in politics,

---

[68] Ibid., 22.

[69] Hearings before the Committee on Foreign Relations United States Senate 89th Congress, 2nd session on S.2793, February 10, 1966, 326.

[70] R. Niebuhr, "Vietnam and the imperial conflict," *The New Leader*, June 6, 1966, 15, 17–18. For judgments as to the trajectory of Niebuhr's views on the Vietnam War see: R. H. Stone, *Reinhold Niebuhr: Prophet to Politicians* (Lanham, MD United Press of America, 1981), pp. 191–5; C. C. Brown, *Niebuhr and His Age* (Harrisburg, PA: Trinity Press International, 2002), pp. 233–8; and E. Naveh, *Reinhold Niebuhr and Non-Utopian Liberalism* (Brighton and Portland: Sussex Academic Press, 2002), pp. 151–6. For a broader view of the spectrum of "Niebuhrians" see M. Hulsether, *Building a Protestant Left* (Knoxville, TN: University of Tennessee Press, 1999), pp. 125–34.

elitism in a democracy, and the exportability of democracy. In spite of their broad area of agreement as political realists, Niebuhr and Kennan had their differences.

The National Interest

Niebuhr had questioned the way in which Kennan presented the national interest as America's sole imperative in his highly influential book *American Diplomacy, 1900–1950*. Niebuhr appreciated Kennan's judgment that many of the weaknesses in U.S. foreign policy were a result of America's "legalistic-moralistic" approach. And he certainly understood the legitimate role that "national interest" played in any sovereign nation. Where Niebuhr had his difficulty was with what he saw as an overly narrow and exclusive emphasis on the national interest in Kennan's proposed solution to the problem – a solution he thought bordered on cynicism. Niebuhr wrote:

> Mr. Kennan's solution for our problem is to return to the policy of making the "national interest" the touchstone of our diplomacy. He does not intend to be morally cynical in the advocacy of this course. He believes that a modest awareness that our own interests represent the limit of our competence should prompt such a policy. His theory is that we may know what is good for us but should be less certain that we know what is good for others. This admonition to modesty is valid as far as it goes. Yet his solution is wrong. For egotism is not the proper cure for an abstract and pretentious idealism.[71]

In the context of his agreement on the potency of power and self-interest in the domain of politics, Niebuhr regarded his differences with both Kennan and Hans Morgenthau to be largely peripheral. He knew the central role that power and interest play in the international arena, and he would no doubt have concurred with Kennan's remark that "we will not improve our performance by trying to dress it up as something else."[72] Yet while Niebuhr cited the "obvious fact that nations are 'moral' in the sense of concerning themselves with interests other than their own only insofar as these interests concur with the nation's own interests,"[73] he was the most forceful among his fellow realists that there is a place within the framework of political realism for considering the issue of national morality.

Niebuhr's conviction concerning the place for morality, even in international politics, is illustrated in a conversation with Hans Morgenthau in 1967. He agreed "that the passion of self-regard is so great – greater in the collective self than in the individual self, and even greater in the modern legally autonomous nation." Nonetheless, he pressed for the need to go beyond mere national self-interest by considering that moral considerations are mixed up with, and serve,

---

[71] R. Niebuhr, *Irony of American History*, p. 148.
[72] G. Kennan, *Memoirs, 1925–1950* (Boston: Little, Brown, 1967), p. 494.
[73] R. Niebuhr, "The Democratic elite and American foreign policy" in M. Childs and J. Reston (eds.), *Walter Lippmann and His Times* (New York: Harcourt, Brace, 1959), pp. 178–9.

those very interests. In his conversation with Morgenthau, Niebuhr used as an example "the Marshall Plan, which might be defined as an act of wise self-interest, really included other interests than our own."[74] At the same time Niebuhr recognized that "the persistence of national self-interest" must be taken into consideration in "trying to find the point of concurrence between the national interest and the wider interest."[75]

Niebuhr thought government can best serve self-interest wisely by using self-interest for moral ends. Because the interests of other nations impinge upon our own, it behooves us to widen our horizons by considering the interests of others, thereby avoiding the potentially disastrous result of indifference. Kennan's desire to return to making the "national interest" the cornerstone of U.S. diplomacy was based on his astute observation that the "legalistic-moralistic" approach so prevalent in America often resulted in a pretentious arrogance that ended up regarding others in its own image. For Niebuhr, however, "The cure for a pretentious idealism which claims to know more about the future and about other men than is given mortal man to know, is not egotism. [The proper cure] is a concern for both the self and the other in which the self, whether individual or collective, preserves a 'decent respect for the opinions of mankind,' derived from a modest awareness of the limits of its own knowledge and power."[76]

The core of Niebuhr's criticism, as Kenneth Thompson put it, was that Niebuhr saw national interest "imperiled at one time by the hazard of moral cynicism and at another time by moral pretension and hypocrisy." In the first instance, Niebuhr saw the exclusive focus on the national interest as self-defeating, leading often to such a narrow conception that "the interests and securities, which depend upon common devotion to principles of justice and upon established mutualities in a community of nations, are sacrificed?" Secondly, according to Thompson, Niebuhr saw "nations which insist on the one hand that they cannot act beyond their interest" often end up proclaiming that they were acting, "not out of self-interest but in obedience to higher objectives like 'civilization' or 'justice.'" Certainly, in the case of America, Niebuhr knew that we tend to "claim more for the benevolence of our policies than they deserve and arouse the resentment of peoples already inclined to envy our power and wealth."[77]

Morality in Politics

In a November 1, 1991, letter to the contributors to the Arthur M. Schlesinger Jr. *festschrift* that he was editing, the historian John Patrick Diggins wrote that he

---

[74] R. Niebuhr in "A dialogue on war and peace in the nuclear age with Reinhold Niebuhr and Hans Morgenthau" in *The War/Peace Report* 7:2 (1967), 3.

[75] R. Niebuhr, "Morals and Cold War," *The New Leader* (April 14, 1958), 26.

[76] R. Niebuhr, *The Irony of American History*, p. 148.

[77] K. W. Thompson, "The limits of principle in international politics: Necessity and the new balance of power," *The Journal of Politics* (August, 1958), 447.

had recently attended "a conference at Bard College on the realist tradition in American foreign policy." He went out of his way to make the point of how "encouraging [it was] to witness the high respect in which Niebuhr, Kennan, and Morgenthau are regarded by younger scholars – not the case two decades ago." Diggins informed them that Schlesinger in his keynote speech gave "a marvelous recollection on the three realists, who were, he accurately noted, skeptical of morality in foreign policy yet themselves deeply and sensitive moral human beings."[78]

Schlesinger was pointing out that both Niebuhr and Kennan were moralists who eschewed moralism. Kennan could be quite cynical about the moralistic approach and posturing of so much American foreign policy. Niebuhr, who had written extensively on moralism in politics, heartily agreed. Indeed, he felt that the moralists involved in policymaking – John Foster Dulles being one of Niebuhr's major examples – posed more danger to America than those realists who inclined toward cynicism. Yet it was Niebuhr's "Christian realism" that strove to provide a framework for relating morality and politics. In 1958, as Niebuhr was thanking Kennan for his "excellent statement on the relationship of the Christian ethic to the process of government," he made one suggestion. He wrote:

You rightly emphasize the place where Christian idealism supplements the coercive powers of government. But this does not leave you room for relating Christian insights to our present human predicament, particularly in mitigating the self-righteousness of the Christian nations. We face the ultimate paradox that a valid faith makes for modesty while a conventional faith always makes for self-righteousness.[79]

If Niebuhr had difficulty in relating ethics to international affairs, Kennan, unlike Niebuhr, had no real desire to do so.[80] So far as Kennan was concerned, morality related to individual self-fulfillment and served civic virtue. "Moral principles," he wrote in 1954, "have their place in the heart of the individual and in the shaping of his own conduct, whether as a citizen or as a government

---

[78] J. P. Diggins, letter "To contributors to the Schlesinger Festschrift" (November 1, 1991), George Kennan Papers, Seeley G. Mudd Manuscript Library, Department of Rare Books and Special Collections, Princeton University Library.

[79] R. Niebuhr to G. Kennan, October 15, 1958. George F. Kennan Papers, Princeton, NJ.

[80] In a 1977 letter to Kenneth Thompson, Kennan appended "a few thoughts on the general subject of ethics and foreign policy" for an upcoming colloquium on that subject that Kennan was unable to attend. He saw the governing of human beings as a practical function and not a moral exercise, "made necessary, regrettably, by the need for order in social relationships and for a collective discipline to control the behavior of that large majority of mankind who are too weak and selfish to control their own behavior usefully on the basis of individual judgment and conscience." He deemed that "the attempt of government to pursue moral purposes in foreign policy [was] impossible given that the principle that government serves as agent in a polyglot society made up of an assemblage of people with widely different views, traditions, beliefs and assumptions." Kennan to K. W. Thompson, April 27, 1977. George F. Kennan Papers, Box 47 Folder 13, Princeton, NJ.

official. In this capacity they are essential to the successful functioning of any political society that rests on popular consent."[81] Kennan insisted:

Morality, then, as the channel to individual self-fulfillment – yes. Morality as the foundation of civic virtue and accordingly as a condition precedent to successful democracy – yes. Morality in governmental method, as a matter of conscience and preference on the part of our people – yes. But morality as a general criterion for the determination of the behavior of states and above all as a criterion for measuring and comparing the behavior of different states – no. Here other criteria, sadder, more limited, more practical, must be allowed to prevail.[82]

Writing on the subject of "Morality and Foreign Policy" in 1985, Kennan felt the position he stated in his 1951 book was "brought forward too cryptically and thus invited a wide variety of interpretations not excluding the thesis that I had advocated an amoral, or even immoral, foreign policy for this country."[83] He then set out to clarify his position. Kennan pointed out that in matters of morality and foreign policy we are talking about governments and not individuals or even entire peoples. Government is not a principal but an agent whose "primary obligation is to the *interests* of the national society it represents, not to the moral impulses that individual elements of that society may experience." Those interests include "its military security, the integrity of its political life and the well-being of its people." Arising from the fact of the nation-state and the sovereignty it enjoys, "these needs have no moral quality." Rather, they "are unavoidable necessities of a national existence and therefore not subject to classification as either "good" or "bad." They may be questioned from a detached philosophic point of view. But the government of the sovereign state cannot make such judgments."[84]

Finally, as Kennan saw it, there were "no internationally accepted standards of morality to which the U.S. government could appeal if it wished to act in the name of moral principles," so "when we talk about the application of moral standards to foreign policy ... we are not talking about compliance with some clear and generally accepted international code of behavior."[85] The "wearisome duty of negotiating and mediating between governments with conflicting interests" runs up against the sad but unavoidable reality of the diplomat having to serve within a system of sovereign national states. Kennan emphasized that this "child of the modern age" – the sovereign national state – often wrapped itself in the garb of moral obligation when, in fact, "in the crucial moments of its own destiny" recognizes "no law but that of its own egoism." He lamented the fact that his recognition of this reality is confused by his critics as approval of the factual state of affairs. Kennan replied to such criticism by claiming that

---

[81] G. Kennan, *Realities of American Foreign Policy* (Princeton, NJ: Princeton University Press, 1954), p. 48.

[82] Ibid., p. 49.

[83] G. Kennan, "Morality and foreign policy," *Foreign Affairs* (Winter, 1985–6), 205.

[84] Ibid., 206.

[85] Ibid., 207–8.

Actually, I think, no one could be more sadly conscious than is the professional diplomat-ist of the primitiveness, the anarchism, the intrinsic absurdity of the modern concept of sovereignty. Could anything be more absurd than a world divided into several dozens of large secular societies, each devoted to the cultivation of the myth of its own overriding importance and virtue, of the sacrosanctity of its own unlimited independence?

As lamentable as this is, the diplomat is, when all is said and done, the servant of this system of national states; it is precisely to the working of this imperfect mechanism that his efforts are dedicated. He is professionally condemned to tinker with its ill-designed parts like a mechanic with a badly built and decrepit car, aware that this function is not to question the design or to grumble over the decrepitude, but to keep the confounded contraption running, some way or other.[86]

Concerning America's claims that its actions are based on moral principles vis-à-vis other governments whose actions it considers morally unacceptable, Kennan advised that we respond only when their actions have an adverse effect on American interests. He put it this way: "Where measures taken by foreign governments affect adversely American interests rather than just American moral sensibilities, protests and retaliation are obviously in order; but then they should be carried forward frankly for what they are, and not allowed to masquerade under the mantle of moral principle."[87]

Kennan, like Hans Morgenthau, relied heavily on finding moral and respon-sible individuals who could then be provided with statesmanlike wisdom and ability to perform the diplomatic function. He yearned, as Greg Russell put it, for "a civilized meritocracy of skill and intellect."[88] Kennan's primary ethical guide-line in the domain of foreign affairs was a disposition for prudence that enabled the statesman to act in accord with national self-interest guided only by the circumstances he or she faced at the time. Niebuhr, while valuing prudence and coming to see it as a norm of statesmanship along with justice, nevertheless thought it limited. He feared that "considerations of prudence inevitably arrest the impulse toward, and concern for, the life of the other."[89] Because he thought prudence alone would inhibit finding a meeting point between parochial inter-ests and the general interest in the art of statecraft, Niebuhr felt it necessary "to draw upon another moral and spiritual resource to widen the conception of interest" – that resource being the "sense of justice" that can "prevent prudence from becoming too prudential in defining [the parochial] interest."[90] In a 1957 letter Niebuhr wrote to Robert C. Good, he stated his view that "prudence is, I think, merely a procedural standard" and went on to contend that "if there is not some residual standard of justice beyond interest, then there is no political ethic

---

[86] G. Kennan, "History and diplomacy as viewed by a diplomatist," *The Review of Politics* (April, 1956), 171.

[87] G. Kennan, "Morality and foreign policy," 211.

[88] G. Russell, "Searching for realism's grand design: George F. Kennan and the ethics of American power in world affairs," *The Political Science Review*, 19 (1990), 203.

[89] R. Niebuhr, "Reply to interpretation and criticism" in C. W. Kegley, *Reinhold Niebuhr*, p. 512.

[90] R. Niebuhr, "Our moral and spiritual resources for international cooperation" *Social Action* (February, 1956), 18–19.

at all."[91] Niebuhr's viewpoint reflected a tension he had with the views of both Kennan and Morgenthau.

Elitism in a Democracy

In a chapter entitled "On Kennan: A Character Sketch," Baton Gellman quoted Kennan in a 1975 interview with George Urban: "I deeply believe that kindness and generosity in our personal behavior, and a refusal to be beastly to others even by way of reaction, are both moral and pragmatic qualities of the highest order." Gellman commented that "this conviction flows not merely from gentlemanliness, but also from the world view of a self-described "inveterate elitist."[92] Kennan's "response to the savagery of the human condition," according to Robert Ivie, "has been to advance the ideal of civility in the orderly and rational pursuit of national self-interest."[93] Ideally, if Kennan were to have his way, the modern world would return to an earlier time in which an aristocratic fraternity of world leaders could speak with one another independently from the people they represented. Kennan was certainly an elitist in his belief that professionals – having in mind primarily the Foreign Service – were the sole source of wisdom in political matters. In a 1955 article published in *Foreign Affairs* on "The Future of Our Professional Diplomacy," Kennan wrote that the question is "whether you want your Foreign Service to be (let us frankly use the abhorred word) an elite, in character and intellect and education, or whether you want its members to be as close as possible to the mean of other Americans of their age." Assured that a tradition going back to the founding fathers would "unhesitatingly have favored the former" he caustically remarked that "it was left for the present generation, given to confusing republican institutions with an egalitarian conformism, to embrace the theory that we should be represented by our average rather than our best."[94]

Kennan believed that "there is always a small minority – perhaps 10 or 15% – who have values, insights, sensitivity far greater than the mass of their fellow beings, and it is very important how this pattern-setting minority behave."[95] In his 1975 interview with Eric Sevareid, Kennan asserted that there was an obvious need for professional training in diplomacy, just as there is in law or medicine. And while he held that there was "room for the talented

---

[91] R. Niebuhr to R. C. Good, October 24, 1957. Reinhold Niebuhr Collection Container 6, Library of Congress.

[92] B. Gellman, *Contending with Kennan: Toward a Philosophy of American Power* (New York: Praeger, 1984), p. 6.

[93] R. L. Ivie, "Realism masking fear: George F. Kennan's political rhetoric" in F. A. Beer and R. Hariman (eds.), *Post-Realism: The Rhetorical Turn in International Relations* (East Lansing, MI: Michigan State University Press, 1996), p. 55.

[94] G. Kennan, "The future of our professional diplomacy," *Foreign Affairs* (July, 1955), 578–9.

[95] Quoted in B. Gellman, *Contending with Kennan: Toward a Philosophy of American Power*. Kennan's remark appears in G. F. Kennan and G. Urban, "A conversation," reprinted in Kennan et al., *Encounters with Kennan: The Great Debate* (London: Frank Cross, 1979), p. 10.

nonprofessional" in diplomatic life, Kennan confessed "a strong belief for professionalism in foreign affairs" along with the conviction that "one of the troubles today with the State Department and the Foreign Service is that they have been administered for decades by people who had no knowledge or experience of the substance of their work."[96]

In response to a follow-up question by Sevareid, Kennan insisted:

I am anything but an egalitarian. I am very much opposed to egalitarian tendencies of all sorts in governmental life and in other walks of life. Sometimes I have been charged with being an elitist. Well, of course I am. What do people expect? God forbid that we should be without an elite. Is everything to be done by gray mediocrity? After all, our whole system is based on the selection of people for different functions in our life. When you talk about selection, you're talking about an elite.[97]

According to Kenneth Thompson, "On the matter of the public and foreign policy, Niebuhr's realism went beyond elitist thinking. He could not bring himself to accept unreservedly that foreign policy should be exclusively the business of professionals, but neither did he subscribe to the view that more democracy was the key to better diplomacy."[98] Niebuhr certainly was ambivalent on this issue, because he often appealed to the "native common sense and earthy wisdom which arrived at conclusions by effecting direct analogies between human problems within their experience and the collective problems of mankind" rather than falling victim to illusions about human nature often found among the intellectual elites.[99]

What Niebuhr did believe was that foreign policy was "the Achilles heel of democracy" for the obvious reason "that the average voter has only enough wisdom and knowledge to judge the politics of government when they impinge directly upon his life, [and that] without aid he cannot come to an adequate judgment when the government affects the life of other nations."[100] As he put it elsewhere, "The problems of foreign policy are too remote and too complex either to interest or to be comprehended by the man in the street."[101] He did value the need – if not the prospect – of education in helping to overcome this problem, claiming that "if it is not to abdicate foreign policy to an elite of experts," a democratic nation must "must be assiduous in expanding both its knowledge and its wisdom in regard to the issues and the facts which are the raw

---

[96] E. Sevareid, "Conversation with George Kennan," 153.

[97] Ibid., 153–4.

[98] K. W. Thompson, "Niebuhr and foreign policy realists" in D. F. Rice (ed.), *Reinhold Niebuhr Revisited: Engagements with an American Original*, p. 140.

[99] R. Niebuhr, "The democratic elite and American foreign policy," 175. Niebuhr here used as an example the taxi drivers who, during the period of World War II, did not espouse the naïve pacifist "illusions that infected the clerical and academic elite of church and university" during the rise of Nazi Germany.

[100] Ibid., 168.

[101] R. Niebuhr, "Democracy and foreign policy," *The New Leader* (April 8, 1957), 9.

stuff of foreign policy."[102] Niebuhr knew very well that "the total public has neither the ability nor the inclination to master all the details required for an adequate policy." Democracy for Niebuhr "requires an aristocracy of knowledgeable and wise leaders in every realm of policy," assuredly "not a tight or self-appointed aristocracy, nor a hereditary one." The kind of aristocracy required in a democracy is "a fluid and, if possible, multiple aristocracy, consisting of classes and of media of education in the community who select themselves and are selected by their interest in and ability to understand the many facets of foreign policy." Niebuhr admitted that "aristocracy" might well be the "wrong word for designating a selected group or groups in a community which have competence above the average public. Ideally, a free society creates various aristocracies or elite groups in various fields of culture and political affairs."[103]

Among Niebuhr's categorization of "elites," there were obviously those in elective office whom one might hope would have some political knowledge, two classes of educators (academic and journalistic), and "those members of the general public who have, either by special training or special interest and capacity, become competent in public, particularly in foreign affairs."[104] The final category dovetailed with the group of individuals that Niebuhr found best represented by George Kennan, namely "all the specialists who must act as the agents of American power and responsibility in every part of the world in which our power impinges and our responsibilities are exercised." This is the group that Kennan himself valued so highly and found so essential to the success of a democratic society with its anti-elitist, egalitarian tendencies.

The Exportability of Democracy

Niebuhr, Kennan, and Morgenthau opposed the idea that America's foreign policy aim should include exporting democracy abroad. Not only should the United States avoid pursuing an interventionist foreign policy aimed at establishing democracy in other societies, it should also refrain from an erroneous conviction that this nation could shape the development of political realities and governmental systems in countries outside its own boundaries. Kennan stated unequivocally: "I think we should note that if America were to try to become, as John Quincy Adams put it disapprovingly, the 'guarantors' instead of the 'friends' of the liberties of half the world, there is no reason to suppose we would make a very good job of it."[105]

---

[102] R. Niebuhr, "The democratic elite and American foreign policy," 171. Niebuhr saw this "raw stuff" of foreign policy involving three categories: "A reassessment of the political philosophy that informs our posture in the world"; "the best possible and most comprehensive knowledge of the world upon which our power impinges"; and "as much comprehension as it is possible for laymen to absorb about the technics of modern warfare." Ibid., 171–2.

[103] Ibid., 173–4.

[104] Ibid., 174.

[105] G. Kennan, *The Cloud of Danger: Current Realities of American Foreign Policy* (Boston: Little, Brown, 1977), p. 43.

Kennan, in his interview with Sevareid, also stated that he was "constantly amazed at the persistence of the view in this country that democracy is the natural state of mankind, and that there is something wrong, that we have been in some way remiss, if other countries don't have it."[106] He saw "no evidence that 'democracy,' or what we picture to ourselves under that word, is the natural state of mankind."[107] This concern was also evident in a 1967 dialogue Niebuhr had with Hans Morgenthau over the issue of war and peace in the nuclear age in the context of the Vietnam War. Niebuhr observed that in South Vietnam, "We are not ... defending a nation. We are trying to create a nation and a democratic nation at that." Morgenthau's response was, "Yes, the very idea of one nation creating, in a completely alien culture, a new nation according to its own prescription seems to me absolutely fantastic." Niebuhr replied, "You know, Morgenthau, I think that it is also fantastic that we regard democracy as a universal option for all people."[108]

All three realists knew that the achievement of democracy had a long and torturous history in the Western World. Insisting that democracy has "a relatively narrow base both in time and space," Kennan claimed that he knew "no reason to suppose that the attempt to develop and employ democratic institutions would necessarily be the best course" and that "the record of attempt of this nature has not been all that good."[109] Niebuhr, believing that although democracy may well be the "ideal instrument of justice in any culture," nonetheless pointed out that the "question remains whether democracy is not also a luxury which only advanced nations can afford."[110] Not only did Kennan agree by pointing out that the soil out of which democracy grew was both unique and limited historically, but he was also suspicious of both America's foreign policy motives and America's pretentions. He was in agreement with Niebuhr who, as early as his 1930 article "Awkward Imperialists," claimed that "we make simple moral judgments, remain unconscious of the self-interest that colors them, support them with an enthusiasm which derives from our ... influential evangelical piety, and are surprised that our contemporaries will not accept us as saviors of the world."[111]

Kennan's way of putting the same point in a book published in 1993 involved making it perfectly clear that he was "emphatically rejecting any and all messianic concepts of America's role in the world: rejecting, that is, the image of ourselves as teachers and redeemers to the rest of humanity, rejecting the

---

[106] E. Sevareid, "Conversation with George F. Kennan," 159. Kennan went on to say that he thought that "democracy is a form of government which has found its seat, you might say in a broad sense, among the countries or people who had their origins on the shores of the North Sea and that it has never been very common elsewhere." Ibid.

[107] G. Kennan, *The Cloud of Danger*, p. 42.

[108] R. Niebuhr, "A dialogue on war and peace in the nuclear age with Reinhold Niebuhr and Hans Morgenthau," 7.

[109] G. Kennan, *The Cloud of Danger*, p. 42.

[110] R. Niebuhr, "Can democracy work?" *The New Leader* (May 28, 1962), 8.

[111] R. Niebuhr, "Awkward imperialists," *The Atlantic Monthly* (May, 1930), 674.

illusions of unique and superior virtue on our part, the prattle about Manifest Destiny or the 'American Century' – all those visions that have so richly commended themselves to Americans of all generations since, and even before, the foundation of our country." He then added:

We are, for the love of God, only human beings, the descendents of human beings, the bearers, like all our ancestors, of all the usual human frailties. Divine hands ... may occasionally reach down to support us in our struggles, as individuals, with our divided nature, but no divine hand has ever reached down to make us, as a national community, anything more than we are, or to elevate us in that capacity over the remainder of mankind.[112]

What Kennan recommended was that America look inward at itself. He was "of the opinion that the best way we – and particularly our government – can influence the political practices of other governments is to apply our axe vigorously to some of the failures and evils of our own society, letting the chips fall where they may."[113] In the case of the Cold War, Kennan believed that "the most important influence that the United States can bring to bear upon internal developments in Russia will continue to be the influence of example: the influence of what it is, and not only what it is to others but what it is to itself. . . . Any message we may try to bring to others will be effective only if it is in accord with what we are to ourselves."[114]

Reinforcing Kennan's view that the soil out of which democracy grew is rather rare, Niebuhr noted that "what should ... be obvious is that Western-style democracy is not immediately relevant to non-European culture," where there is a "lack [of] the standards of literacy, political skill and social equilibria which would make viable political freedom as we have come to know it." It is important to understand that "our treasured democracy is really a necessity of justice ... for a delicate balancing of social forces is required to make justice the end product of democracy."[115] Niebuhr was not being condescending here. He was merely recognizing that, while Western democracy may well be "an ultimate political ideal," it "requires greater political skill, cultural adequacy and a fortunate balance of social forces than are available for many non-Europeans or, more accurately, non-technical nations."[116] Niebuhr's skepticism about exporting democracy was based on his conviction that "organic" factors are fundamental in the development of all communities. He insisted that free and democratic societies could neither be established nor flourish unless the soil is right – unless certain conditions are met. The democracies grew gradually out of bloody soil and are highly intricate systems requiring complex political

---

[112] G. Kennan, *Around the Cragged Hill: A Personal and Political Philosophy* (New York: Norton, 1993), pp. 182–3.
[113] G. Kennan, "In the American mirror" in *At a Century's Ending: Reflections 1982–1995* (New York: Norton, 1996), p. 209.
[114] G. Kennan, *American Diplomacy: 1900–1950* (New York: New American Library, 1951), pp. 143–4.
[115] R. Niebuhr, "After Sputnik and Explorer," *Christianity and Crisis* (March 17, 1958), 30.
[116] R. Niebuhr, "Well-tempered evangelism," *The New Republic* (June 26, 1961), 11–12.

institutions, an acute sense of justice, and highly developed notions of individual freedom, rights, and responsibilities. Moreover, democratic nations "have a culture which demands self-criticism in principle; and institutions which make it possible in practice."[117] In one of his last books, co-authored with Paul Sigmund while jointly teaching a course at Harvard University, the authors claimed that,

Study of European democracy has shown three constant prerequisites of free governments: (1) the unity and solidarity of the community, sufficiently strong to allow the free play of competitive interests without endangering the unity of the community itself; (2) a belief in the freedom of the individual and appreciation of his worth; and (3) a tolerable harmony and equilibrium of social and political and economic forces necessary to establish an approximation of social justice.[118]

---

[117] R. Niebuhr, *The Children of Light and the Children of Darkness* (New York: Charles Scribner's Sons, 1944), p. 183.

[118] R. Niebuhr and P. Sigmund, *The Democratic Experience: Past and Prospects* (New York: Praeger, 1969), p. 73.

CHAPTER 7

Felix Frankfurter (1882–1965)

Felix Frankfurter was appointed to the Supreme Court by Franklin D. Roosevelt in 1939, replacing the recently deceased Benjamin N. Cardozo. He served on the Court until his retirement in 1962. Reinhold Niebuhr claimed that Felix Frankfurter was "the most vital and creative person I have ever known."[1] In his 1965 memorial to his long-time friend, Niebuhr remarked that in addition to being "a great teacher of the Law, a confidant of Presidents and a justice of the Supreme Court," Frankfurter was also "a superb conversationalist with a wide range of interests far beyond his legal expertise and an intense intellectual vitality that was the pride and despair of his friends."[2] Niebuhr knew this firsthand since Frankfurter and he shared many hours conversing during the summer months in Heath, Massachusetts.[3]

Professionally, Niebuhr's and Frankfurter's worlds were divergent and often remote. In spite of their common interests in the political life of the nation, the distance between the world of jurisprudence and that of theological and social polemics was far greater than the simple geographical distance between Washington, DC, and New York City which separated them. Reinhold Niebuhr had many admirers among the ranks of those whom Frederick Schleiermacher called the "cultured despisers of religion," those who appreciated and relied upon Niebuhr's social vision yet were utterly bewildered if not embarrassed by his theological orientation.[4] Frankfurter in an important sense seems to have

---

This chapter is based on my correspondence essay "Felix Frankfurter and Reinhold Niebuhr," *The Journal of Law and Religion*, 1:2 (1984), 325–426.

[1] R. Niebuhr, "Tribute to Felix Frankfurter," *Harvard Law Review*, 76 (1962), 20.

[2] R. Niebuhr, "In memoriam: Felix Frankfurter," *Christianity and Crisis* (April 15, 1965), 69.

[3] The extent and depth of the friendship between them has been ably captured by both Niebuhr's wife Ursula in her book *Remembering Reinhold Niebuhr* (San Francisco: Harper, 1991) and by Niebuhr's daughter Elisabeth Sifton, who in her book *The Serenity Prayer* (New York: Norton, 2003) provides us with highly personal and detailed recollections of their relationship.

[4] One example will suffice. A renowned American historian in writing of Niebuhr's concept of irony once commented: "I realize that Niebuhr's view of human strivings is based on theology, a subject definitely beyond my province. Whatever its theological implications – and I have frankly never

FIG. 7 Frankfurter
Courtesy of the Library of Congress

belonged to this group. He was raised in an "observant" but not "orthodox"
Jewish household, and, in spite of the "warmth of the familiar" which such
elements of the communal life provided, Frankfurter disassociated himself from
"religious" Judaism when he was still a young man. With some reservation, he
referred to himself as a "reverent agnostic" or a "believing unbeliever." Yet this
"reverent agnostic" would go out of his physical and intellectual way to hear
Niebuhr preach. Only the reader can decide whether this was a result of his
esteem and admiration for a friend or an expression of his residual "reverence."
Frankfurter once related the following:

I'm very much interested in theological discussions, theological problems, and one of my
close friends, one of my most esteemed friends, is Dr. Reinhold Niebuhr, and he and I have
had talks on this subject from time to time. We summered together for some years up in
Heath, a small town in western Massachusetts. Once, a few summers ago, I went to a
community church there, a nondenominational church to which the people of the community except the Catholics go, because I heard that Reinhold Niebuhr was going to
deliver the sermon. He did deliver the sermon, a non-denominational sermon, and after
the service I said to him, "Reinie, may a believing unbeliever thank you for your sermon?"

He said, "may an unbelieving believer thank you for appreciating it?"[5]

   explored them – the view has a validity apart from them that appeals to the historian."
   C. V. Woodward, *The Burden of Southern History* (New York: Vintage, 1960), p. 173.
   [5] F. Frankfurter, *Felix Frankfurter Reminisces*, H. B. Phillips (ed.), (New York: Reynal, 1960), p. 291.

Because so much of what Niebuhr and Frankfurter had to say to each other was conducted within the private world they shared each summer, what they said remains forever outside the public view. Yet these men conducted a twenty-five-year correspondence that captures a good measure of their personal relationship as well as their views on the world around them.[6] The fact that men of such eminence should form a bond of deep and lasting friendship is certainly not unusual. But the significant insight into that friendship that is available for public knowledge is owed to Felix Frankfurter's penchant for belles letters. Whereas Niebuhr channeled his indomitable energy into an astonishing production of public writing, Frankfurter was a consummate writer and a meticulous preserver of correspondence, having once written to his wife that "letter writing is the most abidingly fascinating literary form."[7]

The lives of Frankfurter and Niebuhr intersected during the middle third of the twentieth century – a period opening on the eve of America's entry into World War II and closing with the assassination of the thirty-fifth president of the United States and the advent of a decade of national turmoil. By the time the correspondence between Felix Frankfurter (1882–1965) and Reinhold Niebuhr (1892–1971) was underway, both men were well established in their careers. Frankfurter, coming from a prestigious post at the Harvard Law School, took the oath of office as associate justice of the Supreme Court on January 30, 1939. Niebuhr, occupying the Chair of Christian Ethics at Union Theological Seminary in New York, had recently returned from Edinburgh, Scotland, where he had delivered the highly regarded Gifford Lectures soon to be published in two significant volumes, *The Nature and Destiny of Man* (1941–3).

There is no question that these two men found themselves in one another's debt. Frankfurter was a self-confessed admirer of both Niebuhr's books and his editorials and essays in *Christianity and Crisis*, a journal which provided a running commentary on the social and political events of the times. Similarly, Niebuhr paid careful attention to Frankfurter's judicial opinions as well as to his general writings. While differing on occasion over issues both public and private, Frankfurter and Niebuhr had much common ground and a deep mutual respect. Beyond this there was a genuine friendship, illustrated by a letter Frankfurter wrote to Niebuhr in 1940 thanking him for expressing good wishes and acknowledging that Frankfurter needed "the encouragement and confidence of hardheaded spirits like yourself." Then, in jocular fashion, Frankfurter informed Niebuhr that, when asked by a law clerk who was his favorite theologian, "before I had a chance to reply, he told me with enthusiasm that his was Reinhold Niebuhr. I could give reasons for the enthusiasm that you evoke in him and me, but I shall not offend your modesty."[8]

---

[6] A lengthier, more detailed version of this chapter is located in my correspondence essay "Felix Frankfurter and Reinhold Niebuhr: 1940–1964," *Journal of Law and Religion*, 1:2 (1984), 325–426.

[7] F. Frankfurter to his wife (October 3, 1922), Frankfurter Collection, Library of Congress (hereafter cited as FCLC).

[8] F. Frankfurter to R. Niebuhr (February 21, 1940), Niebuhr Collection, Library of Congress (hereafter cited as NCLC).

This carefree mood did not last, however. Within a year, Niebuhr learned that he was being investigated by both the Department of State and the Federal Bureau of Investigation. From the time Niebuhr began warning the nation of the dangers of Hitler's regime he worked tirelessly in assisting victims of Nazi persecution to emigrate from Germany and German-occupied lands. Frankfurter became involved in one such incident when the visa of an immigrant professor was held up by the Department of State because of "loyalty questions" raised against Niebuhr, who was sponsoring the immigration. On November 17, 1941, Niebuhr, with a justifiable note of concern, wrote Frankfurter with the following information:

Dear Mr. Frankfurter:

One of my colleagues has just returned from Washington where *inter alia* he conferred with State Department officials in regard to an emigre professor whom we have been trying to get into the country. He found to his amazement that the visa had been held up for months because my name appeared on his list of sponsors and the department officials showed him a whole file listing my nefarious connections with communism. The whole list was of the Dillinger Red Network type of thing. He said it revealed that the department was very busy with gathering this kind of information and that it was evidently a very ignorant type of snooping which was being engaged in.

Here I have been fighting the communists for years and have never had any contact with them except in those organizations of united front days in which we all stood for collective security. But even in those organizations many of us were constantly on guard against the communists. One should imagine that if the State department went in for such things it would at least employ snoopers who read our magazines to see what the men, whom it is judging are saying. I confess that it is rather disconcerting to think of ignorant files of this type in the State department.

I ought not to bother you with this and I don't know whether there is anything to be done about it. But if you have any good advice to give me on what steps I might take I would be grateful.[9]

Almost three weeks later, after having interceded into this affair, Frankfurter received assurances from Under Secretary of State Sumner Welles that all was well regarding Niebuhr.

During the latter part of 1941, Niebuhr was at work on two significant essays having to do with the position of the Jews in anticipation of the postwar reconstruction effort. These essays first appeared in successive issues of *The Nation* in February, 1942, and were eventually published in a collection of

[9] R. Niebuhr to F. Frankfurter (November 17, 1940, in FCLC).

Niebuhr's shorter writings.[10] Niebuhr argued on behalf of a postwar settlement that would result in a "homeland" for the Jewish people. Although he had abiding respect and appreciation for the degree of toleration in American society, the particular form it had assumed in the "melting pot" theory led him to express the concern that there was "a curious, partly unconscious, cultural imperialism in theories of toleration that looks forward to a complete destruction of all racial distinction. The majority group expects to devour the minority group by way of assimilation. This is a painless death, but it is death nevertheless." Niebuhr went on to level the charge that American Jewry, on the whole, had bought into this form of death-by-assimilation, and citing Justice Louis Brandeis, argued that "Brandeis' Zionism sprang from his understanding of an aspect of human existence to which most of his fellow liberals were blind. He understood 'that whole peoples have an individuality no less marked than that of single persons, that the individuality of a people is irrepressible, and that the misnamed internationalism that seeks the elimination of nationalities or peoples is unattainable. The new nationalism proclaims that each race or people has a right and duty to develop, and that only through such differentiated development will highest civilization be attained.'"[11]

Frankfurter was no stranger to the Zionist cause, having joined Brandeis in 1919 and again in 1920 in the effort to secure the promise of a national homeland for Jews in Palestine.[12] With respect to Niebuhr's articles on "Jews after the War," he felt obliged to convince Niebuhr to try to place them in a journal commanding a wider audience and greater prestige than *The Nation*. So original and profound did he regard Niebuhr's analysis of the relationship between "identity" and "nationality" relative to Jewish survival that Frankfurter wrote to Niebuhr on December 24, 1941, commenting that:

Too many liberals, as you indicate, are still enslaved by their romantic illusions, and cannot face your clean, surgeon-like exposition of reality. I find your essays as refreshing as is cooling spring water to a parched throat. Agreeable to your suggestion, I showed the two papers to Isaiah Berlin [British social and political philosopher and official of the British Embassy in New York City and Washington, DC] and we are of the same mind about them. [My suggestion to you] is that you convey the idea of 'imposing' a settlement in a less startling phrase to people who have never faced these problems with ruthless honesty. Why not speak of it as "part of a world settlement, etc." or some such phrase to indicate that it is not brute force you are talking about, but accommodating the enforcement of global as against mere regional interests.[13]

Three months later, Frankfurter wrote: "I would give a cookie to see the letters that you have had on your Jewish articles insofar as they are merely

---

[10] R. Niebuhr, "Jews after the war: Parts I & II" in D. Robertson (ed.), *Love and Justice: Selections From the Shorter Writings of Reinhold Niebuhr* (Gloucester, MA: Peter Smith, 1957), pp. 132–42.

[11] Ibid., p. 138.

[12] F. Frankfurter reminisced about the personal dynamics involved between himself, Brandeis, and Chaim Weizmann. See Frankfurter and H. Phillips, *Felix Frankfurter Reminisces*, pp. 178–88.

[13] F. Frankfurter to R. Niebuhr (December 24, 1941, in FCLC).

commendatory or merely condemnatory. I hope very much that your articles will be put out in pamphlet form because, as I have told you, I know of nothing in print that faces the Jewish problem more trenchantly and more candidly."[14]

The mutual respect and admiration which existed between Frankfurter and Niebuhr did not preclude a sharp divergence of opinion between them over matters of public importance. However, differences of opinion between them were always conducted within an atmosphere of respect, good will, and levity – and always with a manifest concern for their bond of friendship. One such occasion came in the wake of *McCollum v. Board of Education* (March, 1948), in which the Supreme Court struck down Illinois' "released-time" program operating within the public schools. This program allowed students to receive religious instruction by church leaders in the school's classrooms. In a lengthy concurring opinion (Justice Hugo Black having spoken for the Court), Frankfurter gave voice to a point of view shared by men such as Jefferson and Franklin that the divisiveness of religious sects be prohibited from disrupting the cohesive forces by which the social fabric is maintained.[15] Writing in support of the Court's decision, Frankfurter noted that the "sharp confinement of the public schools to secular education was a recognition of the need of a democratic society to educate its children, insofar as the State undertook to do so, in an atmosphere free from pressures in a realm in which pressures are most resisted and where conflicts are most easily and most bitterly engendered." He insisted because it was "designed to serve as perhaps the most powerful agency for promoting cohesion among a heterogeneous democratic people, the public school must be kept scrupulously free from entanglement in the strife of sects."[16]

Niebuhr's concern with *McCollum v. Board of Education* came on two levels. The first had to do with the issue of a proper interpretation of the "no establishment" clause of the First Amendment and the meaning of separation of Church

---

[14] F. Frankfurter to R. Niebuhr (March 10, 1942, in FCLC).

[15] Jefferson, for example, wrote: "Whatsoever is lawful in the Commonwealth, or permitted to the subject in ordinary way, cannot be forbidden to him for religious uses: and whatever is prejudicial to the Commonwealth in their ordinary uses and therefore prohibited by the laws, ought not to be permitted to churches in their social rites. .... This is the true extent of toleration." T. Jefferson, *Notes on Religion* (dated October, 1776), in S.K. Padiver (ed.), *The Complete Jefferson, Containing His Major Writings, Published and Unpublished Except His Letters* (New York: Duell, Sloan & Pearce, 1943), p. 945.

Franklin, however, put the matter this way in his *Autobiography*: "I never doubted, for instance, the existence of the Deity; that he made the world, and govern'd it by his Providence; that the most acceptable service of God was the doing of good to men; that our souls are immortal; and that all crime will be punished, and virtue rewarded, either here or hereafter. These I esteem'd the essentials of every religion; and, being to be found in all the religions we had in our country, I respected them all, tho' with different degrees of respect, as I found them more or less mix'd with other articles, which, without any tendency to inspire, promote, or confirm morality, serv'd principally to divide us, and make us unfriendly to one another." F. Luther and C.E. Jorgenson Mott (eds.), *Benjamin Franklin, Representative Selections* (New York: American Book Co., 1936), pp. 60–70.

[16] *McCollum v. Board of Education*, 333 U.S. 203, pp. 216–17 (1948).

and State derived from it. On this issue the Supreme Court addressed itself in *McCollum*. Niebuhr's second concern focused on what he regarded as the implicit religiosity of "the democratic way of life," promulgated by the allegedly "secular" system of public education in the United States. This issue was not raised by the Court and was, at best, indirectly relevant to the *McCollum* case. However, knowing Frankfurter's views on the role of public education in the United States, Niebuhr expressed concern over this issue in the wake of recent Supreme Court decisions culminating in *McCollum v. Board of Education*.

The position taken by the Court in *McCollum* interpreted the "no establishment" clause of the Constitution as forbidding the giving of aid to any and all religions, in addition to prohibiting governmental preference of one religion over others. Niebuhr, along with many other religious leaders, argued that governmental programs which benefit all religious bodies, without discrimination against any, would and should be held constitutionally valid. Immediately after the Supreme Court had arrived at its decision in *McCollum*, Niebuhr chose to criticize the Court's position and publish Justice Stanley Reed's minority opinion in the March 29, 1948, issue of *Christianity and Crisis*. In his dissenting opinion, Justice Reed argued against the Court's broadening of the "no establishment" clause, which, he argued, "may have been intended by Congress to be aimed only at a State Church."[17] Of course, the issues here are far more complex and technical than space will now permit. But it should be noted that Niebuhr, while agreeing with Justice Reed's opinion allowing the "released-time" program in Illinois to stand, would reject his position that "our governmental entities ... cannot 'aid' all or any religions. ..." Frankfurter's position on these matters was radically at odds with Niebuhr's. "Separation," Frankfurter wrote, "means separation, not something less."[18]

It was precisely Frankfurter's understanding of the Jeffersonian metaphor "wall of separation" that Niebuhr was attacking. On July 5, 1948, in a "Statement on Church and State" Niebuhr, along with twenty-six major figures within Protestantism, including Niebuhr's brother H. Richard Niebuhr at Yale, put his signature to a statement that insisted that the recent

---

[17] Justice Reed further dissented from what he regarded as a peculiar use of the word "aid." His position was that "passing years ... have brought about acceptance of a broader meaning, although never until today, I believe, has the court widened its interpretation to any such degree as holding that recognition of the interest of our nation in religion, through granting, to qualified representatives of the principal faiths, of opportunity to present religion as an optional, extra-curricular subject during released time in public school buildings, was equivalent to an establishment of religion. I agree that none of our governmental entities can 'set up a church.' I agree that they cannot 'aid' all or any religions or prefer one 'over another.' But 'aid' must be understood as a purposeful assistance directly to the church itself or to some religious group or organization doing religious work of such a character that it may fairly be said to be performing ecclesiastical functions." S. F. Reed, *McCollum v. Board of Education* (dissenting opinion), *Christianity and Crisis* (March 29, 1948), 39.

[18] S. J. Konefsky, *The Constitutional World of Mr. Justice Felix Frankfurter* (New York: Macmillan, 1949), p. 180.

hardening of the idea of 'separation' by the Court will greatly accelerate the trend toward the secularization of our culture. We favor the separation of Church and State in the sense which we believe to have been intended in the first amendment. This prohibited the State from giving any Church or religious body a favored position, and from controlling the religious institutions of the nation. We contend that Jefferson's oft quoted words, 'wall of separation,' which are not in the Constitution but which are used by the Court in the interpretation of the Constitution, are a misleading metaphor.[19]

There was more involved in Niebuhr's discomfort with *McCollum* than his dissent from the "insular" theory of separation which appeared to govern the majority decision. In a preface to Justice Reed's dissenting opinion, the editors of *Christianity and Crisis* asserted that it is "our conviction that the recent Supreme Court Decision on the question of religious instruction in schools is a very fateful one and that it must inevitably lead to an ever more consistent secularization of our education."[20]

While stating in a letter to Justice Harlan F. Stone that "all my bias and predisposition are in favor of giving the fullest elbow room to every variety of religious, political and economic view,"[21] Frankfurter's overriding conviction that the public schools should function as a unifying force in our national life was expressed most vehemently in the widely criticized decision in *Minersville District v. Gobitis*, 310 U.S. 586 (1940). Although raising different constitutional issues from the ones in McCollum, the *Gobitis* decision saw Frankfurter go so far in support of the unifying function of the schools that he let stand a school program that compelled students to salute the flag despite their religious-oriented objections. In writing the majority opinion, Frankfurter held that the issue was clearly one involving the disruption of the social order and that the community had the right to prevent such disruption. He stated that "national unity is the basis of national security. . . . The flag is the symbol of our national unity, transcending all internal differences, however large, within the framework of the Constitution." Insofar as "conscientious scruples have not, in the course of the long struggle for religious toleration, relieved the individual from

---

[19] R. Niebuhr, "Statement on church and state," *Christianity and Crisis* (March 29, 1948), 90.

[20] S. F. Reed, *McCollum v. Board of Education*, 39. Contrary to the notion that "secular" education was the opposite of religion, Niebuhr saw a "secular religiosity" in the democratic way of life propagated by the institutions of public education. Indeed, on August 4, 1947, several months prior to *McCollum v. Board of Education*, he had published an essay on "Democracy as a religion" in the journal, *Christianity and Crisis*. At that time he wrote: "If one may judge by the various commencement utterances of the past month, Americans have only one religion: devotion to democracy. They extol its virtues, are apprehensive about the perils to which it is exposed, pour maledictions upon its foes, rededicate themselves periodically to its purposes and claim unconditioned validity for its ideals. . . . [one] peril of democracy as a religion is that, without a more inclusive religious faith, we identify our particular brand of democracy with the ultimate values of life. This is a sin to which Americans are particularly prone. . . . There are no historic institutions, whether political, economic or religious which can survive a too uncritical devotion. . . . [D]evotion to democracy [is] false as a religion." R. Niebuhr, "Democracy as a religion," *Christianity and Crisis* (August 4, 1947), 1.

[21] F. Frankfurter to H. F. Stone (May 27, 1940, in FCLC).

obedience to a general law not aimed at the promotion or restriction of religious beliefs."[22] The exercise of political authority takes precedence over the religious claims of the individual's exemption from the law.

Frankfurter's view on the nature and function of public education was forged in the crucible of his own experience with the public schools as agents of the "melting pot" theory of Americanization. However else he arrived at his understanding of the "no establishment" clause, his views on education contributed to his vehemence and consistency with respect to public education as a unifying force in American life. Yet to many, including Niebuhr, it became evident that public education was functioning as an agent of "religious" values in the broad sense that the educational institutions were society's instrument for inculcating and disseminating the shared beliefs and values which gave the society its sense of unity and cohesion. The initial correspondence between Frankfurter and Niebuhr on these complex issues is missing from the Frankfurter papers. He had written Niebuhr a letter objecting to the manner in which *Christianity and Crisis* had handled its response to the *McCollum* decision. Evidently, Frankfurter thought the publication of a portion of Justice Reed's dissenting opinion – without a balanced presentation of the majority opinion – was unfair to the integrity of the issues involved. In response, Niebuhr wrote to Frankfurter on March 31, 1948, apologizing for any injustice Frankfurter might have felt, and confessing that

I can quite understand your feeling about our criticism of an opinion which we did not publish, but I don't want to use the paper shortage as an excuse. It is quite obvious that our whole issue, and more, would have been taken by the opinions had we published them all. We, therefore, published the dissenting opinion because it accurately expressed our own apprehensions. I had a rather bad conscience about doing this. Professor [John C] Bennett and I sat up one evening a long while discussing the matter and paying compliments to your opinion and to the thoughtfulness and diligence with which you approach this problem. I can quite understand your statement that "would that a judge had freedom of speech," but I might suggest that you have a more potent freedom-namely the freedom to determine what the law is. So the balances are slightly redressed when those of us who do not agree with your interpretation use our freedom of speech to emphasize a dissenting opinion.

One of the facts which influences my opinion in this matter is that living across the way from Teachers College [at Columbia University], I am convinced that the prevailing philosophy which is pumped into our public schools day after day is itself a religion, and I think a very erroneous one. It preaches the redemption of man by historical development and by the illusory "scientific objectivity." It does not have to worry about the separation of church and state.[23]

Niebuhr knew exactly the source of Frankfurter's view that the public school is "perhaps the most powerful agency for promoting cohesion among a heterogeneous democratic people." Niebuhr's insight is reflected in his 1965 eulogy of

---

[22] *Minersville District v. Gobitis*, 310 U.S. 586, pp. 594–6 (1940).
[23] R. Niebuhr to F. Frankfurter (March 31, 1948, in FCLC).

Frankfurter, wherein he wrote that Frankfurter, "accustomed to the culture of ultramontane Austria ... was tremendously impressed by the multi-racial and multi-religious nature of the public schools. His passion for them as veritable temples of democracy was reflected in many Supreme Court decisions."[24] Yet from Niebuhr's point of view this "veritable temple of democracy" was busily engaged in proclaiming a new faith whose object was the American way of life.[25]

Frankfurter's response to Niebuhr's letter did not engage the issue that Niebuhr raised, but it was indicative of the quality of friendship these men shared. On April 2, 1948, Frankfurter wrote:

> Heavens, Reinie, I feel that you 'have been unjust.' This is indeed a crazy world in which all things seem to be possible, but it is quite beyond my imagining that you should do anything that I deem 'unjust.' I am sorry if in my note you did not find that I was merely making a face at you. But, evidently, I was heavy-tongued in my teasing.
>
> I am greatly troubled to have you tell me that your health has been bad. I hope you use the past tense accurately and that, in any event, you are behaving so that you will become and remain fit and fighting.

Affectionately yours,
Felix Frankfurter[26]

The fact that Niebuhr and Frankfurter should disagree over issues as complex and far-reaching as these is not surprising. And it must be acknowledged that the understanding each man had of the issues was in tension on a fundamental level, not merely on the periphery. They were divided both on the meaning of "separation" in the "no establishment" clause, and, more importantly, on the "religious" aspect inherent in the democratic educational system as it had evolved in the United States.

In his essay "Ten Fateful Years," published in *Christianity and Crisis* on February 5, 1951,[27] Niebuhr reflected on the ten-year period since the journal he had founded was established. Hopeful that the United States had learned some hard lessons from the turbulent period from America's entry into World War II to the advent of the atomic age, Niebuhr outlined a series of issues facing the nation in the coming decade. Frankfurter saw this article as "an impressive piece of writing, or, rather, I should say a profound piece of thinking, not the less

[24] R. Niebuhr, "In memoriam: Felix Frankfurter," *Christianity and Crisis* (April 5, 1965), 69.

[25] The problem of "Civil Religion" in America has preoccupied scholars in theology, church history, and sociology of religion during this period. See W. Herberg, *Protestant, Catholic, Jew: An Essay In American Religious Sociology* (1955); M. E. Marty, *The New Shape of American Religion* (1959); S. Mead, *The Lively Experiment* (1959) and *The Nation With The Soul of a Church* (1975); and R. Bellah, *The Broken Covenant: American Civil Religion in Time of Trial* (1975).

[26] F. Frankfurter to R. Niebuhr (April 2, 1948, in FCLC).

[27] R. Niebuhr, "Ten fateful years," *Christianity and Crisis* (February 5, 1951), 1–4.

so because you have put pithily insights which have informed so much of your recent writing."[28]

Niebuhr was at the zenith of his powers from the time of the appearance of *The Nature and Destiny of Man* in 1941–3 and the onset of his incapacitating illness in the early 1950s. Frankfurter, too, was at the height of his influence during that period and as the years went by they often exchanged requests for information relating to a large range of issues. Frankfurter answered one of Niebuhr's requests that grew out of Niebuhr's labors on his upcoming book *Irony of American History*. Frankfurter wrote to him on October 1, 1951:

Dear Reinie:

You will recall that I undertook to send you two items – (1) a quotation from Brandeis on "separation of powers," and (2) the reference to T. R. Huxley's prophetic remarks at the opening of Johns Hopkins on the difficulties that were bound to confront America, with the superb sentence, "size is not grandeur, and territory does not make a nation."

(1)   These are the Brandeis observations:

The doctrine of the separation of powers was adopted by the Convention of 1787, not to promote efficiency but to preclude the exercise of arbitrary power. The purpose was, not to avoid friction, but, by means of the inevitable friction incident to the distribution of the governmental powers among three departments, to save the people from autocracy.

Brandeis, J., dissenting in *Myers v. United States*, 272 U.S. 52, 293.

(2)   Huxley's remarks you will find in his "American Addresses" (1876, pp. 124–126). If you have any difficulty in putting your hand on this volume let me know and I shall send you the quotation, or you might get hold of a little book of mine called *The Public and Its Government*, published by the Yale Press, in which I quote the relevant portions, at page 164. Unfortunately I have no copy of this little book of mine, otherwise I would send it to you.

Ever yours,
Felix Frankfurter[29]

Frankfurter, in turn, solicited Niebuhr for advice on a variety of matters. With typical humor, on November 7, 1951, he wrote both Reinhold and Ursula Niebuhr requesting "theological goods" relative to a problem he was researching:

Dear Ursula and Reinie:

Being in need of some theological goods of course I turn to the distinguished firm of

Niebuhr & Niebuhr

[28]   F. Frankfurter to R. Niebuhr (February 21, 1952, in FCLC).
[29]   F. Frankfurter to R. Niebuhr (October 1, 1951, in FCLC).

I need some enlightenment on what is deemed from time to time to be "sacrilegious" in the Roman and other churches, and the criteria for determining it. (If in the very way I put my questions I betray ignorance please remember that while judges are supposed to know the law—what hokum that is!—that merely means I should hope profane and not sacred law.)

Anyhow, will you be a good pair and refer me to a few books or authoritative articles on the subject? Perhaps you should know the assumption of my inquiry. If that is wrong throw this in the wastebasket. It is that the concept of sacrilegious is not fixed, final and definite, but has its own history of changes and chances, of diversities and distinctions, of conflicts and controversies. (I hope you will not infer from this that I have reached that stage of senile juvenility where one again indulges in youthful excesses of alliteration.)

I hope the Niebuhrs, both at home and at school, are flourishing. I had a happy talk with Barbara Franks about Familie Niebuhr the other night.

The royal pair managed to impose their easy, human ways even upon our snobbish democracy – at least in Washington.

Affectionately yours,
Felix[30]

Frankfurter's interest in the "sacrilegious" issue owed to a case before the Supreme Court for which he would write a concurring opinion. The Court was considering a case arising out of a challenge to a New York statute which permitted the banning of motion picture films on the ground that they are "sacrilegious." In the case of *Burstyn v. Wilson* (343 U.S. 495, 1952) the Court ruled that under the First and Fourteenth Amendments a state may not ban a film on the basis of a censor's finding that it is "sacrilegious." On November 10, Niebuhr, writing for "the firm," replied:

Dear Felix:

Since you turn to the firm of Niebuhr & Niebuhr and do not specify the alleged head of the household, [I] will take the privilege of answering your letter.

I can give you the gory details about sacrilege fairly briefly. First of all in this, as in many matters, there has been no development of consequence in the theory since Thomas Aquinas, who fixed the definition in his *Summa* II, II, Question xcix. You will find his definitions nicely elaborated in Rickaby's *Moral Teaching of Thomas Aquinas*, also in Slater's *Manual of Moral Theology*.

I can give you the essential points. Sacrilege is defined as violation of a sacred object, but also in the wider sense as "any transgression against the

---

[30] F. Frankfurter to the Niebuhrs (November 7, 1951, in FCLC).

virtue of religion." Thomas distinguishes between real, personal, and local sacrilege: (a) real sacrilege is defined as irreverence toward sacred things. The core of this seems always to be irreverence toward the Eucharist and the Altar. Included here is the improper attitude by the Priest. (b) Personal sacrilege is violation of a sacred person, meaning cleric or member of a religious order. This includes laying violent hands upon them, or upon a total religious community, but also the violation of their vows. (c) Local sacrilege is defined as violation of sacred places, including churches, cemeteries, hospitals, and anything that has been consecrated. This sacrilege includes theft from such places, committing a sin within them which pollutes them, and desecrating them by improper use, such as turning a church into a stable.

This is perhaps too summary an account for your purpose, but it will give you the general idea.

I have finished my book *The Irony of American History* and will turn it into the publishers tomorrow. We are all well and send you our affectionate regards.

Yours,
Reinie[31]

Subsequent to Eisenhower's inauguration to the presidency in 1953, Niebuhr wrote a letter to Frankfurter in which he said that he looked "at the beginnings of the Eisenhower Administration with some degree of satisfaction, though I must say that our mutual friend, [Secretary of State] Mr. [John Foster] Dulles, seems about as tactless as I thought him to be."[32] Although he ardently supported Adlai Stevenson in 1952 and again in 1956, Niebuhr came to admire Eisenhower's basic integrity, his success in winding down the Korean War, and his ability to elicit bipartisan support for both the domestic and foreign policies hammered out during the long period of Democratic control. While increasing the tone of his criticism of the Republican administration throughout the decade, he nonetheless concurred in 1953 with Frankfurter's surprise "at the silly prematureness with which otherwise sensible and informed people commit themselves to judgments on the new administration."[33]

Frankfurter's views on law and his understanding of the relationship between the Supreme Court and the formation of laws have been much debated. On the basis of the doctrine of the separation of powers and the peculiarly unique power vested in the Supreme Court, Frankfurter's insistence on the principle of "judicial restraint" reflected his deep concern both with the proper locus of law in the legislative process and with the possible tyranny and arbitrariness of law if usurped by a court with "absolute" powers. There is, of course, a genuine and

---

[31] R. Niebuhr to F. Frankfurter (November 10, 1951, in FCLC).

[32] R. Niebuhr to F. Frankfurter (February 5, 1953, in FCLC).

[33] F. Frankfurter to R. Niebuhr (February 20, 1953, in FCLC).

honest controversy at this very point. If, for example, one is given a turn of events in which protection under law is denied to segments of the population – as was indeed the case during the individual and civil liberties cases of the 1940s and 1950s – then "justice *under* law" might well require a kind and degree of "judicial activism" which Frankfurter, for sound reasons, resisted and abhorred. What is certainly clear is that the issues surrounding "judicial restraint" versus "judicial activism" are highly complex and the choices made between oft-times unpleasant alternatives ought to give serious pause to those who would be drawn to an oversimplification of the difficulties.

Frankfurter knew that when matters of judgment are involved in troubling cases the totality of a person's experiences is in play. An illuminating glance into the rationale behind his advocacy of "judicial restraint" is seen in his opinion that:

Such judgment will be exercised by two types of men, broadly speaking, but of course with varying emphasis-those who express their private views or revelations, deeming them, if not *vox dei*, at least *vox populi*; or those who feel strongly that they have no authority to promulgate law by their merely personal view and whose whole training and proved performance substantially insure that their conclusions reflect understanding of, and due regard for, law as the expression of the views and feelings that may fairly be deemed representative of the community as a continuing society. ... The outlook of a lawyer fit to be a Justice regarding the role of a judge cuts across all his personal preferences for this or that social arrangement.[34]

Such a statement, of course, does not solve the problem. Rather, it points up the dilemma. For, while Frankfurter held law to be an expression of the community abiding by its formulation within the legislative process, what is to be done when the "laws" or the "views and feelings" of the community deny constitutional protections? The problems are thorny indeed. The manner in which Frankfurter "resolved" the dilemma – at least in principle, if not in wholly consistent practice – is clearly in the direction of "judicial restraint" and a faith in democratic society to make "good law."

Frankfurter was a disciple of Harvard's illustrious professor of constitutional law, James Bradley Thayer. In his book *Felix Frankfurter Reminisces*, Harlan B. Phillips records Frankfurter as saying: "I am of the view that if I were to name one piece of writing on American Constitutional Law – a silly test maybe – I would pick an essay by James Bradley Thayer in the Harvard Law Review, consisting of 26 pages, published in October, 1893, called 'The Origin and Scope of the American Doctrine of Constitutional Law'... "[35] Frankfurter hewed to Thayer's advice that

---

[34] P. Elman (ed.), *Of Law and Men: Papers and Addresses of Felix Frankfurter* (New York: Harcourt, Brace, 1956), pp. 40–1.

[35] F. Frankfurter in H. B. Phillips (ed.), *Felix Frankfurter Reminisces* (New York: Reynal, 1960), pp. 300–1.

the safe and permanent road towards reform is that of impressing upon our people a far stronger sense than they have of the great range of possible mischief *that our system leaves open, and must leave open, to the legislatures*, and of *the clear limits of judicial power*; so that responsibility may be brought sharply home where it belongs. The *checking and cutting down of legislative power, by numerous detailed prohibitions in the constitution, cannot be accomplished without making government petty and incompetent*. This process has already been carried much too far in some of our States. Under *no system can the power of courts go far to save a people from ruin, 'our chief' protection lies elsewhere*. If this be true, it is the greatest public importance to put the matter in its true light. (Italics mine.)[36]

In effect, Frankfurter's views on judicial restraint were grounded in his conception of democracy as a set of procedures – a way of proceeding within certain rules and jurisdictions. In relation to the excerpt from Thayer, Frankfurter remarked: "You know, that's saying something, but that, of course, isn't popular because now many of my friends want me to save them the effort to prevent bad legislation from being passed, and if it is passed even more effort to get it replaced. [They ask] 'What are you there for? You've got the power. Why don't you declare it unconstitutional?' Meaning by 'power' that nobody can overrule me except God by cutting me off and Congress by impeaching me."[37] Frankfurter's claim that "a judge worth his salt is in the grip of his function" supports his attitude that the Supreme Court should adjudicate what is "constitutional," not what is "morally right."[38] In effect, what is constitutional may not coincide with what is "right" by the lights of the individuals exercising decisions in the name of the Court. The passing of laws are legislative acts, not judicial ones. And the loci of "good law" – for which Frankfurter ardently hoped – are the legislative bodies within the political process.[39]

---

[36] Ibid., p. 300.

[37] Ibid., pp. 300–1.

[38] Philip Elman (ed.), *Of Law and Men: Papers and Addresses of Felix Frankfurter*, p. 41.

[39] Frankfurter's position was clearly in evidence in 1934 when he wrote a contribution to the *Encyclopedia of the Social Sciences*. He stated that "judicial adjustments in the English-speaking world operate within traditional limitations. By confining the power of the Supreme Court to the disposition of 'cases' and 'controversies' the Constitution in effect imposed on a tribunal having ultimate power over legislative and executive acts the historic restrictions governing adjudications in common law courts. Most of the problems of modern society, whether of industry, agriculture or finance, of racial interactions or the eternal conflict between liberty and authority, become in the United States sooner or later legal problems for ultimate solution by the Supreme Court. They come before the Court, however, not directly as matters of politics or policy or in the form of principles and abstractions. The Court can only deal with concrete litigation. Its judgment upon a constitutional issue can be invoked only when inextricably entangled with a living and ripe lawsuit. In lawyers' language the Court merely enforces a legal right. . . .
In thus passing on issues only when presented in concrete cases the Supreme Court is true to the empiric process of Anglo-American law. But the attitude of pragmatism which evolved the scope and methods of English judicature, and subsequently its American versions, was powerfully reinforced by considerations of statecraft in defining the sphere of authority for a tribunal of ultimate constitutional adjustments. For in the case of the Supreme Court of the United States questions of jurisdiction are inevitably questions of power as between the several states and the

Thus Frankfurter's "optimism" about the character of democratic society to evolve "good law" is joined with his "realism" regarding the separation-of-powers doctrine and the inordinate powers vested in the Supreme Court – a judicial system in which decisions that lie beyond the range of appeal either block "some attempted exercise of power" or release "the cumbersome procedure of changes of fundamental law." Frankfurter's principle of "judicial restraint" turns on his personal assessment of these issues and their import within the American system of government.

Whatever agreements or disagreements Reinhold Niebuhr and Felix Frankfurter had over the nature and limit of law, they shared a curious fate in recent American history. In their unique and respective ways they proved to be "stumbling blocks" to their "natural" constituencies. American conservatives – who never could grasp the sense of Burkean conservatism that appealed to Niebuhr and Frankfurter – found both men to be dangerous nemeses in regard to all that these alleged "conservatives" deemed to be of value in their reading of society. Both Frankfurter and Niebuhr endured the life-long suspicion and contempt of America's right-wing, except in areas wherein their writings could be twisted to support some outlandish notion or policy which both men abhorred. Yet more surprisingly, Niebuhr and Frankfurter were scorned by their natural allies – the "liberals" – at numerous times in their careers.

Niebuhr, of course, was American liberalism's enfant terrible who relentlessly punctured the illusions of the liberal establishment in order to move it over onto more realistic ground. Finding the theological substructure of the "social gospel liberals" inadequate to the task of effective social reform, Niebuhr undertook a thoroughgoing and comprehensive reassessment of the intellectual assumptions which underlay so much of Western "religious" and "secular" traditions. In the name of a realistic social ethic, Niebuhr launched a broadside into such sacrosanct "liberal" notions as the idea of progress, the rationality of the human being, the individual as master of history and the doctrine of the human's essential goodness. In this endeavor, Niebuhr knew very well that the liberal tradition in American life was the only source of meaningful social reform, however prone it was to grave misjudgments.

Frankfurter was also of "liberal" temperament and came to be identified with the social philosophy of Roosevelt's New Deal. Yet as issues coming before the Supreme Court shifted from those of "social reform" in the 1920s and 1930s to those of "individual" and "civil" liberties in the 1940s and 1950s, Frankfurter's consistent adherence to the principle of "judicial restraint" placed him in an

---

nation or between the Court and the executive and Congress. Every decision of constitutionality is the assertion of some constitutional barrier. However much a judgment of the House of Lords may offend opinion, the Parliament can promptly change the law so declared. But a decision of constitutionality by the Supreme Court either blocks some attempted exercise of power or releases the cumbersome procedure of changes of fundamental law. Therefore the Supreme Court, and very early, evolved canons of judicial self-restraint." F. Frankfurter in A. Macleish and E. F. Prichard Jr. (eds.), *Law and Politics: Occasional Papers of Felix Frankfurter: 1913–1954* (Gloucester, MA: Peter Smith, 1971), pp. 23–4.

adversarial role in relation to many of his friends. During the 1920s and 1930s Frankfurter spoke out against a rampant "judicial activism" in which the Supreme Court interfered in the legislative process by rendering null and void pro-reform legislation. During the 1940s and 1950s Frankfurter was often seen defending the constitutionality of laws that the "liberals" believed to have violated, or at least obstructed, the protection of law regarding individual and civil liberties. Frankfurter's consistency, at least in principle, on the philosophy of "judicial restraint" was what embroiled him in controversy with his former constituency. Because he refused to shift to a stance of "judicial activism" when, according to the liberals, "justice" required it, he was perceived as having abandoned his convictions. His consistency with respect to the place and function of constitutional law in society resulted in decisions within the Court that seemed to obstruct the justice of "protection under law." Because he saw the Supreme Court as "undemocratic," he would "throw back" upon the people and their legislative process the responsibility of formulating "good law." This meant that Frankfurter would on his own admission sometimes render a decision in contradiction to his own conscience.[40]

On May 18, 1954, news broke concerning the famous Supreme Court decision regarding school desegregation in *Brown v. Board of Education*. Niebuhr wrote immediately to Frankfurter:

> Dear Felix:
>
> Together with the whole nation we were thrilled this morning with the news of the unanimous decision of the Supreme Court on the segregation issue. I was particularly thrilled not only because the decision was unanimous, but because it was so wise in the reasons given for the decision, and the time that it permitted most of the States to adjust themselves. I think that this proves that the Supreme Court is operating in terms of the best wisdom of the common law tradition, where both justice and liberty "broaden down from precedent to precedent."

[40] According to one biographer, "Frankfurter did in fact frequently disappoint his 'liberal friends'; and was quickly disowned by them. He spelled out his explanation in a letter to a friend: 'For twenty-five years,' he said, 'my preoccupation as a student of American law was protest against undue assumption of power by judges. I protested when judges declared laws unconstitutional, not because they were laws I favored, but because it was a denial of the democratic process to have our society ruled by judges outside the democratic process. 'After I became a judge,' he continued, 'I could not change my convictions of what I conceive to be the proper function of a judge and nullify legislation simply because I may not like it. But I find that too many of my friends . . . want me . . . to be indifferent to the limits that properly should confine a judge, leaving the remedy for foolish legislation where it mostly belongs, in the hands of an enlightened electorate. I had supposed that that was the best kind of 'liberal' doctrine, but as Holmes said long ago, people on the whole don't want justice, they want you to decide cases their way. . . ." L. Baker, *Felix Frankfurter* (New York: Coward-McCann, 1969), pp. 222–3.

I was also very pleased to get your address before the Philosophical Society at Philadelphia, which expounded the temper and mood which is the basis of such decisions.

I hope that we will see you soon at Heath. We are going up there about June 12th.

With affectionate regards to you and Marion,

Yours,
Reinie[41]

The address to which Niebuhr made reference was "Some Observations on the Nature of the Judicial Process of Supreme Court Litigation," which Frankfurter delivered on April 22, 1954, to the American Philosophical Society meeting in Philadelphia. Niebuhr's mention of this essay in conjunction with his carefully worded appreciation of the "unanimous" decision of the Court might not have been accidental. For although the decision was a unanimous one, there are those who believe that Chief Justice Warren had to perform a miracle in order to overcome Frankfurter's reluctance. It was certainly the case that Frankfurter would have preferred the issue to be resolved in the political arena of American life. The matter of consistency with respect to his judicial philosophy would point unequivocally in that direction.

Frankfurter's role in the historic school desegregation case of 1954 was complex and somewhat confusing. He voted with the Court and revealed in his person and writings an utter detestation of racial inequality. Nonetheless, being "in the grip of his function," he concerned himself first and foremost with the question of law. Liva Baker remarks that "court watchers have speculated that the final decision may have been a rare combination of Frankfurter's intellectual insights and Warren's political insight, as well as Warren's tremendous bargaining power in coming in as a new person whom everyone wanted to work with and who was generally respected."[42]

In his essay before the American Philosophical Society, Frankfurter noted that "broadly speaking, the chief reliance of law in a democracy is the habit of popular respect for law. Especially true is it that law as promulgated by the Supreme Court ultimately depends upon confidence of the people in the Supreme Court as an institution."[43] Frankfurter, above all, knew that the real problem would begin, and not end, with the determination of the constitutional question regarding segregation in the schools. His mind probed the subsequent problems of the enforceability of a desegregation decision and the impact such a decision would have on the issue of public confidence in the Court.

[41] R. Niebuhr to F. Frankfurter (May 18, 1954, in FCLC).

[42] L. Baker, *Felix Frankfurter* (New York: Coward-McCann, 1969), p. 308.

[43] F. Frankfurter, "Some observations on the nature of the judicial process of supreme court litigation," *Proceedings of the American Philosophical Society*, 98:4 (1954), 233.

According to Niebuhr's May 18 letter to Frankfurter, the Niebuhrs expected to be in Heath, Massachusetts, in the vicinity of June 12. Frankfurter was also in Heath that summer but, as Baker put it, "he used a good deal of it pondering the problem of implementation of the May 17 decision which had been postponed by the Court's call for rearguments on implementation."[44] With Niebuhr and Frankfurter together in Massachusetts during the summer of 1954, one cannot but wonder what conversations transpired between them regarding the general climate of the desegregation issue which had so focused America's attention. However, one thing is certain. Frankfurter took the responsibilities of "the veil" with utmost seriousness, and he often voiced a measure of frustration over the restraint which his interpretation of his office had placed upon him. He would never discuss a pending case before the Supreme Court, and he was not receptive to those who sought to discuss such matters with him. Niebuhr's son, Christopher, informed me that his "first knowledge of the law was [his] parents' instruction between a pending case and cases already decided," and in this regard "*no* member of the family ever abused that instruction."[45]

Frankfurter's concern with implementation and public confidence in the Court resonated, nonetheless, with Niebuhr's views regarding the majesty and limits of law. Niebuhr constantly pointed to the precarious balance between force and prestige in both the authority of government and the majesty of law. Certainly Niebuhr's remark to Frankfurter in his May 18 letter stating his approval of the "time that [the decision] permitted most of the States to adjust themselves," would indicate a point at which their thought coincided. One thing seems to be clear. During that summer, according to Liva Baker, Frankfurter

wrote to Chief Justice Warren [in order to assure that the Court] gather as much relevant data in regard to school districting – districting done in a normal fashion without regard for the race issue – to understand legitimate geographical and population factors involved in drawing school district lines. While he hoped the Court would do no more than set general standards, leaving details to be worked out on the local level, Frankfurter felt the Court might benefit from understanding the genuine problems that confront healthy communities. He wanted the Court to understand how these healthy bodies solve their problems so that the Court would not, through ignorance, send the fever of the South higher or attribute normal controversy to inflamed Southern passion.[46]

The Court's phrase "with all deliberate speed" was used to justify procrastination and resistance on the part of those who did not wish to comply with the desegregation decision. Frankfurter, of course, desired to provide for a steady, peaceful, and seamless transition to this revolutionary "reform" of society. Perhaps if the Eisenhower Administration had supplied a tangible moral lead and put its prestige immediately and unequivocally behind the law of the land, the crisis at Little Rock, Arkansas, in the autumn of 1957 could have been

---

[44] L. Baker, *Felix Frankfurter*, p. 319.
[45] C. Niebuhr to D. F. Rice (November 20, 1978).
[46] L. Baker, *Felix Frankfurter*, p. 319.

avoided. At least, this was Niebuhr's view as he wrote of the unfortunate use of force at Little Rock when the Administration finally acted.[47]

In the May 2, 1955, issue of *Christianity and Crisis* Niebuhr published an essay on "'Winston Churchill and Great Britain.'"[48] So enthusiastic was Frankfurter that he suggested to Niebuhr that he, Frankfurter, send a copy of the article to "the great man himself." In his May 14, 1955, letter to Niebuhr, Frankfurter wrote: "My obligations to you are fast reaching the scale of our national debt. And so I must not allow another day to pass by without thanking you for the latest piece of writing [on Churchill] I read that stirred in me exhilarating assent. ... You proved once more, as you frequently do, in the slim pages of *Christianity and Crisis*, how much can be said in how little." Frankfurter then added that

The only thing of yours that I have read recently for which I did not feel full-throated enthusiasm was your review of Walter Lippmann. Am I wrong in thinking that the biblical quotation to him "that hath shall be given" was an ironic utterance. In any event, so far as I am concerned, when it comes to the domain of power and position – moral, intellectual, official – my motto is: from him that hath shall be exacted. I do not see why the great elucidator should be treated with greater charity than some unknown nobody. No, I have not read Walter's book but I know what is in it. I like my Edmund Burke straight and with its own organ-like eloquence.[49]

Frankfurter's reference to Walter Lippmann had to do with Niebuhr's rather kindly review of Lippmann's new book *Essays in the Public Philosophy*, published in 1955. A lively, tongue-in-cheek exchange was to follow on the Lippmann matter. Niebuhr wrote Frankfurter on May 16 stating that

In regard to the review of the Walter Lippmann book, I must confess to a very uneasy conscience and say that if it had been anybody else but Walter Lippmann I would have reviewed it more severely. Your rebuke is justified. Incidentally, I wouldn't say that he talked like Burke. He has been influenced by Mortimer Adler's natural law theories to such a degree that I don't think he quite understands Burke any more.[50]

One day later Niebuhr, continuing to reflect on the Lippmann review, wrote:

I must send you an addendum to my letter lest you think I am really worse than I am. I didn't, at least consciously, go easy on Walter Lippmann because of his reputation. My inhibitions were due to the fact that I met him personally for the first time last year, that he was very kind to me, and that we found ourselves in agreement on many foreign policy questions. So I pulled my punches. I don't think that this mitigates my guilt, but I just wanted to disclose my real motives, as far as I know them.[51]

---

[47] R. Niebuhr, "Bad days at Little Rock," *Christianity and Crisis* (October 14, 1957), 131.
[48] R. Niebuhr, "Winston Churchill and Great Britain," *Christianity and Crisis* (May 2, 1955), 51–2.
[49] F. Frankfurter to R. Niebuhr (May 14, 1955, in FCLC).
[50] R. Niebuhr to F. Frankfurter (May 16, 1955, in FCLC).
[51] R. Niebuhr to F. Frankfurter (May 17, 1955, in FCLC).

Frankfurter, with a somewhat caustic sense of humor, replied:

Dear Reinie:

Of course, it would never occur to me that you would "go easy on Walter Lippmann because of his reputation." Heavens! We lawyers, or, if you like, I, may make crude attributions of motive, but not that crude. I think, however, with all due respect, considering the reviews I have seen by other people, that a fellow like W. L. does exert a kind of hydrolic [sic] pressure on others when he writes about important themes with an air of philosophic seriousness. One of the dearest friends of my life, himself a poet, said to me that when a poet throws a volume of verses out into the open he ought to expect that horses would trample on it. Unless I am greatly misinformed, an eminent professor at Columbia refused to review Lippmann's book because he knew him, though not a great friend of his. What kind of intellectual atmosphere can we have when there are restraints like that to candid utterance?[52]

Late in 1956, Frankfurter expressed a continuing appreciation for Niebuhr's labors as a commentator on the issues of the times. At the same time, he uttered a harsh word for what he termed the "self-righteousness" of certain other contributors to Niebuhr's journal, *Christianity and Crisis*. Frankfurter wrote on December 28, 1956, telling him that,

Increasingly I find satisfaction in the paragraphs signed R.N. in recent issues of Christianity and Crisis. You give me the satisfaction that one derives from agreement, though you express our agreement on the gnarled issues of our time usually with more penetrating analysis than does my own thinking. But I find not merely this satisfaction in what you write, but the satisfaction of making me forget some of the dogmatism and self-righteousness of other contributors. You remember John Morley's remark about Carlyle that he preached the golden gospel of silence in thirty volumes. Am I censorious in finding some of the preachments on humility by some of the editors of C. & C. in cocksure and self-righteous tones?[53]

Three days later Niebuhr replied:

In regard to the substance of your very complimentary letter, Ursula rejoiced and said "You see other people also detect the self-righteousness," which she incidentally detects everywhere among religious people. I agree with you and with her but I am defensive about my profession and maintain that piety only accentuates a common human frailty.

Niebuhr then informed Frankfurter that he had received

an invitation from Oppenheimer to spend a year at the Institute for Advanced Studies writing a book on political ethics or more precisely on "The morality of Nations." Have accepted. The prospect of doing this is both thrilling and frightening because I must

---

[52] F. Frankfurter to R. Niebuhr (May 18, 1955, in FCLC).
[53] F. Frankfurter to R. Niebuhr (December 28, 1956, in FCLC).

elaborate an avocational interest into something which will not make the institute look too silly.[54]

In corresponding with Niebuhr in February, 1957, Frankfurter referred to Niebuhr's "forthcoming year at Princeton" – a year in which Niebuhr would write his book *The Structure of Nations and Empires* (1959) while at the Princeton Institute's School of Historical Studies. On December 17, 1956, its director, J. Robert Oppenheimer, had written to Niebuhr extending the invitation:

> Dear Dr. Niebuhr:
>
> It gives me great pleasure, with the concurrence of the Faculty of the School of Historical Studies, to invite you to accept a membership at the Institute for Advanced Study for next year: the academic year 1957–1958. We understand that this time would be a suitable one for you, and helpful in your work on ethics and the state; of course, we should be happy to consider any other time that would be better for your purposes.
>
> May I add that it is to me a great joy to write this note, and that I hope that the possibility it suggests will indeed be a reality.
>
> With warm good wishes,
>
> Robert Oppenheimer[55]

More central to Frankfurter's February 6, 1957, letter to Niebuhr was his mention of the Richmond Ministers' Association manifesto and his personal reaction to the racial situation since 1954. The years immediately following *Brown v. Board of Education* decision were tumultuous years in American life. Persistent attempts to circumvent the Court's decision, particularly by means of taking refuge behind the "with all deliberate speed" clause, threatened to destroy the delicate social fabric.

Voices of moderation and responsible efforts to encourage public compliance with the rule of law were not entirely absent in the Border States or even in the Deep South. However, such voices were largely overwhelmed by widespread hysteria and open defiance. The mood of the times was sufficiently tense so as to make the occasional voice of sanity and moderation all the more admirable and courageous. One such voice, the Richmond Ministers' Association manifesto, came prior to Arkansas Governor Orval Faubus's obstructionist tactics in Little Rock. Responding to a Virginia constitutional amendment designed to abort the desegregation decision, the Richmond Ministers' Association released a 1,500-word "Statement of Conviction on Race" on January 28, 1957, in which it condemned the tactics of evasion and supported compliance with the law of the land. The ministers claimed the "Governor and a majority of the Legislature ... have, in our opinion, seriously impaired the sacred and historic traditions of

---

[54] R. Niebuhr to F. Frankfurter (Dec. 31, 1956, in FCLC).
[55] J. R. Oppenheimer to R. Niebuhr (Dec. 17, 1956, in NCLC).

Virginia democracy and lowered the prestige of the State in the eyes of thought-ful people."[56] They also argued that "to defy openly the Supreme Court and to encourage others to do so, in our judgment, is not only poor strategy; it is poor citizenship. Therefore, we urge our state government to act with loyalty and with maturity as regards co-operation with all established agencies of American government, and to lead us in a statesmanlike rather than an anarchistic manner."[57]

Frankfurter's February 6 letter to Niebuhr expressed his own hopes on the school desegregation issue:

Dear Reinie:

If you have not seen this manifesto of the Richmond Ministers Association, you will want to. I know one swallow does not make a summer, but sometimes one swallow is a harbinger of others. I know hope rather than prophecy – particularly these days – is behind.

"If winter comes, can spring be far behind?" But at times it does turn out that way.

Of course, I take a serious view of the situation, but not a tragic one. Certainly, for myself, I am not expressing hindsight when I say that I did not anticipate a quicker or more comprehensive acceptance of the Supreme Court decision. Nor was violent resistance, here and there, unanticipated. What one had hoped for was the steady permeation of a conviction of inevitability and the displacement of old habits by the acquisition of new ones in the Border States. Through them and some ferment within the Deep South, one hoped, as I still hope, for an almost imperceptible change of habit by bowing to necessity in the communities having a large percentage of Negroes. I wish you had heard the remarks made by a former colored law clerk of mine, in the intimacy of a private dinner, on the enormous changes that have taken place in the atmosphere and actions of Washington during the few years since he left here, to wit: the summer of 1949. Not remotely do I mean to sound complacent or happy about the situation. That is not the state of my feeling. I am merely trying to convey my own state of mind as of May 17, 1954.[58]

Niebuhr replied on February 8:

Dear Felix,

Thank you for your nice letter and for sending me the manifesto of the Richmond Ministers Association. We have been holding off with a

---

[56] B. Muse, *Virginia's Massive Resistance* (Gloucester, MA: Peter Smith, 1995), p. 39.

[57] T. B. Maston, *Segregation and Desegregation: A Christian Approach* (New York: Macmillan, 1959), p. 34.

[58] F. Frankfurter to R. Niebuhr (February 6, 1957, in FCLC).

statement from Northern ministers because we were told that there was a Conference of Southern ministers from all over the South to make a statement on the race issue, and that anything from the North would seem like Yankee interference.

I was also asked by Martin Luther King to sign a statement to the President asking him to intervene in the situation down South, but I was advised that such a pressure would do more harm than good. A group of Southern preachers are going to see the President privately to try to influence him to act. I confess that I don't know why a Republican President should be so hesitant on this matter. I agree with your analysis of the situation except that I think some evidence points to the fact that the hopeful parts of the South are advancing faster under the lash of your decision, while the recalcitrance of the deep South seems to be accentuated.[59]

Niebuhr had become increasingly critical of the Eisenhower Administration – focusing primarily on the political ineptitude of Eisenhower and the dangerous fusion of self-righteous moralism and strident militarism in Secretary of State John Foster Dulles. Niebuhr had hoped that the debacle of the so-called Suez Crisis, in which the United States had lost control of events in the Mideast by inadvertently driving a wedge between Western allies, might trigger a shattering of America's complacency. He even let himself hope that the Administration's tragic mishandling of events relating to Israel would result in the election of Adlai Stevenson in November, 1956. In a letter written on February 19, 1957, Niebuhr expressed his views on Eisenhower and Dulles to Frankfurter. He referred to the "pettifoggery" and "fantastic stupidity" the Eisenhower administration displayed "in handling all of the relationships between our allies," adding that "for the first time in many decades I feel seriously concerned about the future of this great country, because the two men who seem to be guiding its destiny seem both to be stupid. The one is amiable and the other not, but the stupidity is equal."[60]

In late June, 1957, Niebuhr wrote to Frankfurter in reference to two recent Supreme Court decisions in which he thanked Frankfurter for sending him "two memorable decisions, which are chapters in the Supreme Court's creative influence on the history of our time." Niebuhr wrote:

As I never was happy about the Smith Act I rejoiced with many others that the Court decision makes it quite explicit that it is necessary not only to advocate in the abstract but actually to incite to revolution, to run afoul of the law. I was also glad to see your dissent on the Dupont decision. I don't know anything about it but it seemed to me that the decision was anachronistic.

It is certainly wonderful to see the founding fathers vindicated in having established that very 'undemocratic' institution, the Court, to protect the liberties of democracy. But

[59] R. Niebuhr to F. Frankfurter (February 8, 1957, in FCLC).
[60] R. Niebuhr to F. Frankfurter (February 19, 1957, in FCLC).

perhaps that was not so radical a step because an independent judicatory is by its nature 'undemocratic,' that is, freed from popular and public pressures.[61]

Niebuhr's letter focused on the case of *Yates v. United States*, in which the rights of free speech and free association were addressed by the Court in 1957 after having tolerated a high degree of "red baiting." The case related directly to the Smith Act, or Alien Registration Act of June 28, 1940. The Smith Act ostensibly strengthened laws governing the admission and deportation of aliens in the United States. However, the real aim of the Smith Act was to find means by which to check subversive activities, making it illegal for any person either to advocate or to teach the overthrow – by force or violence – of any government in the United States or to organize or hold membership in any group dedicated to teaching such doctrine. In 1949, during the hysterical days of the "red scare," alleged violation of the Smith Act was used in a New York federal trial of eleven top leaders of the United States Communist Party. The trial commenced on January 17. On October 14, 1949, they were convicted and later, on October 21, sentenced to prison.

Frankfurter had, early in his Supreme Court career, assumed leadership in opposing the position of Hugo Black and William O. Douglas that First Amendment rights were absolute. His conviction that freedom is not absolute, but requires definition by present experience, was expressed in the *Gobitis* case of 1940. Frankfurter had really alienated his "liberal" friends in his opinion in *Dennis v. United States* (1951) – a case figuring prominently in *Yates v. United States* – with his recognition that the nation's interest in self-preservation had validity against the claims of free speech and, more importantly, with his view that legislative acts should have a determining influence in such matters.

What is of particular interest in Niebuhr's letter regarding *Yates* was his statement to Frankfurter: "It is certainly wonderful to see the founding fathers vindicated in having established that very 'undemocratic' institution, the Court, to protect the liberties of democracy." This is especially important in light of Frankfurter's opinion in *Dennis v. United States*. Frankfurter's position is worth quoting in full:

Civil liberties draw at best only limited strength from legal guaranties. Preoccupation by our people with the constitutionality, instead of with the wisdom, of legislation or of executive action is preoccupation with a false value. Even those who would most freely use the judicial brake on the democratic process by invalidating legislation that goes deeply against their grain, acknowledge, at least by paying lip service, that constitutionality does not exact a sense of proportion or the sanity of humor or an absence of fear. Focusing attention on constitutionality tends to make constitutionality synonymous with wisdom. When legislation touches freedom of thought and freedom of speech, such a tendency is a formidable enemy of the free spirit. Much that should be rejected as illiberal, because repressive and envenoming, may well be not unconstitutional. The ultimate reliance for the deepest needs of civilization must be found outside their vindication in courts of law; apart from all else, judges, howsoever they may conscientiously seek to

---

[61] R. Niebuhr to F. Frankfurter (June 26, 1957, in FCLC).

discipline themselves against it, unconsciously are too apt to be moved by the deep undercurrents of public feeling. A persistent, positive translation of the liberating faith into the feelings and thoughts and actions of men and women is the real protection against attempts to strait-jacket the human mind. Such temptations will have their way, if fear and hatred are not exorcized. The mask of a truly civilized man is confidence in the strength and security derived from the inquiring mind. We may be grateful for such honest comforts as it supports, but we must be unafraid of its incertitudes. Without open minds there can be no open society. And if society be not open the spirit of man is mutilated and becomes enslaved.[62]

Yet between *Dennis* (1951) and *Yates* (1957), nearly one hundred convictions and many more indictments had been obtained for alleged Smith Act violations. While *Dennis* upheld the Smith Act as to the criminal offense of conspiring to advocate the forceful overthrow of the government, *Yates* held that the government had too broadly conceived its powers under the Smith Act, ruling that the Smith Act was not to be construed as forbidding advocacy and teaching forcible overthrow as an abstract principle. The crucial distinction rested on a definite effort to incite action to that end. Frankfurter's agreement with *Yates v. United States* had obviously delighted Niebuhr, not least of all because Niebuhr's sympathies appeared to be on the side of Justice Hugo Black in cases pertaining to First Amendment rights. And Frankfurter's decisions on internal security cases during the 1950s were consistently offensive to those of liberal persuasion, with whom Niebuhr largely identified.

In the autumn of 1957, a few months before leaving for the Institute for Advanced Studies at Princeton, Niebuhr wrote to Frankfurter regarding an essay Frankfurter had sent him on Fiorello LaGuardia:

Dear Felix:

We were so glad to get the copy of your address on Mayor LaGuardia. I appreciate it very much for many reasons. This little Napoleon was one of my heroes and 1 still like to hear Christopher's "Hear it Now" record where he says "I could have beaten those bums running on a laundry ticket." I was particularly interested that you had such close contact with him, and your story of the arbitration which you conducted between him and Chandler is superb. We don't often get people who combine political rectitude with dramatic gifts in the way that Fiorello combined them. I still remember his reading the funnies to the children during a newspaper strike here.

We enjoyed our summer in Stockbridge, and are now thinking about Princeton, where we go in February.

With affectionate greetings to you and Marion,

Yours,
Reinie[63]

---

[62] *Dennis v. United States*, 341 U.S. 494, 555–6 (1951).
[63] R. Niebuhr to F. Frankfurter (October 14, 1957, in FCLC).

Two days later, on October 16, Niebuhr received a letter in which Frankfurter requested Niebuhr's views regarding the dilemma of a young pacifist whose pacifism was not theistically grounded. Frankfurter wrote:

Dear Reinie:

The enclosed letter, which I do feel free to trouble you with reading, raises questions on which I would rather have your view than anybody else's. But if you would find it a chore to deal with what the lawyers call the merits of the poor lad's question, send it back to me without another thought. Perhaps second only to Ursula am I mindful of the importance of not putting any extra burden on you.

In any event, I will trouble you to return the letter shortly.

Ever yours,
Felix[64]

Niebuhr's response was indicative of the personal qualities of a man who, after profound and intensive soul-searching, had rejected pacifism as a viable position in a world in which both peace and justice are "gained by strife." Niebuhr had struggled long and hard with the pacifist issue. Once the national chairman of the Fellowship of Reconciliation, Niebuhr had never been completely at ease with the moral absolutes of the pacifist position. From 1932 onward, he became a trenchant critic of those who would obscure the element of coercion in the quest for social justice. Niebuhr's letter to Frankfurter revealed that he was never comfortable with the limited kind of "protection" provided in the law for the pacifist witness. Long before *Welsh v. United States* in June, 1970, Niebuhr held that there was a moral validity in pacifist convictions that arose out of purely humanistic grounds. To hold otherwise, he believed, conflicted with First Amendment rights. On October 18, 1957, Niebuhr wrote Frankfurter:

---

[64] F. Frankfurter to R. Niebuhr (October 16, 1957, in FCLC). The issue with which Frankfurter and Niebuhr concerned themselves was not finally resolved until 1970. On June 15, 1970, the Supreme Court reversed a lower court decision in *Welsh v. United States*. The petitioner to the Court claimed conscientious objector status under #6(j) of the Universal Military Training and Service Act on the grounds that his claim met the conditions of *United States v. Seeger*, 380 U.S. 163, "which held that the test of religious belief under #6(j) is whether it is a sincere and meaningful belief occupying in the life of its possessor a place parallel to that filled by the God of those admittedly qualified for the exemption." Ibid.: 344. The Supreme Court upheld the petitioner's claim and reversed the Court of Appeals. The crucial statement, in the opinion of Justice Hugo Black, affirms that "That section [#6(j)] exempts from military service all those whose consciences, spurred by deeply held moral, ethical, or religious beliefs, would give them no rest or peace if they allowed themselves to become a part of an instrument of war." *Welsh v. United States*, 398 U.S. 333 (1970).

Dear Felix:

Thank you for your letter with the enclosed letter from the 19 year old student, which I return herewith. The predicament of the student shows the limits of the law which tried to prevent exemptions for purely political pacifists by emphasizing the religious ground of the pacifist's belief. I always thought that this was a very dubious part of the law, and this young man's predicament proves that it is. I think the only thing one can say to him is that he should state his convictions clearly and say that they are derived from what he regards to be the ethic of Jesus, that he is an agnostic in regard to any ultimate religious beliefs, but that he has arrived at his conviction not out of political or sociological considerations, but out of a deep personal commitment. I should hope that somewhere along the line the validity of this type of pacifism would be accepted. If not, the law will make belief in God the only haven for pacifistic dissenters. I should assume that if that's what the law really means it is in conflict with the First Amendment.

　　With affectionate regards to you and Marion,

Yours,
Reinie[65]

Niebuhr wrote to Frankfurter on October 30 thanking him for having sent his "volume 'Of Law and Men' with [its] nice dedication. Ursula and I read the volume with great interest and appreciation. Both chapters dealing with the members of the Court and the Court itself and your various eulogies were very discerning and perceptive. Meanwhile we also got the volume 'The Constitutional World of Mr. Justice Frankfurter' (I understand by Professor Konefsky) and I understand that your friend, Mr. Gunther, had a great deal to do with this volume. I am just reading it." Niebuhr then informed Frankfurter that he would be "spending the fall in Princeton ... revising the manuscript of my volume."[66]

　　Frankfurter had suffered a mild heart attack in 1958, and although hospitalized briefly he resumed his work on the Supreme Court with only a moderate curtailment of activity. On January 3, 1959, Niebuhr wrote Frankfurter.

Dear Felix:

During the holidays, visits with the Palfreys, where we saw Professor Handler and with the Feisses, who gave a Washington report of your convalescence, we had frequent occasions to keep current on your condition, which reassured us very much. [We] also had occasion to exchange "Felix" stories with one another, all of them attesting to the deep affection in which you are held by your friends everywhere.

---

[65] R. Niebuhr to F. Frankfurter (October 18, 1957, in FCLC).
[66] R. Niebuhr to F. Frankfurter (October 30, 1958, in FCLC).

We hope your health continues to improve throughout the new year and we wish you and Marion every happiness. Elizabeth was back for the holidays and Christopher didn't stop one day preparing for the exams in the Law School next week. He finds the going pretty tough, but so do young men more gifted or less handicapped than he. We hope he survives. I have finished my book and Ursula and I are editing the chapters in the light of recent criticisms by E. L. Woodward and [Hans] Morgenthau. I would like to send you a copy but one goes to the publishers and the other will become the basis of my lectures this spring. In any case you have more important things to do than to read my outpourings.

Our affectionate regards,

Yours,
Reinie[67]

Frankfurter's heart attack, and his subsequent recuperation, placed additional strain on his wife Marion who had become bedridden with arthritis since 1954. Niebuhr wrote to Frankfurter on February 13, 1959, inquiring about the state of Frankfurter's health and informing him that he had not yet decided upon an exact title for his new book:

Dear Felix:

Our whole family was delighted with your letter for many reasons but first of all about the news of your returning health. These "episodes" or "incidents" as the doctors call them are means of saving our lives. I envy you because your episode was of the heart and not of the brain. I have a more serious reminder of my unwillingness to admit my years because I have a permanent case of spastic paralysis. And I never was quite as profligate with my energy as you have consistently been. But I don't expect justice from the natural process, so I am content with the fact that my life has been prolonged by the shock I suffered. May a justice of the Supreme Court learn wisdom and restrain his native dynamism.

We had a grand time in Princeton and for the first time in my life I spent a whole year on a book. I am anxious to send you a copy when it comes out in July. I think it will be called "Dominion in Nations and Empires."

Niebuhr continues his letter with a personal recollection and a commentary on Archibald MacLeish's play, JB:

I remember that after a service in the church at Heath we defined the difference between us as between a "believing unbeliever" and a "believer with unbelief." Incidentally there are many forms of agnosticism as there are of belief. I say this because Archie [Archibald MacLeish] was with you at that time. While I think his JB is a great work and particularly

[67] R. Niebuhr to F. Frankfurter (January 3, 1959, in FCLC).

good theatre, I suspect he solves the problem of life rather more simply than you would. For he bases his play on the happy ending of the old prose part of Job and leaves out the profound pious impieties of the real poem, which gives the book its real meaning.[68]

Frankfurter, not without serious reservations, had permitted the publication of a series of conversations he had with Harlan B. Phillips. These conversations were published under the title *Felix Frankfurter Reminisces* and were already in their sixth printing by September, 1960. The uneasiness Frankfurter felt regarding the personal nature of this book was somewhat abated in the wake of an enthusiastic response he had received from the Niebuhrs subsequent to the book's publication. On March 10, 1960, Frankfurter wrote to Niebuhr that,

Of course I am enormously pleased by the enthusiasm you express. What is more important, however, is that by hitting you as they do has even more relieved and pleased both Marion and me. Relieved, because both of us have had feeling of unease about getting into print in such a personal fashion. I must confess to a weakness in my character in having consented to this publication. It is the honest truth that I did so fundamentally because of the importunity of the publisher. Gene Reynal (perhaps you know him) who has been a deeply devoted friend of mine over the decades and has to some extent suffered on account of it. What led [me] to yield was my confidence in his taste and judgment. I began to feel that it would be a form of morbidity on my part to feel any impropriety in the publication of what will now appear. The details of your appreciation have set both Marion and my dubiety about the whole business to rest and I am deeply grateful to you.[69]

In that same letter, Frankfurter expressed relief at Niebuhr's "comments on my 'negative' attitude toward Wilson. Not that I am uncertain in what I feel about him (I enclose a piece I wrote on him on the occasion of his hundredth anniversary) but I was afraid that I would hurt the feelings of too many people who idolize him. If ever a great man had clay feet, it was Woodrow Wilson." Frankfurter's attitude toward Woodrow Wilson was largely negative. In *Felix Frankfurter Reminisces*, Frankfurter related several incidents that revealed Wilson's unwillingness to consult with his own key personnel on major political decisions, often leaving his subordinates bewildered and sometimes embarrassed. Frankfurter maintained that "Wilson would act without any kind of respect for orderly consultation if that was what he wanted to do."[70] Moreover, "Wilson was very dogmatic. That was his great limitation, and he didn't believe in debating. He used phrases like 'laying mind against mind' and 'consulting the common council of the nation,' but he didn't carry that out in practice at all – quite the opposite."[71]

While Frankfurter did not wish to hurt the feelings of those who idolized Wilson, he had nonetheless openly confronted Wilson's weaknesses in the essay he had sent to Niebuhr, an essay which was published in *The Times* of London

---

[68] R. Niebuhr to F. Frankfurter (February 13, 1959, in FCLC).
[69] F. Frankfurter to R. Niebuhr (March 10, 1960, in FCLC).
[70] F. Frankfurter in H. B. Phillips (ed.), *Felix Frankfurter Reminisces*, p. 68.
[71] Ibid., p. 75.

on December 28, 1956, commemorating the 100th anniversary of Wilson's birth. Having expressed profound admiration for Wilson's efforts to "adjust by rational methods the inevitable clash and confusion of interests among the different peoples of the world," Frankfurter saw the ironic undermining of that aim in both Wilson's aloofness from personal contacts and in his excessive confidence in reason and ideological abstraction.[72]

Several items pressed in upon the mind of Frankfurter in the early spring of 1960. On May 2, 1960, Niebuhr had written an editorial on "The Church and the South African Tragedy." A rising tide of tension between the black population of South Africa and the South African government precipitated sharp protest from a variety of quarters, both official and unofficial. Included in that protest were condemnations of apartheid by the major religious bodies in England. The Dutch Reformed Church of South Africa, however, openly supported the government's inhumanity. In this context, Niebuhr wrote that the "most disturbing fact, however, is that the Dutch Reformed Church has been the chief bulwark of the National Party. Quite a few of its leaders, former Prime Minister Malan for instance, were former preachers in that church. Fortunately there is an increasing dissent from some of the more sensitive spirits within the church. But the situation is that a Christian church has, on the whole, used an obscurantist version of the Christian faith to elaborate policies as inhumane as those of the Nazis, who were supposed to derive their inhumanity from their paganism."[73]

Commenting on this and other concerns, Frankfurter wrote to Niebuhr on May 24, 1960, confessing that,

From time to time Marion charges me with being a romantic believer in reason. Like you, she knows that evil is an inherent ingredient of man and has a strong belief that public men who do not adequately gauge its extent are dangerous. But when I read what you tell me of the recent report of the Committee on Race Relations of the Federal Council of Dutch Reformed Churches of South Africa, the limits of my credulity assert themselves. I say this, although I know enough of the history of South Africa to know that the social teachings of the Dutch Reformed Churches have always been more obscurantist than that of other Protestant faiths. But to see it in black and white as you set it forth really stops me in my tracks – as does not quite as much but sufficiently so the announcement of the publication of "The Spiritual Heritage of John Foster Dulles." I must believe that people who thus invoke "God" or "Christ" or "spiritual heritage" have not the remotest realization of their blasphemy.[74]

The Dulles book to which Frankfurter referred was called *The Spiritual Heritage of John Foster Dulles*. Encompassing a collection of rather pious and mostly vacuous speeches which Dulles had delivered, this book was certainly

---

[72] F. Frankfurter in P. B. Kurland (ed.), *Of Law and Life and Other Things That Matter: The Papers and Addresses of Felix Frankfurter 1956–1963* (Cambridge, MA: Belknap Press of Harvard University, 1965), p. 64. Ibid., pp. 67–8.

[73] R. Niebuhr, "The church and the South African tragedy," *Christianity and Crisis* (May 2, 1960), 53.

[74] F. Frankfurter to R. Niebuhr (May 24, 1960, in FCLC).

"blasphemous" as Frankfurter had charged. What was most disconcerting to Niebuhr about this book was that the President of Union Theological Seminary in New York, Henry P. van Dusen, edited the Dulles essays and wrote a simplistic but glowing introduction. On May 26, Niebuhr answered Frankfurter's letter of two days before, expressing how heartily he agreed with Frankfurter's assessment of the Dulles book. He remarked that "the introduction to the book by the President of this Seminary makes vivid all the concerns which Ursula and I have increasingly felt about the smugness of the current piety, as revealed in this seminary and indeed in the whole church. It has been reduced to triviality and smugness. You can imagine my state of mind after having devoted all these decades to the religious enterprise."[75]

In his May 24 letter Frankfurter, referring to the summit in Paris that Russian Premier Khrushchev had walked away from, had mentioned that,

Not the least disturbing thing to me is the way all sorts of people are running to cover after the debacle at Paris, full of demands that all the rest of us search our consciences and reexamine our thinking, without the slightest indication that their own thinking also calls for reexamination. Thus, Walter Lippmann tells everybody to beat his breast, but not a word about the geometric demonstrations he made on the very eve of the collapse that all the four leaders, and not the least of all Khrushchev, were absolutely dependent on a détente.

Niebuhr, in his reply of May 26, said:

I am as distressed as you and everyone about the summit meeting, but I don't agree that Khrushchev needed a detente or that this was his chief need. Pressed by the Chinese and his own military on the disarmament issue, and facing a solid front on the Berlin issue by the western powers, he took the only way out by wrecking the conference. We should never have gotten into the position of going to a summit conference without previous successful negotiations. The President sounds very naive when he declares that the shift in Soviet policy is a mystery. We should have known about the internal pressures in the communist empire before the summit. Nobody has come out of that debacle with credit.

Khrushchev had used the Francis Gary Powers U-2 spy plane incident to torpedo the summit conference with France's President Charles de Gaulle, England's Prime Minister Harold Macmillan and President Eisenhower. Eisenhower suffered embarrassment and humiliation as a result of the incident. George Kennan, in *The New York Times* letter to which Frankfurter referred, argued that "at no time, even before the plane incident, was there reason to believe that prospects were good for agreement at the summit on any of the substantive issues involved," and he stressed that "what is needed … is not an orgy of partisan recrimination but a rigorous scrutiny of our own mistakes, a dispassionate reappraisal of our world position, and an airing of the current problems of national policy, all conducted in a spirit which recognizes that America is

[75] R. Niebuhr to F. Frankfurter (May 26, 1960, in FCLC).

today beset by dangers far transcending in their implications the domestic and personal issues of the forthcoming election."[76]

Niebuhr had consistently distrusted negotiation by "summitry," and he cautioned against the precarious position to which such a method of diplomacy might lead. Negotiation on substantive matters is a slow and usually tortuous process requiring both time and privacy. Niebuhr believed that unless the groundwork is carefully worked out in such a manner that a summit meeting merely provides the formalizing of already agreed upon issues, the very thing that happened in Paris becomes all the more likely.

Frankfurter replied to Niebuhr on May 31:

> Dear Reinie:
>
> I hasten to correct any impression I may have given you that I thought that Khrushchev "needed a detente." No such thought was in my mind. I was pointing out the characteristic imperceptiveness of Walter Lippmann when he tries to pierce into the future. It was he who wrote a piece a few days before the day the four were to have met saying that each of them, and not least Khrushchev, needed a detente. (I think Walter is very good at retro-spective interpretation of what happens, but he is totally devoid of pro-phetic instinct.)
>
> I can imagine what a wrench it is for you and Ursula to leave 122nd Street. But you do not tell me where you are moving to.
>
> Affectionately yours,
> Felix[77]

July, 1960, found Niebuhr at the Center for the Study of Democratic Institutions in Santa Barbara, California. The nominating conventions were over and the presidential contest between John F. Kennedy and Richard M. Nixon lay just ahead. Niebuhr, who eventually came to respect the aims of the Kennedy presidency, had serious reservations regarding the Kennedy candidacy. With a delightful sense of self-criticism, Niebuhr related his difficulty accepting Kennedy to his life-long protest against "Protestant purists" and their inability to "come to terms with the moral ambiguity of the political process." In a letter which he characterized as the "aimless confession of a bewildered man," Niebuhr wrote this long and thoughtful letter to Frankfurter on July 23, 1960:

> Dear Felix:
>
> I talked so much about you in the past days, chiefly with Abe Chayes and his wife; and heard so much political gossip from journalists returning from the conventions, mostly old hat to you, that I am inspired to write you a letter.

---

[76] *The New York Times* section 4 (May 22, 1960), 12.
[77] F. Frankfurter to R. Niebuhr (May 31, 1960, in FCLC).

First of all I promised to spend the summer here with the fund people partly for economic reasons and partly because I like the moderate schedule of three hours of meeting per day and partly because people like Harry Ashmore, Prof Harrison Brown, and the journalist Paul Jacobs (Reporter) working in various ways on the project are very interesting. Chayes came here on the way back from the convention. I was surprised to find that he was the original academic Kennedy man in Mass. Three liberal southern journalists, among them McGill of the Atlanta Constitution, also visited us. They were Stevenson men, who had however predicted Kennedy's nomination. Stevenson visited here a week ago. I was among the many academics who were really for Stevenson; but his indecisiveness was revealed in his ambiguous position in the convention, where he was and was not a candidate. I write to you to make a confession, that one who has preached a lifetime to Protestant purists that they must come to terms with the moral ambiguity of the political process, [I] found it very difficult to swallow Kennedy, despite the persuasion of some of our mutual friends. Even now I probably would follow Grenville Clark's example and not vote at all but for the imminent nomination of Nixon. I don't like papa Kennedy at all and the two brothers, Jack and Bob are intelligent, shrewd and tough, also ruthless and unscrupulous.

I know that that great magician of politics, FDR, was not always too scrupulous, but he had a heart; and he never bought primaries as Kennedy did in Wisconsin and West Virginia. Yet a liberal journalist, who expects to support Kennedy, told me yesterday, that he knows of no man who has so wholeheartedly and shrewdly devoted himself to the pursuit of power. He nevertheless expects him to be a good president counting on his cool common sense in this hour of crisis. Perhaps you have heard the story of Kennedy and Nixon. "Twin brothers are going to be in mortal combat in the election and one will murder the other." The point that Nixon will be murdered is probably good prophesy unless Rockefeller helps him out.

The fact that Johnson, who tried to be a bridge between north and south could not be more than a southern candidate, while pathetic for Johnson, is probably an indication how far we have traveled on the race issue since the famous decision of your court.

Incidentally, before closing this aimless confession of a bewildered man, who expects no reaction from one who has, in your phrase, "taken the veil," I must report one more reaction to the moral ambiguity of the political process, at least as conducted in national conventions. A friend said to me "I am critical of Galbraith and Schlesinger for deserting Stevenson for Kennedy before the latter's nomination. Intellectuals must accept political *fait accompli* but they ought not to anticipate it." I thought that was a perfect definition of the irrelevance of the "intellectual" in the political order.

The climate here is wonderful. Cool nights and two hours of warm weather each day, while Los Angeles sizzles just a hundred miles south. No one has explained this phenomenon adequately.

Ursula's and my love to you and Marion and our constant gratitude for your friendship. We do wish we could see you as frequently as we once did in Heath. Vain hopes but precious memories.

Affectionately,
Reinie[78]

Niebuhr retired from Union Theological Seminary in 1960. However, he did not retire in any permanent sense. The autumn term of 1961 found him at Harvard University where he taught on a part-time basis of two hours per week. By 1962, Frankfurter would be forced to step down from the Supreme Court by reason of illness. Both the Frankfurters and Niebuhr endured a continuing decline of vitality during this period, and their correspondence reflected this state of affairs. Niebuhr wrote to the Frankfurters on January 2, 1962:

Dear Marion and Felix:

Ursula and I were tremendously cheered, gratified and complimented by your New Year's telegram to us. We answer more prosaically by letter to wish you both all good things for the New Year; and for Marion particularly new health and vigor.

After suffering from a fall and resultant brain concussion, which seems to have aggravated my paralysis, I have more sympathy than ever with Marion's weakness. I hope she will find new strength in the New Year. I hope for myself that I can fulfill my contract with Harvard in the second semester.

Elisabeth spent the holiday weekend with us and told us enthusiastically of your graciousness to her in her difficult beginning as government bureaucrat. She likes her boss tremendously, at which I am not surprised. Incidentally she owes to you, among many things, her first introduction to Mr. Isenberg in Paris.

Most of all we want to thank you for the friendship of the past and for all the ways it has enriched our lives and that of our children.

Affectionately yours,
Reinie[79]

Felix Frankfurter suffered two strokes in early April, 1962. After his release from the hospital on July 14, 1962, Frankfurter confronted the agonizing decision as to his future on the Supreme Court. His second stroke had left him with slightly impaired speech as well as with partial paralysis of his left limbs. Realizing that he would be unable to fulfill the rigorous and exacting demands of the Court in its upcoming October session, Frankfurter reluctantly tendered his resignation in a letter to President Kennedy on August 28, 1962. His words to Kennedy were:

[78] R. Niebuhr to F. Frankfurter (July 23, 1960, in FCLC).
[79] R. Niebuhr to F. Frankfurter (January 2, 1962, in FCLC).

My dear Mr. President:

Pursuant to the provisions of 28 U.S.A. Section 371 (b), 68 Stat. 12, I hereby retire at the close of this day from regular service as an Associate Justice of the Supreme Court of the United States.

The occasion for my retirement arises from the affliction which I unexpectedly suffered last April. Since then I have undergone substantial improvement. High expectations were earlier expressed by my doctors that I would be able to resume my judicial duties with the beginning of the next Term of the Court, commencing October 1. However, they now advise me that the stepped-up therapy essential to that end involves hazards which might jeopardize the useful years they anticipate still lie ahead of me.

The Court should not enter its new Term with uncertainty as to whether I might later be able to return to unrestricted duty. To retain my seat on the basis of a diminished work schedule would not comport with my own philosophy or with the demands of the business of the Court. I am thus left with no choice but to regard my period of active service on the Court as having run its course.

I need hardly tell you, Mr. President, of the reluctance with which I leave the institution whose concerns have been the absorbing interest of my life. May I again convey to you my gratitude for your call upon me during the summer and for the solicitude you were kind enough to express.

With high respect and esteem,

Faithfully yours,
Felix Frankfurter[80]

Kennedy responded the same day:

My dear Mr. Justice Frankfurter:

Your retirement from regular active service on the Supreme Court ends a long and illustrious chapter in your life, and I understand well how hard a choice you have made. Along with all your host of friends I have followed with admiration your gallant and determined recovery, and I have shared the general hope that you would return soon to the Court's labors. From my own visit I know of your undiminished spirit and your still contagious zest for life. That you now take the judgment of the doctors and set it sternly against your own demanding standard of judicial effectiveness is characteristic, but it comes as an immediate disappointment.

Still, if you allow it, I will say there is also consolation in your decision. I believe it good for you as well as for the rest of us that you should now be free, in reflective leisure, for activities that are impossible in the demanding life of Justice of the Supreme Court. You have been part of the American

---

[80] Kurland, P. (ed.), *Frankfurter, of Law and Live and Other Things That Matter* (1965), pp. 246–47.

public life for well over half a century. What you have learned of the meaning of our country is reflected, of course, in many hundreds of opinions, in thousands of your students, and in dozens of books and articles. But you have a great deal still to tell us, and therefore I am glad to know that the doctors are telling you, in effect, not to retire, but only to turn to a new line of work, with new promise of service to the nation.

Meanwhile, I should like to offer to Mrs. Frankfurter and to you, for myself and for all Americans, our respectful gratitude for the character, courage, learning and judicial dedication with which you have served your country over the last twenty-three years.

Sincerely,
John Kennedy[81]

At approximately the time Frankfurter retired from the Supreme Court, Niebuhr was getting ready to go to Princeton University, where he would spend a semester as a visiting professor. On October 21, 1962, Niebuhr wrote a letter expressing his sentiments regarding the new situation which Frankfurter now faced:

Dear Felix:

I have had the impulse to write to you ever since your retirement, and the spate of highly deserved tributes, from the President, Chief Justice and the journalists, extolling your contributions to American law and our democracy.

But from my own experience with a stroke and with subsequent retirement, I surmised that there were personal problems about retirement, not alluded to in these econiums[sic] I don't pretend that I have solved them and that I could give you wisdom, in any event, about their solution. The years of waning strength, especially for a person of great vitality, present their own problems. I can only say that I have thought of you often in these weeks, wishing that you are happy in directing your vital energies to the law, rather than to the court.

We are spending a semester in Princeton, where I am visiting Professor in their "Council of the Humanities." I enjoy it as much as my failing strength will permit though the Princeton students are a couple of cuts lower than those at Harvard. Our love to you and Marion, whose convalescence, I hope continues with yours.

Affectionately yours,
Reinie[82]

---

[81] Ibid., 247–8.
[82] R. Niebuhr to F. Frankfurter (October 21, 1962, in FCLC).

On November 15, Niebuhr informed Frankfurter that the Harvard "Law School forum did me the honor of inviting a contribution from me for an issue devoted to you. I engaged in the hazardous enterprise as a layman, in interpreting your idea of 'judicial restraint' as a key to the consistency of your judgments which some foolish liberals interpret as moving from left to right. I hope I did you no harm by my amateurish opinion."[83] The *Harvard Law Review* devoted its November, 1962, issue in tribute to Felix Frankfurter. Although mention was made of his essay in the introduction, an extended version of Niebuhr's contribution is in order. Niebuhr remarked that:

Others more competent than I will seek to do justice to [Frankfurter's] distinguished legal career, both as a teacher of law at the Harvard Law School, and during a quarter of a century on the highest court of the nation. But a layman may venture his amateur opinion among experts on this phase of his life. That opinion is strongly informed by the conviction that it is a myth to speak of Frankfurter's development from so-called "liberalism" to so-called "conservatism." Such a description does not truly describe either Frankfurter's temperament or his genius as a legal specialist. ...

Frankfurter has been steadily governed, not by the principles of liberalism or conservatism, but by his respect and veneration for the long democratic tradition not only of this nation but of Great Britain, in which tradition there was always an equal concern for the security of the community on the one hand, and for the rights of the individual on the other. This prevented him from being on the one hand a libertarian or on the other the kind of conservative who is interested merely in preserving the status quo. Among his heroes in public life Henry Stimson was as prominent as F.D.R. It is equally significant that his exemplars on the Court were two great judges of diverse tendencies, Oliver Wendell Holmes and Louis D. Brandeis.

Frankfurter's recently renowned doctrine of "judicial restraint" is an effort to be true to the traditions of a highly complex and diverse national community, which requires laboratory experiments in diverse regions, and prevents the Court from outlawing as unconstitutional legislation which it merely deems unwise. Many of Frankfurter's liberal admirers have criticized some of his opinions, notably on the Smith Act and in dissent to the recent decision ordering more equitable representation in state legislatures [Baker v. Carr, 369 U.S. 186 (1962)]. But only a few have realized that these opinions stem from a consistent political and legal philosophy, neither liberal nor conservative, but based on confidence that the vital forces of a free society, sometimes conflicting, sometimes overlapping and sometimes convergent, will gradually adjust the political forms to the social realities, and will do so more successfully if they are not impeded by judicial fiat. The history of our nation, in which many of these processes were impeded by the court decisions in which the philosophy of *laissez faire* was subtly compounded with, and mistaken for, the precepts of the Constitution, rather suggests that the application of Frankfurter's principles would have hastened the inevitable adjustment of our political life to our social realities.[84]

[83] R. Niebuhr to F. Frankfurter (November 15, 1962, in FCLC).
[84] R. Niebuhr, *Tribute to Felix Frankfurter*, 20-1.

On December 5, 1962, Niebuhr wrote Frankfurter:

Dear Felix:

Thank you for your gracious letter. I am glad that you approved of my interpretation of your doctrine of Judicial Review. I was flattered by the invitation from the Law Review to enter the holy of holies, reserved for lawyers, and wrote the article with a good deal of trepidation, being fearful of betraying my ignorance.

Therefore your kind letter is doubly welcome. I trust that you find retirement not too difficult though I admit it has its difficulties, which must be multiplied for a person with your vitality and exuberance. But just a few essays after you have cast off the 'veil' of which you often spoke, might cure the world of its confusions and might be a vent for your great talent as a guide of the nation.

We hope both you and Marion are in reasonably good health, which is all we old folks can ask. Just about finishing my teaching chores here as visiting Professor.

With great affection,

Yours,
Reinie[85]

The following two years witnessed a steady decline in Frankfurter's health. Writing to Frankfurter on October 7, 1963, about the prospects of the Second Vatican Council dealing with the problem of anti-Semitism, Niebuhr exhibited a rare mood of extreme pessimism regarding his own state of mind:

Dear Felix:

It is so nice to have a letter from you, and incidentally the report from Elisabeth and her husband of the visit they had with you. I am suffering from an intestinal infection, and therefore not completely myself, though I taught my first class this morning.

In regard to Barbara Ward's excellent piece on anti-Semitism, which you were kind enough to send me, I agree with most of her sentiments in regard to the scandal of anti-Semitism. It is exceeded only by the scandal of prejudice against another minority, the Negroes.

I only disagree with her hope that the Vatican Council will do something about it. There is small chance. They have their caps set for the Greek Orthodox. But there is small chance that they will express a MEA CULPA for the long history of anti-Semitism. Catholicism is better than Protestantism on the issue of prejudice against the Negro minority. But on anti-Semitism it is worse, with no signs of righting the wrongs of the ages.

---

[85] R. Niebuhr to F. Frankfurter (December 5, 1962, in FCLC).

We were glad to get such good responses and reports about you and Marion from our children. I am so glad that you have both weathered the storm of your stroke and that you are your usual vibrant self.

Age is creeping up on me more than on you AND I have a difficulty in doing anything significant. I must just bide my time until I pass from this scene. I have several ideas that I would like to express in some essays, but the strength is not there.

My gratitude for our long friendship and for what you have done for this country in your distinguished career.

With love to both of you,

Affectionately yours,
Reinie[86]

Within two days of the Kennedy assassination, Niebuhr wrote Frankfurter a letter in which he commented on the frustrations surrounding Kennedy's civil rights program and the race issue in general:

Dear Felix:

I appreciated so much your brief notes when I was at the hospital. I am now slowly recuperating but still very weak. I hope time will cure the weakness. Living in retirement and unable to do real work, my heart goes out to you who had so much more an active and significant life and have been forced into retirement by the frailties of the flesh. It must be difficult to read the decisions of the Court without having a part in the decisions.

I wish I had some time for unhurried conversations with you as of old. I would ask you about the JFK administration, whether it is bogged down by the old Republican-Southern coalition, or whether the President's lack of FDR's warm humanity makes it impossible for him to appeal to the people over the heads of Congress. His Civil Rights program seems to me courageous, the last chapter in making the South conform to the standards of the nation. How stubborn all racial prejudices are. They seem to dog mankind even in the highest stages of civilization.

Our love to you and Marion.

Affectionately yours,
Reinie[87]

The last letter Niebuhr wrote to Frankfurter came on December 20, 1964, two months prior to Frankfurter's death on February 22, 1965. The depth of friendship between the Niebuhrs and the Frankfurters was foremost in Niebuhr's mind in that epistle:

---

[86] R. Niebuhr to F. Frankfurter (October 7, 1963, in FCLC).
[87] R. Niebuhr to F. Frankfurter (November 20, 1963, in FCLC).

Dear Felix and Marion:

Instead of sending you a holiday greeting, Ursula and I thought we would write you a letter to say how much your friendship has meant to us through the years and to express the hope that the infirmities of age are bearable for you. I have had a second stroke this summer and I am quite lame, so I can sympathize with Felix the more.

I hope Felix is satisfied with the course of events, particularly the smashing defeat of the absurd Goldwater movement. I confess that the millions who voted for this nostalgia leaves me concerned.

We hear rather regularly from Will Scarlett. He suffered because of the Goldwater movement.

Our affectionate greetings and gratitude for the years of your friendship.

Yours,
Reinie[88]

This long and valued friendship was brought to a close when a fatal heart attack resulted in Felix Frankfurter's death on February 22, 1965. Frankfurter's death, in Niebuhr's words, terminated the life "of one of the leading architects of American jurisprudence."[89]

In his final book, published in 1966, six years prior to his own death, Niebuhr claimed that "the guiding principle throughout my mature life of the relation of religious responsibility to political affairs"[90] rested in the conviction "that a realist conception of human nature should be made the servant of an ethic of progressive justice and should not be made into a bastion of conservatism, particularly a conservatism which defends unjust privileges."[91] Niebuhr's sense of "progressive justice" found him in strident support of many issues the resolution of which coincided with the "activist" stance of the Warren Court. Yet he genuinely appreciated the rationale behind Frankfurter's defense of "judicial restraint" as well as the consistence with which Frankfurter sought to apply it in his tenure on the Court.

More than anything else, Niebuhr strove to "explain" Frankfurter and disengage his judicial position from the "liberal-conservative" rhetoric by means of which the serious and engaging issues behind the "restraint" doctrine became obscured. In his final eulogy to Felix Frankfurter, Niebuhr wrote:

Justice Frankfurter was in fact a calculating moderate, aware of both the necessity for guarding the liberties of the people and for allowing an industrial civilization to take measures to ensure collective justice. The doctrine of "judicial restraint," for which he became famous in his later days on the Court, was inspired by the lesson that our nation

[88] R. Niebuhr to F. Frankfurter (December 20, 1964, in FCLC).
[89] R. Niebuhr, see note 1, 70.
[90] R. Niebuhr, *Man's Nature and His Communities* (New York: Charles Scribner's Sons, 1965), p. 25.
[91] Ibid., p. 24.

was tardy in coming to terms with an industrial civilization because the Supreme Court in the nineteenth century invalidated many laws calculated to correct social abuses. This was due to its unconscious presupposition that Adam Smith's *laissez faire* principles were written into the Constitution. This error prompted his theory that the Court must not legislate in passing on the constitutionality of legislation.[92]

[92] R. Niebuhr, *In Memoriam: Felix Frankfurter*, p. 69.

Afterword: Niebuhr's Continuing Relevance

The pursuit of the relevance an individual might have beyond his or her own time is sometimes interesting, always speculative, and definitely fraught with likelihood of embarrassment. Certainly, with regard to seeking relevance in the form of how Niebuhr might react to future events, Arthur Schlesinger Jr. is correct in pointing out, "Nothing is more futile than trying to predict how people now dead would have responded to some later contingency; it is hard enough to predict the reactions of living people."[1] In general terms, however, Niebuhr's stature and the recent publications that have surfaced regarding him deserve some reflection.

Charlie Citrine's confession in Saul Bellow's novel *Humboldt's Gift* that he "was always thinking of statements that must be made and truths of which the world must be reminded"[2] captures perfectly the basis of Reinhold Niebuhr's continuing relevance. So many of Niebuhr's analyses and insights continue to bear the marks of such truths precisely because in America so many things have a habit of recurring in a way that brings them again and again into stark clarity. The list would include America's inordinate view of its own virtue, its persistent declaration of innocence, its penchant for utopianism, its swing between isolationist and interventionist foreign policies, its simplistic moralism, and its excessive individualism. These are just a few among the lingering habits that continually generate patterns and problems that resurface in new guises and in connection with any variety of "new world" events. Clearly, what continues to be relevant about Niebuhr is the intellectual framework and understanding he brought to bear on such patterns and problems. He both recognized and forcefully addressed these ingrained habits of our nation's life. Niebuhr was a man wise about religion, insightful about politics, and astute about the contours and shenanigans of American culture.

---

[1] A. Schlesinger Jr, "Afterword on Niebuhr as a colleague" in G. O. Mazur, (ed.), *Twenty-Five Year Memorial Commemoration to the Life of Hans Morgenthau: 1904–2005* (New York: Semenenko Foundation, 2006), p. 13.

[2] S. Bellow, *Humboldt's Gift* (New York: Penguin, 1996 edition), p. 108.

There are problems associated with this issue of relevance. In 1976, Martin Marty raised an important question respecting the prospect of Niebuhr's future in this regard. He commented on the "lost worlds" of Reinhold Niebuhr, referring to the fact that many of the issues addressed so well by Niebuhr had been replaced by new issues commanding attention. Even during his own life-time, when issues involving racial injustice and gender inequality were gaining increasing prominence, Niebuhr was being criticized for failing to address them adequately. More recently issues such as multiculturalism, post-nationalism, identity politics, ecology, and global pluralism – just to mention a few – have created "new worlds" that were apparently unknown to Niebuhr. In his chapter "After Niebuhr," Mark Hulsether, two generations removed from that of Niebuhr, provides a thoughtful reflection on whether Niebuhr's social Christianity can have any effect on the new worlds of the twenty-first century.[3]

The historian Arthur Schlesinger Jr. took the problem of Niebuhr's "lost worlds" a step further. For Schlesinger the problem is what he saw as Niebuhr's disappearance. In his 2005 *The New York Times* article "Forgetting Reinhold Niebuhr," Schlesinger voiced concern that Niebuhr had become largely invisible at a time when his voice was needed more than ever.[4] In the decades immediately after Niebuhr's death in 1971, however, we do know that he did have an afterlife. With an ironic perversity, so consistently relevant has Niebuhr proved to be that he has been conscripted into the service of virtually every shifting ideology that has appeared in American public life.

What we have witnessed is the shameless misuse and abuse of Niebuhr. Since his death, Niebuhr has been summoned in support of a variety of political and economic positions that he had severely criticized. Conservatives have adopted him as one of their own, although Niebuhr abhorred both the American variety of conservatism and the laissez-faire economics it sought to promulgate. Both neo-conservatives and neo-liberals conscripted Niebuhr in an attempt to defend an aggressive interventionist foreign policy that his brand of political realism had consistently resisted. Niebuhr, in effect, still had enough visibility and prestige to become an ideological weapon for contending factions seeking to ground their own particular causes.

Given both the passing of Niebuhr's worlds and the abuses to which Niebuhr has been subjected, one is given to wonder about the nature of his continuing relevance. Schlesinger saw Niebuhr as a "prophet for a secular age," and he believed that a wide range of contemporary events cried out for the application of Niebuhr's insights and analyses. For Marty, Niebuhr's continuing relevance rested with "what was paradigmatic in [Niebuhr's] effort." He saw Niebuhr's

---

[3] M. Hulsether, "After Niebuhr" in D. F. Rice (ed.), *Reinhold Niebuhr Revisited*, pp. 338–55.

[4] Arthur Schlesinger Jr.'s article "Forgetting Reinhold Niebuhr" appeared in *The New York Times Book Review*, September 18, 2005. Martin Marty wrote a rejoinder entitled "Citing Reinhold" in his M.E.M.O. column in *Christian Century*, October 18, 2005. Both pieces were reprinted with permission in D. F. Rice (ed.), *Reinhold Niebuhr Revisited: Engagements with an American Original* (Grand Rapids, MI: Eerdmans, 2009), pp. 359–56.

voice to be "well attuned to an American environment," because "he combined so well the empirical and pragmatic or activist sense with some deeper philosophical grounding."[5] Echoing Marty, Eyal Naveh maintained that Niebuhr's insights "were articulated within a general liberal framework and [within] the pragmatic orientation that is so central to American culture in general [that they have] the potential to transcend their specific context and particular circumstances."[6] Robin Lovin, seeing that Niebuhr's "Christian realism ... is more than a series of astute observations that [he] made about the events of his time," suggests that Niebuhr's theological understanding can, in our day, be adapted and applied in hopeful ways to the global, pluralistic world that shapes our world.[7]

The center of Niebuhr's intellectual framework was a vantage point often labeled as "Christian realism." As central as this was to Niebuhr's penetrating insights into human nature and behavior, he, taking a cue from William James, was quite willing to draw truth from whatever quarter it appeared – secular or religious. Yet for Niebuhr "biblical faith," critically received and viewed, supplied insights into human nature that served well as a framework for analyzing and interpreting what goes on in society and politics. Aside from the lost and ever-passing worlds through which we move, Niebuhr's teachings on the deleterious effects of self-interest in human affairs, the need to balance power against power in the never-ending quest for justice, the propensity to self-righteousness and pretentions of virtue, and the dangerous and self-deluding arrogance often found in those advancing noble causes all appear to have continuing relevance to the problems and issues facing both our present and our future.

[5] M. E. Marty, "The lost worlds of Reinhold Niebuhr," *American Scholar* (Autumn, 1976), 571.

[6] E. Naveh, *Reinhold Niebuhr and Non-Utopian Liberalism* (Brighton and Portland: Sussex Academic Press, 2002), p. 183.

[7] R. W. Lovin, *Reinhold Niebuhr* (Nashville, TN: Abingdon Press, 2007), p. 60. See Chapter 6, "Christian Realism: Pluralistic and Hopeful," pp. 59–69. See also J. P. Diggins, *Why Niebuhr Now?* (Chicago, IL: University of Chicago Press, 2011). Sadly, Professor Diggins died before completing this book himself.

Index

Note: Page references with letter 'n' followed by locators denote note numbers

A

Acheson, Dean, 119, 180
Age of Jackson
Niebuhr's review, 115
Age of Roosevelt, 126
America's Way Out, 85
American Civil Liberties Union, 81
American Diplomacy, 1900–1950
Niebuhr's criticism of, 194
Americans for Democratic Action (ADA), 3, 99,
116, 121, 125, 140, 142
Augustine, Saint, 4, 158, 159, 160, 163, 166

B

Baker, Liva, 222, 223
Barth, Karl, 6, 21, 37
Niebuhr views Barth as the "Tertullian" of
our day, 39
Bell, Daniel, 93, 94, 95, 106
Bellow, Saul, 247
Bennett, John C., 138
Bernstein, J. B., 123
*Biblical Religion and the Search for Ultimate
Reality*
Niebuhr's criticism of, 39–40
Black, Justice Hugo, 210, 229, 230
Brandeis, Justice Louis, 209
Brown, Charles C., 22, 100
Brown, Robert McAfee, 36
Brunner, Emil, 6
Buckley, William F. Jr., 121
Butterfield, Herbert, 140, 149

C

Cardozo, Justice Benjamin N., 12
Carr, E. H., 147, 149
Chambers, Whittaker, 121, 122

Children of Light and the Children of Darkness,
3, 8, 100, 105, 112, 370
Christianity and Crisis
inaugural issue, 100
Justice Reed's dissenting opinion, 211
on 1948 presidential campaign, 105
on Thomas's eightieth birthday, 112
Coe, George A., 68
Coffin, Henry Sloane, 13
Cogley, John, 138
Columbia University, 3, 7, 13, 35
Commager, Henry Steele, 46
Common Faith, 58, 60
Niebuhr's review 62
Conference for Progressive Political
Action, 82
Congress for Cultural Freedom, 48
Conkin, Paul, 50
Council for a Democratic Germany, 33–34

D

Debs, Eugene, 7, 83, 88
Dewey, John, Chapter Two, *passim,* 1, 2, 4, 5,
44, 82, 85, 88, 121, 127, 129
Christian beliefs, Dewey's opinion of
Niebuhr's relation to traditional
Christianity, 60
conflict with Niebuhr over *Moral Man and
Immoral Society*, 66–68
democracy, comparative views with Niebuhr,
72–79
Dewey–Niebuhr relationship, a brief sketch, 7
God, Dewey's use of the term, 61
humanism, Dewey's problem with the term,
58–59
liberal tradition, conflict with Niebuhr
regarding, 65–72

Dewey, John, Chapter Two (cont.)
  meaning, Dewey and Niebuhr on, 63–65
  natualism, scientific method, and the
    humanistic studies, conflict with
    Niebuhr, 49–57
  religion, dispute with Niebuhr, 57–65
Diggins, John Patrick, 195, 196
Dillenberger, John, 37
Dilthey, Wilhelm, 52
Dorrien, Gary, 79, 112
Douglas, Paul, 47, 82, 85
Douglas, Justice William O., 182, 229
Dulles, John Foster
  Niebuhr's view, 131, 134, 196, 217, 228
  Frankfurter's view, 235

E
Eddy, Sherwood, 16, 80
Eisenhower, Dwight D., 122, 217, 228, 236
End of an Era, 92
Evangelical Herald, 16
  list of articles, 31n10

F
Farmer-Labor Party, 82
Farrell, James T.
  letter to Dewey about Niebuhr, 60
Fellowship of Reconciliation, 8, 81, 99
Fellowship of Socialist Christians, 6, 8, 22, 35
Fleischman, Harry, 95, 96
Ford, Henry, 80
Foreign Affairs, 11, 178
Fox, Richard W., 72, 82, 84, 119, 150, 174,
    176, 185
Frontier Fellowship, 22
Frankfurter, Felix, Chapter Seven, *passim*, 1, 2,
    3, 4
  Brown v. Board of Education, Frankfurter's
    role, 222–224
  Brown vs. Board of Education, desired gradual
    approach in implementation, 223
  Burstyn v. Wilson (1952), request for
    information from Niebuhr on the
    meaning of "sacriligeous", 216–217
  Dennis v. United States and Yates v. United
    States, issues and opinions, 229–230
  Dulles, John Foster, opinion of, 235
  Dutch Reformed Church of South Africa, 235
  enigma to natural constituency, 220–221
  exchange between Frankfurter the "believing
    unbeliver" and Niebuhr an "unbelieving
    believer", 206
  Frankfurter-Niebuhr relationship, a brief
    sketch, 11–12
  Kennedy, John F., letter to Kennedy tendering
    his resignation from the Supreme Court,
    240

  Kennedy's letter in response to Frankfurter's
    reisignation from Supreme Court,
    240–241
  Khrushchev, exchange with Niebuhr over
    failure of Paris summit, 236
  Lippmann, Walter, exchange of views with
    Niebuhr, 224–225, 237
  McCollum v. Board of Education (March
    1948), differences with Niebuhr,
    210–212
  pacifist youth, seeks Niebuhr's advice,
    231–232
  praises Niebuhr for articles on "Jews After the
    War", 208–210
  public education as unifying factor,
    differences with Niebuhr, 212–214
  Richmond Ministers' Association manifesto,
    letter to Niebuhr, 227
  separation of power, answer to Niebuhr's
    request for clarification, 215
  Wilson, Woodrow, view of, 234–235
Frei, Christoph, 145, 169
Friess, Horace S., 13, 14
Fulbright, William J., 192

G
Gaddis, John L., 184, 187
Galbraith, John Kenneth, 113
Gellman, Baton, 199
Gilkey, Langdon, 37
Good, Robert C., 170, 172, 198
Gustafson, James, 156
Gutmann, James, 49

H
Halliwell, Martin, 146
Hamby, Alonzo, 116
Harland, Gordon, 162
Harnack, Adolf von, 6
Harriman, Averell, 123
Harvard Law Review, Niebuhr's article on
    Frankfurter, 242
Harvard Law School, 12
Harvey, Van, 13
Herberg, Will, 106
Hillquit, Morris, 82
Hiss, Alger, 121
Hoffmann, Stanley, 158
Hogan, Michael, 184
Hollander, Ed, 125, 126
Holmes, John Haynes, 82
Hook, Sidney, 48, 49, 59, 61, 79, 106
  Dewey's attitude toward Niebuhr, 49
Hoover, Herbert, 84
Hulsether, Mark, 248
Humphrey, Hubert, 119, 140
Hutchinson, John, 44

I

In Defense of the National Interest, 168
Interpretation of History, 15
Ivie, Robert, 199

J

Jackson, Justice Robert H., 121
James, William, 1, 5, 7, 48, 79, 249
Jefferson, Thomas, 78
Johnson, Lyndon, 133, 137, 138, 139

K

Kairos Circle, 17
"*kairos* moment", 18–19, 23, 34
Kalb, Marvin, 192
Kelsen, Hans, 146
Kennan, George, Chapter Six, *passim*, 1, 2, 3, 4,
    125, 130, 150, 164, 170, 171, 236
  Adams, John Quincy
    quotes Adams on likely failure of exporting
      ideals of democracy, 201
    quotes Adams on recommending that we
      pay attention to our own freedom and
      independence, 193
  Central Europe and the German problem,
    185–186
  Christianity and Crisis, turns down invitation
    as contributing editor, 191
  containment policy toward Soviet Union,
    178–179
  disagreement with militarization of
    containment policy, 179, 182
  elitism in a democracy, comparison with
    Niebuhr, 199–201
  exportability of democracy, comparison with
    Niebuhr, 201–205
  increased militarization, results in departure
    from governmental service in 1953, 184
  Kennan-Niebuhr relationship, a brief sketch,
    10–11
  memorial tribute to Niebuhr in 1971,
    175–176, 177–178
  morality and politics, comparison with
    Niebuhr, 195–199
  national interest, differences with Niebuhr,
    194–195
  NATO, increased dissent from policy,
    183, 188
  Niebuhr referred to as "the father of us
    all", 174
  opposition to Vietnam war, 192–193
  Princeton Institute for Advanced Study,
    involvement in Niebuhr's work on,
    189–190
  Reith Lectures for BBC, 186
  Soviet Union
    inability to accurately assess world realities,
      186–187

peaceful coexistence, unlikelihood of with
      Khrushchev, 191
Kennedy, John F., 113, 137
  letter to Felix Frankfurter on Frankfurter's
    decision to resign from the Supreme
    Court, 240–241
  Niebuhr's letter recommending Stevenson for
    Secretary of State, 139
King, Martin Luther, 140, 228
Khrushchev, Soviet Premier, 191
Kissinger, Henry, 152, 187

L

La Follette, Robert, 82, 83
LaGuardia, Fiorello, 94, 230
Lamont, Corliss, 58
League for Independent Political Action, 47, 85
League for Industrial Democracy, 48, 83, 94
Lindbeck, George A., 5
Lippmann, Walter, 149, 168, 224, 225, 237
Loeb, James, 121, 122, 143
Lovin, Robin, 249

M

MacLeish, Archibald, 233
Madison, James, 78
Marshall Plan, 179, 180, 181, 182, 183
  Niebuhr's use to illustrate the widening of
    national self-interest, 195
Marshall, George C., 150, 180
Martin, James A. Jr., 48, 79
Martin, John B., 122, 124
Marty, Martin, 248. 249
Masaryk, Jan, 181
McCarthy, Eugene, 140
McCarthy, Joseph R., 121
McGovern, George, 140, 142
McKeogh, Colm, 158
Mazur, G. O., 146, 152n30
Meland, Bernard, 58
Miller, Perry, 114
Miller, William Lee, 72
Mollov, Benjamin
  views on Morgenthau's moral and spiritual
    sensitivities, 171–172
Moral Man and Immoral Society, 2, 6, 65, 90
  Norman Thomas's criticism and Niebuhr's
    response, 90–91
Morgenthau, Hans, Chapter Five, *passim*, 1, 2,
    3, 4, 10, 55, 57, 174, 194, 195, 196, 198,
    201, 202
  criticism of Vietnam War, 151–152
  debate over the degree of influence Niebuhr
    had on Morgenthau, 145–146
  ethics and political realism, contrast with
    Niebuhr, 168–173
  interaction with Niebuhr, 147–153
  international politics and world vision, views
    with Niebuhr, 164–168

Morgenthau, Hans, Chapter Five (cont.)
  Lippmann, Walter, criticism of, 149
  Morgenthau-Niebuhr relationship a brief
    sketch, 10
  national interest, differences with Niebuhr,
    161–164
  political man, credits Niebuhr with recovery
    of, 157
  power, differences with Niebuhr, 158–161
  scientific method, agreement with Niebuhr
    over misapplication, 147–148
  "scientism", definition of, 147
  theological orientation, view of in Niebuhr,
    154–157
Mumford, Lewis, 46

N

Naveh, Eyal, 249
Nelson, Anna Kasten, 182, 185
Neo-orthodoxy, 6
Niebuhr, H. Richard, 211
Niebuhr, Reinhold
  admits to excessive criticism of Dewey, 48
  admits late criticim of Vietnnam War, 151
  antisemitism in 1933 Germany, 20–21
  assessement of his own role in theology, 4
  Arab-Israeli crisis, exchange of views with
    Thomas, 108–110
  Barthianism, view of influence in Germany, 21
  Brown v. Board of Education (1954),
    Niebuhr's letter to Frankfurter, 221
  came to Union Theological Seminary in 1928, 2
  Central Europe and the German problem,
    185–186
  Chambers, Whittaker, Niebuhr and
    Schlesinger on, 121–122
  Christianity and Crisis, invites Kennan to join
    editorial board, 190
  class conflict, encourages progressive
    Christians to recognize as a reality, 86
  common ground with Dewey obscured, 48–49
  cultural lag, criticism of Dewey's use of
    theory, 52–53
  democracy, comparative views with Dewey,
    72–79
  differences with Dewey over the issue of
    meaning in life, 63–65
  dispute over influence on Morgenthau,
    146–147
  distinction between the "creed" and the
    "spirit" of liberalism, 71–72
  Dutch Reformed Church of South Africa, 235
  Eisenhower myth, 132
  Eisenhower, opinion of prior to his decision
    which party to represent in 1952,
    122–123
  elitism in a democracy, comparison with
    Kennan, 199–201
  enigma to his natural constituency, 220

ethics and political realism, contrast with
    Morgenthau, 168–173
exportability of democracy, comparison with
    Kennan, 201–205
FBI investigation, seeks advice from
    Frankfurter, 208
German Protestantism, criticism of during the
    rise of Nazism, 21–22
German situation (with Tillich), 13–35
German socialism, reason for failure, 19, 20
Harvard Law Review article on Frankfurter,
    242
Hellenistic and Hebraic thought
  contrasted with Tillich, 43
  contrasted with Dewey, 53–54
  interaction with Morgenthau, 147–153
international politics and world vision, views
    with Morgenthau, 164–168
Kennan delivers memorial tribute to Niebuhr
    in 1971, 175–176, 177–178
Kennedy, John F.
  harsh criticism of Kennedy, 137
  supports Kennedy and recommends
    Stevenson for Secretary of State, 139
Khrushchev, exchange with Frankfurter over
    failure of Paris summit with Khrushchev,
    236
liberal tradition, conflict with Dewey, 65–72
Liberalism and Social Action, criticism of
    Dewey's 1935 book, 70–71
Lippmann, Walter, exchange of views with
    Frankfurter, 224–225, 237
Marshall Plan, support of, 181
McCollum v. Board of Education (1948),
    differences with Frankfurter, 210–212
memorial tribute to Tillich delivered in
    1965, 45
morality and politics, comparison with
    Kennan, 195–199
national interest, differences with Kennan,
    194–195
national interest, differences with
    Morgenthau, 161–164
naturalism, scientific method, and humanistic
    studies, conflict with Dewey, 49–57
Nazi fanaticism, assessing causes, 28–29
Policy Planning Staff, participates in 1949,
    150, 184
post-war Germany and reconstruction, 25–31
power, differences with Morgenthau,
    158–161
pragmatism, Niebuhr's variety, 5–6
public education as a unifying factor,
    differences between Niebuhr and Felix
    Frankfurter, 212–214
religion, dispute with Dewey, 57–65
Richmond Ministers Association manifesto
    and school desegregation, letter to
    Frankfurter, 227–228

Roosevelt
    growing support of FDR in 1939, 98–99
    response to Schlesinger's criticism of
        Niebuhr's belated support, 129–130
    supports FDR and resigns from Socialist
        Party in 1940, 98
Scientific Man and Power Politics, review of
    Morgenthau's book, 148
socialism in America, criticsm of ideological
    baggage, 110
    reasons for failure, 106–107
Socialist Party
    declines Thomas's invitation to rejoin
        party, 104
    reflections on conflict between radicals and
        "old guard" in 1934, 95–96
Stevenson
    opinion of in 1952, 123–124
    supports presidential bid in 1956, 130–132
student radicalism of the 1960s, 141–142
theological disputes with Tillich, 37–45
theological orientation, differences with
    Morgenthau, 154–157
Thomas, Norman
    appreciation of, 111–112
    conflict over WWII, 101–105
    qualified support of presidential run in
        1936, 96–97
Tillich
    and Barth "walking the tightrope" on
        theology and metaphysics, 39–40
    and Barth as the "Origen" and the
        "Tertullian" of our day, 39
    contrast of religious vs. political influence in
        America, 24–25
    personal relationship, 35–37
    role in bringing to the United States, 3,
        13–15
Truman, 1951 meeting, 119
Vital Center, Niebuhr's view of Schlesinger's
    book, 117
Niebuhr, Ursula, 14, 36, 143, 176
Niebuhr-Tillich relationship, 36
Nixon, Richard, 139, 140, 153

O

Office of Strategic Services, 8
Oppenheimer, J. Robert, 135, 189, 226
    Niebuhr and Schlesinger on, 135

P

Pauck, Wilhelm and Marion, 35
Peale, Norman Vincent, 138
Peirce, Charles Sanders, 7
Phillips, Harlan B., 218, 234
Policy Planning Staff of the Department of State
    European Unification, Niebuhr present in
        1949 when issue was being addressed,
        150, 184

first paper, PPS/1 in 1947, led to Marshal
    Plan, 181
purpose of, 150, 180
Poling, Dan, 138
Politics Among Nations, 3, 10, 145
Putnam, Hilary, 51

R

Randall, John Herman, 35, 44
Rauschenbusch, Walter, 80
Reed, Justice Stanley, 211
Reflections on the End of an Era, 21, 69, 127
*Reinhold Niebuhr: His Religious, Social and
    Political Thought,* Tillich's article
    "Reinhold Niebuhr's Doctrine of God",
    41–42
Religious Expectation, 17
Religious Situation, 17
Ritschl, Albrecht, 6
Rorty, Richard, 5, 6
Russell, Bertrand, 49, 64
Russell, Greg, 344
Russell, Richard L., 176
Russia, the Atom and the West
    based on Kennan's 1957 BBC Reith Lectures,
        186–187

S

Schleiermacher, Frederick, 4, 6, 205
Schlesinger, Arthur Jr., Chapter Four, *passim,* 1,
    65, 88, 92, 96, 174, 247, 248
    ADA, criticism of policy in 1953, 125
    Chambers, Whittaker, Schlesinger and
        Niebuhr on, 121–122
    Crisis of the Old Order dedicated to
        Niebuhr, 126
    devestated by by both John's and Robert
        Kennedy's deaths, 139–140
    Faith and History, review, 117–118
    Irony of American History, review,
        120–121
    last letter to Niebuhr arriving after his
        death, 143
    letter to Ursua Niebuhr after learning of
        Niebuhr's death, 143
    Marxism, basis of attraction to Niebuhr., 127
Niebuhr
    account of first impression of
        Niebuhr, 114
    criticized for belated support of FDR,
        128–129
    Oppenheimer, J. Robert, view on
        Oppenheimer case, 135
    review of Niebuhr's *Faith and History,*
        117–118
    review of Niebuhr's *Irony of American
        History,* 120–121
    Schlesinger-Niebuhr relationship, a brief
        sketch, 9

Schlesinger, Arthur Jr., Chapter Four (cont.)
  seeks Niebuhr's support for Kennedy's 1960
    presidential bid, 137
  student radicalism in the 1969s, 140–141
  tribute to Niebuhr in 1971, 144
  Vital Center's main thesis, 116–117
Scientism
  Morgenthau's definition of, 147
  term used by Niebuhr and Morgenthau in
    criticism of Dewey, 35
Seidler, Murray, 82
Sevareid, Eric, 179, 199, 200
Shinn, Roger, 5, 35, 36, 37, 38, 39, 168, 169, 171
  Niebuhr's emphasis on the "personhood" of
    God, 43
  Niebuhr's late awareness of differences from
    Tillich, 38–39
  Tillich, withdrawal from politics, 34
  Union Theological Seminary, perceived
    identity of Niebuhr and Tillich, 39
Sigmund, Paul, 204
Sinclair, Upton, 94
Smith Act, 229
Smith, John E., 44
Smith, Michael J., 146, 156, 159, 160
Social Frontier, 70
Socialist Call, 95, 101
Socialist Decision, 15, 17, 18
Socialist Party of America, 8
Sorel, Georges, 141
Spender, Stephen, 70
Stone, Justice Harlan F., 212
Stone, Ronald, 36, 164, 185
Structure of Nations and Empires
  Niebuhr's doubts about to Schlesinger, 136
  thanks Morgenthau for his help, 150
Swanberg, W. A., 103
Systematic Theology
  Tillich's lectures at Union were basis for his
    writings on systematic theology, 39

T

Thayer, James Bradley, 218
Theology of Paul Tillich
  Niebuhr's crticism of Tillich in his essay
    "Biblical Thought and Ontological
    Speculation in Tillich's Theology",
    39–40
Thomas, Norman, Chapter Three, *passim*, 1, 2,
    4, 46, 78, 127, 128
  Arab-Isareli, exchange of views with Niebuhr,
    108–110
  campaign issues in the 1932 election, 87–88
  fascism, agreement with Niebuhr that
    America was drifting towards fascism in
    the mid-1930s, 92
  Moral Man and Immoral Society, Thomas's
    criticism and Niebuhr's reply, 90–91

Niebuhr
  at odds with over WWII, 101–105
  criticized for abandoning the Socialist
    Party, 104
Old Guard/radical conflict, 94–96
policy changes sought for in 1928 election, 84
political parties, describes differences between
    the competing parties in 1932, 88
Roosevelt, F. D.
  FDR attacked on drift toward War, 101
  expanded attack on FDR in 1936, 96
  views of FDR in wake of 1932 election,
    91–93
socialism
  cites three distinguishing features in 1931,
    85–86
  reasons for failure in America, 106
Socialist Party of America, Thomas joins in
    1918, 82
socialists, given credit for whatever minimal
    good came out of FDR's election of 1932,
    91–92
Thomas-Niebuhr relationship, a brief sketch,
    7–8
Thompson, Kenneth, 11, 150, 151, 153,
    157, 161, 168, 169, 172, 174, 176, 195,
    200
  Niebuhr's contribution to Kennan's Policy
    Planning Staff, 151
Tillich, Paul, Chapter One, *passim*, 1, 2, 3, 7,
    61, 129
  Barth, K., 21
  first non-Jew dismissed from a teaching post
    in Nazi Germany, 15
  German Protestantism, criticism of during the
    rise of Nazism, 21–22
  German situation, 13–35
  Kairos Circle, 17
  "kairos moment", 18–19, 23, 34
  Nazi fanaticism assessing causes, 28–29
  Niebuhr
    charged with being unphilosophical, 44
    credited with role in bringing Tillich to the
      United States, 14
    delivers memorial tribute to Tillich in
      1965, 45
  post-war Germany and reconstruction, 25–31
  Strasbourg meeting with Niebuhr in 1936,
    23–24
  theological disputes with Niebuhr, 37–45
  Tillich-Niebuhr relationship, a brief sketch,
    6–7 and 35–37
  Tillich mistaken in viewing Niebuhr as
    intending to produce a theological
    system, 38
  views Tillich as the "Origen" or our day, 39
Tocqueville, Alexis de, 4
Truman, Harry, 119, 123, 180

U

Union for Democratic Action, 103, 116
Union Seminary Quarterly Review
    Niebuhr's "Paul Tillich in
        Memorian"published in November,
        1965 issue, 45
Union Theological Seminary, 1, 3, 7, 13
United States Supreme Court, Frankfurter joins
    in January, 1939, 12, 205
Urban, George, 199

V

van Dusen, Henry Pitt, 138, 236
Vandenberg Resolution, 182
Vital Center
    main thesis, 116–117
    Niebuhr's influence on Schlesinger's
        book, 116

W

Waldman, Louis, 95
Wallace, Henry, 32
Waltz, Kenneth, 154
Warren, Earl, 222
Welles, Sumner, 208
Westbrook, Robert, 73
White, Morton, 59, 115, 120, 121
Whitehead, Alfred North, 53
Willkie, Wendell, 173
Wilson, Woodrow
    Frankfurter's view, 234–235
Wolfers, Arnold, 150
World Tomorrow
    Norman Thomas becomes editor in 1917, 81

X

"X" article, 11, 178